AUTO-BIO

VEHICLE DETAILS

This page enables you to compile a list of useful data on your car, so that whether you're ordering spares or just checking the tyre pressures, all the key information - the information that is 'personal' to your car - is easily within reach.

Registration number: ....
Model: ....
Engine type/size: ....
Fuel type/grade: ....
Body colour: ....
Paint code number: ....
Date of first registration: ....
Date of manufacture (if different): ....
VIN (or 'chassis') number: ....
Engine number: ....
Ignition key/key tag number: ....

Door lock key/s number/s: ....
Fuel locking cap key number (if fitted): ....
Alarm remote code (if fitted): ....
Radio/cassette security code (if fitted): ....

Tyre size
Front: ....Rear: ....

Tyre pressures (normally laden)
Front: ....Rear: ....

Tyre pressures (fully laden)
Front: ....Rear: ....

Insurance

    Name and address of insurer: ....
....
    Policy number: ....

Modifications

    Information that might be useful when you need to purchase parts: ....
....

Suppliers

    Address and telephone number of your local dealership: ....
....
....

First published in 1997 by: **Porter Publishing Ltd.**

The Storehouse
Little Hereford Street
Bromyard
Hereford HR7 4DE
England

Tel: 01885 488800
Fax: 01885 483012

© Copyright Lindsay Porter
and Porter Publishing Ltd, 1997.

All rights reserved. No part of this publication may be reproduced, stored in a retrieval system, or transmitted in any form including electronic, electrical, mechanical, optical, photocopying, recording or by any other means without prior written permission of the publisher. All enquiries should be addressed to the publisher at the address shown on this page.

British Library Cataloguing in Publication Data.

A catalogue record for this book is available from the British Library.

ISBN 1-899238-22-0

Series Editor: Lindsay Porter
Front cover design: Crazy Horse 1842 Ltd - Porter Publishing Ltd.
Back cover design: Porter Publishing Ltd
Layout and Typesetting: Mark Leonard
Printed in England by The Trinity Press, Worcester.

GREAT CARS ON VIDEO

PP Video has a truly great range of video tapes, mostly original 'archive' footage, and covering the finest cars ever built. We present the official Jaguar Cars Archive, Dunlop Archive, Audi AG Archive films, among others. There are profiles on the greatest classic cars, motor racing from the '30s, the '50s, the '60s and '70s, and much more besides. For a FREE VIDEO CATALOGUE, please write to: PP Video Ltd, at the address shown at the top of this page.

MORE TOP-SELLING Step-by-Step PORTER MANUALS

All with 100s of clear illustrations!

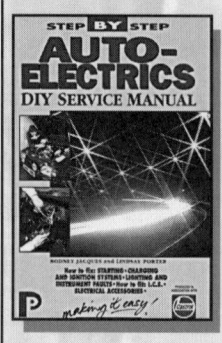

AUTO-ELECTRICS DIY Service Manual
Covers every electrical component on the car. Explains how it works AND how to fix it! Packed with simple instructions. Comprehensive and easy to follow.

The Complete TRAILER MANUAL
The ONLY complete trailer manual! How to build your own; how to use, service and repair; the towing and weight laws. All trailer types covered. Car tow limits listed car-by-car.

THE CARAVAN MANUAL
Keep your caravan in super, safe condition with the help of this book. Every aspect of servicing electrics, brakes, hitch, interior, accessories and more. User's guide and car tow limits listed, car-by-car.

THE MOTOR CARAVAN MANUAL
Step-by-Step service jobs on every type of petrol and diesel Motor Caravan; every type of body and all interior fittings. Buyer's guide; user's guide; step-by-step servicing and much more besides.

DIESEL CAR ENGINES Service Guide
See how your car's Diesel engine works; follow the step-by-step service instructions; fix it when it goes wrong. Thorough, comprehensive step-by-step DIY service manual, covering all Diesel car types.

ABSOLUTE BEGINNERS Service Guide
If you've never serviced a car before, this manual 'holds your hand' through every step, from topping-up and changing oil to overhauling brakes and bodywork.

PORTER MANUALS:

- Packed with information.
- The best for quality.
- The *easiest* to use!

From your local stockist, or contact us at the address at the top of this page for availability and a full list of titles.

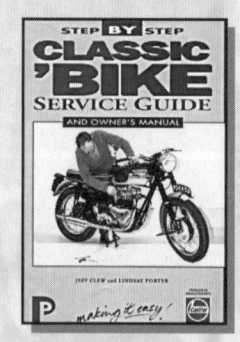

CLASSIC 'BIKE Service Guide
For all those enthusiasts of old British motor bikes. The complete step-by-step guide to Buying, Selling, Running, Servicing and Maintaining every model of classic British 'bike.

The remainder of the Porter Manuals range - those not covering FIAT cars - are at present not FIAT approved.

F I A T Panda

Repair Manual and Service Guide

by
Lindsay Porter
and Roy Stenning

Every care has been taken to ensure that the material in this book is correct. However, should any matter not be clear after reading this book, you are advised to consult your nearest franchised dealer. Liability cannot be accepted for damage, loss, accidents or injury, due to failure to follow instructions or to consult expert advice if this is required.

CONTENTS

Detailed Contents are shown at the start of each chapter.

CONTENTS

	Auto-Biography	1
CHAPTER 1:	Safety First!	5
CHAPTER 2:	Using Your Car	9
CHAPTER 3:	Facts and Figures	15
CHAPTER 4:	Getting Through the MoT	21
CHAPTER 5:	Servicing Your Car	25
CHAPTER 6:	Repairs and Replacements	69
CHAPTER 7:	Wiring Diagrams	135
	Spark Plug Conditions and Recommended Lubricants	142
	Index	143

FACT FILE: 'LEFT AND 'RIGHT' SIDES OF THE CAR

● Throughout this manual, we refer to the 'left' and 'right' sides of the car. They refer to the sides of the car that you would see if you were sitting in the driver's seat, looking forwards.

Please be sure to read the whole of this Chapter before carrying out any work on your car.

CHAPTER 1
SAFETY FIRST!

You must always ensure that safety is the first consideration in any job you carry out. A slight lack of concentration, or a rush to finish the job quickly can easily result in an accident, as can failure to follow the precautions outlined in this manual.

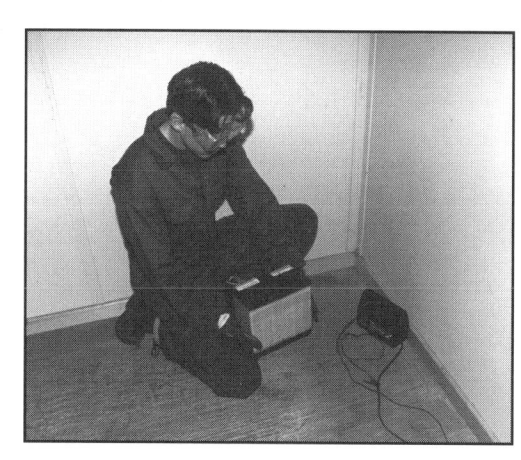

Be sure to consult the suppliers of any materials and equipment you may use, and to obtain and read carefully any operating and health and safety instructions that may be available on packaging or from manufacturers and suppliers.

GENERAL

Raising the Car Safely

ALWAYS ensure that the vehicle is properly supported when raised off the ground. Don't work on, around, or underneath a raised vehicle unless axle stands are positioned under secure, load bearing underbody areas, or the vehicle is driven onto ramps, with the wheels remaining on the ground securely chocked to prevent movement.

NEVER work on a vehicle supported on a jack. Jacks are made for lifting the vehicle only, not for holding it off the ground while it is being worked on.

ALWAYS ensure that the safe working load rating of any jacks, hoists or lifting gear used is sufficient for the job, and that lifting gear is used only as recommended by the manufacturer.

NEVER attempt to loosen or tighten nuts that require a lot of force to turn (e.g. a tight oil drain plug) with the vehicle raised, unless it is safely supported. Take care not to pull the vehicle off its supports when applying force to a spanner. Wherever possible, initially slacken tight fastenings before raising the car off the ground.

ALWAYS wear eye protection when working under the vehicle and when using power tools.

Working On The Vehicle

ALWAYS seek specialist advice unless you are justifiably confident about carrying out each job. The safety of your vehicle affects you, your passengers and other road users.

DON'T lean over, or work on, a running engine unless it is strictly necessary, and keep long hair and loose clothing well out of the way of moving mechanical parts. Note that it is theoretically possible for fluorescent striplighting to make an engine fan appear to be stationary - double check whether it is spinning or not! This is the sort of error that happens when you're really tired and not thinking straight. So...

...DON'T work on your car when you're over tired.

ALWAYS work in a well ventilated area and don't inhale dust - it may contain asbestos or other harmful substances.

NEVER run the engine indoors, in a confined space or over a pit.

REMOVE your wrist watch, rings and all other jewellery before doing any work on the vehicle - and especially when working on the electrical system.

DON'T remove the radiator or expansion tank filler cap when the cooling system is hot, or you may get scalded by escaping coolant or steam. Let the system cool down first and even then, if the engine is not completely cold, cover the cap with a cloth and gradually release the pressure.

NEVER drain oil, coolant or automatic transmission fluid when the engine is hot. Allow time for it to cool sufficiently to avoid scalding you.

ALWAYS keep antifreeze, brake and clutch fluid away from vehicle paintwork. Wash off any spills immediately.

TAKE CARE to avoid touching any engine or exhaust system component unless it is cool enough not to burn you.

CHAPTER 1 SAFETY FIRST!

Running The Vehicle

NEVER start the engine unless the gearbox is in neutral (or 'Park' in the case of automatic transmission) and the hand brake is fully applied.

NEVER run catalytic converter equipped vehicles without the exhaust system heat shields in place.

TAKE CARE when parking vehicles fitted with catalytic converters. The 'cat' reaches extremely high temperatures and any combustible materials under the car, such as long dry grass, could be ignited.

Personal Safety

NEVER siphon fuel, antifreeze, brake fluid or other such toxic liquids by mouth, or allow contact with your skin. Use a suitable hand pump and wear gloves.

BEFORE undertaking dirty jobs, use a barrier cream on your hands as a protection against infection. Preferably, wear suitable gloves, available from DIY outlets.

WEAR IMPERVIOUS GLOVES for sure when there is a risk of used engine oil coming into contact with your skin. It can cause cancer.

WIPE UP any spilt oil, grease or water off the floor immediately.

MAKE SURE that spanners and all other tools are the right size for the job and are not likely to slip. Never try to 'double-up' spanners to gain more leverage.

SEEK HELP if you need to lift something heavy which may be beyond your capability. Don't forget that when lifting a heavy weight, you should keep your back straight and bend your knees to avoid injuring your back.

NEVER take risky short-cuts or rush to finish a job. Plan ahead and allow plenty of time.

BE METICULOUS and keep the work area tidy - you'll avoid frustration, work better and lose less.

KEEP children and animals right-away from the work area and from unattended vehicles.

ALWAYS tell someone what you're doing and have them regularly check that all is well, especially when working alone on, or under, the vehicle.

HAZARDS

Fire!

Petrol (gasoline) is a dangerous and highly flammable liquid requiring special precautions. When working on the fuel system, disconnect the vehicle battery earth (ground) terminal whenever possible and always work outside, or in a very well ventilated area. Any form of spark, such as that caused by an electrical fault, by two metal surfaces striking against each other, by a central heating boiler in the garage 'firing up', or even by static electricity built up in your clothing can, in a confined space, ignite petrol vapour causing an explosion. Take great care not to spill petrol on to the engine or exhaust system, never allow any naked flame anywhere near the work area and, above all, don't smoke.

Invest in a workshop-sized fire extinguisher. Choose the carbon dioxide type or preferably, dry powder but NEVER a water type extinguisher for workshop use.

DON'T disconnect any fuel pipes on a fuel injected engine without following the advice in this manual. The fuel in the line is under very high pressure - sufficient to cause serious injury. Remember that many injection systems have residual pressure in the pipes for days after switching off. If necessary seek specialist advice.

Fumes

Petrol (gasoline) vapour and that given off by many solvents, thinners, and adhesives are highly toxic and under certain conditions can lead to unconsciousness or even death, if inhaled. The risks are increased if such fluids are used in a confined space so always ensure adequate ventilation. Always read the maker's instructions and follow them with care.

Never drain petrol (gasoline) or use solvents, thinners adhesives or other toxic substances in an inspection pit. It is also dangerous to park a vehicle for any length of time over an inspection pit. The fumes from even a slight fuel leak can cause an explosion when the engine is started.

Mains Electricity

Avoid the use of mains electricity when working on the vehicle, whenever possible. Use rechargeable tools and a DC inspection lamp, powered from a remote 12V battery - both are much safer. However, if you do use mains-powered equipment, ensure that the appliance is wired correctly to its plug, that where necessary it is properly earthed (grounded), and that the fuse is of the correct rating for the appliance. Do not use any mains powered equipment in damp conditions or in the vicinity of fuel, fuel vapour or the vehicle battery.

Always use an RCD (Residual Current Device) circuit breaker with mains electricity. Then, if there is a short, the RCD circuit breaker minimises the risk of electrocution by instantly cutting the power supply.

Ignition System

Never work on the ignition system with the ignition switched on, or with the engine being turned over on the starter, or running and you are recommended never to do so.

Touching certain parts of the ignition system, such as the HT leads, distributor cap, ignition coil etc., can result in a severe electric shock or physical injury as a hand is pulled sharply away. Voltages produced by electronic ignition systems are much higher than those produced by conventional systems and could prove fatal, particularly to people with cardiac pacemaker implants. Consult your handbook or main dealer if in any doubt.

Cooling Fan

On many vehicles, the electric cooling fan can switch itself on even with the ignition turned off. This is especially likely after driving the car and parking it before turning off, after which heat rises to the top of the engine and turns the fan on, suddenly and without warning. If you intend working in the engine bay, it's best to do so when the engine is cold, to disconnect the battery, or keep away from the fan, if neither of these are possible.

Battery

Never cause a spark, smoke, or allow a naked light near the vehicle's battery, even in a well ventilated area. Highly explosive hydrogen gas is given off as part of the charging process.

Battery terminals on the car should be shielded, since a spark can be caused by any metal object which touches the battery's terminals or connecting straps.

IMPORTANT NOTE: Before disconnecting the battery earth (ground) terminal read the relevant FACT FILE in Chapter 5 regarding saving computer and radio settings.)

When using a battery charger, switch off the power supply before the battery charger leads are connected or disconnected. If the battery is not of the 'sealed-for-life' type, loosen the filler plugs or remove the cover before charging. For best results the battery should be given a low rate trickle charge overnight. Do not charge at an excessive rate or the battery may burst.

Always wear gloves and goggles when carrying or when topping up the battery. Acid electrolyte is extremely corrosive and must not be allowed to contact the eyes, skin or clothes.

Brakes and Asbestos

Obviously, a car's brakes are among its most important safety related items. ONLY work on your vehicle's braking system if you are trained and competent to do so. If you have not been trained in this work, but wish to carry out the jobs described in this book, we strongly recommend that you have a garage or qualified mechanic check your work before using the car.

Whenever you work on the braking system components, or remove front or rear brake pads or shoes: i) wear an efficient particle mask; ii) wipe off all brake dust from the brakes after spraying on a proprietary brand of brake cleaner (never blow dust off with compressed air); iii) dispose of brake dust and discarded shoes or pads in a sealed plastic bag; iv) wash your hands thoroughly after you have finished working on the brakes and certainly before you eat or smoke; v) replace shoes and pads only with asbestos-free shoes or pads. Note that asbestos brake dust can cause cancer if inhaled; vi) always replace brake pads and/or shoes in complete 'axle' sets of four - never replace the pads/shoes on one wheel only.

Brake Fluid

Brake fluid absorbs moisture rapidly from the air and can become dangerous resulting in brake failure. You should change the fluid in accordance with your vehicle manufacturer's recommendations or as advised in this book. Never store (or use) an opened container of brake fluid. Dispose of the remainder at your Local Authority Waste Disposal Site, in the designated disposal unit, not with general waste or with waste oil.

Engine Oils

Always wear disposable plastic or rubber gloves when draining the oil from your engine. i) Note that the drain plug and the oil are often hotter than you expect. Wear gloves if the plug is too hot to touch and keep your hand to one side so that you are not scalded by the spurt of oil as the plug comes away; ii) There are very real health hazards associated with used engine oil. In the words of one manufacturer's handbook "Prolonged and repeated contact may cause serious skin disorders, including dermatitis and cancer." Use a barrier cream on your hands and try not to get oil on them. Always wear gloves and wash your hands with hand cleaner soon after carrying out the work. Keep oil out of the reach of children; iii) NEVER, EVER dispose of old engine oil into the ground or down a drain. In the UK, and in most EC countries, every local authority must provide a safe means of oil disposal. In the UK, try your local Environmental Health Department for advice on waste disposal facilities.

Plastic Materials

Many of the materials used (polymers, resins, adhesives and materials acting as catalysts and accelerators) contain dangers in the form of poisonous fumes, skin irritants, and the risk of fire and explosions. Do not allow resin or 2-pack adhesive hardener, or that supplied with filler or 2-pack stopper, to come into contact with skin or eyes. Read carefully the safety notes supplied on the can, tube or packaging and always wear impervious gloves and goggles when working with them.

Fluoroelastomers

Fluoroelastomers are commonly used for oil seals, wiring and cabling, bearing surfaces, gaskets, diaphragms, hoses and 'O' rings. If they are subjected to temperatures greater than 315 degrees C, they will decompose and can be potentially hazardous. Some decomposition may occur at temperatures above 200 degrees C, and it is obvious that when a car has been in a fire or has been dismantled with the assistance of a cutting torch or blow torch, the fluoroelastomers can decompose in the manner indicated above.

According to the Health and Safety Executive, "Skin contact with this liquid or decomposition residues can cause painful and penetrating burns. Permanent irreversible skin and tissue damage can occur". Damage can also be caused to eyes or by the inhalation of fumes created as fluoroelastomers are burned or heated.

After a vehicle has been exposed to fire or high temperatures:

1. Do not touch blackened or charred seals or equipment.

2. Preferably, don't handle parts containing decomposed fluoroelastomers, but if you must, wear goggles and PVC (polyvinyl chloride) or neoprene protective gloves whilst doing so. Never handle such parts unless they are completely cool.

3. Contaminated parts, residues, materials and clothing, including protective clothing and gloves, should be disposed of by an approved contractor to landfill or by incineration according to national or local regulations. Oil seals, gaskets and 'O' rings, along with contaminated material, must not be burned.

WORKSHOP

1. Always have a fire extinguisher of the correct type at arm's length when working on the fuel system. If you do have a fire, DON'T PANIC. Use the extinguisher effectively by directing it at the base of the fire.

2. NEVER use a naked flame anywhere in the workplace.

3. KEEP your inspection lamp well away from any source of petrol (gasoline) such as when disconnecting a carburettor float bowl or fuel line.

4. NEVER use petrol (gasoline) to clean parts. Use paraffin (kerosene), white spirits, or, a proprietary degreaser.

5. NO SMOKING. There's a risk of fire or of transferring dangerous substances to your mouth and, in any case, ash falling into mechanical components is to be avoided.

FACT FILE: FOUR WHEEL DRIVE CARS

● Whenever you have to raise a wheel off the ground and turn it by hand, always ensure that the opposite-side's wheel to the one being lifted is also off the ground and free to turn and that both wheels remaining on the ground are held by the parking brake (if possible) and securely chocked in both directions.

● ALWAYS have the gearbox in neutral (or 'N' in the case of automatics). In the case of some 4 wheel drive automatics and those with permanent 4WD, it is necessary to disengage the 4WD system by special means.

● Consult your handbook or seek advice from your main dealer.

---

6. BE METHODICAL in everything you do, use common sense, and think of safety at all times.

ENVIRONMENT FIRST!

The used oil from the sump of just one car can cover an area of water the size of two football pitches, cutting off the oxygen supply and harming swans, ducks, fish and other river lift.

When you drain your engine oil - don't oil the drain!

Pouring oil down the drain will cause pollution. It is also an offense. Don't mix used oil with other materials, such as paint and solvents, because this makes recycling difficult. Take used oil to an oil recycling bank. Telephone FREE on 0800 663366 to find the location of your nearest oil bank, or contact you local authority recycling officer.

OIL POLLUTES WATER USE YOUR BRAIN - NOT THE DRAIN!

Please read the whole of the CHAPTER 1, SAFETY FIRST! before carrying out any work on your car.

CHAPTER 2
USING YOUR CAR

This Chapter is taken from FIAT's own official Handbooks on the Panda. It contains important and helpful information for the operation of your FIAT Panda.

We recommend that you read this chapter carefully, so that you will become familiar with your vehicle's controls and instruments.

KEYS AND LOCKS

❑ 1. DOORS AND BONNET

DOOR LOCKS
Most FIAT Pandas have manual locking. You turn the key in the lock in the normal way to lock and unlock the door.

TYPES OF KEYS
1A. 'Earlier Cars' models are supplied with two keys which are:

● Ignition and steering lock key (**A**).

● This key (**B**) is used to lock and unlock the car doors and tailgate/boot.

'Later cars' are supplied with just one master key:

1B. The Master key combines the features of keys (**1A-A**) and (**1A-B**) and operates all the door and car locks as well as the ignition and steering lock.

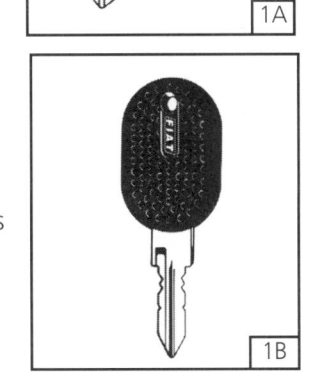

IMPORTANT NOTE: Replacement keys can be obtained from FIAT Sales network by quoting the number stamped on the key. Keep a record of the key numbers and store the record in a safe place.

SAFETY FIRST!

● Never remove the key when the car is moving. If you do, the steering wheel will lock the first time you turn it.

● If the ignition lock has been tampered with or shows any sign of damage (e.g. attempted theft), have the lock checked at your nearest FIAT Service Centre.

❑ 2. IGNITION SWITCH AND STEERING COLUMN LOCK

IGNITION SWITCH
2. The ignition/steering column lock key, once inserted in the ignition lock, can be placed in any of the following four positions:

● **PARK** - With the key in this position the side and tail lights can be turned on, the steering column locked and the keys can be removed.

● **STOP** - When the key is turned to the STOP position the steering column will be locked, and the keys can be removed.

● **MAR** - This is the driving position. When the key is in this position all the electrical devices are energised.

● **AVV** - Turning the key to this position starts the engine.

STEERING COLUMN LOCK
● **LOCKING** - To apply the steering wheel lock turn the steering wheel slightly to the left or right when the key is at STOP or PARK.

● **UNLOCKING** - Rock the steering wheel gently back and forth while turning the ignition key to MAR unlocks the steering wheel.

CHAPTER 2 — USING YOUR CAR

DASHBOARD

❑ 3. PANEL INDICATORS

Instrument Display Panel

3A. These are the instrument panel warning LED indicators for all FIAT Panda models. Your vehicle will only have the Panel Indicators relevant to your

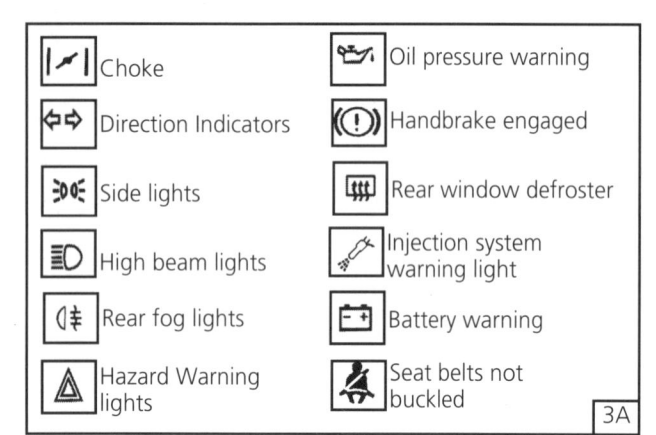

↙	Choke	🛢	Oil pressure warning
⇦⇨	Direction Indicators	⚠	Handbrake engaged
≡D≡	Side lights	⚟	Rear window defroster
≡D	High beam lights	🔧	Injection system warning light
(≣	Rear fog lights	🔋	Battery warning
⚠	Hazard Warning lights	🔔	Seat belts not buckled

particular model:

IMPORTANT NOTE: The check panel will not indicate if the side and tail light fuses blow at the same time, or if there is a circuit failure within the panel display.

HEATING AND VENTILATION CONTROLS

The heating and ventilation control panel on all Pandas is situated on the dashboard to the left of the steering wheel.

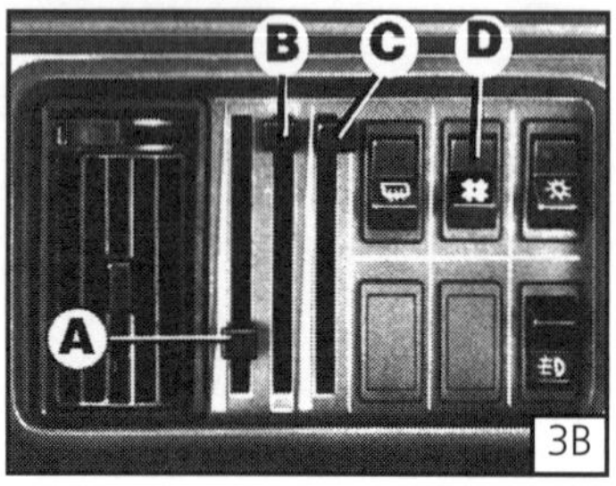

3B. The ventilation controls for the earlier Panda models are:

- **A** - Air flow control lever.

- **B** - Cold air temperature slide control (blue sector).

- **C** - Warm air temperature slide control (red sector).

- **D** - Fan ON/OFF switch.

3C. On later models of FIAT Panda the ventilation controls are:

- **A** - Increases or decreases air flow.

- **B** - Temperature control lever (blue sector for cold air, red sector for warm air).

- **C** - Air distribution knob-up for footwell and down for windscreen.

- **D** - Passenger air vent distribution ON/OFF switch.

- **E** - Fan speed selection switch.

CONTROLS

❑ 4. LIGHTING CONTROLS

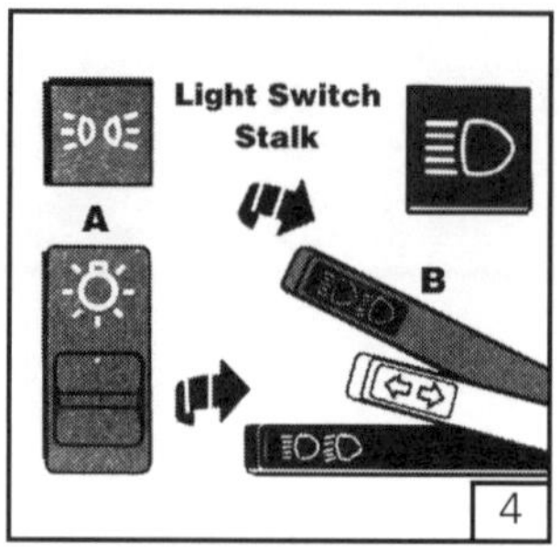

4. Side lights and headlights are controlled by a combination of switch (**A**) and stalk (**B**).

SIDE/TAIL LIGHT SWITCH

The light control switch (**A**), is located on the dashboard to the left of the steering wheel.

The lights only operate when the ignition key is at MAR.

With the ignition key at MAR, slide the light control switch (**A**):

- Up to switch all lights off.

- Centre position to turn on the side/tail lights, number plate light and all internal panel lighting.

LOW BEAM HEADLIGHTS

- Slide switch (**A**) down to the last click to turn on all of the above and the low beam headlights.

HIGH BEAM HEADLIGHTS

- Push the headlight stalk (**B**) down to turn the full beam headlights on, and push (**B**) back up to switch back to low beam.

❑ 5. DIRECTION INDICATORS

5. Move the left-hand indicator stalk (**C**) from its central position:

- Up = right turn.

- Down = left turn.

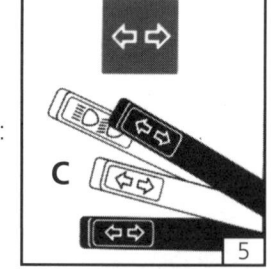

The panel direction indicator LED flashes when the indicators are operating. The stalk returns to the centre position after completing the turn.

❑ 6. WINDSCREEN WASHER/WIPER

6. The washer and wiper right-hand stalk (**D**) only operates when the ignition key is at MAR.

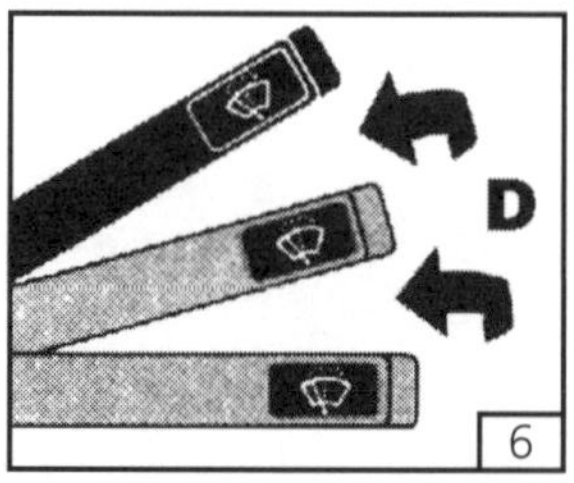

To operate the windscreen washer/wipers, push the stalk:

- Up to switch the wipers OFF.

- Centre position for intermittent operation.

- Down for continuous operation.

- Pull the wiper stalk (**D**) towards the steering wheel to turn on the windscreen washer/wiper.

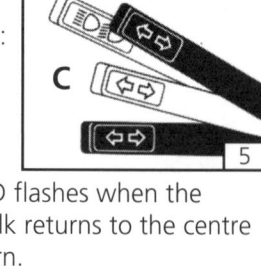

❑ 7. CONTROL SWITCH BANK

Most models are fitted with a switch bank, which is located on the dashboard to the left of the steering wheel.

EARLIER MODELS

7A. To operate the control bank switches on earlier models you must first place the ignition key at MAR:

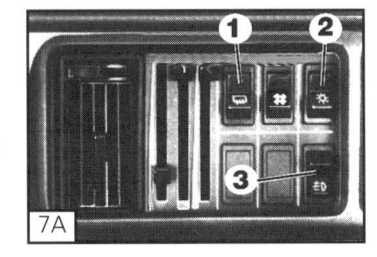

- Push down button (**1**) to operate the rear windscreen demister.

- Press switch (**2**) to turn lights on.

- Press button (**3**) to turn on the fog lights.

LATER MODELS

7B. To operate the controls on the later style of switch bank:

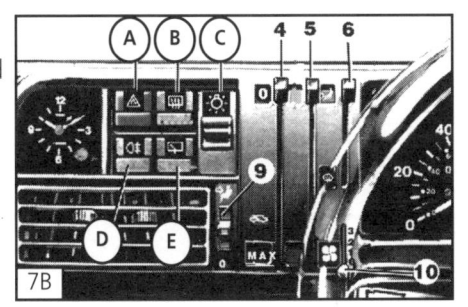

- **A** - Press to turn the hazard warning lights on or off. All the directional indicator lights and the panel indicator will flash. The hazard warning lights work whether the key is inserted or not.

- **B** - Press to switch the rear demister ON/OFF.

- **C** - Slide this switch to turn the lights ON/OFF.

- **D** - Push this button turn on the rear fog lights.

- **E** - Press to operate the rear windscreen wiper.

❑ 8. FUEL CUT-OFF SWITCH (VERY LATE MODELS ONLY)

8. This safety switch comes into action in the event of a collision, when it will cut off the fuel supply and stop the engine.

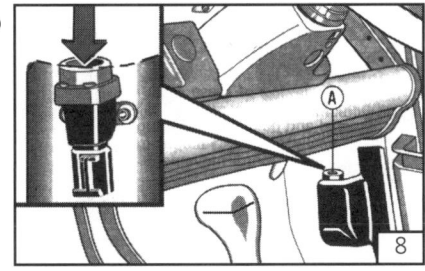

IMPORTANT

NOTE: If the cut-off switch has been activated, to prevent the battery from being run down, remember to turn the ignition key to STOP.

If there are no signs of a fuel leak and the car is in good enough condition to set off again, reactivate the fuel supply system by pressing button (**A**), which is situated on the right-hand side of the steering wheel underneath the dashboard.

INDIVIDUAL SETTINGS

❑ 9. FRONT SEAT ADJUSTMENT (EARLIER MODELS)

LEGROOM ADJUSTMENT

9. Lift lever (**A**) and exert body pressure in the direction desired to set the seats fore and aft position.

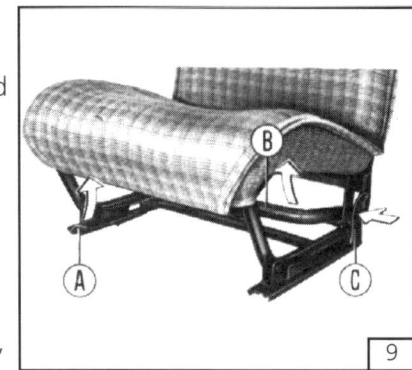

- Release lever (**A**), to ensure that the seat is locked in the desired position.

FRONT SEAT ANGLE ADJUSTMENT

- To adjust the angle of the front seats backrest cushion lift lever (**B**) to recline or raise the backrest.

ACCESS TO THE REAR SEATS

- The front seats can be released and folded forwards by lifting lever (**C**) and then tipping the seat forwards.

❑ 10. FRONT SEAT ADJUSTMENT (LATER MODELS)

LEGROOM ADJUSTMENT

10. Pull up lever (**A**) and exert body pressure to make fore and aft seat adjustments.

FRONT SEAT ANGLE ADJUSTMENT

- To adjust the angle of the front seat backrest cushions lift lever (**B**) to recline or raise the backrest.

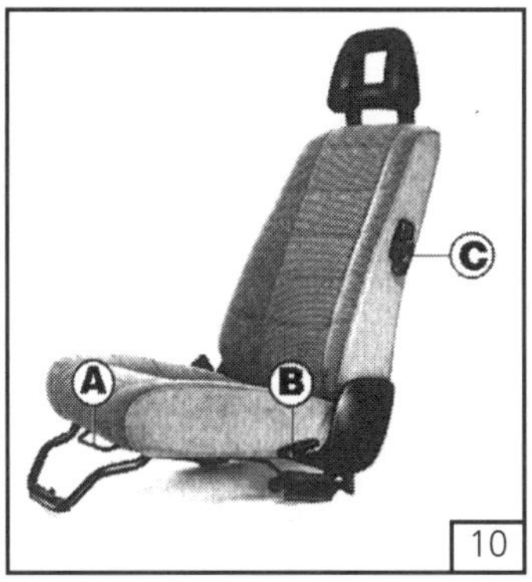

ACCESS TO THE REAR SEATS

- The front seats can be released and folded forwards by sliding lever (**C**) upwards.

❑ 11. DOOR MIRROR ADJUSTMENT

MANUAL ADJUSTMENT

11A. On these vehicles you can adjust the door mirrors angle using lever (**C**) from inside the passenger compartment.

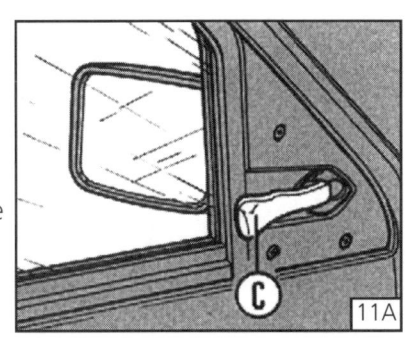

The mirror can be folded flush against the car when driving through a car wash.

CHAPTER 2 USING YOUR CAR

CHAPTER 2 USING YOUR CAR

POWER ADJUSTMENT

11B. When fitted, the two electric powered window switches are located in the driver's side armrest. They operate when the key is at MAR.

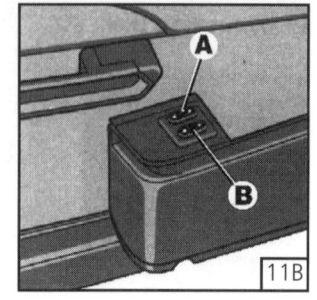

- **A** - Opens and closes the driver's door window.
- **B** - Opens and closes the passenger's door window.

There is also a single switch in the passenger's side door armrest which will only open and close the front passenger's window.

BONNET AND LUGGAGE COMPARTMENT

❏ 12. BONNET

OPENING THE BONNET

12A. First pull the bonnet release lever '**A**' (underneath the dashboard on the passenger side, or driver's side on later cars), towards you.

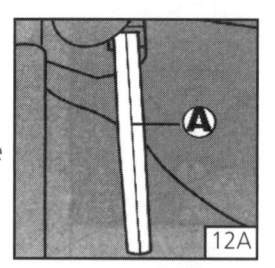

12B. Positioned underneath the front of the bonnet is the bonnet release catch (**B**). Lift the catch up to release.

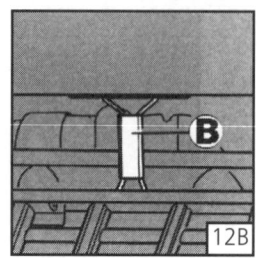

- Lift the bonnet and pull the support rod out of its holder.
- When the bonnet is fully raised, place the tip of the rod in the recess located in the bonnet.

❏ 13. LUGGAGE COMPARTMENT

INCREASING THE CARGO AREA (EARLIER MODELS)
To collapse the back seats on early Panda models use the following procedure to fold the rear seat down:

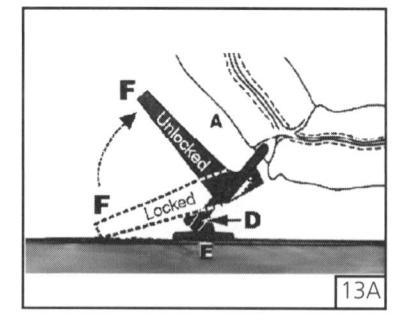

13A. Release the back rest catches (**A**) using levers (**F**) to unhook loop (**D**) from hooks (**E**).

13B. Release the seat backrest frame bar (**B**) by pulling the locking levers back while lifting the ends of the frame bar.

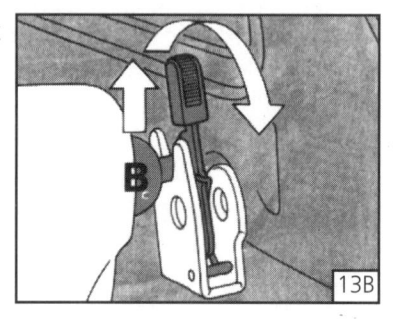

- Remove the frame bar by pulling the left side diagonally upwards out of the recess panel, then remove the right side by pulling the bar towards the inside of the car.

13C. Shown below are backseat positions for the earlier style Panda.

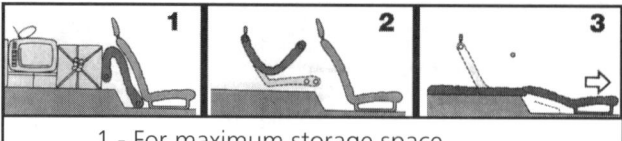

1 - For maximum storage space.
2 - Hammock position.
3 - Sleeping position.

INCREASING THE CARGO AREA (LATER CARS)
13D. Use the following procedure to fold the rear seat down:

- Press levers (**B**) down to release the seat backrest.
- Push the backrest down then forwards.

Reverse the procedure to replace the backseat to its original position, ensuring that: i) the seat belt buckles are resting on the backseats cushion, ii) the seat belt straps are not trapped behind the backrest and iii) the levers (**B**) are locked in the correct position.

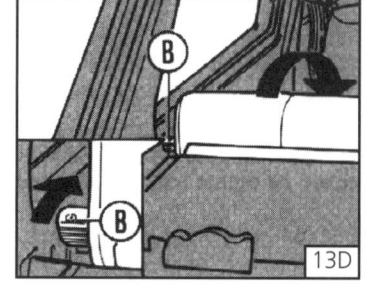

ACCESSORIES

❏ 14. INTERIOR LIGHTS

COURTESY LIGHT
On most models the courtesy light is positioned in the centre of the roof. The light turns on when either of the front doors are opened.

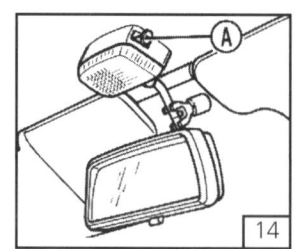

14. When the doors are closed flicking switch '**A**' (on the right-hand side of the courtesy light) will switch the light ON/OFF.

❏ 15. SUNROOF OPERATION

Some models are fitted with with a sunroof, which consists of two fabric coverings which are both opened and closed in the same way as each other.

TO OPEN THE SUNROOF
15A. Release lever (**A**) and fold the fabric forwards, making sure it does not get trapped under the frame.

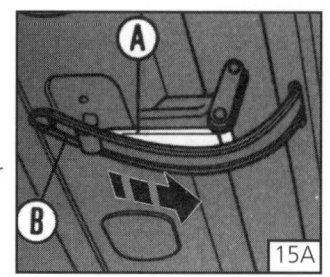

15B. Roll the canvas back and secure with strap (**B**) by fastening to the hook on the roof.

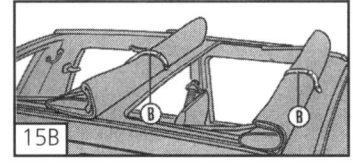

- Lever (**A**) should be positioned between the rubber strap and the fabric.

TO CLOSE THE SUNROOF

15C. Reverse the previous operations. Make sure that pin (**C**) of lever (**A**) is housed in seat (**D**).

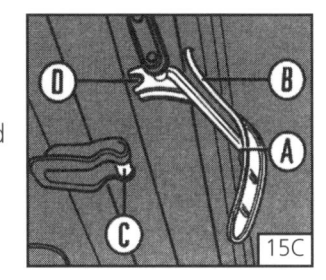

- Finally, hook strap (**B**) to the end of lever (**A**).

PARTIAL OPENING

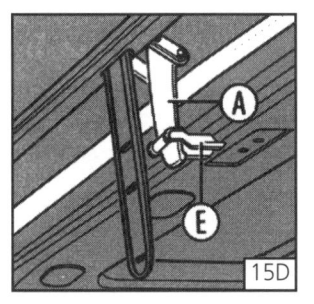

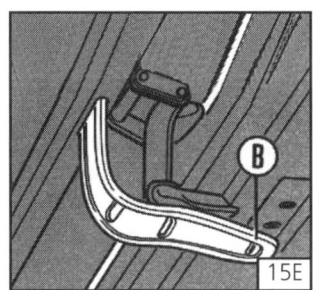

15D. Insert the end of lever (**A**) into hook (**E**).

15E. Position the elastic strap (**B**) as shown above.

WHEEL CHANGING

❏ 16. CHANGING THE WHEEL IN AN EMERGENCY

CHANGING THE WHEEL

Whenever possible park the car on firm level ground. Put the car into first or reverse gear and pull on the handbrake. It's a good idea to keep a chock or piece of wood in the boot of your car, which can be wedged under the wheels to prevent the car from rolling. If you haven't got a piece of wood handy you can always use a large rock or stone.

> **SAFETY FIRST!**
>
> - Before jacking the car, always make sure that the vehicle is on firm even ground.
>
> - Always place the spare wheel, or the wheel you've just removed, under the car: partly for safety to guard against being crushed; partly so that if the car topples off the jack you won't damage the underneath of the car and you'll be able to reposition the jack.

The spare wheel, jack and wheel bolt spanner are located under the bonnet in the engine compartment.

- Open the bonnet and remove the spare wheel from the engine compartment.

16A. Release the jack from the tool kit housing by unhooking the elastic strap (**A**).

- Remove the wheel bolt spanner (**B**) from its housing on the windscreen washer reservoir.

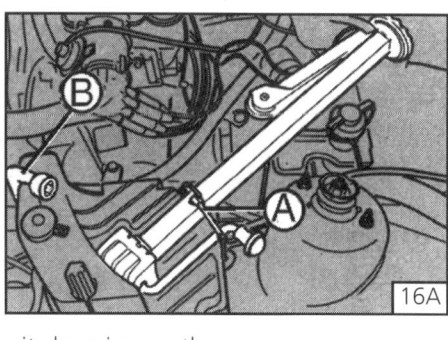

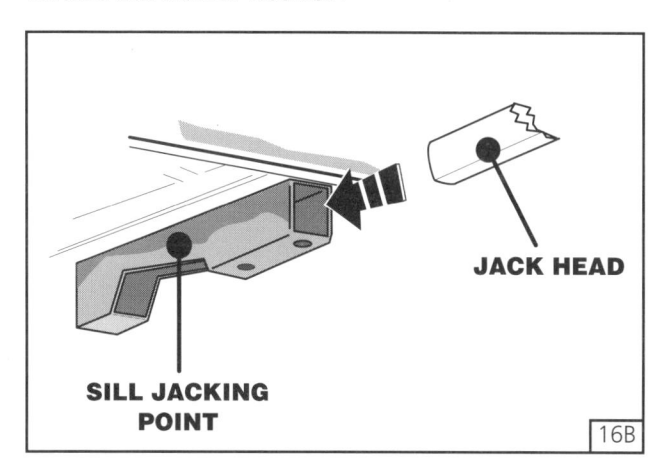

16B. Position the head of the jack so that it slides into the jacking point.

JACK SUPPORT

16C. Panda 4x4s are equipped with a jack support.

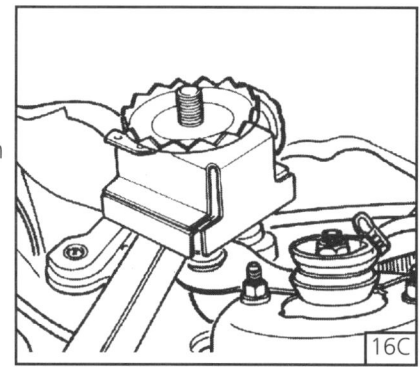

16D. If when fully extended, the jack does not raise the car high enough off the ground, place the jack support (serrated edge face down) under the jack to raise the car a little higher.

CHAPTER 2 USING YOUR CAR

CHAPTER 2 USING YOUR CAR

REMOVING THE WHEEL

16E. Using the wrench provided, loosen all the wheel bolts about one turn, in the order shown in the inset illustration.

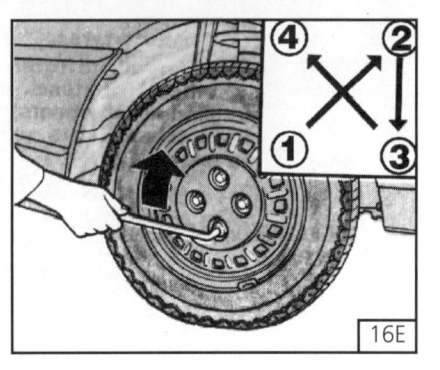

- Lift the car until the wheel is about 25 mm (1 in.) off the ground.

- The hub cap is only secured by three of the four wheel bolts.

- Remove the hub cap by unscrewing the three bolts, then unscrew the fourth wheel bolt, and remove the wheel.

- Put the spare wheel on, making sure that the aligning peg on the hub fits into one of the holes in the rim.

Some models are fitted with press fit wheel covers. To remove this type of cover pry off the cover to reach the wheel bolts.

EMERGENCY STARTING

❑ 17. ENGINE STARTING

JUMP STARTING YOUR CAR
Choose a fully charged battery with the same or higher capacity than the flat battery in your car, then proceed as follows:

- Make sure that the car with the flat batteries electrical equipment is turned off and that the ignition keys are removed.

17. Connect one of the jump lead clamps to the positive battery post of your flat battery. Then clamp the other end of the same lead on to the positive post of the second (charged) battery.

- Connect one end of the second jump lead to the negative pole of the charged battery, and attach the other end to the metal terminal (as shown) of the earth cable from your car's flat battery.

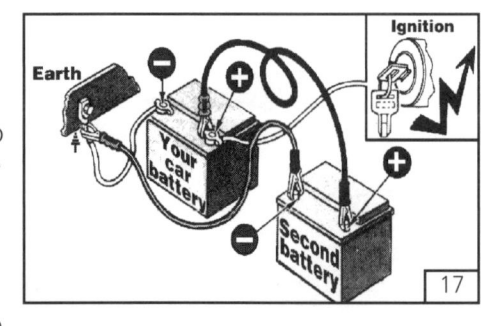

- Run the engine of the car with the charged battery at a medium to slow speed.

- Start the engine of the car with the flat battery, and run the engines of both cars for about three minutes.

- To reduce voltage peaks when disconnecting the jump leads, turn on the air fan and the heated rear screen of the car that had the flat battery.

- Remove the jumpleads, starting with the negative clamp connected to the car with the flat battery's earth.

IMPORTANT NOTE: When disconnecting the jump leads DO NOT switch on the headlights in place of the heated rear screen, as the peak voltage may blow the headlight bulbs.

BUMP STARTING
The best method of starting the engine in an emergency is using an auxiliary battery and jump leads, as described above. But in the case of extreme emergency, as long as your car does not have automatic transmission and is not fitted with a catalytic converter, the alternative method would be to bump start your car.

IMPORTANT NOTE: Never bump start a car fitted with a catalytic converter, as the sudden rush of unburnt fuel into the catalytic converter during the initial moments of engine operation could damage the converter beyond repair.

On models fitted with automatic transmission bump starting is made impossible by the features of the automatic transmission (i.e. no manual clutch).

To bump start a car not fitted with automatic transmission or a catalytic converter:

- Place the key in the ignition and turn to MAR.

- Engage a high gear (3rd or 4th) NOT REVERSE.

- Hold the clutch pedal down and get someone to push the car.

- When the pushed car has reached a fair speed, with the car still in gear gradually release the clutch pedal.

- As soon as the gear kicks in the engine should turn over and start running. Keep the engine running!

Get the battery charged and the car checked immediately.

IMPORTANT NOTE: Ensure that the key is in the ignition and is not removed at any time during bump starting. If the key is not in the ignition the steering wheel will lock the first time you turn it.

CHAPTER 3
FACTS AND FIGURES

This chapter provides you with all the information you will need about your car, especially in connection with servicing and repairing it. First, you'll need to identify the engine type. If you don't know it already, see **Chapter 6, Repairs and Replacements**.

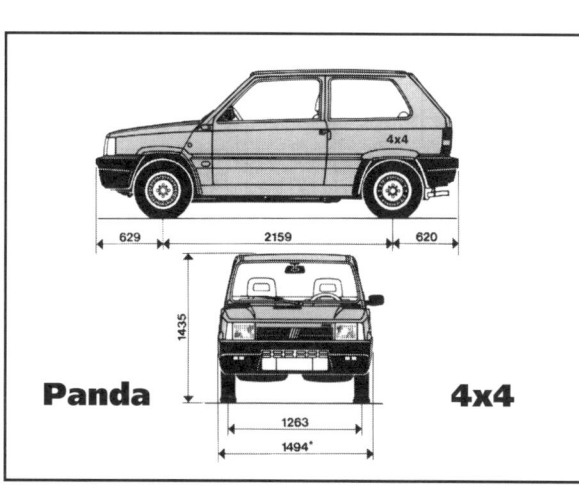

Before buying parts, be sure to take your vehicle's chassis (VIN) and spares numbers with you - see **Auto-Biography** on page 1 and **PART G: IDENTIFICATION NUMBERS** in this chapter.

Chapter Contents

	Page No.		Page No.
PART A: MAJOR MILESTONES	15	PART E: REPAIR DATA	17
PART B: VITAL STATISTICS	16	PART F: TORQUE WRENCH SETTINGS	18
PART C: CAPACITIES	16	PART G: IDENTIFICATION NUMBERS	20
PART D: SERVICE DATA	17		

IMPORTANT NOTE: Many detail changes have taken place over the years, and there have been many different Special Editions and Options available. The following information will be true of most cases but can only be taken as a general guide. Consult your local FIAT dealer for confirmation.

PART A: MAJOR MILESTONES

Overview When introduced, the Panda was fitted with either a FIAT 126-style 2-cylinder engine, or a 127-type 903cc, 4-cylinder overhead valve (OHV) unit. Later, a more sophisticated range of overhead camshaft (OHC) FIRE (Fully Integrated Robotised Engine) units became available and, later still, a diesel engine. The mainland Europe's 2-cylinder engine, the 899cc FIRE and the diesel were not available in the UK, nor was the van version of the Panda. Important to note: at times, both the OHC FIRE engine and the OHV engine were offered on Pandas.

However, the Panda's new coil spring rear suspension, in 1986, did replace the old leaf-spring set up, except on 4 x 4 models.

Limited Editions Too many were produced to list here. Only those which throw up anomalies are shown.

June 1981 *Panda* introduced into UK with 903cc OHV engine.

January 1986 *Panda 4 x 4* introduced, with 965cc OHV engine. Not available in UK.

April 1986 *Panda 4 x 4* fitted with 999cc FIRE OHC engine and launched in UK. Leaf-spring rear suspension retained.

April 1986 FIRE OHC engines introduced to front-drive cars, in 769cc (*750L*) and 999cc (*1000CL*) forms. OHV engines discontinued. 'Omega' rear suspension (on non-4 x 4 models), with coil springs instead of leaf.

June/July 1989 *Bella* limited edition, with 903cc OHV engine produced.

January 1990 *Panda 900 Dance* limited edition, with 903cc OHV engine introduced. Later, 500 *Italia '90* 903cc cars imported.

December 1991 *Panda 4 x 4* discontinued.

August 1991 *Panda Selecta* with constantly variable automatic transmission introduced. 999cc FIRE engine.

1992/1993 Pandas with fuel injection and catalytic converters (unleaded petrol only) introduced. Relatively small numbers produced.

April 1993 *Panda Selecta* fitted with 1108cc FIRE engine.

Mid-1995 No longer imported into UK.

PART B: VITAL STATISTICS

KEY TO MODELS

A = 1981-86 Panda 45
B = 1986-91 Panda 750
C = 1986-91 Panda 1000 (OHV engine)
D = 1986-91 Panda 1000 (OHC 'FIRE')
E = 1986-91 Panda 4x4
F = 1991-on Panda 4x4
G = 1991-on, manual gearbox
H = 1991-on Selecta Automatic

Wheels and tyres

WHEELS: 4.00 B X 13

TYRES SIZES: Most 'basic' versions - 135 SR 13. 'Super' versions - 145/70 SR 13 (pre-1986); 155/65 SR 13 (post-1986) Panda 1000 (optional) - 155/65 SR 13. Panda 4 x 4 - 145 SR 13 M&S.

TYRE PRESSURES (cold)

	Normal Load		Fully Loaded	
	Front	Rear	Front	Rear
135 SR 13 and 145/70 SR 13	2 bar/29 psi	2 bar/29 psi	2.2 bar/32 psi	2.2 bar/32 psi
155/65 SR 13	2.2 bar/32 psi	2.2 bar/32 psi	2.2 bar/32 psi	2.2 bar/32 psi
145 SR 13 (4 x 4)	2 bar/29 psi	2 bar/29 psi	2 bar/29 psi	2 bar/29 psi

Weights

Vehicle weights

NB Maximum load = Maximum Laden Weight minus Unladen Weight.

MODELS	Unladen Weight	Maximum Laden Weight
A	680 kg	1080 kg
B, C, D	700 kg	1100 kg
E	790 kg	1190 kg
F	800 kg	1220 kg
G	715 kg	1150 kg
H	745 kg	1150 kg

Max. roof load - 50 kg, all models.

Towable limits	Panda	Panda 4 x 4
Trailer with brakes	800 kg	900 kg
Trailer without brakes	350 kg	400 kg
Max. towball load	56 kg	56 kg

Dimensions (vehicle unladen)

Non-4 x 4 models - Overall length: 3408 mm; Overall width: 1494 mm; Wheelbase: 2159 mm; Front track: 1263 mm; Rear track: 1265 mm; Height: 1435 mm.

4 x 4 models - Overall length: 3408 mm; Overall width: 1500 mm; Wheelbase: 2170 mm; Front track: 1260 mm (1254 mm, later models); Rear track: 1264 mm (1258 mm, later models); Height: 1468 mm (1485 mm, later models).

PART C: CAPACITIES

KEY TO MODELS: See **PART B: VITAL STATISTICS**.

All fluid figures are given in litres.

FUEL TANK: A - 35 (inc. 7 to 8 reserve); B, C & D - 40 (inc. 5 to 7.5 reserve); E - 35 (inc. 5.5 to 6.5 reserve); F - 32 (inc. 5.5 to 6.5 reserve); G & H - 38 (inc. 5 to 7.5 reserve).

COOLANT CAPACITY INC. HEATER: All models - 5.2. **Paraflu** 50%, distilled water 50% protects down to - 35 degrees Celsius.

ENGINE OIL CAPACITY INC. FILTER: All models - 3.88 **Selenia** engine oil.

GEARBOX/TRANSAXLE: H - 2.8 drain and change **Tutela** ATF; All other models - 2.4 **Tutela** ZC 90.

STEERING GEAR: All models - 0.1 kg **Tutela** K 854 grease.

CV JOINT CAVITIES AND BOOTS: E & F - 0.045 kg. All other models - 0.095 kg **Tutela** MRM 2.

UNIVERSAL JOINTS: E & F only: **Tutela** MRM 2.

BRAKE FLUID: All models - 0.39 **Tutela** PLUS 3 240 degrees C.

PART D: SERVICE DATA

All settings in mm unless stated otherwise.

Engine

FIRING ORDER: All models - 1-3-4-2
DISTRIBUTOR POINTS GAP: (Non-electronic types only) Cars with Ducellier distributor - 0.37 to 0.43; With Marelli distributor - 0.42 to 0.48
DWELL ANGLE: (Non-electronic types only) Ducellier distributor - 52 to 58 degrees. Marelli distributor - 51 to 55 degrees.
TIMING - DEGREES BEFORE TOP-DEAD CENTRE (BTDC): OHV engines and 750 L - 5 degrees static or with vacuum pipe disconnected. All other models to 1991- 2 degrees. 1992-on (with electronic ignition and automatic speed control) - 7 to 13 degrees.
MAXIMUM VACUUM ADVANCE: All models - 12 to 13 degrees BTDC.
SPARK PLUG GAP:
All non-electronic ignition models - 0.7 to 0.8 mm
Electronic ignition models - 0.85 to 0.95 mm

SPARK PLUG TYPES:
Non-electronic ignition - FIAT - WGLSR. Champion - RC9YC
Electronic ignition - FIAT - 9FYSSR. Champion - RN9YCC
IDLE SPEED: All models: 750 to 800 rpm up to 1991. Then 850-950 rpm.
CO CONTENT AT IDLE (MAX): Early models: 2 to 3%. Later carburettor models: 1.5 to 2%. Fuel injected models (not adjustable): 0.4 to 1%.
UNBURNED HYDROCARBONS: <70 p.p.m. at 900 rpm, +/-50 rpm (1992-on).
VALVE CLEARANCES: OHV engines: Inlet - 0.15 mm; Exhaust - 0.2 mm. OHC 'FIRE' engines: Inlet - 0.3 mm +/-0.05; Exhaust - 0.4 mm +/- 0.05

Other settings

CLUTCH PEDAL POSITION: 8 to 12 mm below brake pedal level.
BRAKE DISC PAD MINIMUM THICKNESS: 1.5 mm
BRAKE SHOE FRICTION LINING MINIMUM THICKNESS: 1.5 mm
TYRE PRESSURES. (See **PART B: VITAL STATISTICS**.)

PART E: REPAIR DATA

All dimensions given in mm unless stated otherwise.

NB The 1108cc engine was used in very small numbers. Most engine dimensions are as for the 999cc engine. Note the following 1108 cc engine dimensions, however: **BORE** - 70 to 70.05; **STROKE** - 72.0.

Engine 'bottom end'

	903cc OHV	769cc FIRE	999cc FIRE
BORE	65 - 65.05	65 - 65.05	70 - 70.05
MAX. BORE TAPER OR OVALITY:	0.015	0.015	0.015

ENGINE CAMSHAFT BEARING DIAMETERS - FRONT (TIMING GEAR) END (OHV engines only):

Grade B	50.5 - 50.51	N/A	N/A
Grade C	50.51 - 50.52	N/A	N/A
Grade D	50.7 - 50.71	N/A	N/A
Grade E	50.71 - 50.72	N/A	N/A

NOTE: Oversize bearings are not available for centre and rear camshaft bearings.

STROKE:	68.0	58.0	64.9

PISTON SIZES:

SIZE A	64.94-64.95	64.96-64.97	69.96-69.97
SIZE C	64.96-64.97	64.98-64.99	69.98-69.99
SIZE E	64.98-64.99	65-65.01	70-70.01

OVERSIZES: 0.2, 0.4, 0.6
PISTON CLEARANCE IN BORE
	0.05-0.07	0.03-0.05	0.03-0.05

	903cc OHV	769cc FIRE	999cc FIRE

PISTON RING THICKNESS:

TOP	1.728-1.74	1.48-1.49	1.478-1.49
SECOND	1.978-1.99	1.478-1.49	1.478-1.49
BOTTOM	2.925-2.937	2.975-2.99	2.975-2.99

PISTON RING CLEARANCES - RING-TO-GROOVE

TOP	0.045-0.077	0.04-0.07	0.04-0.072
SECOND	0.025-0.057	0.025-0.057	0.025-0.057
BOTTOM	0.020-0.055	0.020-0.055	0.020-0.055

PISTON RING END GAP
	0.2-0.45	0.2-0.45	0.2-0.45

PISTON RING OVERSIZES: 0.2, 0.4, 0.6

CRANK JOURNAL DIAMETER
	50.785-50.805	43.99-44	43.99-44

CRANK, BIG-END DIAMETER
	39.985-40.005	37.988-38.008	37.988-38.008

MAIN BEARING SHELL THICKNESS
SIZE 1	1.832-1.837	1.834-1.84	1.834-1.84
SIZE 2	1.837-1.843	1.839-1.845	1.839-1.845

MAIN BEARING CLEARANCE
	0.028-0.073	0.025-0.06	0.025-0.06

MAIN BEARING UNDERSIZES: 0.254-0.508

BIG-END BEARING SHELL THICKNESS (STANDARD):
	1.807-1.813	1.542-1.548	1.542-1.548

BIG-END BEARING CLEARANCE
	0.026-0.071	0.024-0.068	0.024-0.068

BIG-END BEARING UNDERSIZES: 0.25, 0.5, 0.76, 1.0

THRUST WASHER THICKNESS
	2.31-2.36	2.31-2.36	2.31-2.36

THRUST WASHER OVERSIZE
	0.0127	0.0127	0.0127

CRANKSHAFT END FLOAT
	0.055-0.265	0.055-0.265	0.055-0.265

Engine 'top end' and valve gear

	903cc OHV	769cc FIRE	999cc FIRE

ENGINE CAMSHAFT BEARING OUTER DIAMETERS (OHC Engines only)

FRONT	N/A	24.045-24.070	24.045-24.070
CENTRE	N/A	23.545-23.57	23.545-23.57
REAR	N/A	24.045-24.070	24.045-24.070

CAM FOLLOWER DIAMETER

| 13.982-14 | 34.975-34.995 | 34.975-34.995 |

OVERSIZES AVAILABLE

| 0.05-0.1 | N/A | N/A |

INLET VALVE HEAD SIZE

| 28.8-29.1 | 26.2-26.5 | 30.2-30.5 |

EXHAUST VALVE HEAD SIZE

| 28.8-29.1 | 23.2-23.5 | 27.2-27.5 |

VALVE SEAT RE-CUTTING ANGLE: 45 degrees, +/-5' (all types)
VALVE FACE RE-CUTTING ANGLE: 45 degrees 30', +/-5' (all types)
OHC VALVE SHIM THICKNESSES: Between 3.2 and 4.7 mm in shim increments of 0.05 mm.

Cooling system

THERMOSTAT - Starts to open - 85 degrees C. Fully open - 100 degrees C
PRESSURE CAP RATING - 0.98 bar (14 lbf/sq.in.)
FAN SWITCH THERMOSTAT - Cut in - 90-94 degrees C. Cut out 85 to 89 C
WATER TIGHTNESS PRESSURE CHECK - at 0.98 bar (14 lbf/sq.in.)

Brakes

GAP - SERVO PISTON ROD TO MASTER CYL. SUPPORT - 0.825 to 1.025
MINIMUM ALLOWED DISC THICKNESS - 9.0 mm
MAXIMUM ALLOWED BRAKE DRUM INTERNAL DIAMETER: 186.83 mm

Running gear - front (Not 4 x 4)

CAMBER: Front - 1 degree +/-30'(not adjustable). Rear - 0 (not adjustable)
FRONT CASTER: 2 degrees 30' +/-30' (not adjustable)
TOE-IN: Front - 0 to -4 mm. Rear - 0
FRONT SPRING HEIGHT, RELEASED: 354 mm
FRONT SPRING HEIGHT, LOADED TO 2200 Nm: 213 mm
REPLACEMENT FRONT SPRING COLOURS:
Height >213 - Yellow. Height <213 - Green (Both springs must be same colour)

Running gear - front (4 x 4 Only)

CAMBER: Front - 2 degrees 20' +/-30'(not adjustable). Rear - 0 (not adjustable)
FRONT CASTER: 3 degrees 30' +/-30'
TOE-IN: Front - -2 to -6 mm. Rear - 0 (not adjustable)
FRONT SPRING HEIGHT, LOADED TO 2410 Nm: 231 mm
REPLACEMENT FRONT SPRING COLOURS:
Height >231 - Yellow. Height <231 - Green (Both springs must be same colour)

Rear suspension - (up to 1986 and 4 x 4)

Tubular axle, leaf springs, telescopic shock absorbers.

Rear suspension - (1986-on)

Tubular 'Omega' shaped axle, reaction arms, coil springs, telescopic shock absorbers
REAR COIL SPRING HEIGHT, RELEASED: 170 mm
REAR COIL SPRING HEIGHT, LOADED TO 2570 Nm: 170 mm
REPLACEMENT FRONT COIL SPRING COLOURS:
Height >170 - Yellow. Height <170 - Green (Both springs must be same colour)

PART F: TORQUE WRENCH SETTINGS

IMPORTANT NOTE: All torque settings shown in newton-metres (Nm).

Engine

	'FIRE' OHC	OHV
Main bearing cap, bolt (M10 x 1.25)	40 + 90 degrees	69
Cylinder head fixing, nut or bolt (M9 x 1.25)	30 + 90 degrees + 90 degrees	30 + 59
Big end, nut or bolt (M8 x 1)	41	41
Flywheel to crankshaft fixing, bolt (M8 x 1.25)	44	44
Rocker shaft pedestal nuts (M8)	N/A	39
Camshaft caps fixing (M8 x 1.25)	20	N/A
Camshaft caps fixing (M6 x 1)	10	N/A
Camshaft sprocket bolt	N/A	49
Belt tensioner fixing, nut (M8 x 1.25)	28	N/A
Timing driven gear fixing bolt, (M10 x 1.25)	70	N/A
Cambelt drive gear to crankshaft fixing, bolt (M10 x 1.25)	80	N/A
Crankshaft pulley nut (M8 x 1.25 FIRE only)	25	98
Water temperature sender unit (M14 x 1.25)	25	49
Carburettor to inlet manifold fixing, bolt (M6 x 1)	12	N/A
Inlet manifold to cylinder head fixing bolt (M8 x 1.25)	27	N/A
Water pump to cylinder block/crankcase fixing nut (M6 x 1)	8	25
Water pump cover fixing nuts	N/A	27

Gearbox and Clutch (All models)

Clutch to flywheel fixing, bolt (M6) - - - - - - - - - - - - - - - - - - - 16
Clutch selector fork, bolt (M8) - 26
Gearbox casing to bell housing fixing, bolt (M8) - - - - - - - - - 25
Bell housing to engine fixing, nuts and bolts (M12 x 1.25) - - - 78
Starter motor to bell housing fixing, bolt (M8) - - - - - - - - - - - 25
Cover to bell housing fixing, bolt (M6) - - - - - - - - - - - - - - - - 10
Cover for oil seal boot to bell housing mounting
fixing, bolt (M6) - 7.8
Flange retaining differential casing to gearbox
casing fixing, bolt (M8) - 25
Gearbox oil drain plug (M22 x 1.5) - - - - - - - - - - - - - - - - - - - 46

EXTERNAL GEARBOX CONTROLS

Gear lever mounting fixing, 'Nyloc' nut (M6) - - - - - - - - - - - - 4
Selector linkage to gear lever, nut for bolt (M6) - - - - - - - - - 7
Selector linkage support brackets fixing, bolt (M8 x 1.25) - - - 24

4x4 Components

Rear drive power take off mounting, nut for stud (M10 x 1.25) - 50
Power take off relay mounting to cover fixing, bolt (M8) - - - - 27
Selector spring push rod cover (M14 x 1.25) - - - - - - - - - - - - 40
Reduction gear power take off cover drain plug (M12 x 1.5) - 30
Rear wheel drive engagement fork fixing, bolt (M6 x 1) - - - - 10
Relay lever mounting to bodyshell fixing, bolt (M6) - - - - - - - - 4
Rod to relay lever fixing, nut (M6) - - - - - - - - - - - - - - - - - - - 7
Relay lever to mounting fixing, nut for bolt (M10) - - - - - - - - 31
Rod to relay lever fixing, nut (M6) - - - - - - - - - - - - - - - - - - - 7
Propeller shaft, gearbox side fixing, bolt (M8) - - - - - - - - - - 44
Propeller shaft, differential side, fixing, nut (M8) - - - - - - - - - 32
Connecting sleeve to mounting fixing, nut (M16 x 1.5) - - - - - 29
Constant velocity joint to propeller shaft fixing, bolt (M8) - - - 37
Constant velocity joint, gearbox side fixing, bolt (M8) - - - - - - 44

Braking System

Front brake caliper support mounting bolts
(manual gearbox) (M10 x 1.25) - 53
Front brake caliper mounting bolt (Selecta) - - - - - - - - - - - - 53
Handbrake lever assembly to bodywork
fixing, bolt (M10 x 1.25) - 39
Rear wheel cylinder to backplate (M6) - - - - - - - - - - - - - - - - 10
Load proportioning valve, nut for bolt (M6) - - - - - - - - - - - - 4.4
Complete pedal mounting fixing, nut (M8) - - - - - - - - - - - - - 15
Master cylinder fixing, nut for bolt (M8) - - - - - - - - - - - - - - - 25
Master cylinder to servo brake fixing, nut (M8) - - - - - - - - - - 20
Brake back plate fixing, bolt (M8) - - - - - - - - - - - - - - - - - - - 24
Front brake pipe to caliper union - 4x4 ONLY
    cast iron (M10 x 1) - 16
    aluminium (M10 x 1) - 11

Steering

Steering wheel to column fixing, nut (M16 x 1.5) - - - - - - - - - 49
Universal joint fork to column fixing, nut for bolt (M8) - - - - - 27
Steering box to bodywork fixing, bolt (M8) - - - - - - - - - - - - - 25
Ball joint to side steering rod fixing, nut (M14 x 1) - - - - - - - - 49
Ball joint to lever on shock absorber fixing, nut (M10 x 1.25) - 34

Front Suspension

Wheel nuts (M12 x 1.25) - 86
Wheel bearing fixing, nut (to be staked) (M20 x 1.5) - - - - - - 216
Front hub and brake backplate fixing bolts (M10 x 1.25) - - - 64
Radius rod to bodywork fixing, nut (M10 x 1.25) - - - - - - - - - 44
Front suspension lower ball joint fixing, nut (M10 x 1.25) - - - 34
Front suspension, strut lower fixing bolts -
front wheel drive cars (M10 x 1.25) - - - - - - - - - - - - - - - - - - 66
Front suspension, strut lower fixing bolts -
4 x 4 cars (M12 x 1.25) - 123
Front suspension strut upper fixings, (M8 and M10) - - - - - - - 25
Radius rod to front suspension lower arm
fixing, nut for bolt (M12 x 1.25) - 69
Radius rod to body, nut (M12 x 1.25) - - - - - - - - - - - - - - - - 69
Radius rod to front suspension lower arm
attachment bracket fixing, bolt (M8) - - - - - - - - - - - - - - - - - 15
Radius rod mounting to bodywork
fixing, bolt (M10 x 1.25) - 39
Track rod end nut (M8) - 25

Rear Suspension

Wheel nuts (M12 x 1.25) - 86
Upper and lower shock absorber, fixing nuts (M12 x 1.25) - - - 49
Wheel hub fixing, nut (M20 x 1.5) - - - - - - - - - - - - - - - - - - 216

LEAF SPRING REAR SUSPENSION ONLY

Leaf spring U-bolt nuts (M10 x 1.25) - - - - - - - - - - - - - - - - - 49
Spring shackle fixing (M10 x 1.25) - - - - - - - - - - - - - - - - - - 29
Spring, front pivot bolt (M12 x 1.25) - - - - - - - - - - - - - - - - - 49

COIL SPRING REAR SUSPENSION ONLY

Central axle fixing, nut (M12 x 1.25) - - - - - - - - - - - - - - - - 123
Central axle mounting, to bodywork fixing, bolt (M8) - - - - - - 24
Side strut to bodywork front fixing, nut (M10 x 1.25) - - - - - - 70
Side strut to axle rear fixing, bolt (M10 x 1.25) - - - - - - - - - - 49

Rear Axle - 4x4 Only

Oil filler plug (M22 x 1.5 taper) - 46
Oil drain plug (M22 x 1.5 taper) - 46
Leaf spring U-bolt, nuts (M10 x 1.25) - - - - - - - - - - - - - - - - 49
Rear suspension leaf spring shackle
fixing, nut (M10 x 1.25) - 29
Spring, front pivot bolt nut (M12 x 1.25) - - - - - - - - - - - - - - 49
Rear suspension upper and lower shock absorber
fixings, nuts (M12 x 1.25) - 49
Rear suspension upper shock absorber
fixing, nut (M12 x 1.25) - 49
Bearing complete with hub to rear axle
fixing, bolt (M10 x 1.25) - 70

CHAPTER 3 Facts and Figures

19

PART G: IDENTIFICATION NUMBERS

Finding the Numbers

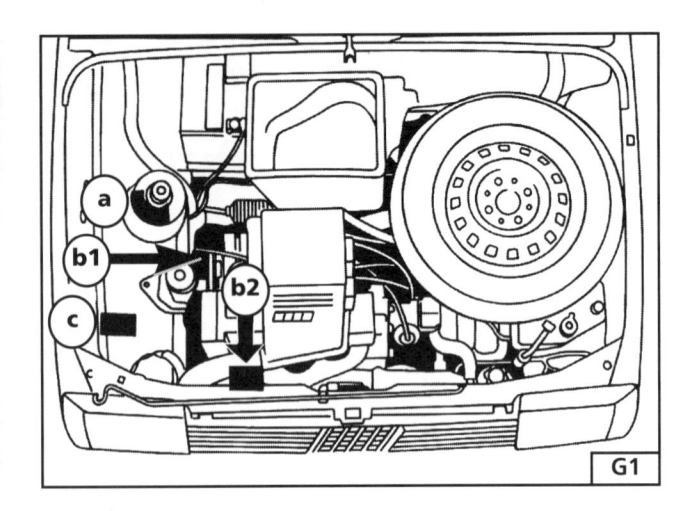

Model and Data Plate

G1: There are four sets of identification numbers in all. First, there is the Vehicle Identification (V.I.N.) Number, or chassis number (**a**). Second, is the engine number. Position (**b1**) is the engine number on OHV engines and (**b2**) the position on FIRE OHC engines. Also, see **G4** and **G5**.

Third, there is the Model and Data Plate (**c**).

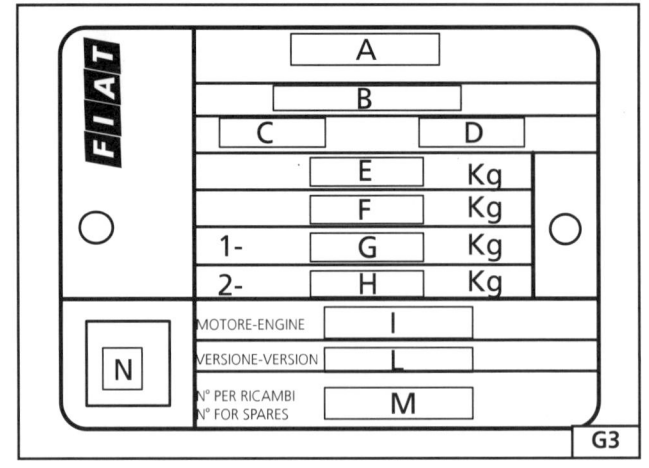

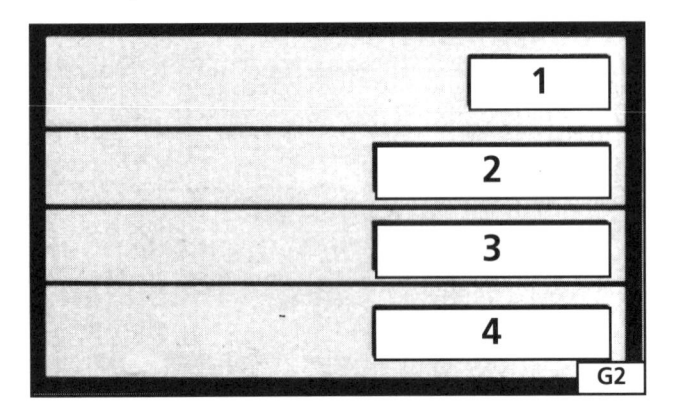

G3: The numbers stamped on the plate stand for the following: **A** - Manufacturer; **B** - Homologation number; **C** - Vehicle identity code; **D** - Chassis serial number; **E** - Maximum authorised weight of vehicle, fully laden; **F** - Maximum authorised weight of vehicle, fully laden plus trailer; **G** - Maximum authorised weight on front axle; **H** - Maximum authorised weight on rear axle; **I** - Engine type; **L** - Body code (see below); **M** - Number for buying spares; **N** - Smoke opacity index (diesel engines only) - not UK.

INSIDE INFORMATION: The number stamped at position 'L' will tell you whether the vehicle was originally fitted with a four-speed or five-speed gearbox. If the last three numbers are 43A, 43C or 43D, the vehicle was fitted with the four-speed gearbox. If the last numbers are 53A (or any other letter), the vehicle was fitted with a five-speed gearbox.

G2: Fourth, you will need the Paint Identification Plate if you need to need to buy paint. You'll find it on the inside of the hatchback door. The numbers shown on the plate give the following information: **1** - Paint manufacturer; **2** - Colour name; **3** - Colour code; **4** - Respray and touch-up code.

Engine Numbers

G4: This is the position of the engine numbers on OHV engines. Note the position relative to the oil filler cap.

G5: Here is the position on all FIRE OHC engines.

Vehicle Identification Numbers

See illustration **G1**, part **a**. There are two groups of codes which are unique to your car. You should never buy a car without checking first that the V.I.N. shown on the car matches that on the vehicle registration document. The vehicle code is also shown at position **C** on the model plate and the chassis serial number is also shown at position **D**.

Please read the whole of the CHAPTER 1, SAFETY FIRST! before carrying out any work on your car.

CHAPTER 4
GETTING THROUGH THE MOT

This chapter is for owners in Britain whose vehicles need to pass the 'MoT' test. Obviously, you won't be able to examine your car to the same degree of thoroughness as the MoT testing station. But you can reduce the risk of being one of the 4 out of 10 who fail the test first time by following this check-list.

The checks shown below are correct at the time of writing but do note that they are becoming stricter all the time. Your local MoT testing station will have the latest information, should you need it.

Chapter Contents

	Page No.		Page No.
PART A: INSIDE THE CAR	21	PART C: VEHICLE RAISED OFF THE GROUND	23
PART B: VEHICLE ON THE GROUND	22	PART D: EXHAUST EMISSIONS	24

PART A: INSIDE THE CAR

Steering Wheel and Column

○ **1.** Try to move the steering wheel towards and away from you and then from side to side. There should be no appreciable movement or play. Check that the steering wheel is not loose on the column.

○ **2.** Lightly grip the steering wheel between thumb and finger and turn from side to side. **Cars with a steering rack:** free play should not exceed approximately 13 mm (0.5 in.), assuming a 380 mm (15 in.) diameter steering wheel. **Cars fitted with a steering box:** free play should not exceed approximately 75 mm (3.0 in.), assuming a 380 mm (15 in.) diameter steering wheel.

○ **3.** If there is a universal joint at the bottom of the steering column inside the car, check for movement. Place your hand over the joint while turning the steering wheel to-and-fro a little way with your other hand. If ANY free play can be felt, the joint must be replaced.

○ **4.** Ensure that there are no breaks or loose components on the steering wheel itself.

Electrical Equipment

○ **5.** With the ignition turned on, ensure that the horn works okay.

○ **6.** Check that the front wipers work.

○ **7.** Check that the windscreen washers work.

○ **8.** Check that the internal warnings for the indicator and hazard warning lights work okay.

Checks With An Assistant

○ **9.** Check that the front and rear side lights and number plate lights work and that the lenses and reflectors are secure, clean and undamaged.

○ **10.** Check the operation of the headlights (you won't be able to check the alignment yourself) and check that the lenses are undamaged. The reflectors inside the headlights must not be tarnished, nor must there be condensation inside the headlight.

○ **11.** Turn on the ignition and check the direction indicators, front and rear and on the side markers.

○ **12.** Check that the hazard warning lights operate on the outside of the vehicle, front and rear.

○ **13.** Check that the rear fog light/s, including the warning light inside the car, all work correctly.

○ **14.** Check that the rear brake lights work correctly. These checks are carried out all around the vehicle with all four wheels on the ground.

○ **15.** Operate the brake lights, side lights and each indicator in turn, all at the same time. None should affect the operation of the others.

SAFETY FIRST!

- *Follow the Safety information in **CHAPTER 1, SAFETY FIRST!** but bear in mind that the vehicle needs to be even more stable than usual when raised off the ground.*

- *There must be no risk of it toppling off its stands or ramps while suspension and steering components are being pushed and pulled in order to test them.*

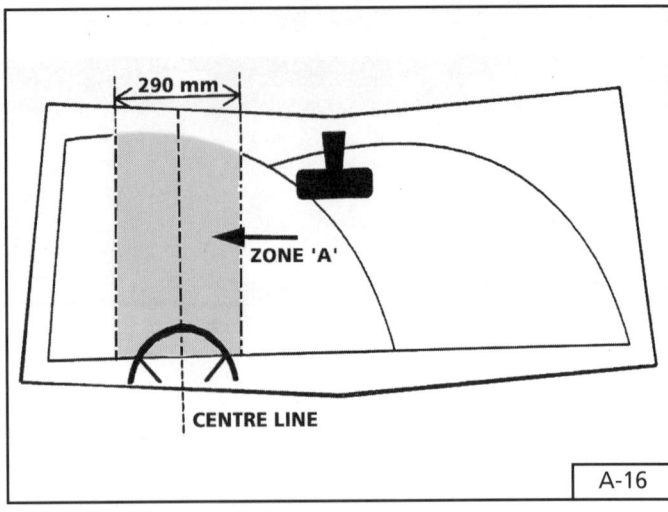

Windscreen and Mirrors

⭕ **16.** In zone 'A' of your windscreen, no items of damage larger than 10 mm in diameter will be allowed. In the rest of the area swept by the windscreen wipers, no damage greater than 40 mm in diameter will be allowed, nor should windscreen stickers or other obstructions encroach on this area.

⭕ **17.** Check that the exterior mirror on the driver's side is in good condition.

⭕ **18.** There must be one other mirror in good condition, either inside the car or an external mirror on the passenger's side.

Brakes

⭕ **19.** You cannot check the brakes properly without a rolling road brake tester but you can carry out the following checks:

⭕ **20.** Pull on the handbrake. It should be fully ON before the handbrake reaches the end of its travel.

⭕ **21.** Knock the handbrake from side to side and check that it does not then release itself.

⭕ **22.** Check the security of the handbrake mountings and check the floor around it for rust or splits.

⭕ **23.** Check that the brake pedal is in good condition and that, when you take hold of it and move it from side to side, there is not too much play.

⭕ **24.** Push the footbrake down hard, with your foot. If it creeps slowly down to the floor, there is probably a problem with the master cylinder. Release the pedal, and after a few seconds, press down again. If the pedal feels spongy or it travels nearly to the floor, there is air in the system or another MoT-failing fault with the brakes.

⭕ **25.** Check the servo unit (when fitted) as follows: Pump the pedal several times then hold it down hard. Start the engine. As the engine starts, the pedal should move down slightly. If it doesn't the servo or the vacuum hose leading to it may be faulty.

Seat Belts and Seats

⭕ **26.** Examine all of the webbing (pull out the belts from the inertia reel if necessary) for cuts, fraying or deterioration.

⭕ **27.** Check that each inertia reel belt retracts correctly.

⭕ **28.** Fasten and unfasten each belt to ensure that the buckles work correctly.

⭕ **29.** Tug hard on each belt and inspect the mountings, as far as possible, to ensure that all are okay.

IMPORTANT NOTE: Checks apply to rear seat belts as much as front ones.

⭕ **30.** Make sure that the seat runners and mountings are secure and that the back rest locks in the upright position.

Doors and Door Locks

⭕ **31.** Check that both front doors latch securely when closed and that both can be opened and closed from both outside and inside the car.

PART B: VEHICLE ON THE GROUND

Electrical Equipment

See *Part A: INSIDE THE CAR* for checks on the operation of the electrical equipment.

⭕ **1.** Examine the wiper blades and replace those that show any damage.

Vehicle Identification Numbers (VIN)

⭕ **2.** The VIN (or chassis number on older vehicles) must be clearly displayed and legible.

⭕ **3.** Number plates must be secure, legible and in good condition with correct spacing between letters and numbers. Any non-standard spacing will not be accepted.

Braking System

⭕ **4.** Inside the engine bay inspect the master cylinder, servo unit (if fitted), brake pipes and mountings. Look for corrosion, loose fitting or leaks.

Steering and Suspension

⭕ **5.** While still in the engine bay, have your assistant turn the steering wheel lightly from side to side and look for play in steering universal joints or steering rack mountings and any other steering connections.

⭕ **6.** If your vehicle is fitted with power steering, check the security and condition of the steering pump, hoses and drivebelt, in the engine bay.

⭕ **7.** Look and reach under the car while your assistant turns the steering wheel more vigorously from side to side. Place your hand over each track rod end in turn and inspect all of the steering linkages, joints and attachments for wear.

⭕ **8.** Go around the vehicle and 'bounce' each corner of the vehicle in turn. Release at the lowest point and the vehicle should rise and settle in its normal position without continuing to 'bounce' of its own accord.

PART C: VEHICLE RAISED OFF THE GROUND

Bodywork Structure

○ **1.** Any sharp edges on the external bodywork, caused by damage or corrosion will cause the vehicle to fail.

○ **2.** Check all load bearing areas for corrosion. Open the doors and check the sills inside and out, above and below. Any corrosion in structural metalwork within 30 cm (12 in.) of seat belt mounting, steering and suspension attachment points will cause the vehicle to fail.

Wheels and Tyres

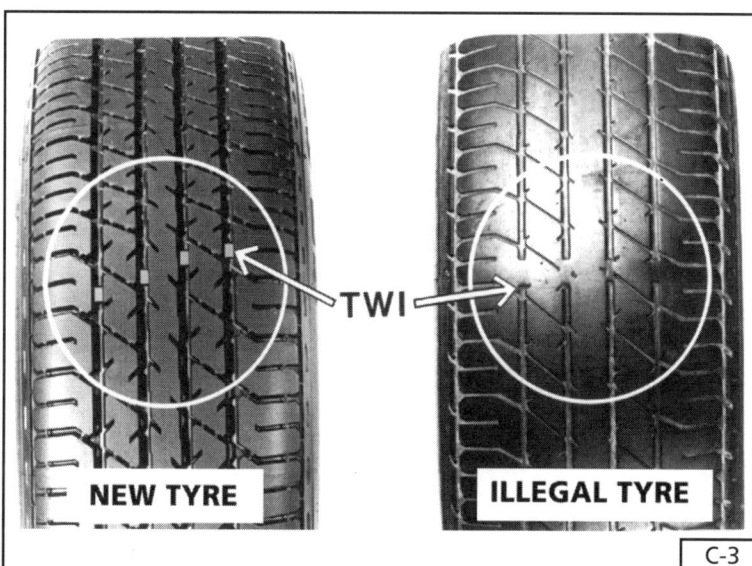

NEW TYRE — TWI — **ILLEGAL TYRE**

C-3

○ **3.** To pass the test, the tread must be at least 1.6 mm deep throughout a continuous band comprising the central three-quarters of the width of the tread. The Tread Wear Indicators (TWI) will tell you when the limit has been reached, on most tyres.

IMPORTANT NOTE: Tyres are past their best, especially in wet conditions, well before this point is reached!

○ **4.** Check that the front tyres match and that the rear tyres match each other - in terms of size and type but not necessarily make. They must be the correct size for the vehicle and the pressures must be correct.

○ **5.** With each wheel off the ground in turn, check the inside and the outside of the tyre wall for cuts, lumps and bulges and check the wheel for damage. Note that tyres deteriorate progressively over a period of time and if they have degraded to this extent, replace them.

Under the Front of the Car

You will need to support the front of the car on axle stands with the rear wheels firmly chocked in both directions.

○ **6.** Have your helper turn the steering from lock to lock and check that the steering turns smoothly and that the brake hoses or pipes do not contact the wheel, tyre or any part of the steering or suspension.

○ **7.** Have your assistant hold down the brake pedal firmly. Check each brake flexible hose for bulges or leaks.

○ **8.** Inspect all the rigid brake pipes underneath the front of the vehicle for corrosion or leaks and also look for signs of fluid leaks at the brake calipers. Rigid fuel pipes need to be checked in the same way.

○ **9.** At each full lock position, check the steering rack rubber gaiters for splits, leaks or loose retaining clips.

○ **10.** Check the track rod end dust covers to make sure they are in place.

○ **11.** Inspect each constant velocity joint gaiter - both inners and outers - for splits or damage. You will have to rotate each wheel to see the gaiters all the way round.

○ **12.** Check all of the suspension rubber mountings, including the anti-rollbar mountings (when fitted). Take a firm grip on each shock absorber in turn with both hands and try to twist the damper to check for deterioration in the top and bottom mounting bushes.

○ **13.** Underneath the front wheel arches, check that the shock absorbers are not corroded, that the springs have not cracked and that there are no fluid leaks down the body of the shock absorber.

○ **14.** While under the front end of the car, check the front of the exhaust system for security of fixing at the manifold, for corrosion and secure fixing to the mounting points.

○ **15.** Preferably working with a helper, grasp each front road wheel at the 12 o'clock and 6 o'clock positions and try rocking the wheel. Look for movement or wear at the suspension ball joints, suspension mountings, steering mountings and at the wheel bearing - look for movement between the wheel and hub. Repeat the test by grasping the road wheel at 3 o'clock and 9 o'clock and rocking once more.

○ **16.** Spin each wheel and check for noise or roughness in the wheel bearing and binding in either the wheel bearing or the brake.

IMPORTANT NOTE: Don't forget that on front wheel drive cars, the gearbox must be in neutral. There will be a certain amount of noise and drag from the drivetrain components.

○ **17.** If you suspect wear at any of the suspension points, try levering with a screwdriver to see whether or not you can confirm any movement in that area.

○ **18.** Vehicles fitted with other suspension types such as hydraulic suspension, torsion bar suspension etc. need to be checked in a similar way with the additional point that there must be no fluid leaks or damaged pipes on vehicles with hydraulic suspension.

Underneath the Rear of the Car

○ **19.** Inspect the rear springs for security at their mounting points and for cracks, severe corrosion or damage.

○ **20.** Check the rear shock absorbers in the same way as the checks carried out for the fronts.

○ **21.** Check all rear suspension mounting points, including the rubbers to any locating rods or anti-rollbar that may be fitted.

○ **22.** Check all of the flexible and rigid brake pipes and the fuel pipes just as for the front of the vehicle.

◯ **23.** Have your assistant press down firmly on the brake pedal while you check the rear brake flexible hoses for bulges, splits or other deterioration.

◯ **24.** Check the fuel tank for leaks or corrosion. Remember also to check the fuel filler cap - a correctly sealing filler cap is a part of the MoT test.

◯ **25.** Examine the handbrake mechanism. Frayed or broken cables or worn mounting points, either to the bodywork or in the linkage will all be failure points.

◯ **26.** Check each of the rear wheel bearings as for the fronts.

◯ **27.** Spin each rear wheel and check that neither the wheel bearings nor the brakes are binding. Pull on and let off the handbrake and check once again to make sure that the handbrake mechanism is releasing.

SAFETY FIRST!
- Only run the car out of doors.
- Beware of burning yourself on a hot exhaust system.

◯ **28.** While you are out from under the car, but with the rear end still raised off the ground, run the engine. Hold a rag over the end of the exhaust pipe and listen for blows or leaks in the system. You can now get back under the car and investigate further if necessary.

◯ **29.** Check the exhaust system mountings and check for rust, corrosion or holes in the rear part of the system.

◯ **30.** Check the rear brake back plate or calipers (as appropriate) for any signs of fluid leakage.

◯ **31.** Check the insides and the outsides of the tyres as well as the tyre treads for damage, as for the front tyres.

PART D: EXHAUST EMISSIONS

This is an area that is impossible to check accurately at home. However, the following rule-of-thumb tests will give you a good idea whether your car is likely to fail or not.

i INSIDE INFORMATION: If you feel that your car is likely to fail because of the emission test, have your MoT testing station carry out the emission part of the test first so that if it fails, you don't waste money on having the rest of the test carried out. *i*

◯ **1. PETROL ENGINES BEFORE 1 AUGUST 1973 AND DIESEL ENGINES BEFORE 1 AUGUST 1979** only have to pass visible smoke check. Rev the engine to about 2,500 rpm (about half maximum speed) for 20 seconds and then allow it to return to idle. If too much smoke is emitted (in the opinion of the tester) the car will fail.

◯ **2. DIESEL ENGINES FROM 1 AUGUST 1979** The engine will have to be taken up to maximum revs several times by the tester, so make certain that your timing belt is in good condition, otherwise severe damage could be caused to your engine. If the latter happens, it will be your responsibility!

FACT FILE: VEHICLE EMISSIONS

PETROL ENGINED VEHICLES WITHOUT CATALYSER

Vehicles first used before 1 August 1973
- visual smoke check only.

Vehicles first used between 1 August 1973 and 31 July 1986
- 4.5% carbon monoxide and 1,200 parts per million, unburned hydrocarbons.

Vehicles first used between 1 August 1986 and 31 July 1992
- 3.5% carbon monoxide and 1,200 parts per million, unburned hydrocarbons.

PETROL ENGINED VEHICLES FITTED WITH CATALYTIC CONVERTERS

Vehicles first used from 1 August 1992 (K-registration on)

- All have to be tested at an MoT Testing Station specially equipped to handle cars fitted with catalytic converters whether or not the vehicle is fitted with a 'cat'. If the test, or the garage's data, shows that the vehicle was not fitted with a 'cat' by the manufacturer, the owner is permitted to take the vehicle to a Testing Station not equipped for catalysed cars, if he/she prefers to do so (up to 1998-only). Required maxima are - 3.5% carbon monoxide and 1,200 parts per million, unburned hydrocarbons. The simple emissions test (as above) will be supplemented by a further check to make sure that the catalyst is maintained in good and efficient working order.

- The tester also has to check that the engine oil is up to a specified temperature before carrying out the test. (This is because 'cats' don't work properly at lower temperatures - ensure *your* engine is fully warm!)

DIESEL ENGINES' EMISSIONS STANDARDS

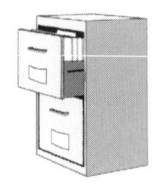

- The Tester will have to rev your engine hard, several times. If it is not in good condition, he is entitled to refuse to test it. This is the full range of tests, even though all may not apply to your car.

Vehicles first used before 1 August, 1979

- Engine run at normal running temperature; engine speed taken to around 2,500 rpm (or half governed max. speed, if lower) and held for 20 seconds. FAILURE, if engine emits dense blue or black smoke for next 5 seconds, at tick-over. (NOTE: Testers are allowed to be more lenient with pre-1960 vehicles.)

Vehicles first used on or after 1 August, 1979

- After checking engine condition, and with the engine at normal running temperature, the engine will be run up to full revs between three and six times to see whether your engine passes the prescribed smoke density test. (For what it's worth - 2.5k for non-turbo cars; 3.0k for turbo diesels. An opacity meter probe will be placed in your car's exhaust pipe and this is not something you can replicate at home.) Irrespective of the meter readings, the car will fail if smoke or vapour obscures the view of other road users.

- IMPORTANT NOTE: The diesel engine test puts a lot of stress on the engine. It is IMPERATIVE that your car's engine is properly serviced, and the cam belt changed on schedule, before you take it in for the MoT test. The tester is entitled to refuse to test the car if he feels that the engine is not in serviceable condition and there are a number of pre-Test checks he may carry out.

Please read the whole of the Introduction to this Chapter before carrying out any work on your car.

CHAPTER 5
SERVICING YOUR CAR

Everyone wants to own a car that starts first time, runs reliably and lasts longer than the average. And it's all a question of thorough maintenance!

If you follow the FIAT-approved Service Jobs listed here you can almost guarantee that your car will still be going strong when others have fallen by the wayside - or the hard shoulder.

How To Use This Chapter

This chapter contains all of the servicing Jobs recommended by FIAT for all models of Uno imported into the UK. To use the schedule, note that:
- Each letter code tells you the Service Interval at which you should carry out each Service Job.
- Look the code up in the Service Intervals Key.
- Each Service Job has a Job number. Look up the number in the relevant part of this chapter and you will see a complete explanation of how to carry out the work.

SAFETY FIRST!

- *SAFETY FIRST information must always be read with care and always taken seriously.*
- *In addition, please read the whole of **Chapter 1, Safety First!** before carrying out any work on your car.*
- *There are many hazards associated with working on a car but all of them can be avoided by adhering strictly to the safety rules.*
- *Don't skimp on safety!*

SERVICE INTERVALS - INTRODUCTION

Over the years, FIAT, in common with all other manufacturers, have lengthened their recommended service intervals. For instance, oil changes on later FIATs don't have to take place as often as on earlier ones. In the main, these changes have not come about because of specific modifications to the cars themselves. They have come about because of a number of factors: Lubricants, spark plugs, seals and other components have improved and mechanical parts are better made due to improved materials and production techniques.

As a result, you are recommended to follow the maker's recommendations on how often to service your car. If your car lies right on a change-over point, the choice of which schedule to follow will be yours, unless the specific advice given here recommends otherwise - as we said earlier, most change points came about for a number of reasons, so it generally isn't necessary to identify with pinpoint accuracy which bracket your car belongs to, if it isn't obvious.

making it easy! • We think it is very important to keep things as straight forward as possible. And where you see this heading, you'll know there's an extra tip to help 'make it easy' for you!

Thanks are due to FIAT agents, Steels of Hereford, and in particular, Graham Evans and David Beaumont, for their assistance with this chapter.

Some of the suggested inspection/replacement intervals may not correspond to those shown in the original handbook. The suggested schedule takes in to account the age of the vehicle and the annual MOT test.

IMPORTANT NOTE: Each service should be carried out at EITHER the recommended mileage OR the recommended time interval, whichever comes first.

SERVICE INTERVALS: KEY

A - Every week, or before every long journey.
B - Every year or 9,000 miles.
C - Every 2 years or 18,000 miles.
D - Every 3 years or 27,000 miles.
E - Every 4 years or 36,000 miles.
F - Every 5 years or 45,000 miles.
G - Every 6 years or 54,000 miles.
H - Every 7 years or 63,000 miles.
I - Every 8 years or 72,000 miles..

SERVICE INTERVALS CHART

PART A: REGULAR CHECKS

Job	Description	Service Intervals
Job 1.	Engine oil - check level	A
Job 2.	Cooling system - check level	A
Job 3.	Brake fluid - check level	A
Job 4.	Battery - check electrolyte level	A
Job 5.	Screen washer fluid - check level	A
Job 6.	Tyres - check pressures and condition	A
Job 7.	Check lights/change bulbs	A
Job 8.	Check/clean/gap spark plugs	B
Job 9.	Check spare tyre pressure	B
Job 10.	Check front brake pads	B

PART B: ENGINE AND COOLING SYSTEM

Job	Description	Service Intervals
Job 11.	Change engine oil and filter	B
Job 12.	Check/adjust valve clearances	C
Job 13.	Check crankcase ventilation	F
Job 14.	Check camshaft timing belt	E
Job 15.	Change camshaft timing belt	H
Job 16.	Check cooling system	B
Job 17.	Change engine coolant	C

PART C: TRANSMISSION

Job	Description	Service Intervals
Job 18.	Check manual gearbox oil level	C
Job 19.	Change manual gearbox oil (4 x 4 intervals in brackets)	I
Job 20.	Check auto. transmission fluid level	B
Job 21.	Change auto. transmission fluid and filter	D
Job 22.	Check driveshaft gaiters	B
Job 23.	Check/adjust clutch pedal/cable	B
Job 24.	Check auto. transmission selector cable	C
Job 25.	Check/lubricate propshaft (4 x 4 MODELS ONLY)	C
Job 26.	Change rear axle oil (4 x 4 MODELS ONLY)	D

PART D: IGNITION AND ELECTRICS

Job	Description	Service Intervals
Job 27.	Check/adjust alternator drive belt	C
Job 28.	Check/clean HT leads and distributor cap	B
Job 29.	Check/adjust contact breaker points (DISTRIBUTORS WITH CONTACT BREAKERS ONLY)	B
Job 30.	Replace contact breaker points (DISTRIBUTORS WITH CONTACT BREAKERS ONLY)	C
Job 31.	Check ignition timing	C
Job 32.	Change spark plugs	C
Job 33.	Check electric fan operation	B

PART E: FUEL AND EXHAUST

Job	Description	Service Intervals
Job 34.	Check fuel pipes for leaks	B
Job 35.	Change air filter	C
Job 36.	Change fuel filter	C
Job 37.	Check/adjust idle speed, mixture and emissions	C
Job 38.	Check/service emission control systems	D
Job 39.	Check lambda sensor	D
Job 40.	Check inlet and exhaust manifold fixings	D
Job 41.	Check exhaust system	B

PART F: STEERING AND SUSPENSION

	SERVICE INTERVALS
Job 42. Check front wheel bearings	B
Job 43. Check front suspension	B
Job 44. Check track rod ends	B
Job 45. Check steering column and rack	B
Job 46. Check rear wheel bearings	B
Job 47. Check rear suspension	B
Job 48. Check wheel bolts for tightness	B

PART G: BRAKING SYSTEM

	SERVICE INTERVALS
Job 49. Check front brakes, change pads	B
Job 50. Check rear brakes	C
Job 51. Check/adjust handbrake	B
Job 52. Check brake pipes	B
Job 53. Change brake hydraulic fluid	C

PART H: BODYWORK & INTERIOR

	SERVICE INTERVALS
Job 54. Lubricate hinges and locks	B
Job 55. Check windscreen	B
Job 56. Check seat and seat belt mountings	B
Job 57. Check headlight alignment	B
Job 58. Check underbody	B

PART I: ROAD TEST

Job 59. Road test and specialist check *AFTER EVERY SERVICE.*

ENGINE BAY LAYOUTS

These are the engine bay layouts common to almost all Pandas. Note that later vehicles do not have a radiator - mounted coolant cap. There is no carburettor fitted to fuel injected vehicles.

EARLY MODELS

LATER MODELS

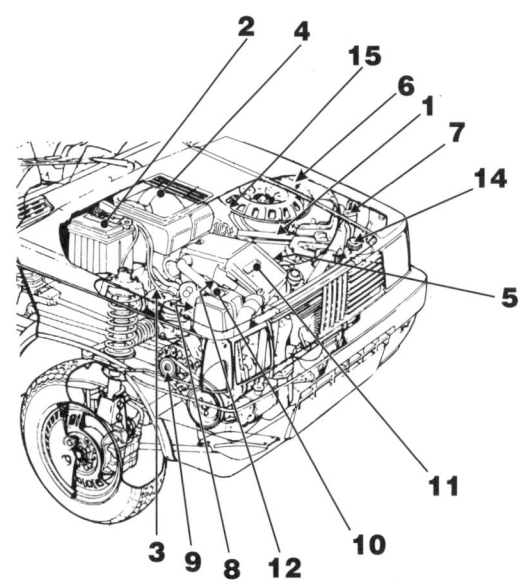

1. Jack position.
2. Battery.
3. Brake master cylinder (r.h. drive).
4. Air intake opening.
5. Distributor.
6. Spare wheel position.
7. Windscreen washer reservoir.
8. Dipstick.
9. Alternator position.
10. Oil filler cap.
11. Air filter.
12. Carburettor position.
13. Radiator filler cap.
14. Coolant expansion tank.
15. Automatic gearbox filler/dipstick.

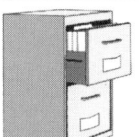

FACT FILE: PANDA ENGINE TYPES

● There have been two basic types of Panda engine. The OHV (overhead valve) engine which was used exclusively up until 1986 and then was joined by an OHC (overhead camshaft) engine. OHV engines continued alongside OHC engines, although with modifications, for several years.

● All OHC Panda engines belong to the advanced 'FIRE' (Fully Integrated Robotised Engine) category of lightweight, robot-produced FIAT engines.

● All OHV engines have a vertically mounted distributor on the right-hand end of the engine while 'FIRE' OHC engines have a horizontally-mounted distributor, on the left-hand end of the camshaft.

PART A: REGULAR CHECKS

We recommend that these jobs are carried out on a weekly basis, as well as before every long journey. They consist of checks that are essential for your safety and to help prevent vehicle breakdown.

❏ Job 1. Engine oil - check level.

Check the engine oil level, with the vehicle standing on level ground. If the engine has been running, leave it turned off for several minutes to let the oil drain into the sump.

1A. The dipstick is located at the rear of the engine on all cars: Near the distributor on OHV engines...

1B. ...between the alternator and engine on 'FIRE' OHC engines. Lift the dipstick out, wipe it dry with a clean cloth and re-insert it. The oil level is correct when between the MAX and MIN marks - see *inset*.

1D. On later, overhead camshaft (OHC) engines the oil filler cap is a square plastic moulding fitted to the top of the cam cover and is simply removed by pulling upwards. It can be very tight - take care not to bash the back of your hand as it comes free! Pour slowly into these engines!

IMPORTANT NOTE: Regularly check the ground over which the car has been parked for traces of oil or other fluid leaks. If a leak is found, do not drive the car without first finding out where the leak has come from and, if necessary, putting things right - it could be from a major failure in the braking system!

❏ Job 2. Cooling system - check level.

SAFETY FIRST!

- ALWAYS check the coolant level with the engine COLD.
- If the engine is hot there is a real danger of scalding from boiling coolant gushing from the tank when the cap is removed.

Never allow the coolant level to fall below the MIN mark on the expansion tank. It is vitally important that all engines have the correct proportion of anti-freeze in the coolant. So-called 'anti-freeze' doesn't only help prevent freezing in the winter, but also helps prevent overheating in summer temperatures. In addition, anti-freeze also cuts down on internal engine corrosion. Its use is ESSENTIAL in engines fitted with alloy blocks and/or cylinder heads - all Panda engines, in fact.

i INSIDE INFORMATION: You will give your Panda engine's aluminium alloy parts the best possible protection against corrosion if you follow FIAT's advice and use a 50% solution of *FL Paraflu* coolant fluid, with distilled water. *i*

EARLY MODELS AND ALL 4x4s, WITH SEPARATE HEADER TANK.

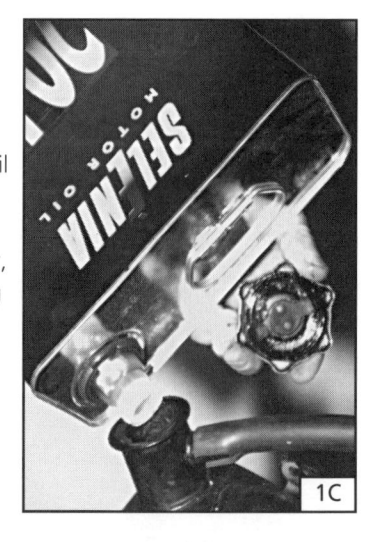

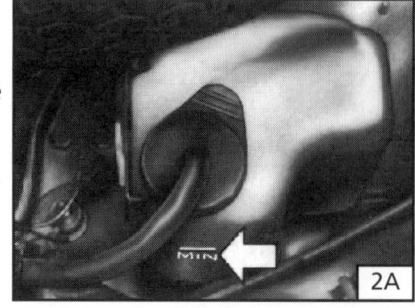

i INSIDE INFORMATION: The difference between the MIN and MAX marks is approximately one litre of oil. *i*

TOPPING-UP

1C. On earlier, overhead valve (OHV) engines the oil filler cap is located at the end of the rocker cover adjacent to the distributor, and is removed by turning a quarter turn to the left and lifting.

2A. The coolant should be about 25 mm (1 in.) above the MIN mark (arrowed) on the header tank. This is the early non-4x4 header tank, in front of the spare wheel.

2B. This is the 4x4 header tank style and position.

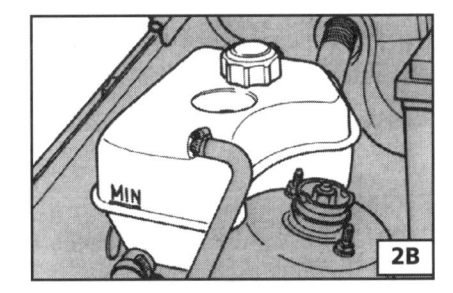

LATER MODELS WITH HEADER TANK INTEGRAL WITH RADIATOR

2C. The coolant should be 25 to 30 mm (about 1 in.) above the MIN mark (arrowed) on the header tank.

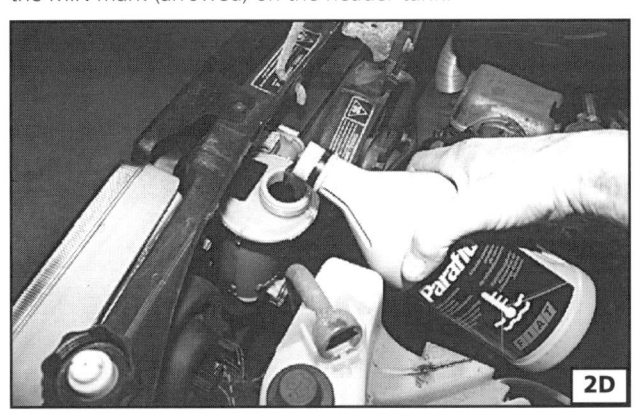

2D. Top-up the coolant using a 50:50 mixture of water and **FL Paraflu** anti-freeze. However, in an emergency, water or (better still) neat anti-freeze can be used provided that the 50:50 ratio is not noticeably altered.

SAFETY FIRST!

- If brake fluid should come into contact with the skin or eyes, rinse immediately with plenty of water.
- It is acceptable for the brake fluid level to fall slightly during normal use, but if it falls significantly below the MIN mark on the reservoir there is probably a leak or an internal seal failure. Stop using the car until the problem has been put right.
- If you let dirt get into the hydraulic system it can cause brake failure. Wipe the filler cap clean before removing it.
- You should only ever use new brake fluid from a sealed container - FIAT recommend **FL Tutela DOT 3** brake fluid. Old fluid absorbs moisture and this could cause the brakes to fail when carrying out an emergency stop or during another heavy use of the brakes - just when you need them most and are least able to do anything about it, in fact!

☐ **Job 3. Brake fluid - check level.**

On all models, the brake fluid reservoir is positioned above the master cylinder on the rear right-hand corner of the engine bay. The reservoir is semi-transparent so the level can be checked without disturbing the cap and risking the introduction of dirt or grit into the fluid.

IMPORTANT NOTE: Ensure that the fluid level is high enough to allow fluid to flow internally between the front and rear sections of the reservoir. The level will then be correct.

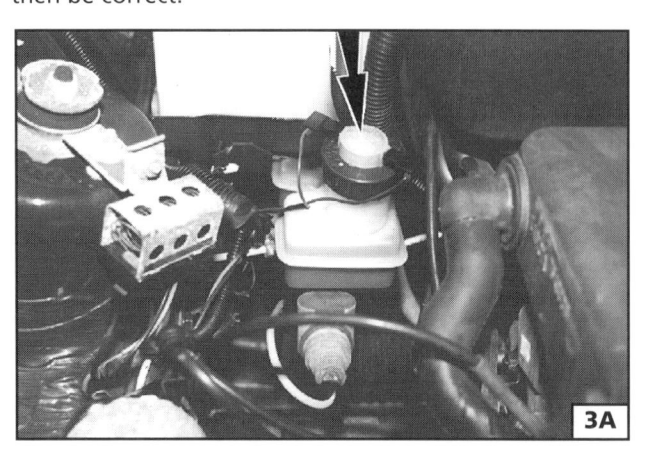

3A. If topping-up is required, turn the cap without allowing the centre section to turn. This section (arrowed), with two wires attached to it, swivels in the cap. If you turn this centre section with the cap, the wires or terminals could be damaged.

3B. Place the cap and float to one side - take care not to drip fluid from the float, and top up with **FL Tutela DOT 3**.

Check that the brake fluid-level warning-light is operating. Turn the ignition key to the MAR position and press down the button between the two terminals on the reservoir cap, when fitted. The warning light on the dash should light up. When no button if fitted, unscrew and raise the cap (ignition key at MAR) to check the warning lights.

If the warning light does not light up, and the fluid level is satisfactory, check the relevant fuse and then have the electrical circuit checked (by a specialist, if necessary) without delay.

CHAPTER 5 REGULAR CHECKS

❑ **Job 4. Battery - check electrolyte level.**

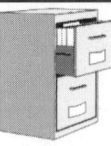

FACT FILE: DISCONNECTING THE BATTERY

● Many vehicles depend on a constant power supply from the battery and you can find yourself in all sorts of trouble if you simply disconnect the battery on those vehicles. You might find that the car alarm will go off, you could find that the engine management system forgets all it ever 'learned' and the car will feel very strange to drive until it has re-programmed itself, and you could find that your radio refuses to operate again unless you key in the correct code. And if you've bought the car second-hand and don't know the code, you would have to send the set back to the manufacturer for re-programming.

● So, on later cars with engine management systems you must ensure that the vehicle has a constant power supply even though the battery is removed. To do so, you will need a separate 12 volt battery supply. You could put a self tapping screw into the positive lead near the battery terminal before disconnecting it, and put a positive connection to your other battery via this screw.

● But you would have to be EXTREMELY CAREFUL to wrap insulation tape around the connection so that no short is caused. The negative terminal on the other battery would also have to be connected to the car's bodywork.

SAFETY FIRST!

● *The gas given off by a battery is highly explosive. Never smoke, use a naked flame or allow a spark to occur in the battery compartment.*

● *Never disconnect the battery (it can cause sparking) with the battery caps removed.*

● *All vehicle batteries contain sulphuric acid. If the acid comes into contact with the skin or eyes, wash immediately with copious amounts of cold water and seek medical advice.*

● *Do not check the battery levels within half an hour of the battery being charged with a separate battery charger because the addition of fresh water could cause electrolyte to flood out of the battery.*

4A. Check the electrolyte level in the battery. MAX and MIN lines (arrowed) are moulded into the translucent battery casing. In the case of non-FIAT-supplied batteries, the cell caps or strip may need to be removed to see the liquid level.

i **INSIDE INFORMATION:** The translucent battery casing becomes clouded over the years. Try wiping the surface clean and shining an electric torch light through the battery. If this doesn't work, remove the cover strips and look down into the cells - see below. *i*

4B. Original FIAT batteries are of the 'maintenance-free' type and usually do not need topping-up. However, if necessary, top up after prising off the cell sealing strip with a screwdriver. Top-up each cell ONLY with distilled or de-ionised water.

❑ **Job 5. Screen washer fluid - check level.**

Top-up with a mixture of water and screen-wash additive, mixed according to the instructions on the container. FIAT recommend **Arexons DP1**. The reservoir - the same one for both front and rear screen-washers (when fitted) - is located in the engine bay.

5A. On early models it takes the form of a stout plastic bag, located in the front right-hand corner, underneath the jack.

5B. Later models have a rigid, translucent container, located in the left-hand corner, adjacent to the spare wheel.

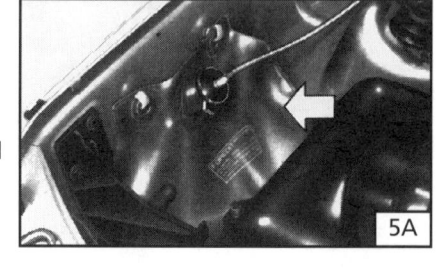

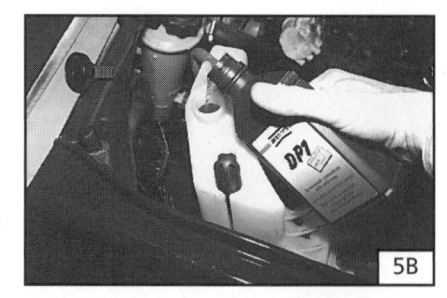

❑ **Job 6. Tyres - check pressures and condition.**

6A. Check the tyre pressures using a reliable and accurate gauge. Note that the recommended pressures (see **Chapter 3, Facts and Figures**)

30

- are given for COLD tyres. Tyres warm up as the car is used - and warm tyres will give a false (high) reading. You should also check for wear or damage, at the same time.

> **SAFETY FIRST!**
>
> - Tyres which show uneven wear tell their own story, if only you know how to speak the language!
> - If a tyre is worn more on one side than the other, consult your main dealer or a tyre specialist. It probably means that the steering tracking needs setting - a simple job for a specialist - but it could indicate suspension damage, so have it checked.
> - If a tyre is worn more in the centre or on the edges, it could mean that your tyre pressures are wrong, but if they're not, have the car checked.
> - Incorrectly inflated tyres wear rapidly, can cause the car's handling to become dangerous and can make fuel consumption worse.

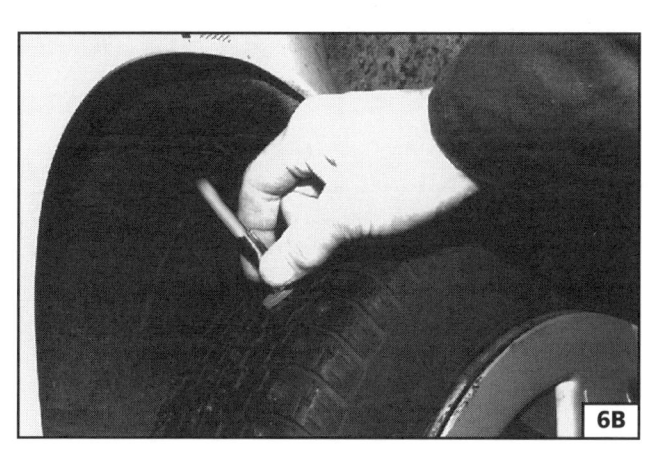

6B. Every few weeks, examine the tyre treads for wear using a tread-depth gauge. It won't take more than a few moments and it keeps you safe and legal. Check visually, every time you check the pressures, just to keep your eye on things.

Every three months, raise each wheel in turn off the ground and turn it slowly between your hands, looking and feeling for any bulges, tears or splits in the tyre walls, especially the inner sidewalls which are seldom seen. Every few months, you should also check the spare tyre. See *Job 9* for further information.

i INSIDE INFORMATION: Tyre manufacturers recommend replacing tyres every seven years, whether they are worn out or not. In time, rubber deteriorates, with an increased risk of blow-out. Keep your eye on the sidewalls of older tyres. If you see **any** cracking, splits or other damage scrap the tyre. If you're not sure, consult your FIAT dealer or tyre specialist. *i*

☐ **Job 7. Check lights/change bulbs.**

making it easy - Whenever a light fails to work, check the fuses before replacing the bulb. The cause might be the fuse rather than the bulb.
- The bulb might be okay, but a blown bulb often causes a fuse to 'go' in sympathy.
- See *Job 7M, FACT FILE: FUSES*.

HEADLIGHTS - EARLIEST MODELS

7A. First remove the cover (**A**) by turning it anti-clockwise.

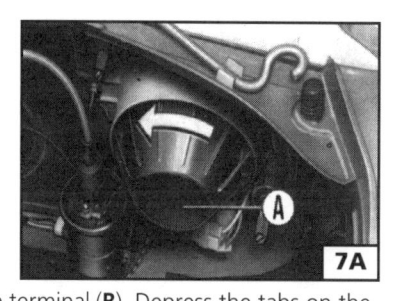

7B. Carefully pull off the terminal (**B**). Depress the tabs on the spring retainer (**C**) and turn anti-clockwise. When fitting a new bulb (**D**), make sure that the pin on the bulb locates in its seat in the holder. Check headlight alignment - see *Job 57*.

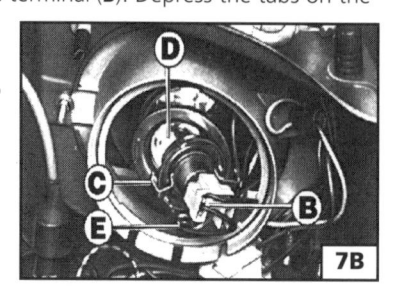

HEADLIGHTS - LATER MODELS

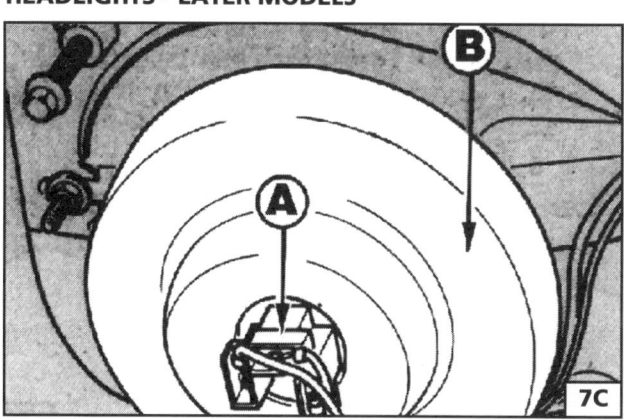

7C. First carefully remove the terminal (**A**) and then pull off the rubber boot (**B**).

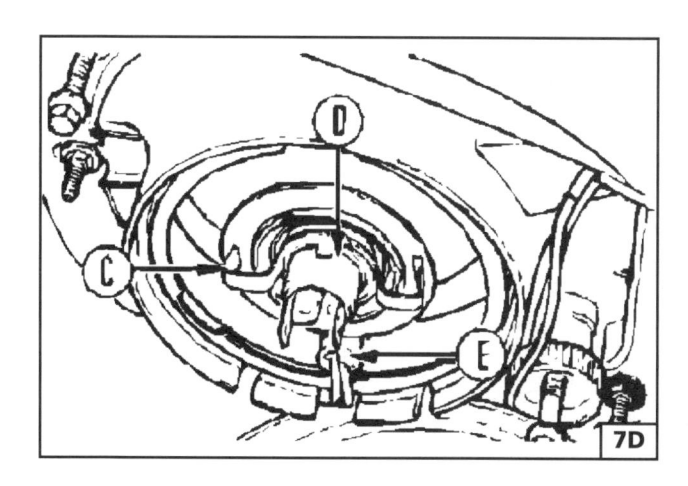

7D. Push in the two side tabs of the spring clip (**C**) and turn it anti-clockwise to remove it. When fitting a new bulb (**D**), make sure that the pin on the bulb locates in its seat in the holder. Make sure that the rubber boot seals properly when refitted. Check headlight alignment - see *Job 57*.

SIDE LIGHTS - ALL MODELS

First remove the headlight bulb holder. (See **7B-E** and **7D-E**, above.) The bayonet-type bulb is pushed in slightly, turned anti-clockwise and removed.

CHAPTER 5 REGULAR CHECKS

CHAPTER 5 REGULAR CHECKS

making it easy!
- If you touch a halogen headlight or driving light bulb with bare fingers, the microscopic transfer of grease will shorten its life.
- Handle with a piece of tissue paper if the original wrapping is no longer there.
- If the bulb is touched - no worries! Just wipe clean with methylated spirit on a fresh, clean tissue or cloth.

FRONT DIRECTION INDICATORS - ALL MODELS

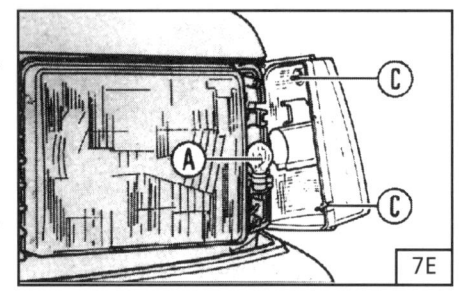

7E. Remove the two screws (**C**) and take off the lens. The bayonet-type bulb (**A**) is pushed in slightly, turned anti-clockwise and removed. Check the lens seals and replace if they are letting in water, otherwise the bulb holder will quickly corrode.

DIRECTION INDICATORS, SIDE REPEATERS - ALL MODELS

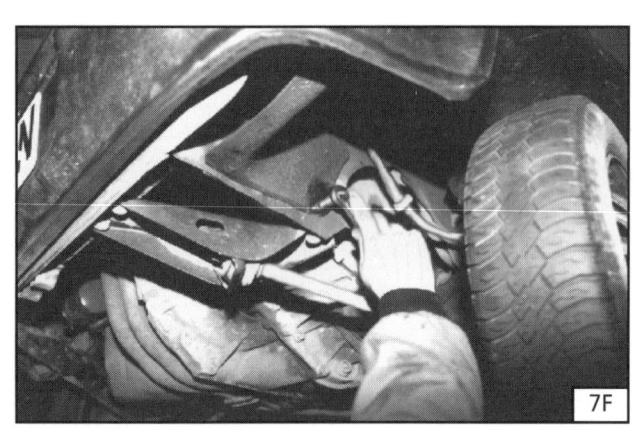

7F. On some models, the bulb is sealed into the unit. If it fails, buy a complete replacement unit from your FIAT dealer. Most have replaceable bulbs, however. Before you can get at the light unit, you will have to take out the hex-head screws holding the wing liner in place and remove the wing liner.

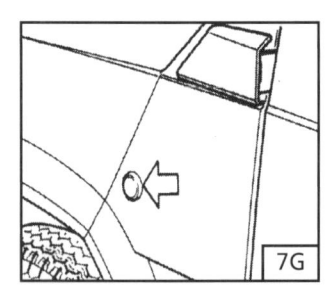

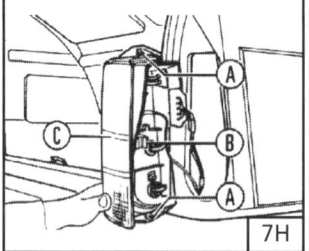

7G. From inside the wing, free the spring retainers, carefully remove the wiring connector so as not to damage the wiring and pull out the light unit from the outside of the wing.

REAR LIGHT UNIT - ALL MODELS

7H. Remove the two screws (**A**), top and bottom, and take off the lens (**C**) and bulb holders complete. Push in the plastic tab (**B**) and pull the bulb holder out of the lens.

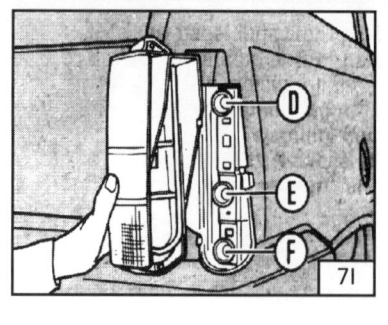

7I. The bayonet-type bulbs are pushed in slightly, turned anti-clockwise and removed. Bulb (**D**) is the combined Rear/Stop bulb (ensure that the pegs on the bulb are the right way round when attempting to refit - they only go one way); bulb (**E**) is the Direction Indicator bulb, and (**F**) is the rear Fog Light bulb (left-side) or the Reversing Light bulb (right-side).

NUMBER PLATE LIGHT - EARLY MODELS

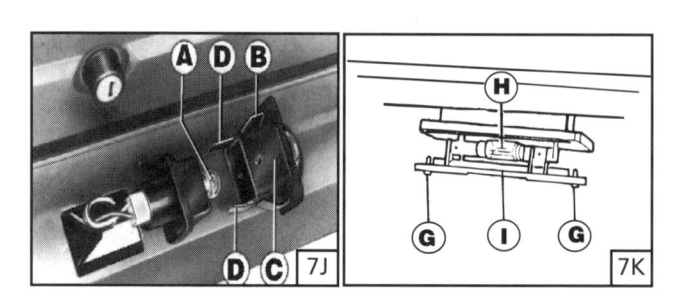

7J. Slightly depress the spring retainer (**B**) and withdraw the bulb holder and lens (**C**). Depress retainers (**D**) and remove the lens from the bulb holder. The bayonet-type bulb (**A**) is pushed in slightly, turned anti-clockwise and removed.

NUMBER PLATE LIGHT - LATER MODELS

7K. Remove the two screws (**G**) and remove the lens (**I**). The festoon-type bulb (**H**) is pulled out after easing the retainers carefully apart with the finger nails and the replacement is fitted in a similar way.

INTERIOR LIGHT - ALL MODELS

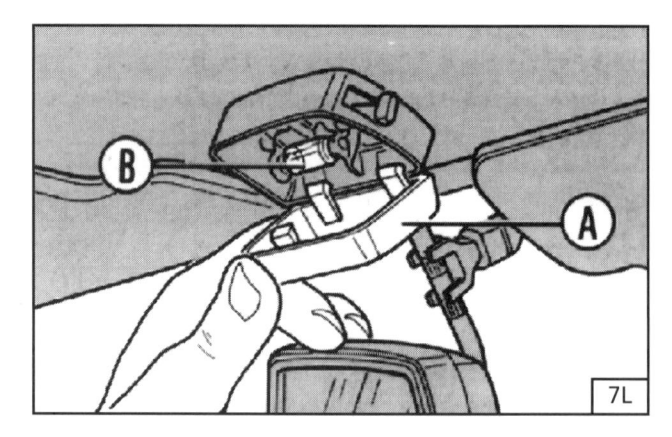

7L. Slightly squeeze in the sides of the lens (**A**). The festoon-type bulb (**B**) is pulled out after easing the retainers carefully apart with the finger nails and the replacement is fitted in a similar way.

DASH BULBS

See **Chapter 6, Repairs and Replacements** for details of how to replace bulbs in the dashboard.

FACT FILE: FUSES

- **7M.** The fuse box is found in the left-hand side of the engine bay (early cars), or under either left or right-ends of the dashboard (later cars) according to year.

- On later cars, a symbol above each fuse tells you which circuit it protects.

- The **amperage** is clearly marked on each fuse. ALWAYS replace a blown fuse with one of the correct amperage. NEVER 'fix' a fault by using a fuse of a higher amperage, nor 'bridge' a blown fuse. You could easily set your car on fire if you attempt to do so.

- You can easily see if a fuse is 'blown' because the conductor wire (A) will have a gap in it.

- If a fuse blows, find out why and put it right before fitting

---

7N. On early cars, with fuse box in the engine bay, the fuse positions are as follows:

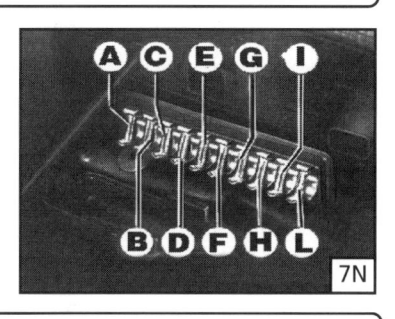

Fuse	Protected Circuit
A (8 Amp)	Reversing light; stop lights, direction indicator lights; heater fan motor; low brake fluid level indicator and check switch; low engine oil pressure warning light; fuel gauge and warning light.
B (8 Amp)	Screen wiper motor; heated rear window relay winding; rear window wipers.
C (8 Amp)	L.H. high beam and headlamp warning light.
D (8 Amp)	R.H. high beam.
E (8 Amp)	L.H. dipped beam; rear fog-guard light and warning light.
F (8 Amp)	R.H. dipped beam.
G (8 Amp)	L.H. side light and R.H. rear light; number plate light; panel light; side light warning light.
H (8 Amp)	R.H. side light and L.H. rear light.
I (16 Amp)	Horn; courtesy light.
L (16 Amp)	Heated rear window; hazard warning circuit (where mandatory).

❑ **Job 8. Check/clean/gap spark plugs.**

OHV ENGINES ONLY

8A. On the earlier, OHV engine, the plugs face forwards. Removing the air cleaner housing gives much easier access to the spark plugs on OHC cars.

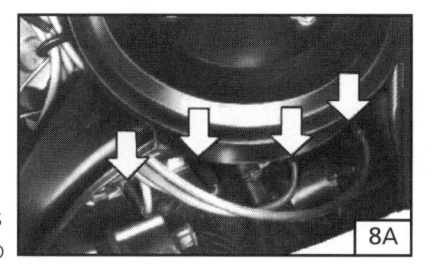

To remove the circular air cleaner from earlier cars, undo the wing nuts, take off the top casing and take out the filter. See *illustration, Job 35A*. Also, disconnect the air intake hose. Remove the two mounting nuts, one each side of the carburettor air intake, and remove the bolt holding the bracket on the outside of the casing. As you lift the casing, you will see the crankcase vent hose fitted to the bottom of the casing. Pull it off.

i INSIDE INFORMATION: Now is a good time to inspect the crankcase vent hose. Trace it back to the crankcase and inspect both ends and all the way along it. See *Job 13*. *i*

OHC 'FIRE' ENGINES ONLY

8B. You have to remove the air cleaner on OHC 'FIRE'-engined cars. The (rectangular) air cleaner housing is released by undoing this single 10 mm nut, releasing the clip on the front of the cam cover, and unclipping the intake hose (arrowed) which is enough to allow the housing to be swivelled to one side.

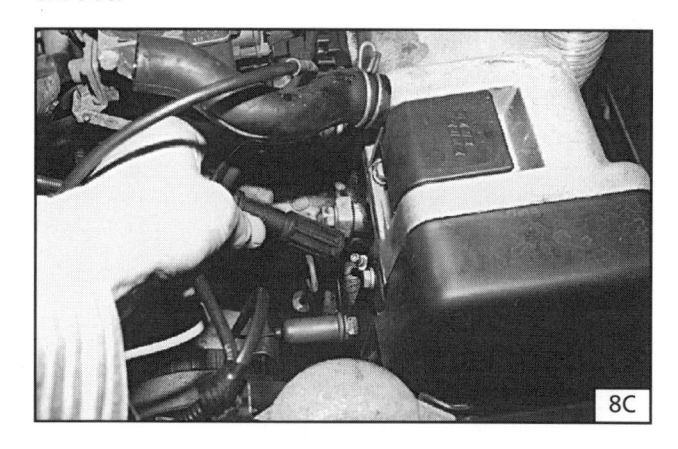

8C. Carefully removed the plug caps, being careful to pull only on the cap itself and not on the HT lead.

8D. Unscrew the plug using the correct type of spark plug socket and taking care to keep the spanner strictly in line with the plug so as not to crack the electrode.

CHAPTER 5 REGULAR CHECKS

33

CHAPTER 5 ENGINE AND COOLING SYSTEM

8E. Clean the plug electrodes by getting vigorous with a brass-bristled brush. If the electrodes of the plug look rounded and worn (compare them with a new plug) replace them.

making it easy! ● Leave the spark plug in the socket spanner while using the wire brush - this is kinder on the fingers and reduces the risk of dropping the plug and breaking it.

i INSIDE INFORMATION: Both engine types use aluminium cylinder heads, into which the plugs are screwed. This is very easily damaged if the spark plugs do not engage their threads properly: It is important therefore to screw in the plugs by hand initially, say two or three turns, before using the plug spanner. A slight smear of copper grease on the plug threads will enable them to turn more freely and also make them easier to remove next time. Finally, don't over tighten the spark plugs - firm hand pressure on the spanner is sufficient. *i*

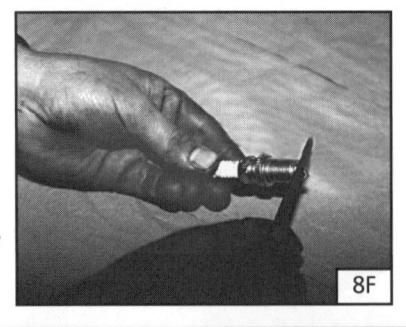

8F. It is essential that the plug is gapped correctly. See **Chapter 3, Facts and Figures**. Use a feeler blade of the correct thickness sliding it between the electrodes. It should be a firm sliding fit. Use a gapping tool or

carefully wielded pliers to bend the curved electrode towards or away from the centre electrode. Take GREAT CARE not to damage the insulator near the tip of the plug. If any of the plug's insulation is damaged, or if the plug is heavily contaminated, throw it away and fit a new one.

i INSIDE INFORMATION: If you are trying to remove a plug which becomes tighter as you turn it, there's every possibility that it is cross-threaded. Once out, it probably won't go back in again. Tighten it up again and take the car to a FIAT dealer who may be able to clean up the threads with a purpose-made tool. If this can't be done, he will have to add a thread insert to your cylinder head. It pays to take great care when removing and fitting spark plugs, especially when dealing with aluminium cylinder heads! *i*

❑ **Job 9. Check spare tyre pressure.**

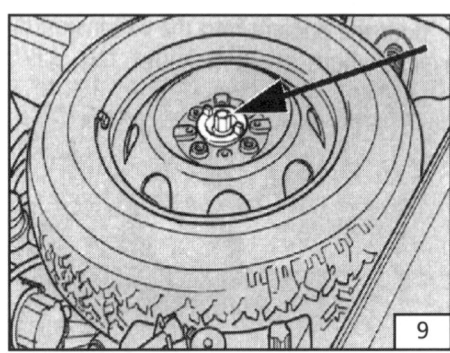

9. This job should ideally be carried out every month or two - you never know when you're going to need that spare! But if you haven't remembered, do it at the time shown on the Service Interval Chart at the latest.

i INSIDE INFORMATION: Put in the maximum recommended pressure for heavy-duty use - it's always easier to let some air out if necessary, than to put some in. Lift the spare out of the engine bay after unscrewing the hold-down nut (arrowed) and check the 'hidden' lower sidewall (see **Job 6**) for cracking. The rubber of a tyre that spends its life in the heat and fumes of the engine bay will deteriorate faster than those on the car. *i*

❑ **Job 10. Check front brake pads.**

We recommend that you check the condition of the (front) brake pads every six months. See **Job 49** for full details.

PART B: ENGINE AND COOLING SYSTEM

SAFETY FIRST!

● Refer to the sections on **ENGINE OILS** and **RAISING THE CAR SAFELY** in **Chapter 1, Safety First!** before carrying out the following work.
● You must always wear rubber or plastic gloves when changing the oil. Used engine oil can severely irritate the skin and may be carcinogenic.
● Oil drain plugs are often over tightened. Take care that the spanner does not slip, causing injury.
● Take great care that the effort needed to undo the drain plug does not cause the vehicle to fall on you or to slide off ramps - remember those wheel chocks, which must be placed back and front of the rear wheels!

❑ Job 11. Change engine oil and filter.

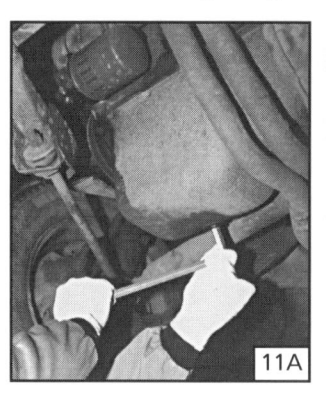

11A. The sump drain plug is on the rear-side of the sump. The plug has a recessed hexagonal head and you will need either a sump plug spanner, a large Allen key, or a 'Hex' headed socket fitted to a socket wrench to undo it. Your local FIAT dealer can supply you with the correct spanner.

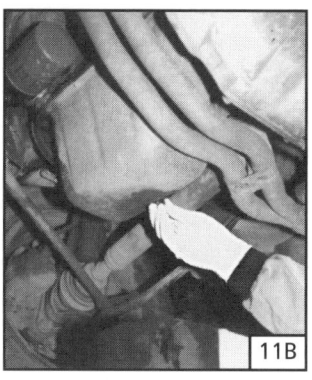

11B. Once the initial tightness of the plug has been released, unscrew the last few turns by (gloved!) hand, holding the plug in place until the threads have cleared. then withdrawing it smartly and allowing the oil to flow into a suitable receptacle beneath.

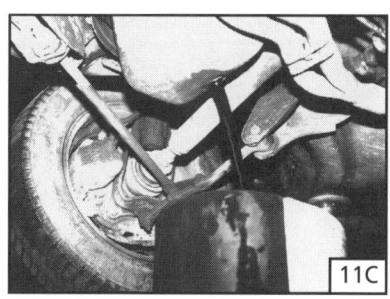

i **11C. INSIDE INFORMATION:** As the oil empties, the angle of 'spurt' will change, so be prepared to move the container. *i*

making it easy!
- Only drain the oil from an engine which is warm - but not so hot that the oil can scald!
- Allow the oil to drain for at least ten minutes before replacing the sump plug. You can use this time to remove the old oil filter and fit the replacement.

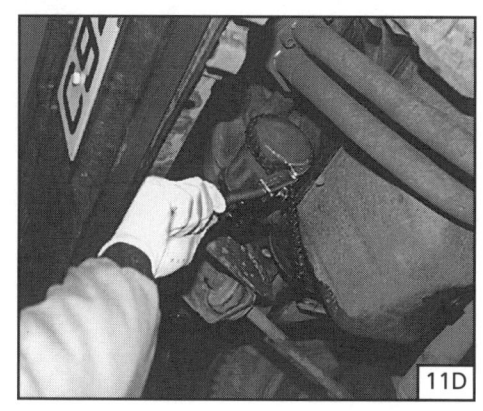

11D. The oil filter on the earlier OHV engines is located on the rearward-facing side of the engine, and on 'FIRE' OHC engines at the front. Use a chain wrench like the one shown here, to unscrew the old filter. Note that there will be some oil spillage as the filter seal is broken, so ensure that a drip tray is positioned beneath it.

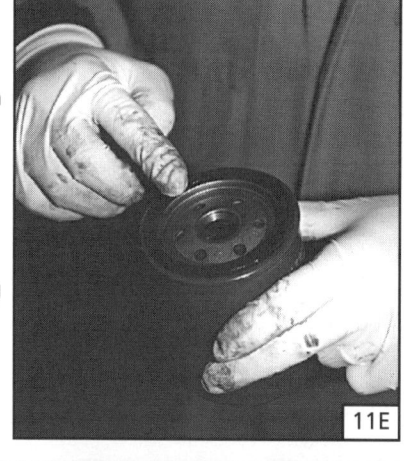

11E. To prevent the rubber sealing ring on the new filter from buckling or twisting out of shape as it's tightened, lightly smear the seal with clean oil before fitting it, and ensure that the ring is correctly seated in its groove.

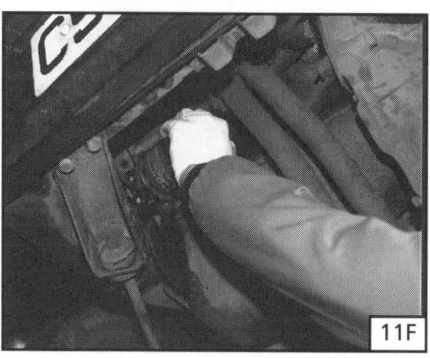

11F. Screw the new filter onto the stud by hand. When the rubber sealing ring contacts its seat, continue to turn the filter a further 3/4 of a turn, *by hand only*. Over-tightening the filter makes it difficult to remove at the next oil change and can buckle the seal, causing a leak.

i **INSIDE INFORMATION:** It isn't necessary to use excessive force when refitting the sump plug. Simply grip the spanner so that the thumb rests on the spanner head, limiting the amount of leverage that can be applied. Use firm pressure only. Before refitting the plug, wipe around the drain hole with a piece of clean cloth to remove any dirt. *i*

11G. Using a funnel or pouring jug, pour in the correct quantity of oil (see **Chapter 3, Facts and Figures**) and check the level against the dipstick.

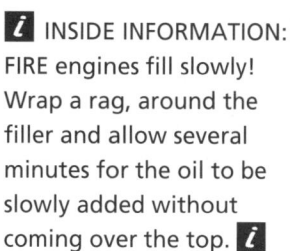

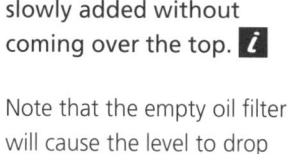

i **INSIDE INFORMATION:** FIRE engines fill slowly! Wrap a rag, around the filler and allow several minutes for the oil to be slowly added without coming over the top. *i*

Note that the empty oil filter will cause the level to drop slightly when the engine is started and the oil flows into it. You should run the engine at idle speed until the oil pressure warning light goes out, turn off and leave to stand for a few minutes and then check that there are no leaks and correct the oil `level before using the car.

CHAPTER 5 ENGINE AND COOLING SYSTEM

35

Job 12. Check/adjust valve clearances.

Two types of valve gear have been used on Panda engines - OHV (overhead valve) and OHC (overhead camshaft) types:

IMPORTANT NOTE: Valve clearances should be checked and set only when the engine is cold.

- EARLIER OHV ENGINES have conventional valve rockers on show beneath the rocker covers. (See **12A** for details.)

- 'FIRE' OHC ENGINES have a belt-driven overhead camshaft. See **12E** and **12F** for details, where the measuring technique is described.

EARLIER OHV ENGINES
12A. Start by removing the spare wheel, and the air cleaner and the four bolts holding the rocker cover in place. If the cover sticks on its gasket, jar it with the flat of your hand or a rubber mallet. Do not attempt to lever it off or it will distort. The carburettor and other ancillaries happen to have already been removed from this engine.

FACT FILE: SETTING VALVE CLEARANCES
- It is essential that valve clearances are set when there is no pressure on the valve. The 'Rule of Nine' ensures that valves are always adjusted at the right time.

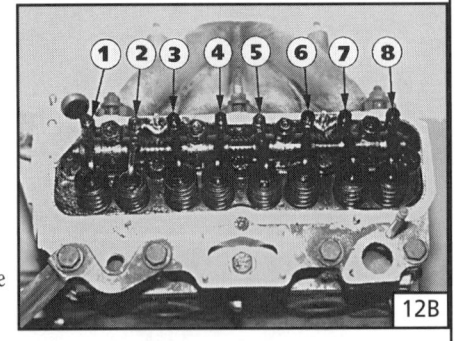

- **12B.** Number the valves counting them from the timing cover end of the engine. With the gearbox in neutral and the spark plugs removed, turn the engine over by hand so that number 8 valve is fully open - in other words, it's fully depressed by the rocker. You can now safely check or adjust the clearance for valve number 1. Following the chart below, you should now fully open valve number 6 while adjusting the clearance for valve number 3. (8 + 1 = 9; 6 + 3 = 9 - it works every time!)

IMPORTANT NOTE: Valve clearances for inlet and exhaust valves are different - see **Chapter 3, Facts and Figures**.

FACT FILE: CONTINUED
In the following chart, EX stands for Exhaust Valve and IN stands for Inlet Valve.

Check and Adjust	Valve Fully Open
1 - EX	8 - EX
3 - IN	6 - IN
5 - EX	4 - EX
2 - IN	7 - IN
8 - EX	1 - EX
6 - IN	3 - IN
4 - EX	5 - EX
7 - IN	2 - IN

N.B. If you adjust the valves in the above order, you will have the minimum amount of engine turning to carry out.

12C. Slide the end of the appropriate feeler gauge between the end of the valve stem and the rocker arm. It should just slide in but be in contact with both the valve and the rocker, giving a slightly stiff, sliding fit.

12D. To adjust the clearance, if necessary, put a ring spanner on the lock nut, free off the lock nut and turn the adjuster screw with a small open-ended or adjustable spanner. The idea is to use the adjuster screw to set the gap correctly and then re-tighten the lock nut without moving the adjuster screw.

It's a good idea to fit a new rocker cover gasket to avoid irritating leaks of oil running down the engine block.

> *making it easy!*
> - The lock nut will tend to tighten the adjuster screw as it is fastened down.
> - You may need to ease the adjuster screw back a very small amount so that it is pulled into its correct position as the lock nut is tightened.
> - After a couple of trial runs, you will quickly be able to judge the correct amount for yourself.

'FIRE' OHC ENGINES

12E. After removing the air cleaner, remove the four bolts holding the camshaft cover in place and take it off.

12F. The valve clearance is measured directly beneath the cam and must be checked when the high point of the cam is pointing directly upwards and away from the cam follower.

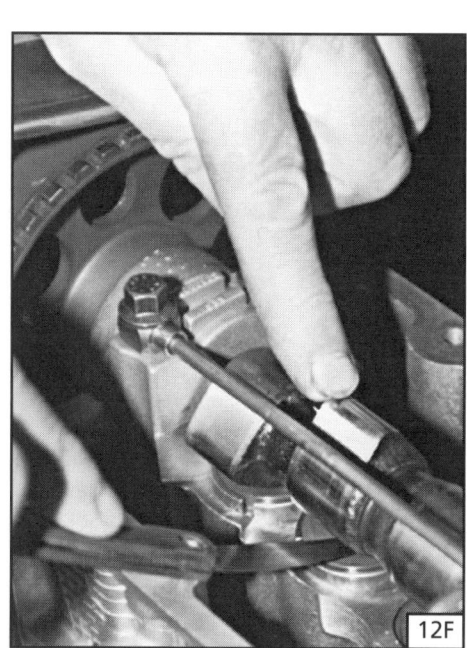

Try different feeler gauge thicknesses until you find one that is a tight sliding fit in between the cam and the cam follower. Make a note of the clearance between each valves cam follower and the cam, starting with number 1, at the timing belt end of the engine.

i INSIDE INFORMATION: Remember that the clearances for inlet and exhaust valves differ. See **Chapter 3, Facts and Figures.** Counting from the timing belt end of the engine, the valves are: 1, 3, 6, 8 - exhaust; 2, 4, 5, 7 - inlet. *i*

If a clearance is outside the tolerances shown in **Chapter 3, Facts and Figures**, the relevant shim will have to be changed. New shims are available from your FIAT dealer. This work is outside the normal service schedule and is fully described in **Chapter 6, Repairs and Replacements.**

❑ **Job 13. Check crankcase ventilation.**

13. Check the condition of the breather hose from the valve cover or cam cover (depending on engine type) to the air cleaner housing. The one shown has split lengthways due to the effects of oil contamination and needs replacing. If the pipe has become blocked or damaged, replace it, transferring the flame trap from inside the old pipe to the new one.

EARLIER, OHV ENGINES ONLY

You will have to remove the air filter housing to get at the crankcase ventilation pipe beneath it.

❑ **Job 14. Check camshaft timing belt.**

'FIRE' OVERHEAD CAMSHAFT ENGINES ONLY

14A. Take out the three bolts holding the camshaft belt cover in place. One is in the position arrowed, a second is directly opposite it...

CHAPTER 5 ENGINE AND COOLING SYSTEM

37

14B. ...and the third is easy to miss at the base, just above the alternator belt. (This is an engine removed from the car.)

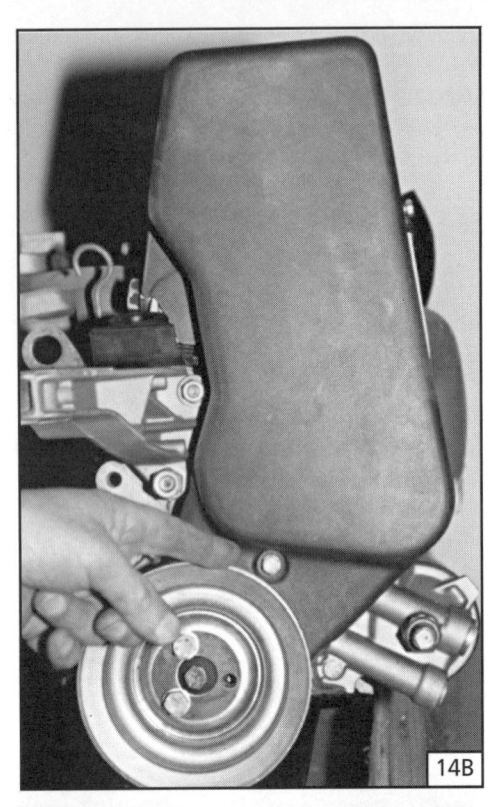

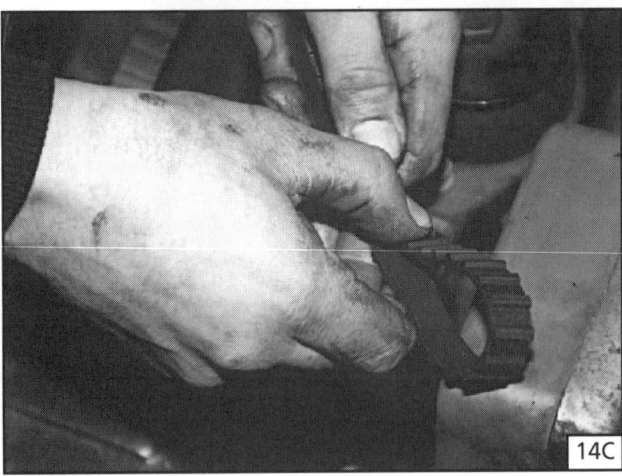

14C. Examine the belt for wear. If there is any sign of cracking, or if the toothed side appears worn or there are any 'teeth' missing, replace the belt straight away, without waiting for the recommended replacement interval. If the belt breaks, all engine power will suddenly be lost. Camshaft belt replacement is described in *Chapter 6, Repairs and Replacements*, or you may wish to have your FIAT dealer carry out the work for you.

❏ **Job 15. Change camshaft timing belt.**

'FIRE' OVERHEAD CAMSHAFT ENGINES ONLY

It is ESSENTIAL that you renew the camshaft drive belt at the recommended interval. See the *Service Interval Chart* at the start of this chapter and *Job 14*, above. *Chapter 6, Repairs and Replacements* explains how to carry out the work.

❏ **Job 16. Check cooling system.**

SAFETY FIRST!

• The coolant level should only be checked WHEN THE SYSTEM IS COLD. If you remove the pressure cap when the engine is hot, the release of pressure can cause the water in the cooling system to boil and spurt several feet in the air with the risk of severe scalding.

• Take precautions to prevent anti-freeze being swallowed or coming in contact with the skin or eyes and keep it away from children. If this should happen, rinse immediately with plenty of water. Seek immediate medical help if necessary.

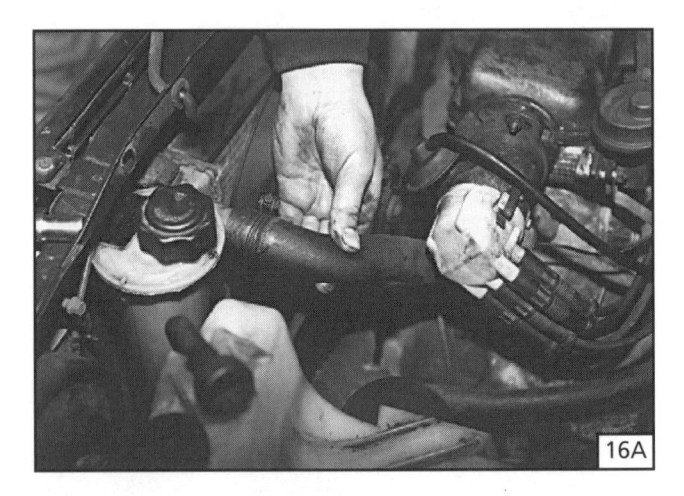

16A. Examine the cooling system hoses, looking for signs of splitting, chafing and perishing of the rubber hoses. Squeeze the top and bottom radiator hoses. Any hard, brittle areas or crackling sounds or feelings tell you that the hoses are decomposing from the inside - replace any found with such warning signs.

16B. Ensure that any worm-drive hose clips are secure and firm, but do not over tighten them. This is the bottom hose clip (arrowed) being checked for tightness from beneath the car.

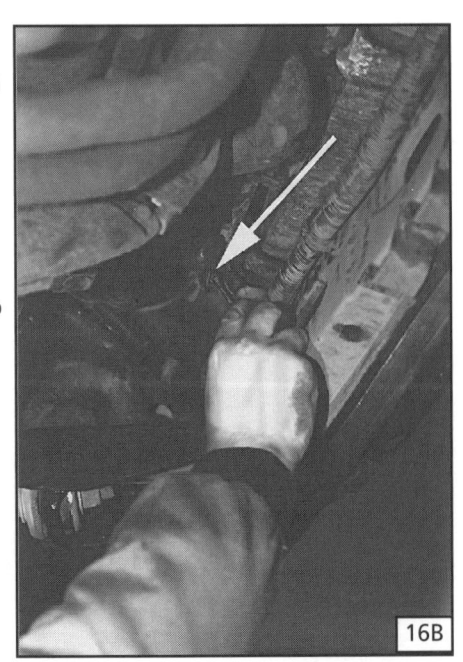

☐ **Job 17. Change engine coolant.**

> **SAFETY FIRST!**
>
> ● See **SAFETY FIRST!** at the start of **Job 16**.

Remove the expansion tank cap and, on early models only, the radiator filler cap.

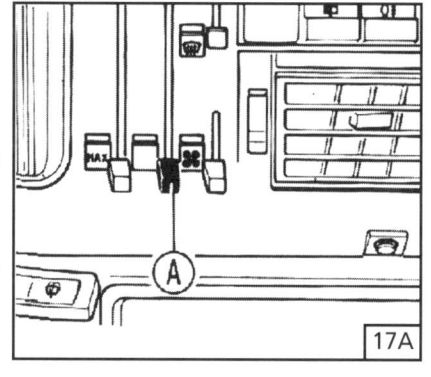

17A. Move the heater control (**A**) down to the red position. Loosen the worm-drive clip and pull off the bottom radiator hose (see **Job 16B**). Drain the coolant into a container. On earlier cars, where the expansion tank is connected to the radiator by a hose, detach the hose from the expansion tank and drain the expansion tank.

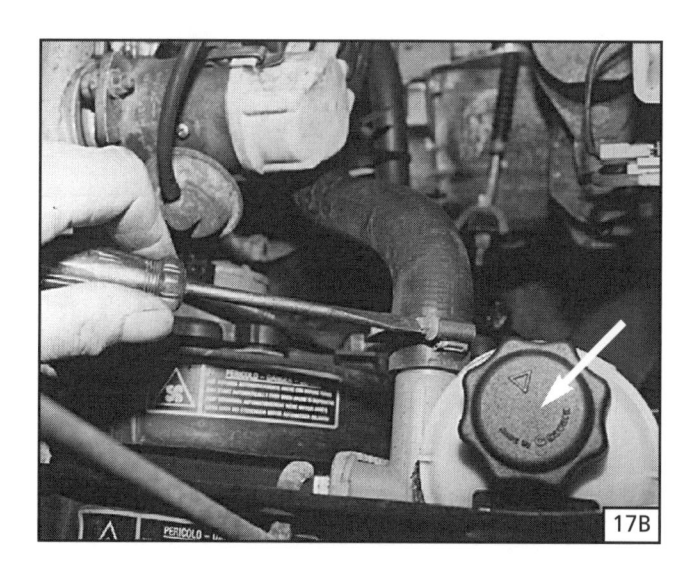

17B. INSIDE INFORMATION: After a very high mileage, sediment will gather in the cooling system, preventing it from working efficiently. Your engine could then overheat, or the heater may not work properly. From time to time, it is a good idea to flush the cooling system. With the bottom hose re-connected, disconnect the top hose clip (arrowed) and remove the top hose from the radiator. (You don't want to be working on the ground with water pouring over you!) Insert the end of a garden hose first into the hose (packing the gap with a rag) and then the radiator inlet, flushing the system in both directions until the water comes out clear. IMPORTANT NOTE: Flush first with the heater control turned off (fully 'up') until the engine and radiator are clear, so that you don't flush sediment into the heater system, then with the heater turned on, to flush the heater system out.

EARLIER OHV ENGINES ONLY

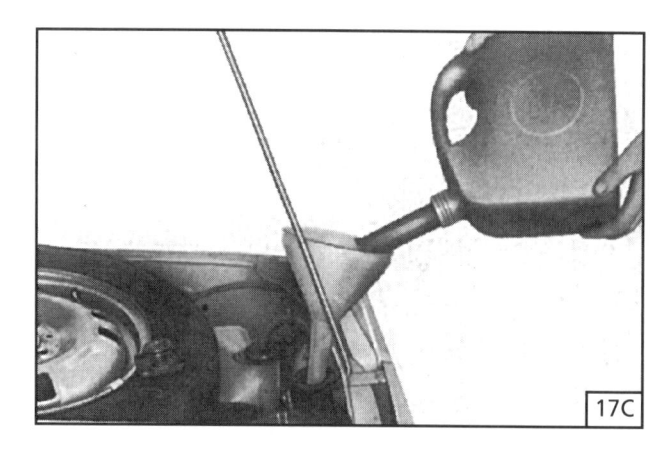

17C. Where there is a cap on the radiator *and* on the expansion tank, follow the following procedure:

● heater control fully down (see illustration **17A part A**).
● have all hoses reconnected *except* the one to the expansion tank.
● fill radiator through the radiator filler cap.
● reconnect the expansion tank and fill as shown to the normal level.
● refit the radiator filler cap.
● run the engine until air bubbles stop rising through the expansion tank.
● if water 'disappears' from the expansion tank, turn engine off. When coolant is cold, remove radiator filler cap, refill radiator and expansion tank and try again.
● check levels after running engine for several minutes, and after running the car a short distance on the road, top up the coolant when cold.
● use 50% water (preferably distilled) and 50% **Paraflu** coolant fluid (anti-freeze).

IMPORTANT NOTE: After refilling and bleeding the system (see **17D** and **17E**), it is highly likely that more air will be dislodged when you first use the car. Keep your eye on the coolant level (See **Job 2**) - perhaps carrying some 50/50 diluted coolant with you for the first few journeys.

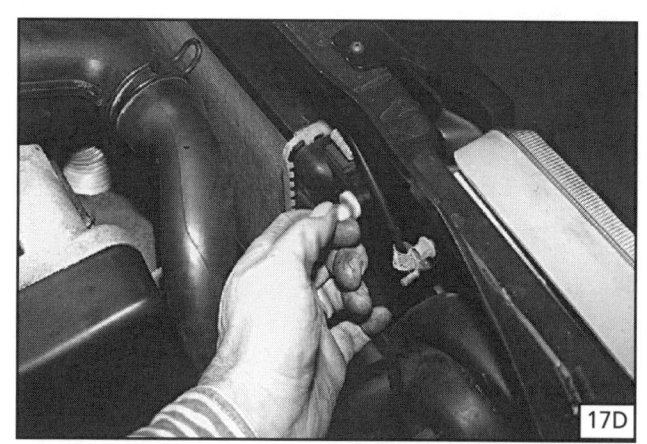

17D. When there is only an expansion cap, and to prevent potential air-locks forming in the cooling system as it is refilled (all hoses reconnected, of course!), two air-bleed screws are provided at strategic places in the system which should be opened before refilling. The first is located on the right-hand side of the radiator...

17E. ... and the second (arrowed) is found on the left-hand heater hose in front of the bulkhead. It is only necessary to undo the screws by two or three full turns.

Refill the cooling system, with a 50/50 mixture of clean water and fresh **Paraflu anti-freeze.** Tighten the bleed screws when coolant, and not air, comes out steadily. Run the engine for a few minutes (but not for so long that the coolant gets hot) and bleed them again.

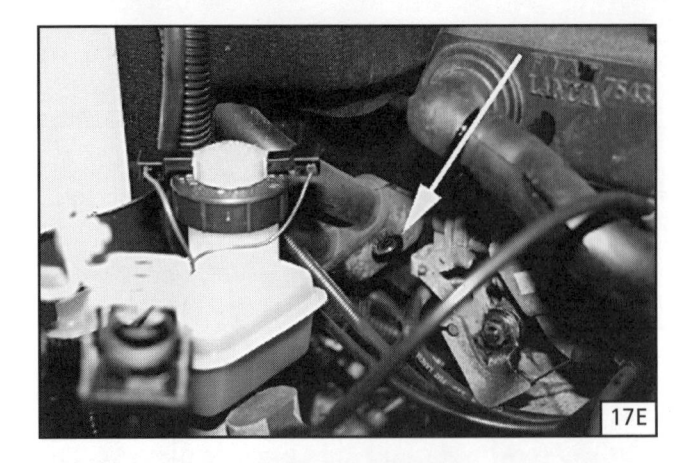

PART C: TRANSMISSION

❑ **Job 18. Check manual gearbox oil level.**

18. The gearbox and final drive (differential) unit run in the same oil. Their combined oil level and filler plug is located on the forward-facing side of the gearbox: When checking the level, the car must be on level ground. From beneath the car, wipe around the filler plug with a rag so that no dirt can get into the gearbox. If the area is encrusted, use engine cleaner or even aerosol releasing fluid to help move greasy dirt.

Remove the plug with a 10 mm Allen key and top-up if necessary, using the specified **Tutela** transmission oil (see *Chapter 3, Facts and Figures*), until oil just dribbles from the filler hole.

❑ **Job 19. Change manual gearbox oil.**

19. The combined gearbox and final drive oil should be drained at the time shown in the **Service Interval Chart.** Do so only after the car has been used and with the gearbox oil warm, so that it flows out well. Remove the 10 mm plug and drain the oil into a container.

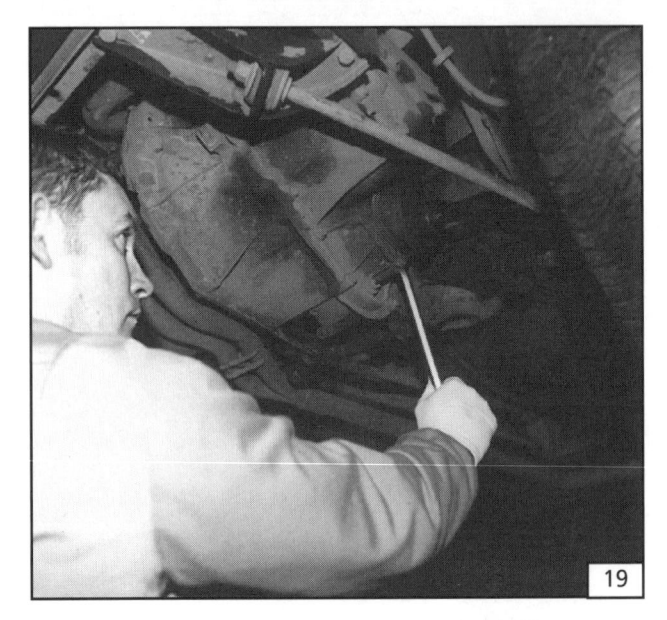

Leave for 10 minutes, to drain completely, and refill with the correct grade of **Tutela** transmission oil, through the level/filler plug, as described in *Job 18.*

❑ **Job 20. Check auto. transmission fluid level.**

20A. The automatic transmission system should be checked with the engine either cold or at normal running temperature, not in-between. FIAT recommend that the level is checked when the oil is hot. There are two sets of level marks - one for HOT and one for COLD - one on each side of the dipstick.

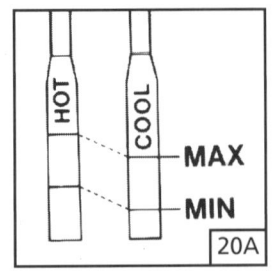

IMPORTANT NOTE: i) The automatic transmission fluid (ATF) both lubricates and cools the transmission system. It is especially important that the ATF is at the correct level. If the system need regular topping up because of leaks, fix them as rapidly as possible or have your FIAT dealer check the system. ii) Wipe the dipstick only with a lint-free rag so as to avoid clogging up the delicate valves in the gearbox. Keep dirt out!

20B. The automatic transmission fluid dipstick (**A**) is located

SAFETY FIRST!

- Beware of hot or moving parts when working on a running engine.
- The electric cooling fan can start up without warning!
- DON'T wear loose clothing, jewellery or long hair left loose.
- Wear suitable work gloves if the engine is hot.

towards the rear of the engine/transmission unit. See page 27.

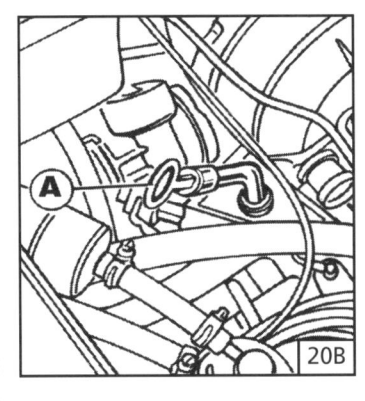

To check the level, first start the engine and firmly hold down the brake pedal. Move the gear selector lever several times from D to R and back to make sure all the hydraulic circuits are filled with fluid. Then select P and rev the engine a couple of times. WITH THE ENGINE STILL RUNNING, pull out the dipstick, wipe it clean with a lint-free cloth or paper kitchen towel, re-insert it and check the level. MAKE SURE YOU USE THE CORRECT SIDE OF THE LEVEL - 'HOT' OR 'COOL'.

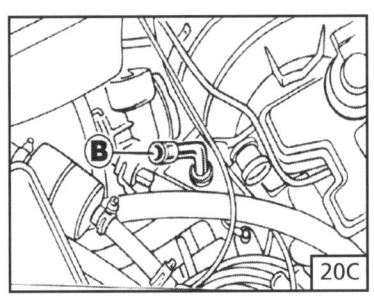

20C. If necessary, fresh **Tutela** ATF should be poured in through the dipstick tube (**B**), using a dispenser with a small spout. You may have to leave the fresh oil to clear the tube before you will be able to see a clear reading on the dipstick.

❏ **Job 21. Change auto. transmission fluid and filter.**

As well as **Tutela** Automatic Transmission Fluid, you will need a new sump plug washer, a sump gasket and a new gearbox oil filter, from your FIAT dealer. The filter should be changed every time the oil is replaced.

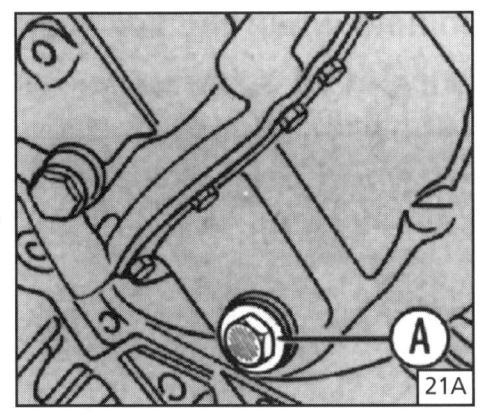

21A. Always drain the ATF when the transmission fluid is warm, such as after a run. Raise the front of the car on ramps, so that the ATF will drain well out of the rear corner of the gearbox sump where the drain plug (**A**) is situated.

21B. Remove the drain plug with a ring spanner and allow the fluid to drain into a container placed beneath the transmission - allow ten minutes for the fluid to drain completely.

21C. From underneath the car, take out the 13 cross-head machine screws holding the automatic gearbox sump in place.

21D. Two more bolts (arrowed) can be seen once the sump is removed, holding the oil filter in place.

i INSIDE INFORMATION: The sump is easy to distort when being refitted, leading to oil leaks. Refit all of the machine screws before tightening any of them. Screw them all in, and then go round again, tightening them all to the recommended torque. *i*

CHAPTER 5 TRANSMISSION

41

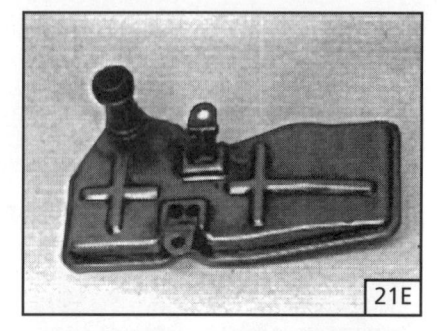

21E. Remove the filter discard it and fit the new replacement. Refit the sump, using a new gasket and non-setting gasket sealer, every time.

21F. Replace the drain plug (use a new washer) and fill the gearbox through the dipstick tube. (See **Job 20**.)

IMPORTANT NOTE: At every stage, take very great care not to allow any dirt or grit to get into the gearbox. An auto. 'box has delicate internal components, machined to very fine tolerances. The introduction of any dirt or grit will greatly reduce its life!

making it easy!
- FIAT dealers are recommended to use a special anti-blowback device when refilling with ATF.
- The bore of the filler tube is small and ATF will certainly 'glug' back out if you try to fill up using a funnel. Some brands of ATF are sold with a specially small dispensing tube made to be inserted right into a dipstick tube.
- Make sure that you use this type of dispenser - and when empty, save the container for future use.

❑ **Job 22. Check inner and outer driveshaft gaiters.**

22. Grasp and turn the inner driveshafts and gaiters, checking all round for any signs of splitting or damage that could allow the grease inside the joint to leak out, and ensure that the clips securing the gaiters are secure.

Repeat the same procedure for the outer gaiters, which are more prone to wear as their range of movement is greater.

IMPORTANT NOTE: Change any split, damaged or suspect gaiter as soon as possible - preferably before using the car. If water, road dirt or grit enters and the joint runs without lubricant, it will be ruined in no time at all - and the repair will become a very expensive one! See **Chapter 6, Repairs and Replacements**.

❑ **Job 23. Check/adjust clutch pedal/cable.**

The clutch mechanism itself is self-adjusting, although the cable linkage can stretch over a period of time and this will need adjusting.

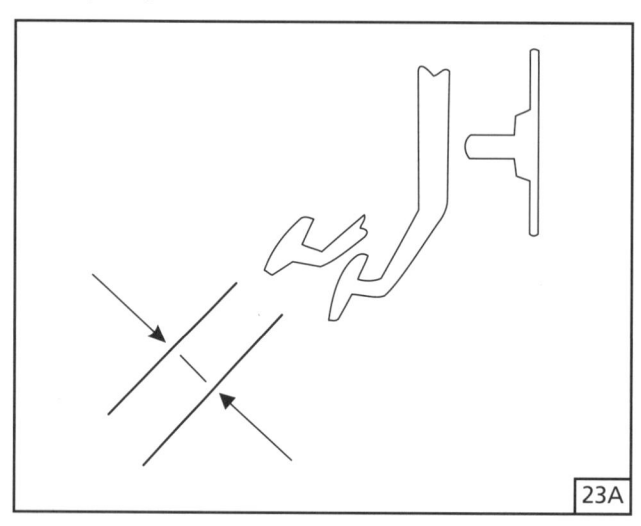

23A. Inside the car, measure the difference in height between the clutch and brake pedals. The clutch pedal should be 8 to 12 mm lower than the brake pedal. If it is not, adjust the cable as follows:

23B. The clutch adjuster can be reached from inside the engine bay; it's on top of the gearbox.

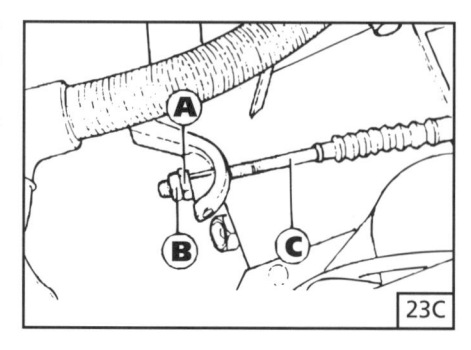

23C. Slacken the outer locknut (**B**) from the inner adjusting nut (**A**) using two spanners in opposition. Turning the adjusting nut inwards along the threaded rod will increase the pedal travel, while unscrewing it will reduce the travel. Tighten the locknut against the inner nut after adjustment.

❑ Job 24. Check auto. transmission selector cable.

It should only be possible - for obvious and important safety reasons - to start the engine when the gear selector is in the 'P' or 'N' position. Place it in each of the other positions and try to start the car. If it does, the fault must be put right! Also, check that, with the ignition switched off, and the selector lever in 'D' (Drive), 'L' (Low), 'R' (Reverse) or 'N' (Neutral), the timed warning buzzer sounds. If it doesn't, the fault is also probably one of faulty selector cable adjustment.

See *Chapter 6, Repairs and Replacements, PART B* under Automatic Transmission Selector Cable Replacement for adjustment details.

❑ Job 25. Check/lubricate propshaft.

4x4 MODELS ONLY

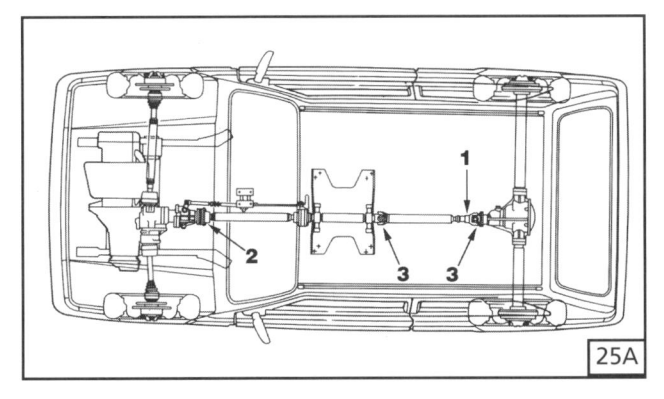

25A. LUBRICATE PROPSHAFT: Apply two or three strokes of a grease gun to the grease nipple (**1**) located on the sliding coupling at the rear of the propshaft, adjacent to the rear universal joint.

CHECK C.V. JOINT BOOT: Check carefully for splits (**2**). If any are found, replace the boot before using the vehicle, if at all possible.

CHECK UNIVERSAL JOINTS: Move both joints (**3**) by hand and insert a screwdriver into each joint. Lever carefully and check for wear. Any movement - replacement necessary!

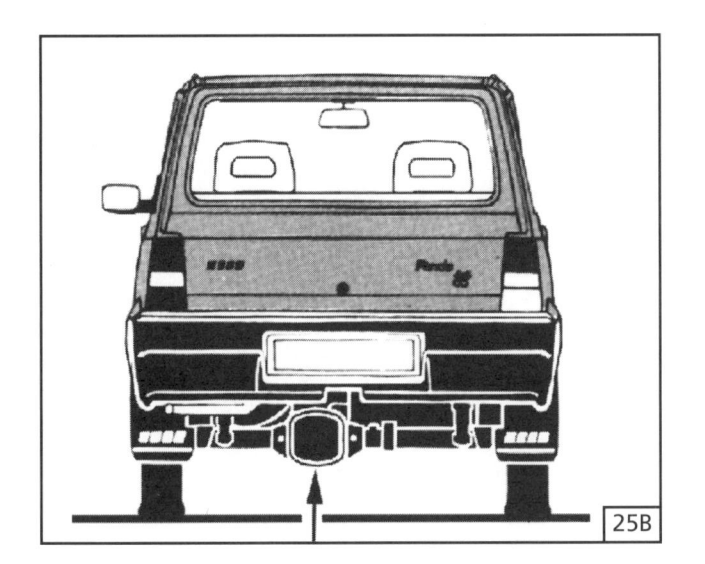

25B. CHECK REAR AXLE OIL LEVEL: With the car on level ground, clean around the oil filler/level plug (see *Job 26*) so that no dirt can get into the differential housing, and remove the level plug. Oil should just start to dribble out. If it doesn't top-up with the recommended grade of **Tutela** oil.

25C. CHECK PROPSHAFT BOLTS: These can come loose, especially if the vehicle is used over rough ground. Use a pair of spanners, as shown: one to hold the bolt; the other to tighten the nut.

❑ Job 26. Change rear axle oil.

4x4 MODELS ONLY

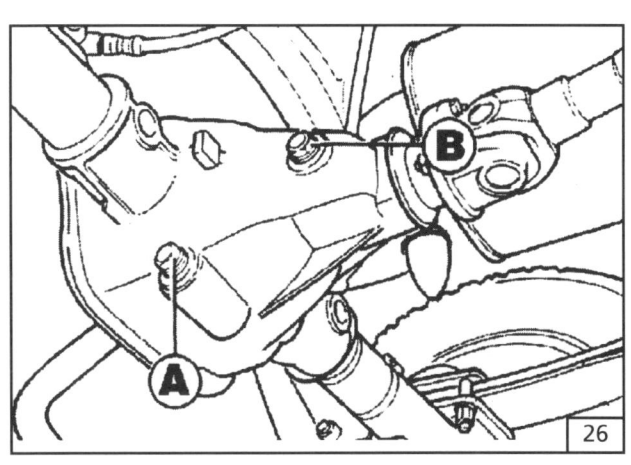

26. Carefully clean around the drain plug (**A**) and the filler/level plug (**B**) so that, when removed, no dirt can get into the differential housing. Remove the drain plug (**A**) and allow the old oil to drain completely - as the oil is thick, this can take up to 15 minutes. Replace the drain plug and remove the filler/level plug (**B**) refilling with the correct grade of **Tutela** oil. Fill until the oil is level with the filler hole and just starts to seep out. Refit the drain plug.

CHAPTER 5 TRANSMISSION

43

PART D: IGNITION AND ELECTRICS

SAFETY FIRST!

• You may minimise the risk of shock when the engine is running by wearing thick rubber gloves and by NEVER working on the system in damp weather or when standing on damp ground. Read **Chapter 1, Safety First!** before carrying out any work on the ignition system.

• The ELECTRONIC IGNITION SYSTEM INVOLVES VERY HIGH VOLTAGES! All manufacturers recommend that only trained personnel should go near the high-tension circuit (coil, distributor and HT wiring) and it is ESSENTIAL that anyone wearing a medical pacemaker device does not go near the ignition system. Also, stroboscopic timing requires the engine to be running - take great care that parts of the timing light or parts of you don't get caught up in the moving parts! Don't wear loose clothing or hair.

❑ **Job 27. Check/adjust alternator drive belt.**

27A. Check the belt and if any sign of cracking, fraying or severe wear on the inner face is found, replace it.

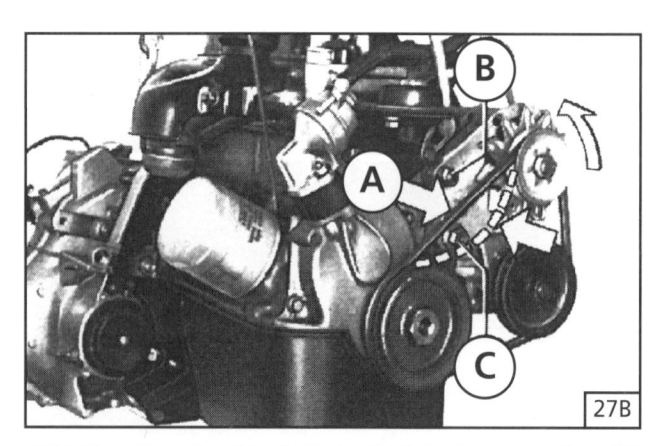

27B. The alternator drive belt should deflect no more than 10 mm when firm thumb pressure is applied to the belt between the pulleys in the direction of the arrow (**A**), with the dotted line showing the direction of deflection in exaggerated form. This is the alternator on early, OHV engines.

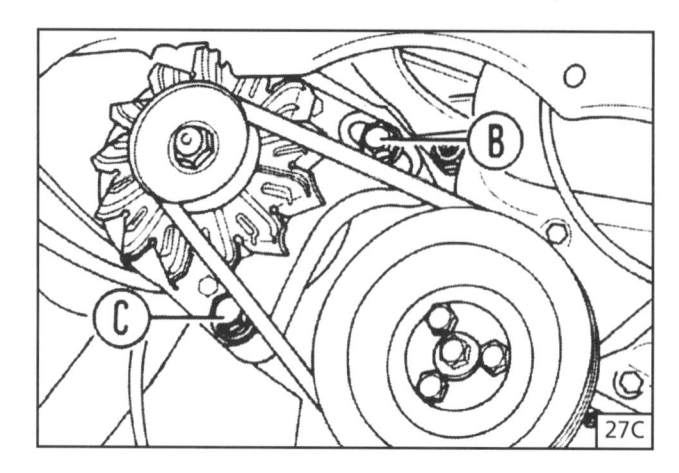

27C. If adjustment is necessary, slacken the upper pivot bolt (**B**) and the lower bolt (**C**), on all models. This is the later, FIRE, OHC engine.

Also check the general condition of the belt, looking for signs of cracking and frayed edges, and also for signs of 'polishing' of the belt's surface that can lead to 'squeal'. That shown is a later type of 'ribbed' belt.

making it easy! • **27D.** On FIRE, OHC engines access to the lower bolt is improved if this splash-shield is removed from inside the wheel arch - it is secured by three screws.

27E. Inside the wheelarch, with the right-hand wheel removed, the mounting can now be reached.

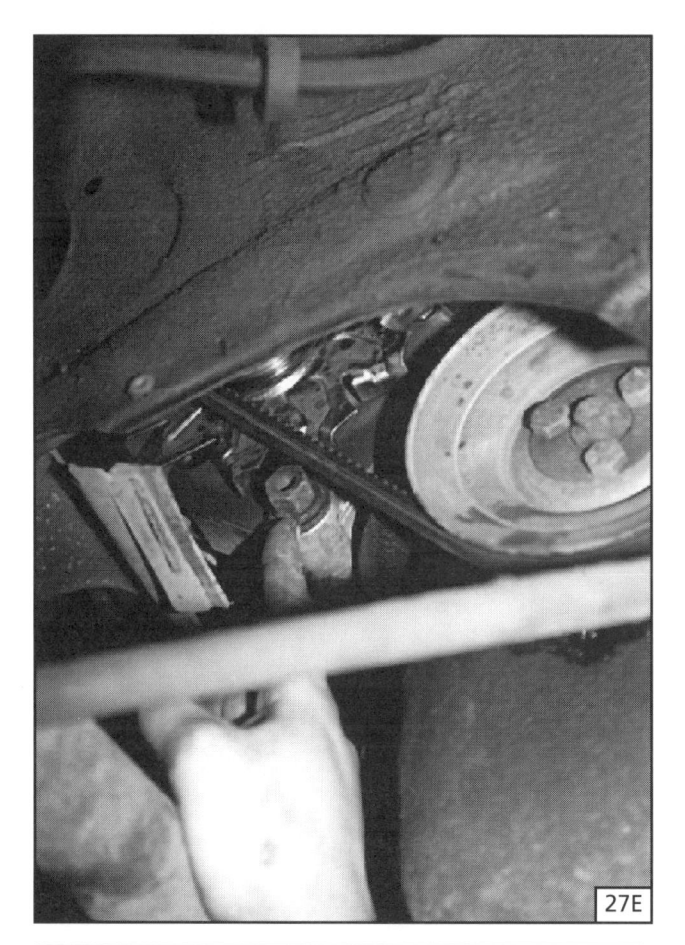

making it easy!

27F. Use a length of wood to pivot the alternator away from the engine block but take great care not to damage the alternator casing - you don't need to lever too hard! Tighten the bolts when the tension is correct. You may need some help to apply tension while the bolt is tightened.

❑ **Job 28. Check/clean HT leads and distributor cap.**

SAFETY FIRST!

● See **SAFETY FIRST!** at the start of this section and **Chapter 1, Safety First!**

28A. Remove each plug lead from the spark plugs, pulling only on the plug caps, not on the HT cables. Also, remove the large HT lead from the coil...

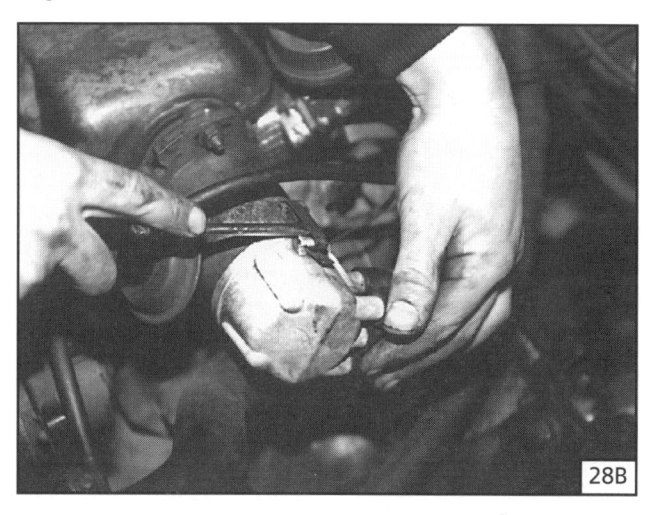

28B. ...and take off the distributor cap. Clean the cap and cables with a clean rag, applying a little aerosol water dispellant spray to help shift oil and grime.

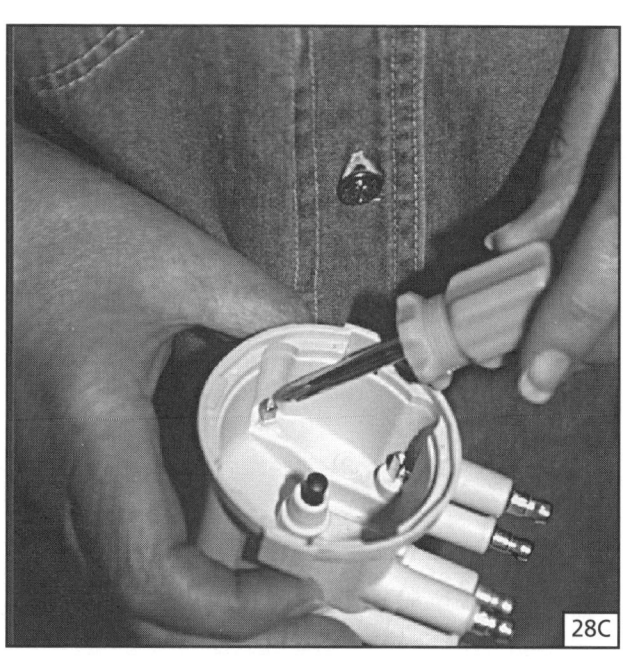

28C. Check each of the posts for burning or damage, and the central carbon brush, to ensure that it's not worn down and that the spring loading is okay.

CHAPTER 5 IGNITION AND ELECTRICS

45

CHAPTER 5 IGNITION AND ELECTRICS

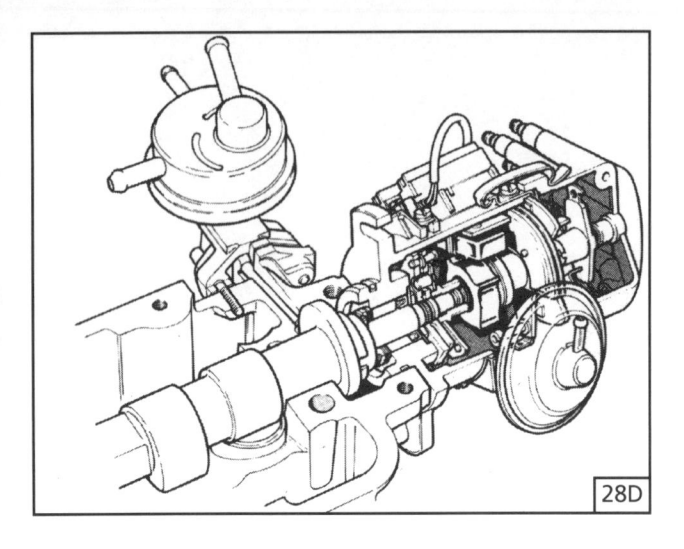

28D. IMPORTANT NOTE: The distributor illustrated is the Marelli SE 101 C contact breakerless ignition distributor. DO NOT spray water dispellant or apply lubricant of any sort to any part of an electronic ignition distributor. (It's okay to clean the cap, as described, however.)

☐ **Job 29. Check/adjust contact breaker points.**

DISTRIBUTORS WITH CONTACT BREAKERS ONLY - POINTS INSPECTION

29A. Remove the distributor cap as described in *Job 28*...

29B. ...and pull off the rotor arm...

29C. ...the cover...

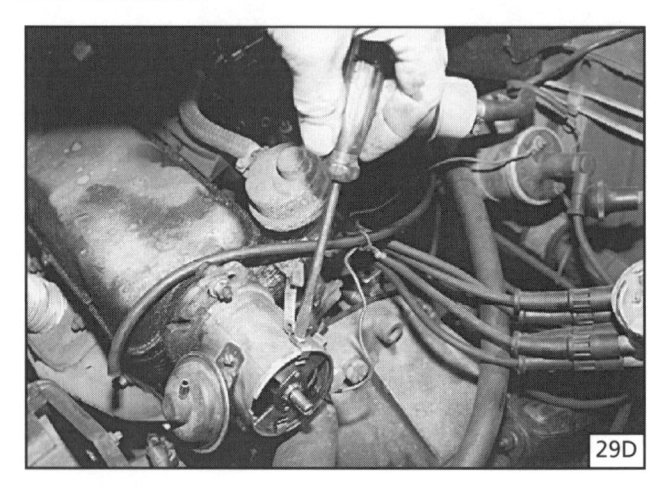

29D. ...and the bearing support, if fitted by removing the two fixing screws.

29E. With the ignition turned off, push the contact breaker points apart with a screwdriver and examine the points faces (arrowed).

FACT FILE: CONTACT BREAKER POINTS FAULTS

● If a metal build-up or 'pip' is clearly visible on one of the points, they are excessively worn.
● If there is any visible burning on the face of the points, they should be replaced.
● If the faces or the points are badly burned or bluish in colour, the condenser unit is probably defective and should also be replaced.
● Points are cheap to replace and it isn't worth cleaning them up, as described in some manuals.

> **SAFETY FIRST!**
>
> ● See **SAFETY FIRST!** on **page 44** at the start of this section and **Chapter 1, Safety First!**

The size of the points gap is affected by moving the fixed contact plate in the distributor away from or nearer to the cam in the centre of the distributor. The wider the gap, the earlier the points open (and the longer the points are open for), and so the size of the points gap has a direct bearing on the ignition timing.

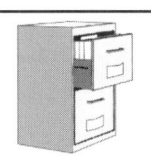

> FACT FILE: DISTRIBUTOR TYPES
>
> ● Two types of distributor have been fitted to FIAT Pandas with contact breaker distributors.
> ● The earlier Ducellier distributor was fitted to Overhead Valve engines and is adjusted with a screwdriver, with the distributor cap removed.
> ● The Marelli distributor was fitted to earlier Overhead Camshaft engines and has a hole in the side of the body, so the points gap can be adjusted (though the points cannot be examined) without removing the cap.
> ● The Marelli unit has a bearing support over the points, easily seen with the cap removed.

i INSIDE INFORMATION: If the distributor is badly worn, the dwell angle/points gap, and thus the timing, will fluctuate as the engine runs. If this is the case, you will have to set the points to an 'average' of the various readings you will obtain. *i*

> *making it easy!*
>
> ● The old-fashioned way of setting points, using a feeler gauge to set the gap, is not a very accurate way of doing things. Far better is to use a dwell meter, which sets the 'gap' by measuring the time for which the points are open - which is what matters!
> ● The use of a dwell meter is highly recommended when checking or adjusting the points on either engine type, but particularly on the OHC engine, where access to the points is awkward.
> ● Connect up the dwell meter as described on the instructions that come with the dwell meter you are using and measure the points dwell - the amount of time for which the points are open in each rotation. See **Chapter 3, Facts and Figures** for your engine's setting.
> ● Checking and adjusting the points with a feeler gauge requires the engine to be turned slowly, by hand, in the normal direction of rotation. However, the closeness of the engine to the inner wing panel makes use of a spanner on the pulley bolt awkward.
> ● A far easier method is to apply the handbrake firmly, select second gear and jack up the right-hand (driver's-side) wheel until just clear of the ground. Secure the car on an axle stand. Now, when the road wheel is turned by hand, the engine will also turn - easily if you also remove the spark plugs.

SETTING THE POINTS GAP

In an emergency, or if you don't own a dwell meter, you could set the points gap using a feeler gauge. Follow the instructions for adjusting the points given below, but with these differences. Select a feeler gauge of the correct thickness. (See **Chapter 3, Facts and Figures.**)

The points gap must be set when the heel of the points is on the highest part of the cam, so that the points are at their maximum opening.

Adjust the gap so that the feeler gauge is a sliding fit, making contact with both sides of the points as it goes in. Be careful not to let the spring in the points fool you into thinking you have a tight sliding fit, when in fact you don't. But a loose fit is just as bad. Use an electric torch to help you to see what is going on.

29F. Always disconnect the rubber vacuum advance pipe connection to the distributor and plug the rubber pipe (not the stub on the distributor) before setting the points gap with a dwell meter.

DUCELLIER (OHV ENGINE) DISTRIBUTORS

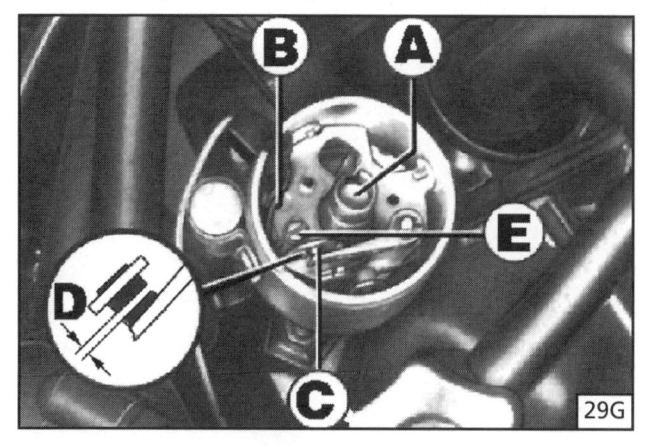

29G. Ensure that the ignition is turned off. Before adjusting the points, first remove the distributor cap and rotor arm as described in **Job 28**. Slacken the contact breaker locking screw (**E**) and use a screwdriver, inserted into the adjuster slot (**B**) to move the fixed contact in or out as necessary, adjusting the points gap (**C** and **D**). Turn the engine over by hand, as described in **MAKING IT EASY** and adjust the position of the fixed contact until the dwell figure given in **Chapter 3, Facts and Figures** is achieved, with the engine being turned.

CHAPTER 5 IGNITION AND ELECTRICS

LUBRICATE DISTRIBUTOR: Apply a couple of drops of oil to the felt pad (**A**) to provide lubrication for the distributor shaft. Apply a tiny smear of grease to the side of the cam face, using the tip of a small screwdriver.

LATER OHV-ENGINE DISTRIBUTORS

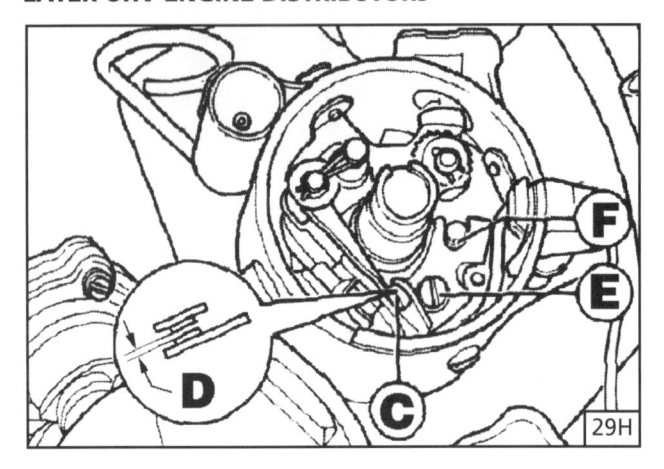

29H. Slacken the screw (**E**) and adjust the points gap (**C** and **D**) by inserting and carefully twisting a screwdriver in the slot (**F**).

MARELLI (OHC ENGINE) DISTRIBUTORS

29I. For the position and appearance of the Marelli distributor,
see **Job 28A**. Make sure the ignition is turned off. The points gap (**1**) on this distributor can be set by connecting a dwell meter and adjusting the gap with a 3 mm Allen key (**2**), inserted through the body of the distributor. See **Job 30** for more detailed information.

29J. This screwdriver is pointing out the position of the hole in the distributor body...

29K. ...and this is the Allen-head adjuster screw (arrowed) on the points, inside the distributor.

❑ **Job 30. Replace contact breaker points.**

DISTRIBUTORS WITH CONTACT BREAKERS ONLY

It is important to correctly identify the type of distributor fitted to your Panda. See **FACT FILE: DISTRIBUTOR TYPES** in **Job 29.** You should wipe both faces of the new contact breaker points with a cloth dipped in methylated spirits or cellulose thinners to remove any protective varnish that may have been put there by the manufacturer.

DUCELLIER (OHV ENGINE) DISTRIBUTORS

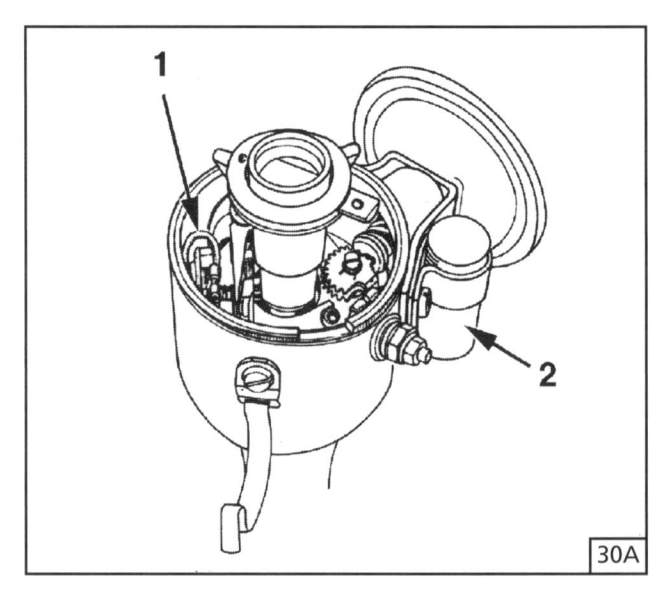

30A. Remove the low tension cable (**1**) and the cable from the condenser (**2**) remove the terminal screw and washer.
Unscrew and remove the contact breaker locking screw (see **29G** and **29H**) and lift off the points.

MARELLI (OHC ENGINE) DISTRIBUTORS

After removing the distributor cap, lift off the rotor arm and remove the bearing support. See **Job 29A** to **29C**.

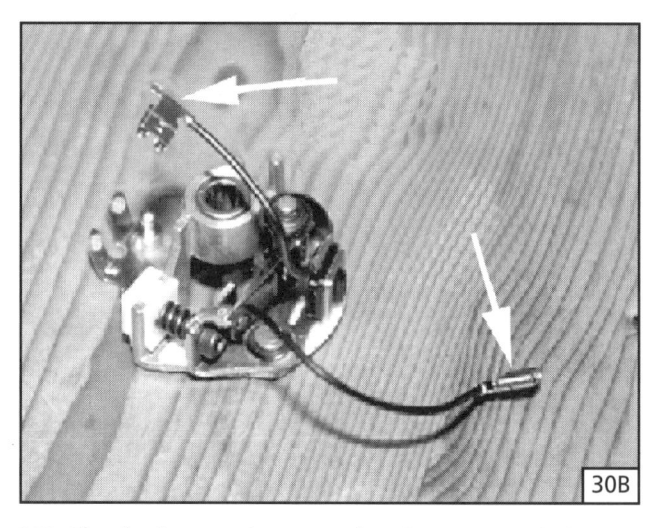

30B. The distributor points are replaced as a unit with the entire base plate - they are not separable. Later, the two leads (arrowed) will have to be disconnected from their terminals inside the body.

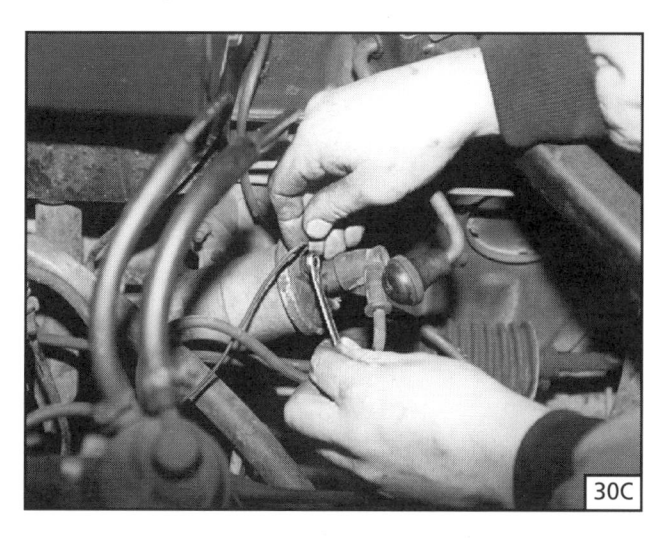

i **30C. INSIDE INFORMATION:** FIAT dealers recommend that these points are replaced with the distributor out of the car. Disconnect the low tension lead from the condenser at the coil, take off the distributor cap...

30D. ...and the advance control pipe from the stub (arrowed). So that the distributor can be replaced without 'losing' the ignition timing, put a dab of typists' correction fluid across the base of the distributor and onto its mounting, as shown. *i*

IMPORTANT NOTE: If the ignition timing is 'lost' for any reason, or you are not sure that it is correct, see **Job 31**.

30E. Take off the two nuts and washers holding the distributor in place and take it out of its housing.

30F. On the bench (vice jaws protected with card), lift off the rotor arm and cover...

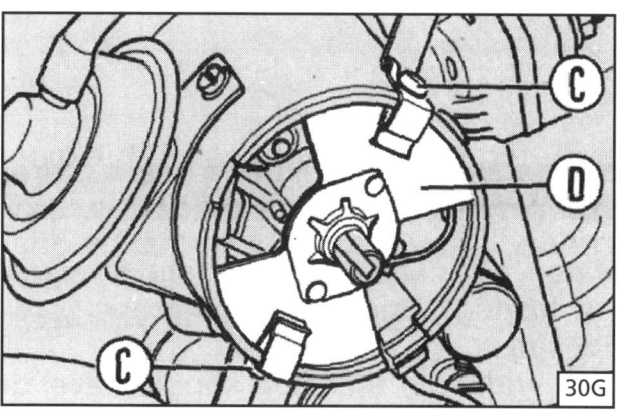

30G. ...remove the two screws and clips (**C**) holding the bearing support (**D**) in place, and lift away.

30H. Take out the two screws (**1**) holding the vacuum advance unit (**2**) in place and lift it away. Remove the hairclip (**3**), detach the two leads (see **30B**) and lift the points out.

IMPORTANT NOTE: There may be shim washers beneath the plate. Leave them in place or retrieve for refitting later.

LUBRICATE DISTRIBUTOR: When fitting a new contact breaker assembly, and whenever inspecting the condition of the points, put a couple of drops of oil on the sintered bush in the middle of the assembly.

CHECK DISTRIBUTOR SHAFT - ALL TYPES

While replacing the points, try moving the distributor shaft from side to side. If there is any noticeable movement, the points gap and timing will fluctuate as the engine runs, leading to inefficiency in the ignition system. The only solution is a replacement - see your FIAT dealer.

☐ **Job 31. Check ignition timing.**

SAFETY FIRST!

● You may minimise the risk of shock when the engine is running by wearing thick rubber gloves and by NEVER working on the system in damp weather or when standing on damp ground. Read **Chapter 1, Safety First!** before carrying out any work on the ignition system.

● The ELECTRONIC IGNITION SYSTEM INVOLVES VERY HIGH VOLTAGES! all manufacturers recommend that only trained personnel should go near the high-tension circuit (coil, distributor and HT wiring) and it is ESSENTIAL that anyone wearing a medical pacemaker device does not go near the ignition system. Also, stroboscopic timing requires the engine to be running - take great care that parts of the timing light or parts of you don't get caught up in the moving parts! Don't wear loose clothing or hair.

● The engine needs to be running for you to use a strobe lamp, so make sure all tools, cloths and your clothing are well away from any moving parts, particularly the drive belt. Running the engine with the car stationary will heat the coolant and it is quite likely that the thermostatic electric fan will start suddenly. Make sure no tools, cloths or clothing or fingers are near it. Work out of doors to avoid a build up of exhaust fumes.

● **IMPORTANT NOTE:** For engines with BREAKERLESS ELECTRONIC IGNITION, there is no gap to set - only the timing can be set.

i **INSIDE INFORMATION:** Check the vacuum device by disconnecting the pipe at the manifold and sucking. If air comes from the advance assembley, the diaphragm is probably leaking and a new unit should be fitted. otherwise the vacuum advance won't work and performance will suffer badly. *i*

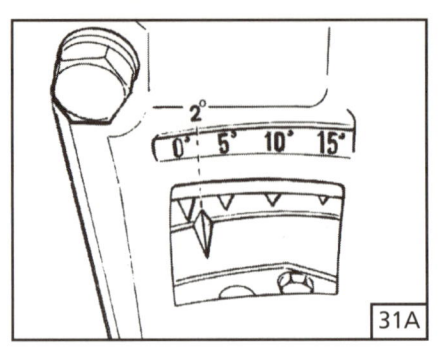

31A. The static timing marks are located in a 'window' on the clutch bell-housing and consist of three pointers: The larger pointer represents zero degrees (or Top Dead Centre), the centre pointer 4 degrees advance (Before Top Dead Centre - BTDC) and the right pointer 8 degrees BTDC. A timing mark, an engraved line, is also provided, on the rim of the flywheel.

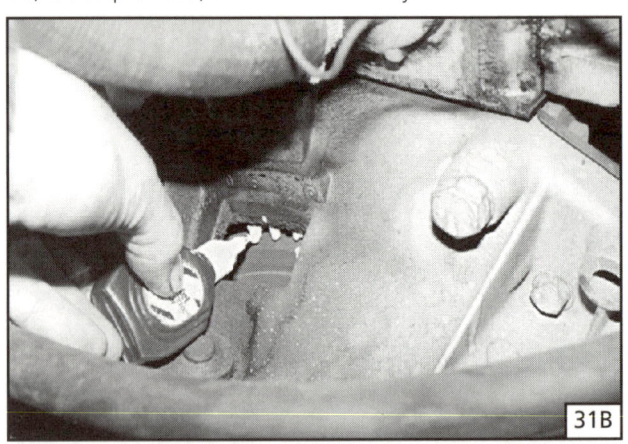

● **31B.** Use typists' correction fluid to highlight the timing marks and make them easier to see in the beam from the timing light.

31C. Connect up a timing light according to the maker's instructions, making sure none of the wires to the light can come into contact with any hot or moving parts of the engine. Disconnect and block the vacuum pipe to the distributor advance mechanism . (The distributor cap has been removed here, so that you can see the position of the timing marks. You have to carry out this job with everything connected up, of course!)

Check the timing by directing the flashing beam of the timing light at the timing marks on the engine, which will appear 'frozen'. If the timing is not as specified in **Chapter 3, Facts and Figures**, adjust the timing as follows.

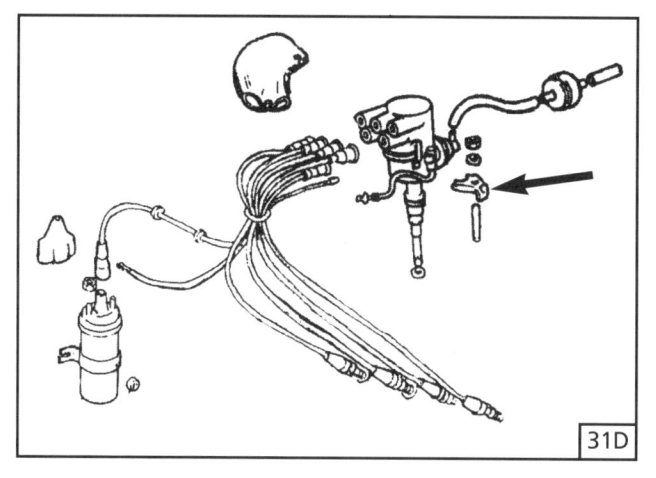

31D. On OHV engines, slacken the distributor clamp nut (arrowed) just sufficiently to allow the distributor to turn under firm hand pressure.

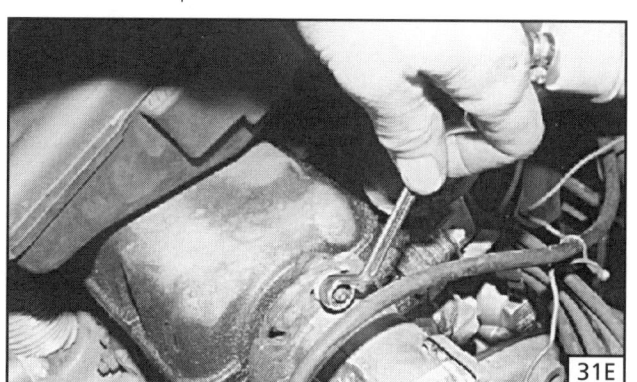

31E. On 'FIRE' OHC engines, the top clamp nut is situated here. Its 'twin' is immediately opposite and beneath. Slacken both but initially, just retighten the top one when the ignition timing is correct. Retighten the bottom one (with an extension on your socket spanner) when you have finished.

ON BOTH TYPES: With the engine running, as the distributor is turned (clockwise to advance, anti-clockwise to retard) so the timing mark on the flywheel will be seen to move relative to the pointers. Move the distributor so the timing marks are aligned correctly and retighten the clamp nut.

❏ **Job 32. Change spark plugs.**

Spark plugs 'tire' and lose efficiency over a period of time, even if they look okay. See **Job 8 - Check/clean/gap spark plugs.** for information on their removal and replacement.

❏ **Job 33. Check electric fan operation.**

Drive the car until it is warm enough for the engine to run without use of the choke. Park out of doors and, with the gearbox in neutral (or 'P' in the case of an automatic) leave the engine running until the engine's temperature climbs towards its normal running position. At just above this position, the electric cooling fan should come on, to compensate for the lack of cooling air passing through the moving car's radiator, and then go off again when the temperature drops. Refer to your coolant temperature gauge on the dash, if fitted.

PART E: FUEL AND EXHAUST

❏ **Job 34. Check fuel pipes for leaks.**

Check the fuel lines in the engine compartment, looking for signs of chafing, splits and perishing of the rubber and plastic parts. Ensure any worm-drive hose clips used on the connections are firm and secure.

34. Underneath the car, look out for physical damage to fuel lines and ensure that all pipe clips are in place.

❏ **Job 35. Change air filter.**

EARLIER OHV CARS

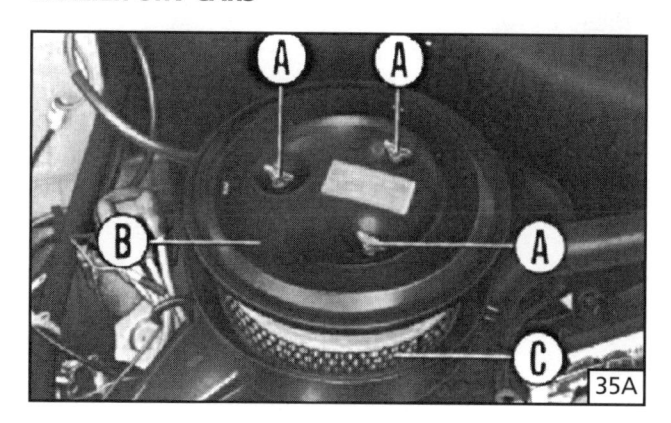

35A. Start by unscrewing the wing nuts (**A**) and lifting off the cover (**B**) followed by the filter element (**C**). Wipe out the insides of the housing, to remove any oil or debris before fitting the new element. Take care to seat the filter properly in the housing and to replace the sealing washers beneath the wing nuts.

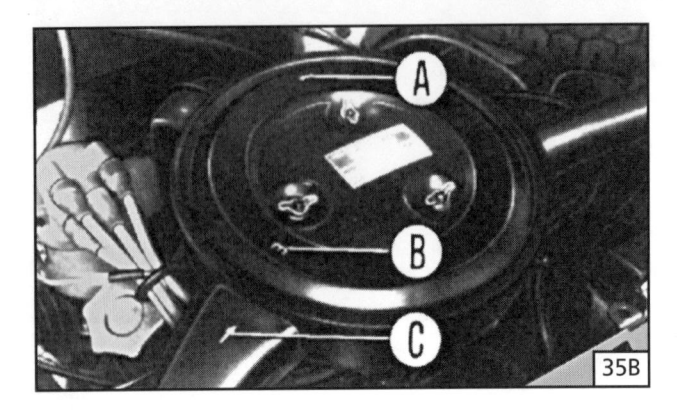

35B. The air intake has a SUMMER and a WINTER setting. The latter directs the air over the hot, manifold part of the engine. Set yours to the correct position for the time of the year. In winter, symbol **A** should line up with arrow **C**. In summer, symbol **B** should line up with the arrow.

LATER OHV CARS

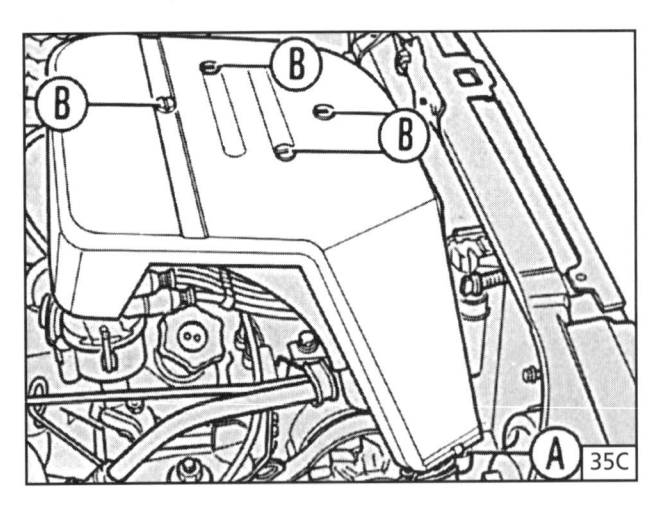

35C. Reach the filter element by unscrewing the four clips (**B**) and releasing the spring clips (**A**).

OHC 'FIRE' ENGINE CARS

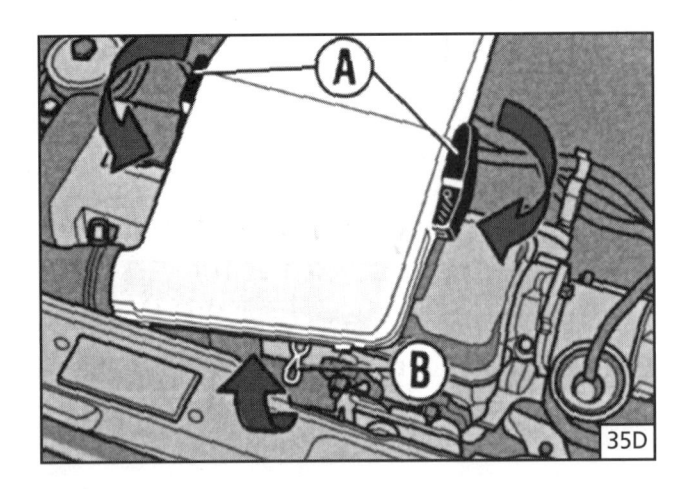

35D. Release the two plastic spring clips (**A**), one on each side of the air cleaner housing, by pulling outwards, and disconnect spring clip (**B**) at the front of the housing.

35E. Pull the front part of the housing forwards so that the filter element can be pulled out and replaced. When you push the new element into position, make sure the outer seal is properly fitted to the channel. Replace the front of the housing and secure the clips.

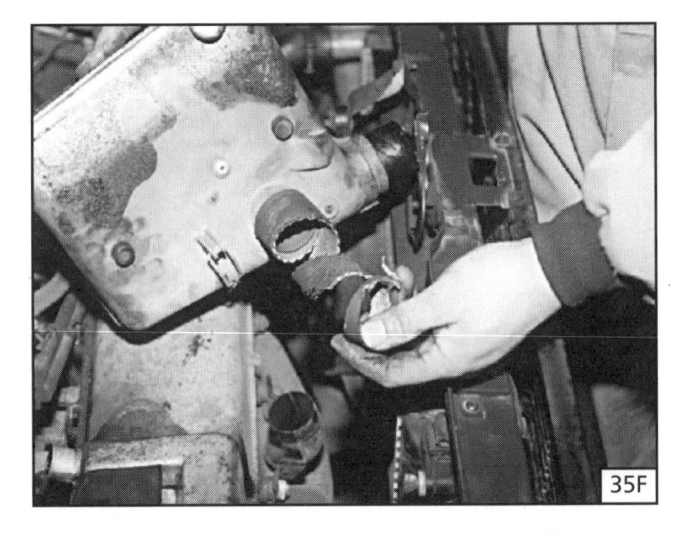

35F. Inspect the air intake pipe. If it's missing or badly damaged, the engine may ice up and intermittently cut out, especially in cold or damp weather. Replace it if necessary.

❏ **Job 36. Change fuel filter.**

WEBER CARBURETTOR ENGINES ONLY

36A. If your engine is fitted with a Weber carburettor (see **Job 37, FACT FILE: CARBURETTOR TYPES**) you will find a filter plug at the fuel inlet. Disconnect the earth battery lead, detach the supply hose from the carburetttor and mop up spilt fuel witha rag. Unscrew the filter plug, take out the gauze, clean, and replace it.

SAFETY FIRST!

- *Fuel injection systems inject fuel at extremely high pressure and all of the fuel in the pipes from the injection pump to the injectors in the cylinder head is at this pressure.*
- *If the pressure is released, the resulting jet of petrol can penetrate skin or cause blindness if it hits the eyes.*
- *The fuel lines remain pressurised for some considerable time after the ignition is switched off.*
- *IMPORTANT NOTE: Removing pressure from the fuel lines, as described below, will not remove pressure from each of the components - they will still be pressurised. Do not work on any of the components as part of the service schedule, and take appropriate action to depressurise them before carrying out any other work on them.*
- *Before working on any part of the system it is necessary to relieve the pressure, as follows:*
- *Disconnect the battery negative terminal. (See FACT FILE: DISCONNECTING THE BATTERY under Job 4.)*
- *Work out of doors and away from any sources of flame or ignition. Wear rubber or plastic gloves and goggles. Have a large rag ready.*
- *Place a container beneath the filter to catch the fuel that is likely to be spilt.*
- *Place your spanner on the first connection to be undone. Before undoing it, place the rag, folded to give several thicknesses, over the joint.*
- *Undo the connection very slowly and carefully, allowing the pressure within the pipework to be let out without causing a dangerous jet of fuel.*
- *Release the pressure from each of the pipes in the same way.*
- *Mop up all traces of fuel and allow to dry thoroughly before starting the car or taking it back indoors.*

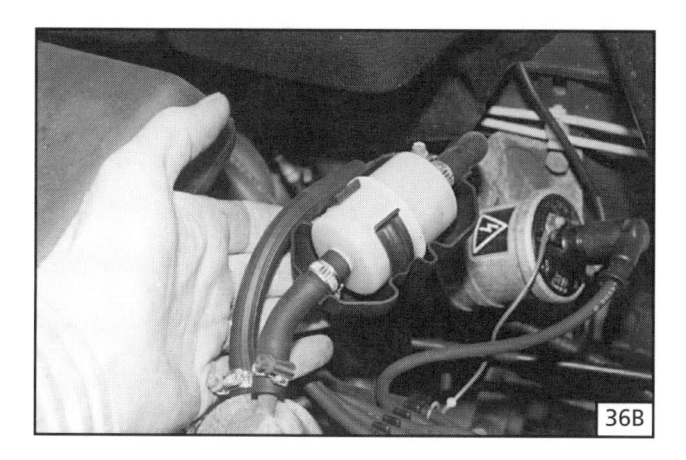

FUEL INJECTION MODELS ONLY

36B. The in-line filter must be renewed at the specified service interval to prevent damaging sediment from getting into the delicate injection mechanism. This type fits into a spring clip in a plastic casing, alongside the air filter, near the coil.

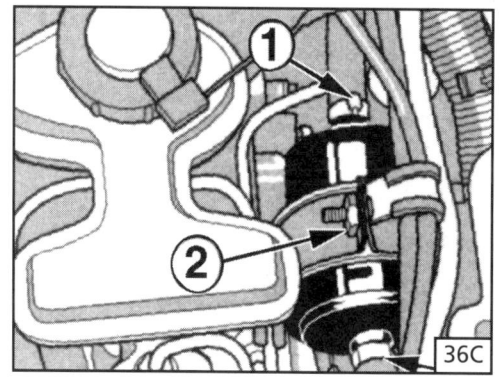

36C. This in-line filter is in a similar position, shown in the handbook as being below the brake fluid reservoir but on a left-hand drive car. If original FIAT clips are fitted (**1**), cut off the crimped part with side-cutters and use standard fuel hose clips when refitting. Pull off the pipes: Slacken the clamp nut (**2**) and slide the filter out.

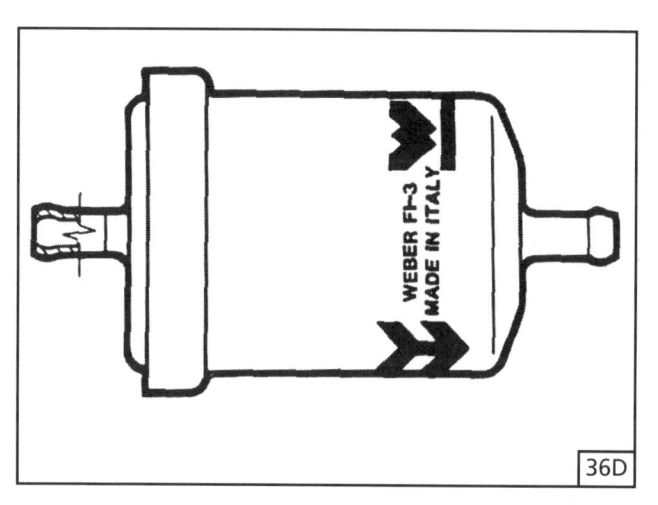

36D. On many vehicles there is also a low pressure filter to be replaced at the same time. It is fitted under the bodyshell, close to the fuel tank, along the fuel supply pipe.

IMPORTANT NOTE: The new filter will have an arrow on it. Make sure that it points in the direction of the fuel flow - towards the throttle body - when it is fitted. After clamping the new filter in place, refit the hoses, ensure no traces of fuel are left in the engine bay, reconnect the battery and restart the engine. Check carefully to ensure that there are no leaks

❑ Job 37. Check/adjust idle speed, mixture and emissions.

Setting the idle speed and mixture is not just a matter of making the car run smoothly and economically: it's also a question of allowing the car to run within the legal hydrocarbon (HC), Nitrous Oxide (NO) and carbon monoxide (CO) emission limits. If it is outside the permissible limits, the car will fail the annual test. Be warned, though, that a worn engine may fail the test, even if the carburation or injection system is correctly set up.

IMPORTANT NOTE: When tuning the engine, you should tune the carburettor or injection last of all. Their settings will be affected by the state of tune of the rest of the engine, so carry out ignition tuning, change the air filter, and so on, first.

CHAPTER 5 FUEL AND EXHAUST

i **INSIDE INFORMATION:** These jobs require the use of a tachometer (rev. counter) and an exhaust gas analyser to achieve any degree of accuracy. If you don't own them - and relatively inexpensive tools are now available - you may wish to have the work carried out by your local FIAT dealer. *i*

ROUGH GUIDE: Within each section is a description of how you can get the car running tolerably well without any specialist equipment, so that you can take it to your FIAT dealership for accurate (and MoT-able!) tuning.

CARBURETTOR MODELS ONLY

ADJUSTMENT SCREWS: There are two setting screws on all carburettors fitted to Pandas. The idle speed adjustment adjusts the tick-over speed, and the idle mixture adjustment sets the richness of the mixture at tick-over.

TAMPER PROOFING: All Panda carburettors have a tamper-proof seal (some plastic; some aluminium) placed over the mixture adjustment screw. These seals are there to prevent anyone unauthorised from altering the mixture, and thus the exhaust emissions. In certain countries, these seals must be retained, by law.

If the seal is a plastic cap placed over the adjuster screw, it can be removed with a pair of pliers. If it is a plug within the screw recess, it will have to be forced out with a sharp object.

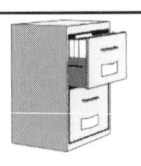

> FACT FILE: CARBURETTOR TYPES AND ADJUSTER SCREWS
> ● Two types of carburettor were fitted to the early, OHV engines. The Solex C32 DISA carburettor can be identified by the two threaded studs which protrude up into the air filter housing when the filter is removed. The Weber 32 ICEV carburettor has no such studs.
> ● Some 'FIRE' OHC engines were also fitted with a carburettor - always a Weber.

IMPORTANT NOTE: All of the following photographs show the adjusters being pointed out with air cleaner removed. The air cleaner MUST be fitted, and the filter element in good condition when you set the carburettor, otherwise you will achieve a grossly distorted setting.

> **KEY:** In each of the following three illustrations: **A** = idle speed screw, and **B** = mixture screw (probably covered with a plug - see **TAMPER PROOFING** above).

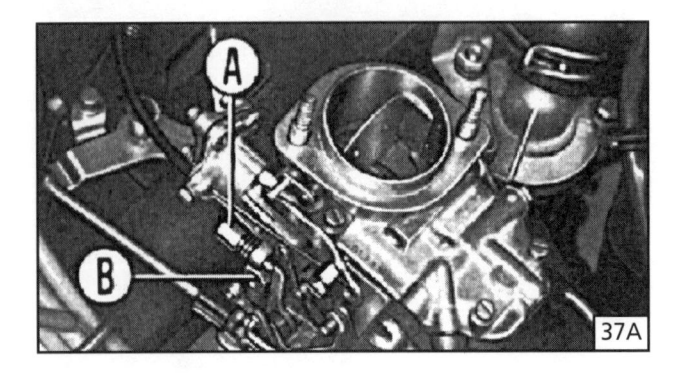

37A. These are the adjuster screws on an early car's Solex C32 DISA/7 carburettor. Several different models of Solex carburettor have been used, and the screw positions vary considerably. Look for the throttle stop screw - the one that is indirectly connected to the throttle arm and cable - and that's the idle speed adjuster. The mixture screw may be harder to find and you might have to ask your FIAT dealer for advice. Put a dab of paint on it when you've found it, for future identification!

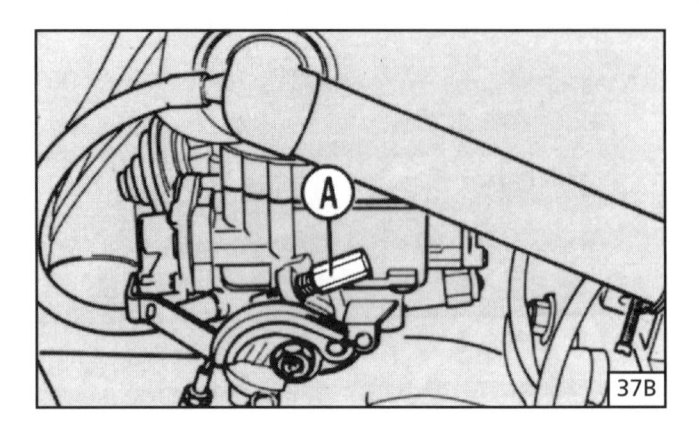

37B. This is the idle speed screw on the Weber carburettor.

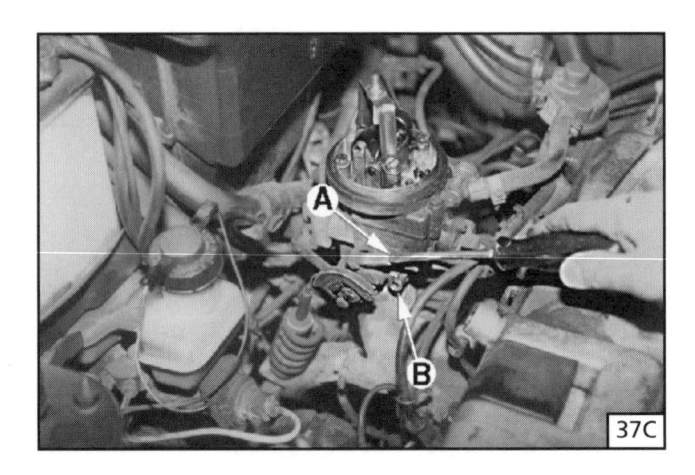

37C. These are the positions of the adjuster screws on the Weber carburettor in situ. Sometimes, there is a steel support plate, as shown in **37D** and **37F**.

37D. IDLE SPEED ADJUSTMENT: Out of doors, run the car, until it is at its normal running temperature. Connect up a tachometer according to the maker's instructions, and check the idle speed. Turning the screw clockwise increases the idle speed, anti-clockwise reduces it. Set the idle speed in accordance with **Chapter 3, Facts and Figures**.

ROUGH GUIDE: Turn the screw until the engine is running at
the slowest speed at which it runs smoothly and evenly.

37E. MIXTURE ADJUSTMENT: Check that the idle speed is correct and make sure that the engine is at full operating temperature. Connect an exhaust gas analyser as instructed by the maker: If the CO reading is outside the range shown in **Chapter 3, Facts and Figures**, adjustment is required, as follows:

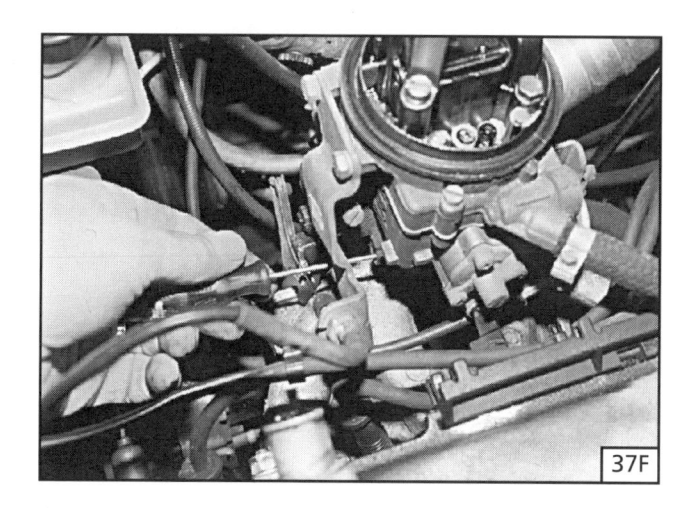

37F. Use a narrow-blade screwdriver and turn the screw clockwise to weaken (reduce) or anti-clockwise to richen (increase) the reading.
ROUGH GUIDE: Turn the mixture screw in (clockwise). As you do so, the tick-over speed will increase, until the point comes where the engine starts to run 'lumpily'. Back off the screw until the engine runs smooth again, and then some more until the speed just starts to drop. At this point, screw the adjuster back in a fraction and you'll be at or near the optimum setting for smooth running.

FUEL INJECTION MODELS

The idle speed and mixture settings are controlled by the Electronic Control Unit (ECU) which is 'self-learning' and is programmed to adjust itself to give the ideal settings under all conditions. No manual adjustment is possible, or provided for. If there is a problem, you will need to take your car to a FIAT dealer with the appropriate diagnostic equipment.

☐ **Job 38. Check/service emission control systems.**

FUEL INJECTION MODELS ONLY

On later Pandas, there are sophisticated emission control systems, similar to those fitted to other vehicles of the same age, to enable the car to comply with contemporary

> **FACT FILE: EMISSION CONTROL SYSTEMS**
> The main features of the system are:
> • an **Electronic Control Module (ECU)**, or 'computer brain' which is programmed to alter the car's fuel and ignition settings according to information received from various sensors.
> • a **catalytic converter** in the exhaust system, to convert CO and other gases to less harmful gases.
> • a **lambda sensor** in the exhaust manifold or front pipe (according to model) to detect the 'tune' of the exhaust gases and give a signal to the **ECU**.
> • a **fuel evaporation control system** to cut down on petrol vapour emissions from the fuel tank.

regulations.

ELECTRONIC CONTROL MODULE: This is not an item that requires any servicing. If you think it might be faulty, ask you FIAT dealer or fuel injection specialist to check it for you. This must be done by someone with the correct FIAT plug-in diagnostic equipment and data.

CATALYTIC CONVERTER: This is not serviceable. If it fails, you will be told at the MoT test. Since replacement is expensive - we recommend that you obtain a second opinion - no need to have the full test carried out - before replacing the 'cat'. See **Chapter 6, Repairs and Replacements** for replacement information.

LAMBDA SENSOR: See **Job 39**.

FUEL EVAPORATION CONTROL SYSTEM

38. The charcoal canister (**1**) should not normally need to be replaced check the canister one-way valve (**2**) to make sure it's working. They are under the left wheelarch - see **Job 7F** for details of wheelarch liner removal.

CHAPTER 5 FUEL AND EXHAUST

55

To change the one-way valve:

1. Disconnect the battery. (See **FACT FILE: DISCONNECTING THE BATTERY** under **Job 4**.). Raise the front of the car on axle stands (see **Chapter 1, Safety First!**) Remove the left-hand inner wheel arch after taking out the retaining screws.

2. If the original FIAT hose clips are fitted, cut through the crimped section with side-cutters. (Fit standard screw-tight hose clips when fitting the new valve.) Remove the hoses.

3. Remove the retaining clips and remove the one-way valve from the canister inlet hose.

4. Test the one-way valve by trying to blow through both ends. You should only be able to blow air towards the canister, not away from it. If the valve is faulty, renew it, making sure that is fitted the right way round.

i INSIDE INFORMATION: If the charcoal canister is flooded with petrol, it is probable that one of the **purge valves** or purge valve floats is faulty. See the relevant part of **Chapter 6, Repairs and Replacements** for replacement details. If the engine cuts out and then restarts after a while, it could be the **breather hose valve**, fitted under the fuel filler neck. This one-way valve allows air to enter the tank as the fuel level falls, otherwise an air lock can prevent fuel reaching the engine. To test the valve, take off the pipe clips, remove the valve and test it as for the canister one-way valve, above. It should allow air to pass into the tank, but not the other way. *i*

❏ **Job 39. Check lambda sensor.**

FUEL INJECTION MODELS ONLY

For a description of how the sensor works, see **Job 38, FACT FILE: EMISSION CONTROL SYSTEMS**. It should be checked at the recommended interval - the cost of checking and replacing the sensor would be far less than that of having to replace the catalytic converter, polluted because of a faulty lambda sensor.

making it easy **39.** ● Replacement of the sensor (**1**) is a simple job, but it can only be tested by your FIAT dealer or a specialist with the correct diagnostic equipment.
● If the sensor is found to be faulty, have it replaced by your specialist. They can then re-test, which will confirm if the sensor was, in fact fault,. Lambda sensors are very delicate and easily damaged.
● It is not likely that you would be able to return one to the supplier if you had fitted it yourself. Lambda sensors are only fitted to cars with a catalytic converter (**2**).

❏ **Job 40. Check inlet and exhaust manifold fixings.**

40. Check that all of the inlet and exhaust manifold nuts and bolts are tight - they can vibrate loose.

❏ **Job 41. Check exhaust system.**

41A. Examine the silencer and exhaust pipes for corrosion and signs of leaking, indicated by a 'sooty' deposit, at the point of the leak. Look carefully, especially around the section joints.

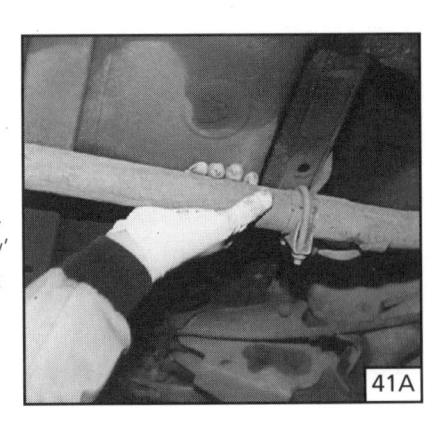

making it easy ● If you suspect a leak but it's location isn't obvious, start the engine and try pressurising the system by holding a piece of board or something similar so that it blocks off the tailpipe.

● Under pressure, the leak should be more noisy, enabling you to track down its position.

● Get an assistant to help you if you can, but remember that an exhaust system can get very hot and touching the pipework can cause nasty burns!

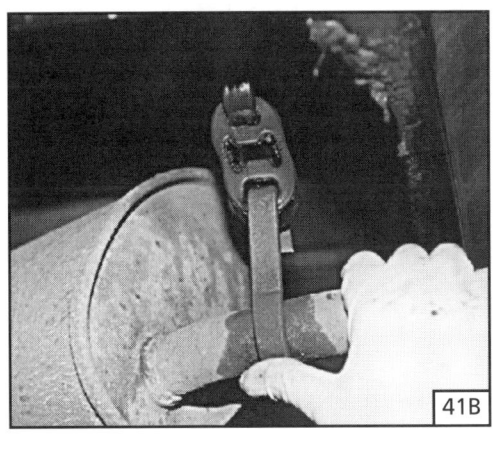

41B. Also check the condition of the rubber 'hangers' that hold the exhaust system to the car while allowing some movement: If any are missing or broken, the exhaust system can quite rapidly fracture because of the extra stresses placed upon it. Pull and stretch the rubber of the rear mount, looking for cracks.

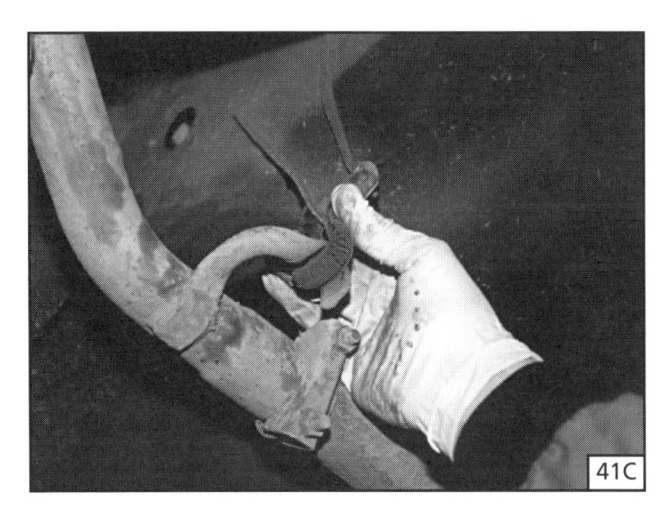

41C. This centre mount is a prime candidate for replacement!

PART F: STEERING AND SUSPENSION

❏ Job 42. Check front wheel bearings.

FIAT Panda wheel bearings are sealed within their hubs and cannot be separately replaced. However, this method of manufacture does give a much longer bearing life. In order to check for wear:
- raise the front of the car on axle stands (see **Chapter 1, Safety First!**).
- place the gearbox in neutral (or 'N' in the case of an automatic).
- pull the handbrake securely on and chock the rear wheels.

❏ Job 43. Check front suspension.

BOTTOM BALL JOINT

Jack the car from underneath the suspension lower arm inner mounting, so that the wheel is off the ground and fit an axle stand under the trolley-jacking point under the middle of the car, at the front. (See **Chapter 1, Safety First!**) Lower the car until it is just touching the axle stand - the wheel a few inches off the ground and the weight of the car supported by the jack.

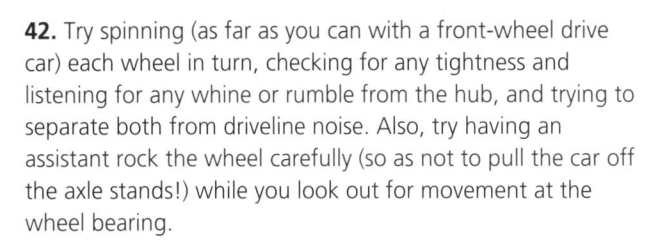

42. Try spinning (as far as you can with a front-wheel drive car) each wheel in turn, checking for any tightness and listening for any whine or rumble from the hub, and trying to separate both from driveline noise. Also, try having an assistant rock the wheel carefully (so as not to pull the car off the axle stands!) while you look out for movement at the wheel bearing.

i **INSIDE INFORMATION:** If a wheel bearing is worn, you will normally hear a noise on the outer, loaded bearing when cornering. *i*

43A. To examine the ball joint, have a helper grip the top and bottom of the road wheel and try 'rocking' it, using a pull-push motion, while you observe the ball joint for any movement. Quite a considerable effort is needed to pull and push the wheel, so make CERTAIN that the car is not rocked off its supports.

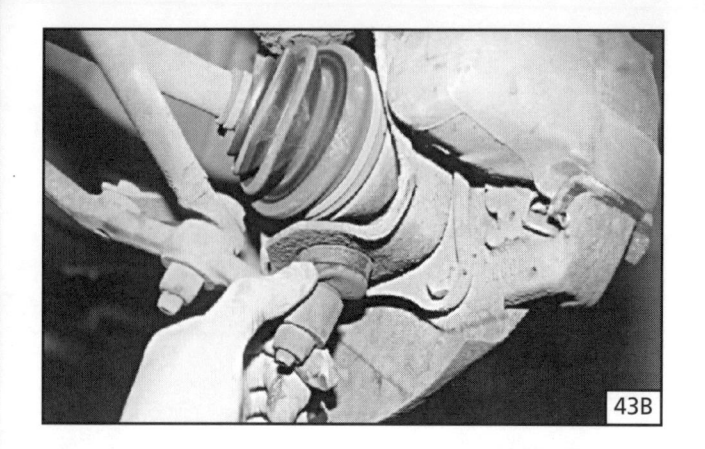

CHAPTER 5 Steering and Suspension

43B. The ball joint boot also has to be examined for any damage or leakage of grease - a simple, visual examination. Replace straight away if necessary. See **Chapter 6, Repairs and Replacements** for replacement information.

LOWER TRACK CONTROL ARM INNER BUSHES

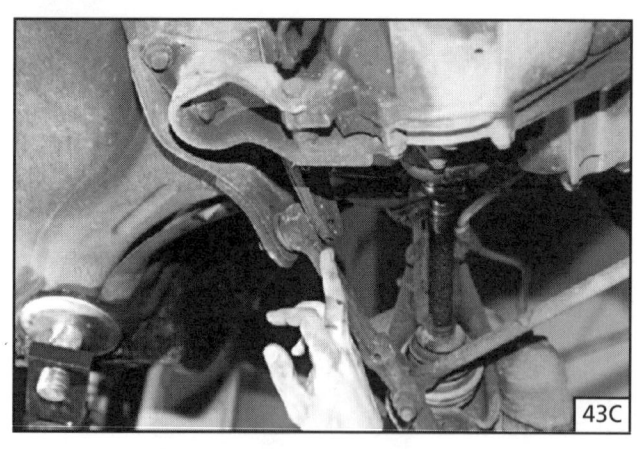

43C. Remove the jack so that the car is properly supported on the axle stand and allow the suspension to hang free. Get your helper to push and pull the bottom of the road wheel in and out, while you check the inner rubber bushes for any signs of movement. See **Chapter 6, Repairs and Replacements** for replacement information.

SUSPENSION STRUT/SHOCK ABSORBER

43D. Examine the shock absorber, which is enclosed inside the coil spring, for leaks, looking for signs of a 'damp' oil stain seeping from underneath the top half of the shock absorber body.

i INSIDE INFORMATION: A very common MoT failure point is the front shock absorber shroud, which splits and drops down, opening the shock absorber to the elements. To replace, you have to remove and dismantle the strut so that you can 'get at' the shock absorber body. *i*

The top of the strut/shock absorber is mounted in a metal bonded rubber bush which can be checked for softness, cracking or deterioration from inside the engine bay.

BOUNCE TEST: Try 'bouncing' each front corner of the car in a rhythmical motion, pressing down as hard as you can. When you let go, the movement should continue for no more than one-and-a-half rebounds. If it does so, this is a sure indication that that particular shock absorber is worn and should be replaced. If one of the front shock absorbers needs replacing, replace both, for safety reasons.

RADIUS ARM

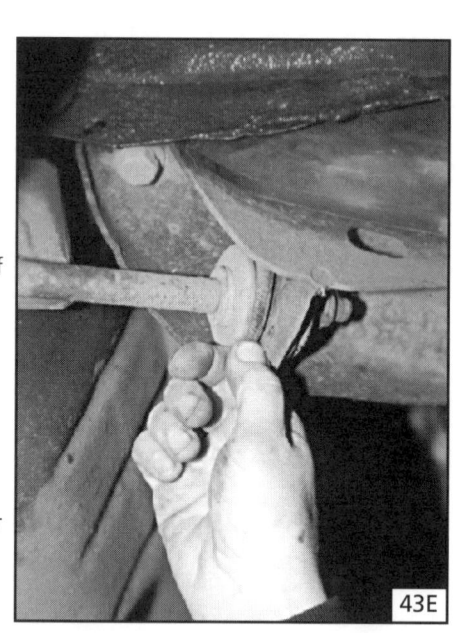

43E. The radius arm controls the camber angle so it is important that its bushes are in good condition and that the arm itself is not bent. From underneath the car, check the inner and outer bushes for any signs of deterioration. Look for cracks or spreading. Grip the radius arm firmly and attempt to move it while observing the bushes. If necessary, replace the bushes as described in **Chapter 6, Repairs and Replacements.** If the radius arm itself is bent, cracked or damaged in any way, renew it.

☐ **Job 44. Check track rod ends.**

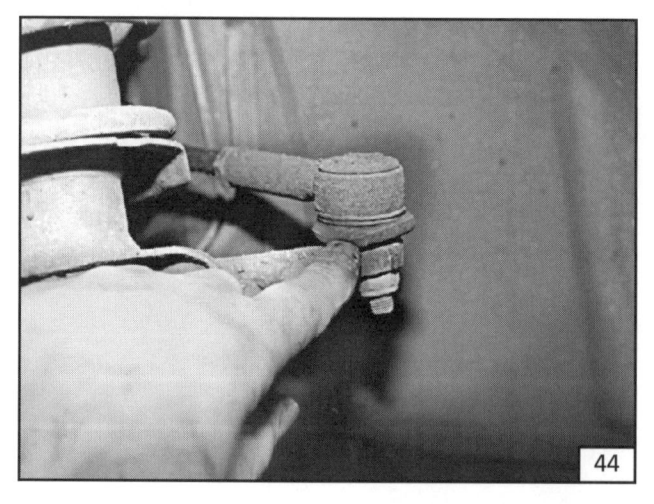

44. Drive the car on to car ramps, firmly apply the handbrake and chock the rear wheels. Get your helper to sit inside the car, turn the ignition key to the 'MAR' position to release the steering column lock. Now, turn the steering wheel about 100 mm (4 inches) from lock to lock - steadily, without jerking. From underneath the car, look for any free movement in each TRE. Also, look out for a split gaiter. Replace the TRE if the gaiter is split - it will rapidly wear and fail even if it appears sound.

i INSIDE INFORMATION: Try placing your hand over the joint and also feeling for any signs of wear. If there are any signs of wear, replace the track rod end. ***i***

❏ **Job 45. Check steering column and rack.**

STEERING COLUMN

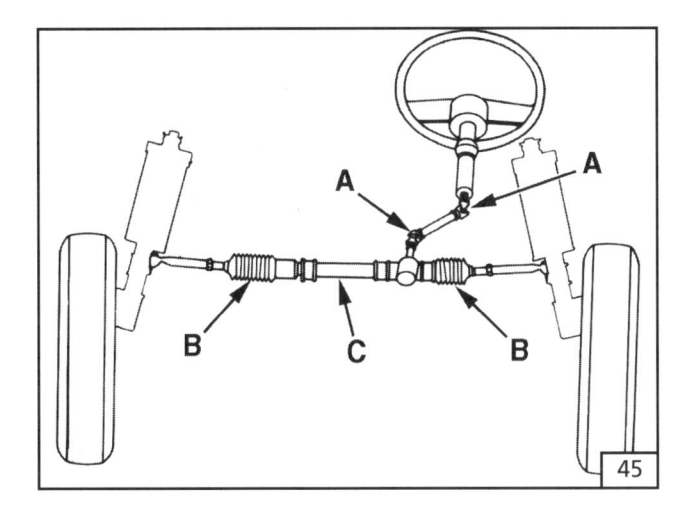

[Figure 45: Steering column and rack diagram with labels A, A, B, C, B]

45. The steering column has two universal joints (A) which need to be examined for wear. While your assistant is turning the steering wheel, check to see if there is any movement in the universal joints.

i INSIDE INFORMATION: Place your hand over the joint - you can usually feel the movement better than you can see it. If there is ANY movement at all, play at the steering wheel will be greatly exaggerated - replace the faulty universal joint. ***i***

STEERING RACK GAITERS

Turn the ignition key to the 'MAR' position but take care not to start the engine. Turn the steering wheel to full right lock. From underneath the bonnet, examine the gaiter (**B**) on the left-hand side, which will now be fully extended. Check visually for splits or oil leakage. Turn the steering wheel to the opposite lock and examine the gaiter (**B**) on the other side of the rack. If necessary, replace IMMEDIATELY - an expensive rack will rapidly ruin if the gaiter is split.

Also, watch the steering rack body (**C**) to see if it is firmly attached. If there is any movement between the rack and its mountings, check the securing bolts for tightness.

❏ **Job 46. Check rear wheel bearings.**

Panda rear wheel bearings are sealed in their hubs and are usually very long lived. See the checking procedures described in **Job 42**, but remember not to apply the handbrake! Also note that the rear wheels will be easier to spin than the fronts, with no interference from driveline components turning at the same time.

❏ **Job 47. Check rear suspension.**

Jack up the rear of the car at the trolley-jacking point in the centre, at the rear, and place the axle stands under the axle, as close to the wheels as possible. Lower the car onto the axle stands.

LEAF SPRING CARS UP TO 1986 AND ALL 4x4s

Examine the leaf springs for any signs of cracks - it may be necessary to clean the spring with a wire brush to remove any road dirt first. Examine the spring eye bushes. Place a lever between each of the spring eyes and the mounting bracket and pull the lever while watching for any movement around the bushes. At the rear end of each spring is a swinging shackle. Place a lever between the spring eye and the body frame, pull on the lever and look for any signs of movement. If the spring bushes are worn, replace them.
See **Chapter 6, Repairs and Replacements.**

[Figure 47A: Rear suspension with labels - Bodyshell support plane, Axle buffer plane, Nuts fixing leaf spring shackles, Nut for bolt fixing front leaf spring]

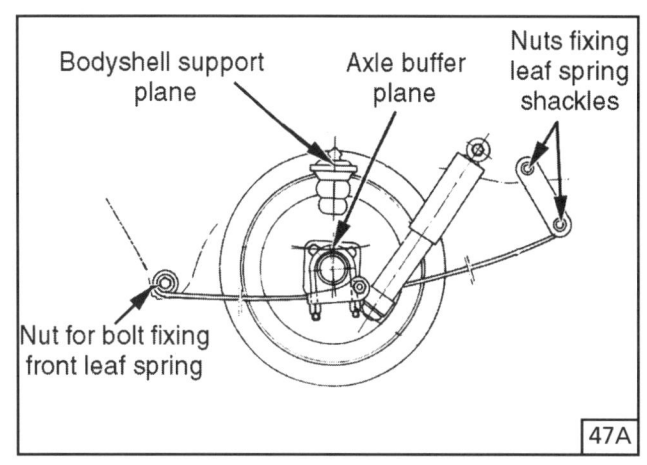

47A. Check all securing bolts and nuts for tightness, including the U-bolts which hold the axle to the spring. This is the Panda 4x4 rear suspension arrangement.

i INSIDE INFORMATION: Use a small hammer and tap the nuts: if they are loose, they will move. ***i***

COIL SPRING CARS FROM 1986-ON ONLY

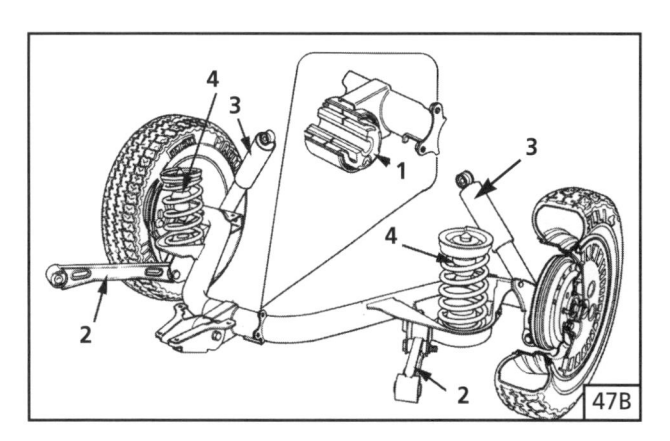

[Figure 47B: Omega coil spring suspension diagram with labels 1, 2, 3, 4]

47B. This is the layout of the 'Omega' coil spring suspension.

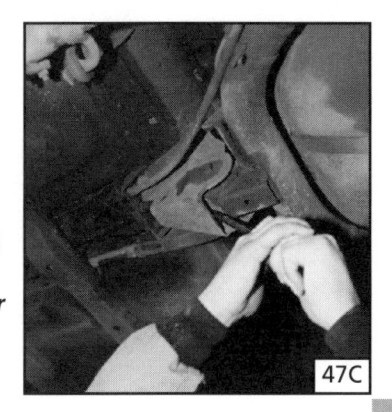

47C. CENTRE SUSPENSION MOUNTING BLOCK: Check the large rubber bushes in the mounting block (See **47B-1**) for wear, splitting, spreading or deterioration. Replace if necessary. See **Chapter 6, Repairs and Replacements.**

CHAPTER 5 STEERING AND SUSPENSION

47D. RADIUS ARMS: Check the bushes in both ends of the radius arms (see **47B-2**) and replace if necessary.

IMPORTANT NOTE: If either of the radius arms is bent or damaged, don't attempt to straighten it; replace it. A bent radius arm will affect the handling and steering of the car and must be replaced immediately.

REAR SHOCK ABSORBERS

47E. Look for signs of leaks coming from underneath the top part of each rear shock absorber (see **47B-3**) and replace if necessary.

47F. Also check the top and bottom rubber mounting bushes. If any are soft, split - or missing! - they must be replaced.

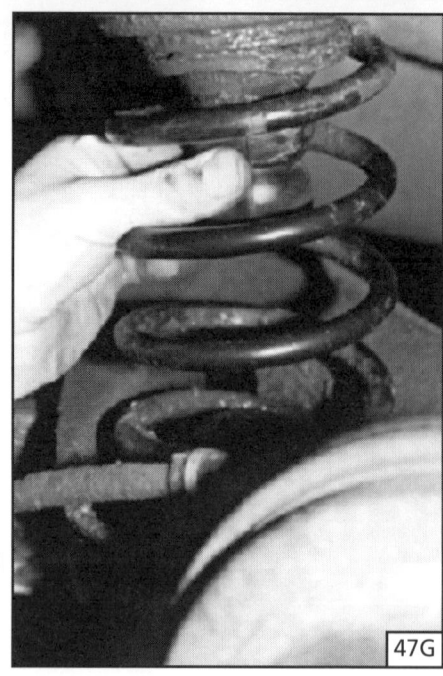

47G. Check that the full-compression bump stops (see **47B-4**) are present and correct.

BOUNCE TEST: Try 'bouncing' each rear corner of the car in a rhythmical motion, pressing down as hard as you can. When you let go, the movement should continue for no more than one-and-a-half rebounds. If it does so, this is a sure indication that that particular shock absorber is worn and should be replaced. If one of the rear shock absorbers needs replacing, replace both, for safety reasons.

❏ **Job 48. Check wheel bolts for tightness.**

48. Remove each wheel bolt in turn and ensure that they run smoothly. Clean the threads, if necessary. Refit and check that all are tightened to the correct torque - see **Chapter 3, Facts and Figures** - using a torque wrench.

60

PART G: BRAKING SYSTEM

❏ **Job 49. Check front brakes, change pads.**

Checking a Panda's brake pads involves the same amount of work as changing them. For that reason, brake pad replacement is covered here in detail rather than in **Chapter 6, Repairs and Replacements**.

> **SAFETY FIRST!**
>
> • Before raising the front of the car off the ground, see **Chapter 1, Safety First!**
> • Also, be sure to read the section on **BRAKES AND ASBESTOS** in **Chapter 1, Safety First!** for further important information before starting work.
> • Obviously, your car's brakes are among its most important safety related items. Do NOT dismantle or attempt to perform any work on the braking system unless you are fully competent to do so.
> • If you have not been trained in this work, but wish to carry it out, we strongly recommend that you have a garage or qualified mechanic check your work before using the car on the road.
> • Always start by cleaning the brakes with a proprietary brand of brake cleaner - brake drums removed where appropriate - but never use compressed air to clean off brake dust.
> • Always replace brake pads and/or shoes in complete 'axle' sets of four - never replace the pads/shoes on one wheel only.
> • After fitting new brake shoes or pads, avoid heavy braking - except in an emergency - for the first 150 to 200 miles (250 to 300 km).

Start by raising the wheel to be worked on and supporting it on an axle stand. Remove the road wheel - see **Chapter 1, Safety First!**. Clean the brake assembly off with aerosol brake cleaner.

MANUAL GEARBOX MODELS ONLY (See later on in this section for Selecta automatic gearbox models.)

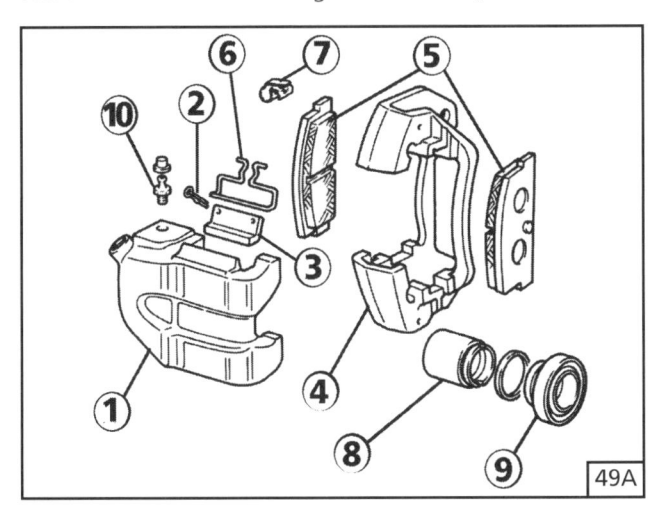

49A. This drawing illustrates the various components of the front brake assembly.

49B. You can't see the pads without first removing the caliper. On later models start by removing the TWO spring clips (see **49A-2** - only the top ones shown here): one at the top of the caliper assembly; another at the bottom. (Earlier models have four clips - one at each end of each locking plate.) Grasp the outer eyes of the pins and pull.

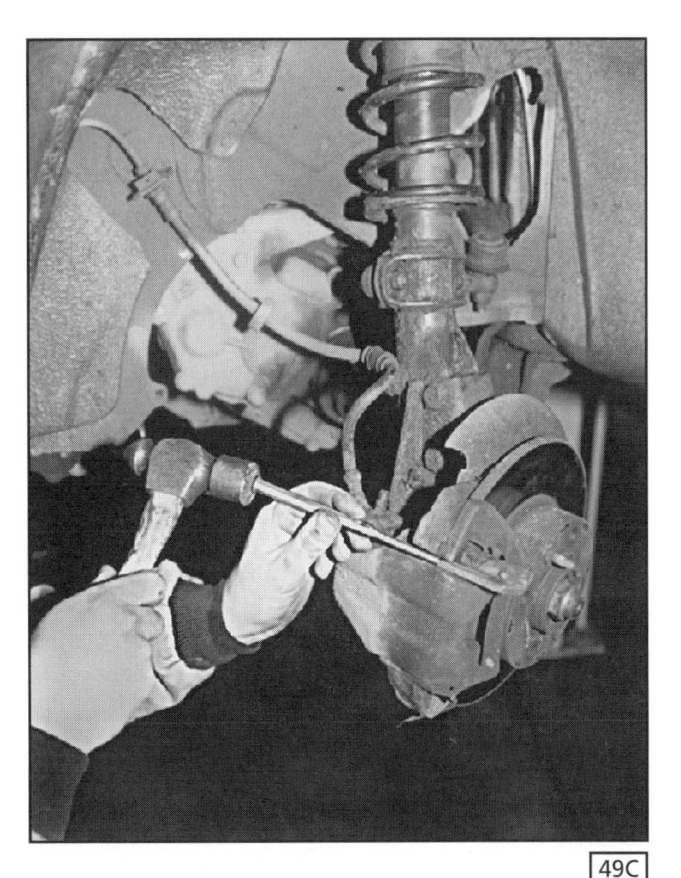

49C. You can now drive the TWO tapered locking plates (see **49A-3** - start with the top one, shown here) from between the caliper and the caliper support bracket. Because they are tapered, start by pushing the caliper towards the support bracket, to help relieve pressure, and pull or tap OUTWARDS.

61

CHAPTER 5 BRAKING SYSTEM

i INSIDE INFORMATION: Packed brake dust and corrosion usually make it difficult to move the plates. Start them off by drifting the top one out with a hammer and a suitable drift. *i*

49D. With both upper and lower locking plates removed...

49E. ...the caliper (see **49A-1**) can be lifted away.

IMPORTANT NOTE: DO NOT allow the weight of the caliper to hang from the flexible hose - position it to rest on the driveshaft, or support it from the road spring using a length of wire.

49F. First, **compare the thickness** of the two pads - there should be no significant difference them. Also **check the thickness** of each pad. The minimum recommended thickness of lining material is 1.5 mm, but bearing in mind the amount of time before the next service, you may wish to replace the pads before they get to this stage.

49G. In practice, of course, having got this far, you'll want to remove the pads (see **49A-5**). They lift away. The two large spring clips (see **49A-6**) are **NOT** removed.

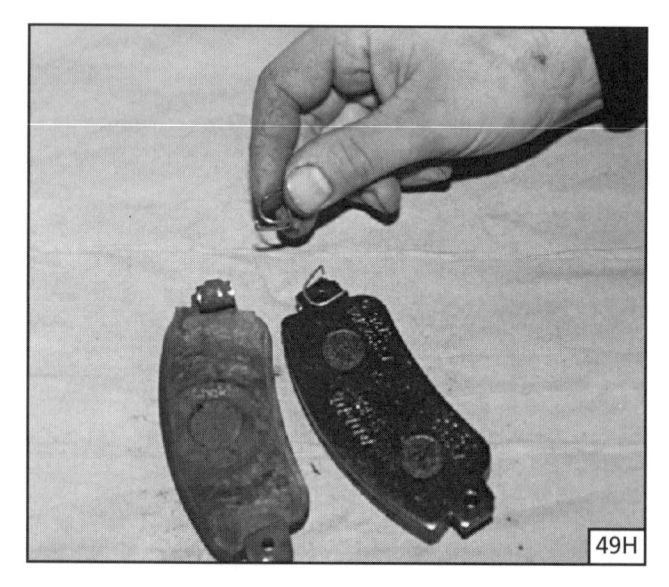

49H. Don't forget the two anti-rattle springs (see **49A-7**), one at the top and bottom of each pad. The pad on the left has the old-style bent-steel spring clips; the new FIAT ones on the right come complete with the correct spring clips. **We STRONGLY** recommend the use of FIAT original-equipment brake components.

62

49I. All parts of the assembly - including the caliper - should be washed off, once again, with a proprietary brand of brake cleaner.

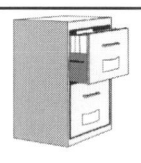

FACT FILE: BRAKE DISC WEAR SYMPTOMS
There are certain essential checks you should carry out for yourself, with brake pads removed:
- Look out for any obvious grooves that may have been worn into the disc. Slight undulations are acceptable, but anything worse, and the disc should be replaced.
- Look and feel for any wear-ridge on the outer edges of the disc. The depth of these ridges will give an indication of how much the disc may have worn.
- Check for signs of surface flaking on both sides of the disc. If any flaking is found, the disc must be replaced.
- Check for any signs of corrosion on the surface of the disc. If any is found, you can be certain that the brake caliper is faulty (unless the car has been standing, unused for some time) and urgent repair work is needed.
- If you are not certain about whether any of the wear symptoms mentioned in this FACT FILE are acceptable or not, ask your specialist or FIAT dealer to check.

49J. You can now check the thickness of the brake disc, which should not be below 9.00 mm at any point. Unless you have a micrometer and know how to use it accurately, you won't be able to carry out this check, of course, in which case this check should be carried out by your specialist or FIAT agent.

49K. Before reassembling the brake assembly, check the condition of the brake caliper. Have an assistant VERY SLOWLY AND GENTLY apply pressure to the brake pedal while you watch the piston (See **49A-8**), which should move outwards. If it doesn't easily move outwards, it is seized and the caliper should be replaced. DO NOT allow the piston to project more than 10 mm or the piston may be forced from the caliper - use a woodworker's G-clamp to act as 'end stop' to prevent the piston from popping out. Examine the piston seal (see **49A-9**), looking for signs of splitting and fluid leaks. This one has a split and requires immediate replacement.

Also, see **FACT FILE: BRAKE DISC WEAR SYMPTOMS**, for further evidence of whether the piston is seized or sticking. Check inside the caliper housing for any signs of abrasion or corrosion. If any are found, or the seal appears split or damaged in any way, the caliper assembly should be replaced with a new genuine FIAT assembly.

---

making it easy!
- *In order to refit the pads or (especially) if you are fitting new ones, the caliper piston will have to be pushed back into the bore.*
- *Use an old battery hydrometer, or something similar, to draw about half the brake fluid out of the master cylinder.*
- *Push the piston back into the caliper, using a woodworker's G-clamp.*
- *Have a helper keep an eye on the master cylinder so that it doesn't overflow as fluid is pushed back up the pipe.*
- *Remove more fluid if necessary.*
- *Top up with fresh brake fluid.*

CHAPTER 5 BRAKING SYSTEM

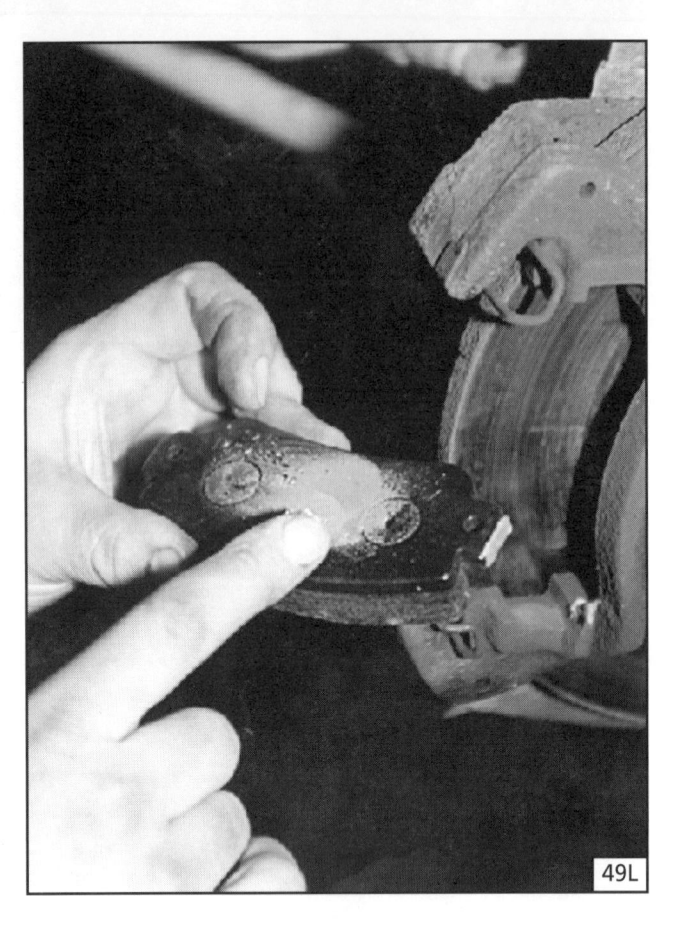

49L. Before fitting the pads, put a light smear of lithium brake grease (NOT ordinary grease) on the pads' metal backplates, at the points shown but, **IMPORTANT NOTE:** If you apply more than the lightest smear, grease could get onto the friction linings. This would ruin your pads and - worse still - prevent the brakes from working!

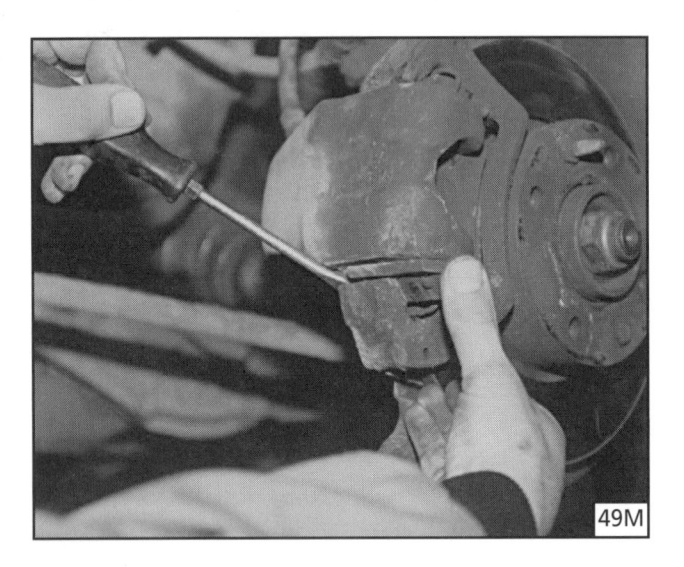

49M. When refitting the locking plates, start with the lower one. Lever the caliper up with a screwdriver while pushing, then tapping with a hammer, until they are fully home. Don't forget the retaining clips (See **49A-2**), one at the top and one at the bottom.

IMPORTANT NOTE: After fitting the pads, apply the brakes firmly several times to ensure that the pads are correctly adjusted.

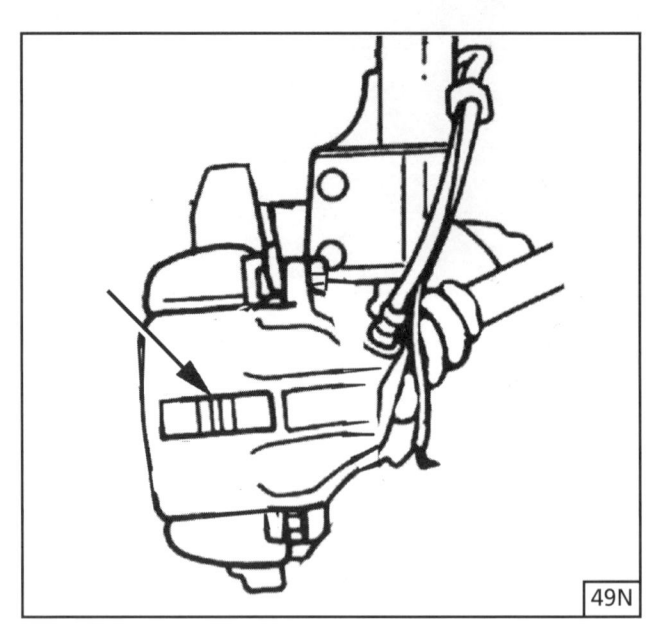

'SELECTA' AUTOMATIC GEARBOX MODELS ONLY

49N. When working on the different brakes fitted to automatics, all of the above information on the brakes fitted to manual gearbox cars must be read and followed carefully, except for the specific information shown here.

It is possible to inspect the pads through the aperture in the caliper (arrowed). However, if you are not fully familiar with these brakes, we recommend that you remove the calipers, which will also enable you to inspect the piston seals. See **Chapter 6, Repairs and Replacements, Part H, Jobs 1, 2** and **3**.

☐ **Job 50. Check rear brakes.**

SAFETY FIRST!

• Before raising the front of the car off the ground, see **Chapter 1, Safety First!**
• Also, be sure to read the section on **BRAKES AND ASBESTOS** in **Chapter 1, Safety First!** for further important information before starting work, in case your car is fitted with old pads containing asbestos.
• Obviously, your car's brakes are among its most important safety related items. **Do NOT** dismantle or attempt to perform any work on the braking system unless you are fully competent to do so.
• If you have not been trained in this work, but wish to carry it out, we strongly recommend that you have a garage or qualified mechanic check your work before using the car on the road.
• Always start by washing the brakes with a proprietary brand of brake cleaner - brake drums removed where appropriate - but never use compressed air to clean off brake dust.
• Always replace brake pads and/or shoes in complete 'axle' sets of four - never replace the pads/shoes on one wheel only.
• After fitting new brake shoes or pads, avoid heavy braking - except in an emergency - for the first 150 to 200 miles (250 to 300 km).

Raise the wheel off the ground, remove it and support the car with an axle stand. Make sure that the wheels remaining on the ground are chocked in both directions.

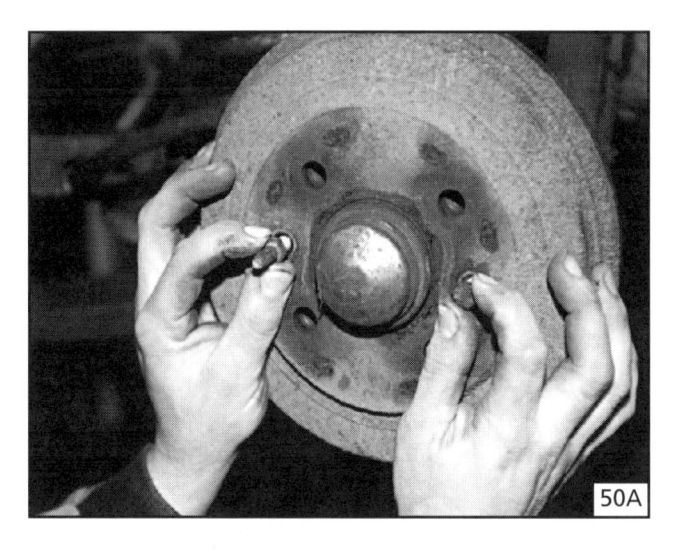

50A. Remove the two bolts (one of them also the wheel positioning stud)...

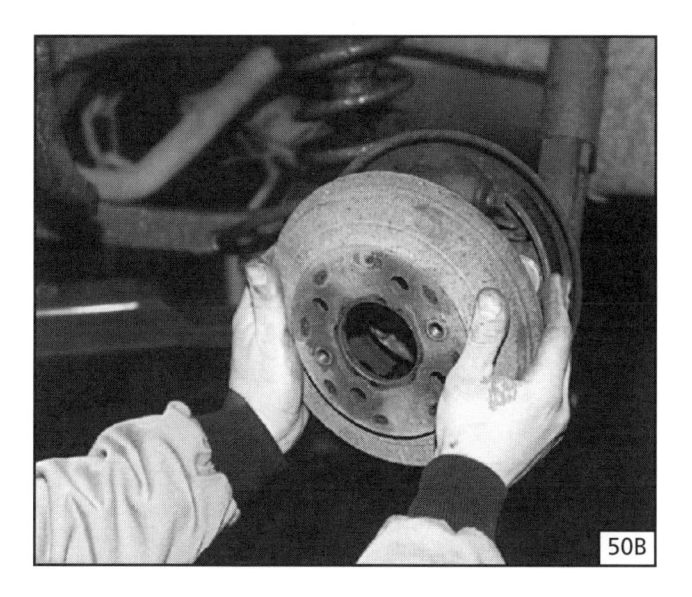

50B. ...and remove the drum.

making it easy! There is no manual adjuster to slacken off and the drum usually - but not always! - pulls off easily! If it sticks, try:
- disconnecting the handbrake cable from beneath the car.
- cleaning any build-up of rust from around the edges of the drum, as far as you can get to it.
- screwing a pair of bolts into the two threaded holes in the drum. Tighten the bolts up evenly and they will force the drum off the shoes.
- tapping carefully around the drum with a hide mallet (NOT a steel hammer!) to help loosen it.

50C. Clean the inside of the drum and the brake assembly with aerosol brake cleaner. If the drum is badly scored inside replace it.

i **INSIDE INFORMATION:** Test for cracks by hanging the drum on a piece of wire. Tap it lightly with the end of a spanner. If it 'rings', it's probably fine; if it 'clunks', it isn't - replace, don't use it. Ask your FIAT dealer for advice on scoring and cracks if you find any and you're not sure about them. *i*

50D. Examine the brake shoes for wear or oil contamination. If the latter, the wheel cylinder is probably leaking (see **50F**) and the shoes will have to be scrapped - they can NOT be safely cleaned.

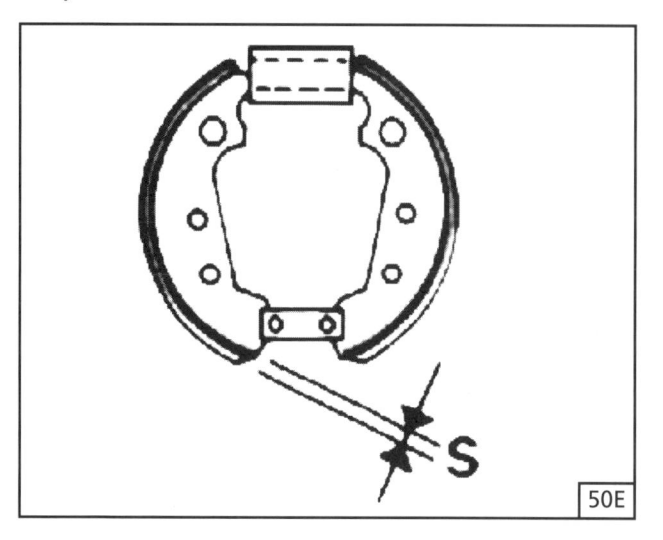

50E. FIAT recommend a minimum of 1.5 mm shoe thickness (**S**, in the diagram). In view of the amount of time between checks, you may wish to replace yours (with genuine FIAT components) before they get to this stage.

CHAPTER 5 BRAKING SYSTEM

65

CHAPTER 5 BRAKING SYSTEM

50F. Carefully fold back each of the two rubbers on the wheel cylinder. Any fluid found inside - as in this case - requires that a new cylinder is fitted straight away.

IMPORTANT NOTE: For information on replacing rear brake shoes or wheel cylinders, see **Chapter 6, Repairs and Replacements.**

☐ **Job 51. Check/adjust handbrake.**

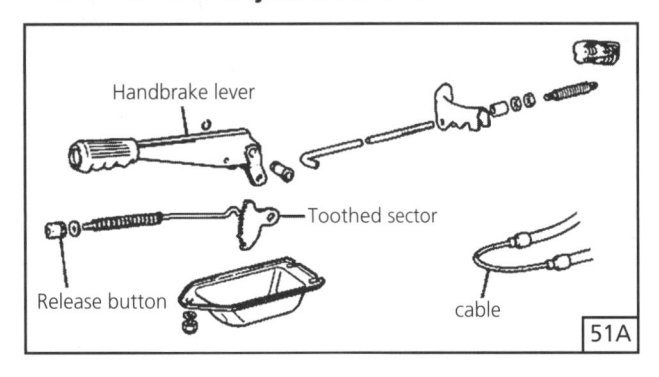

51A. The handbrake is intended to 'set' itself, in use, as the rear brake self-adjusters operate. If the handbrake seems not to work, even though the travel is not excessive, strip the rear drums off and examine the rear brake shoes (see **Job 50**) rather than over-tightening the handbrake cable. However, if the travel is excessive, even though the brakes are correctly adjusted at the wheels, the handbrake may need adjusting to compensate for a stretched handbrake cable.

SAFETY FIRST!

- You will have to raise the rear of the vehicle in order to adjust the handbrake: It is ESSENTIAL to ensure that the front wheels are securely chocked in both directions, and that axle stands or ramps are used to support the vehicle's weight after jacking.

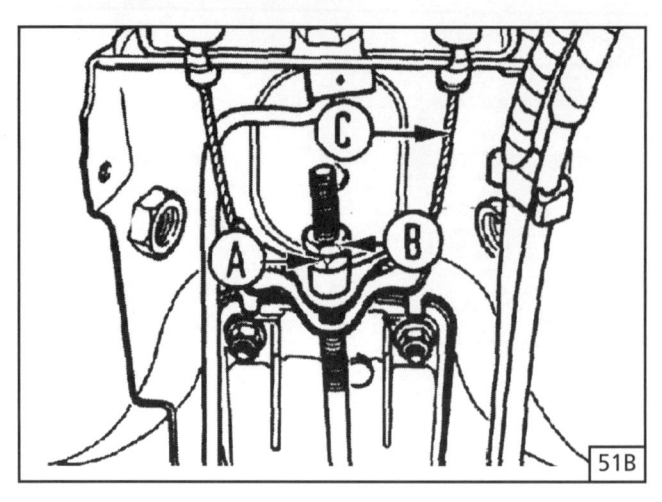

51B. Pull on the handbrake lever by three to five notches (or 'clicks') on the ratchet. From underneath the car, slacken the locknut (**B**) and turn the adjusting nut (**A**) until the cable (**C**) is drawn taut. Check that both rear wheels are 'locked' when the handbrake is 'on', and that both rear wheels are completely free when it is fully 'off'. When everything works properly, tighten the locknut (**B**) and lower the vehicle to the ground. Check again that moving the handbrake through not more than four or five notches is sufficient to hold the car stationary.

51C. Grease all of the adjuster mechanism and the cable ends. Remove the cover beneath the handbrake lever and grease the toothed ratchet mechanism.

☐ **Job 52. Check brake pipes.**

FLEXIBLE HOSES

52A. Check the flexible brake pipes that connect the calipers to the metal pipes on the body. Try bending back on themselves those that are not contained in a protective coil, ⇨

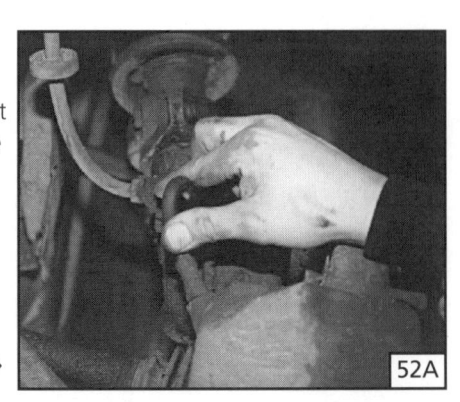

66

and look for any signs of cracking. Check them all for signs of rubbing, splitting, kinks and perishing of the rubber. Have an assistant depress the brake pedal and check the hoses for any signs of 'ballooning' or swelling of the hoses when under pressure.

RIGID PIPES

52B. Check all rigid pipes for signs of damage or corrosion and check that all of the mounting clips are sound and in place.

❏ **Job 53. Change brake hydraulic fluid.**

Change the brake fluid at the recommended interval. Brake fluid is hygroscopic, which means that it absorbs water vapour from the air. This has the serious effect of corroding brake components, and the potentially ***disastrous*** effect of causing the brakes to fail totally under heavy use.

i INSIDE INFORMATION: When brakes are applied very heavily, the fluid can heat up to over the boiling point of water. Any vapour in the fluid will then vaporise, producing a vapour lock in the pipe. The vapour compresses, the brake pedal goes to the floor and brakes are lost - just when you need them most! *i*

PART H: BODYWORK

❏ **Job 54. Lubricate hinges and locks.**
54. Apply a few drops of light oil (from either an aerosol or oil can) to the hinges on the bonnet, doors and tailgate. Use an aerosol with injector nozzle for the insides of the door locks - this will also stop them freezing in winter. Grease the door and tailgate striker mechanism with silicone grease (so as not to stain clothes) and grease the bonnet release mechanism and cable end.

❏ **Job 55. Check windscreen.**

Clean the windscreen with a proprietary glass cleaner and examine the screen for stone chips, cracks and scoring. While some degree of damage is acceptable, the strict MoT Test regulations limit the amount and position of such defects. Check with your local FIAT dealer or MoT Test station, if you're not sure. If you catch it early enough, a small chip can often be inexpensively repaired, before the crack spreads and ruins the windscreen.

❏ **Job 56. Check seat and seat belt mountings.**

Your car's seat and safety belt mountings and backrest adjustment locking mechanism will be checked as part of the annual test, but it pays to check them beforehand. Also, regularly check that the seat belts: a) retract easily and smoothly, b) 'hold' when you snatch them, or under sharp braking, and c) are not frayed at any point along the whole length.

❏ **Job 57. Check headlight alignment.**

Have the headlight alignment checked by your FIAT dealer, who will have the necessary beam-setting equipment to carry out the work accurately. This job will also be carried out as part of the MoT Test.

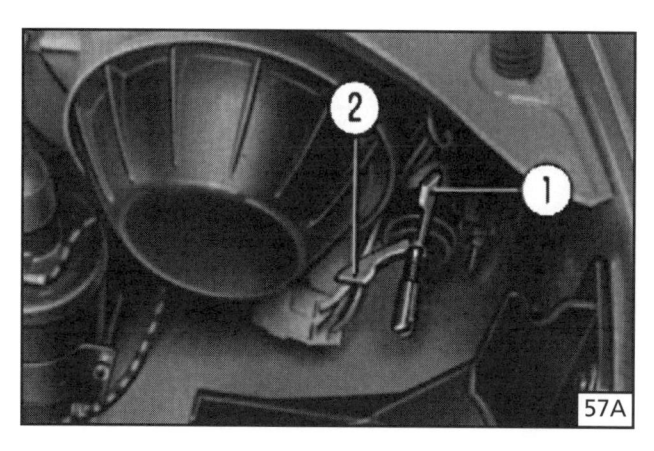

57A. On early cars, ensure that the beam correction levers are in position '1' (light loads) and not position '2' (heavy loads) before the beams are set.

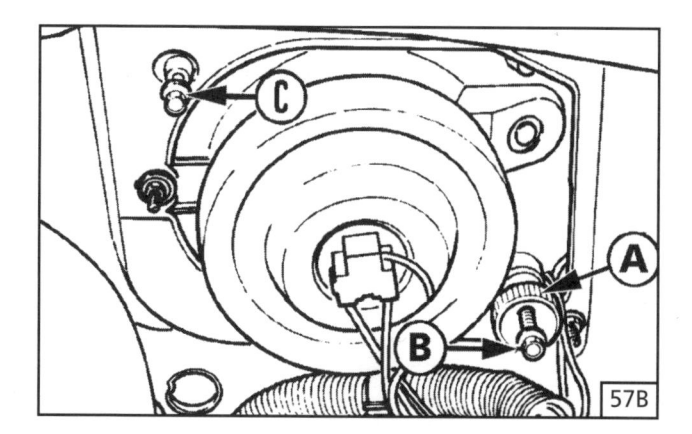

57B. On some later cars, the beam correction adjuster is the knurled nut (**A**). The headlight beam setting adjusters - (**B**) for vertical adjustments and (**C**) for horizontal - are only used for setting beams with a professional beam-setting device.

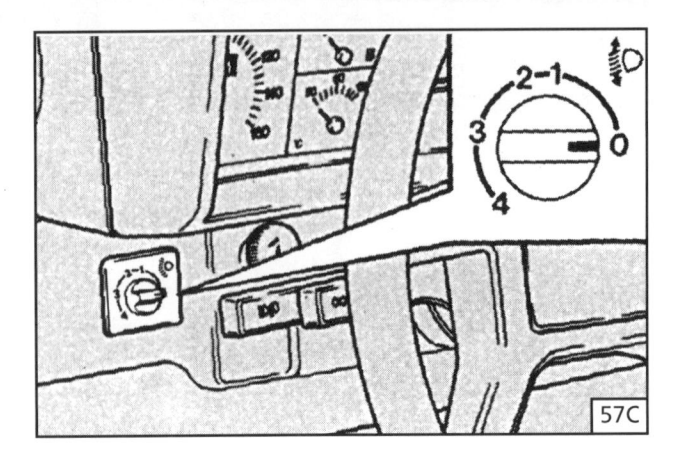

57C. Some later cars have a beam adjuster on the dash. Set it to position '0' before the beams are set.

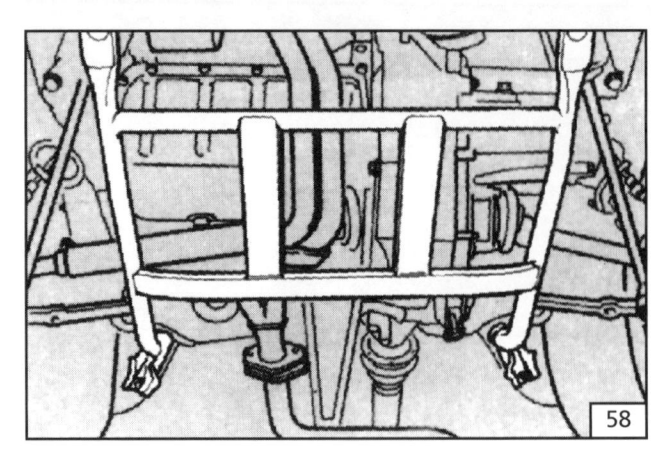

❑ **Job 58. Check underbody.**

58. Check the condition of the underbody for damage and corrosion. Take a tin of waxy underbody seal and a brush under the car and replace any missing underbody seal. Check the 4x4 underbody particularly carefully, especially the front underbody guard and the propshaft shield which, on vehicles used off-road, can easily become damaged. Repair, or replace if necessary, so as to protect the engine and front transmission assemblies.

PART I: ROAD TEST

❑ **Job 59. Road test and specialist check - after every service.**

Before you can claim to have 'finished' working on your car, you must check it, test it and, if necessary, have a qualified mechanic check it over for you.

If you are not a qualified mechanic, we strongly recommend having someone who is a properly qualified mechanic - your FIAT dealership perhaps - inspect all of the car's safety-related items after they have been worked on at home and before using the car on the road.

● Before setting out, check that the lights, indicators and in-car controls, as well as seat belts and seat adjustments, all work correctly.

● Run the car for several minutes before setting out then turn off, check fluid levels and check underneath for leaks.

● Check that the steering moves freely in both directions and that the car does not 'pull' one way or the other when driving in a straight line - but do bear in mind the effect of the camber on the road.

● Make sure that the brakes work effectively, smoothly and without the need for 'pumping'. There should be no juddering or squealing.

● Check that the car does not 'pull' from one side to the other when you brake firmly from around 40 mph. (Don't cause a skid and don't try this if there is any following traffic.)

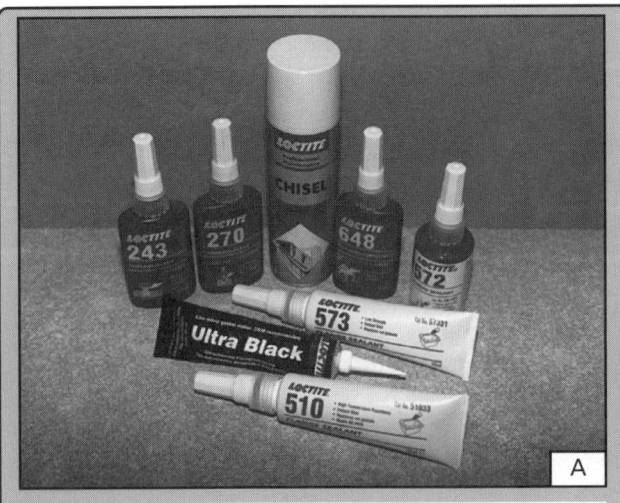

A. FIAT sell and recommend Loctite products. There is a range of gasket sealants and 'CHISEL' aerosol gasket shifter ...

B. ... as well as a bio-degradable spray-on engine degreaser.

Please read the whole of CHAPTER 1, SAFETY FIRST before carrying out any work on your car.

CHAPTER 6
REPAIRS AND REPLACEMENT

This chapter shows you how to remove and overhaul all the major 'wearing' parts of the car. We deliberately *don't* show how to rebuild major components, such as the gearbox, or differential. You are much better off, in terms of time, cost and the provision of a guarantee, to buy a replacement unit.

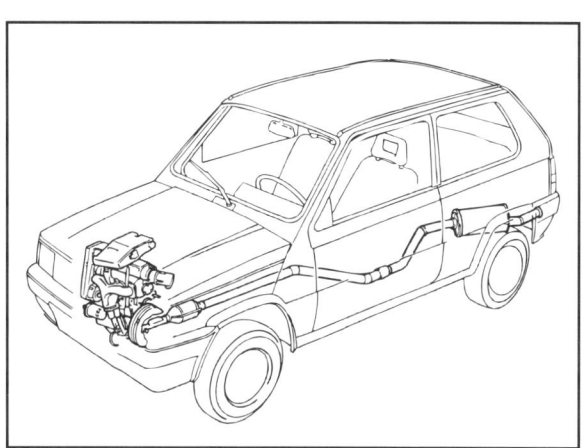

The same applies to major electrical components, such as alternator and starter motor. If as we recommend you stick to 'original' FIAT replacement parts, you will maintain the original quality of your car.

Chapter Contents

	Page No.		Page No.
PART A: ENGINE	69	PART E: ELECTRICAL AND INSTRUMENTS	109
PART B: TRANSMISSION AND CLUTCH	101	PART F: FUEL AND EXHAUST SYSTEMS	114
PART C: COOLING SYSTEM	106	PART G: STEERING AND SUSPENSION	117
PART D: IGNITION	108	PART H: BRAKES	124
		PART I: BODY AND INTERIOR	132

Illustration and Section Numbers

- In this chapter, each area of the car is dealt with in a different PART of the chapter, such as, *PART A: ENGINE*.

- Each Job in each PART has a separate identifying number. For example **Job 4. OHC Cylinder Head Removal.**

- Every Job is broken down into easy-to-follow Steps, numbered from 1-on.

- Illustrations are numbered so that you can see at a glance where they belong!

- The illustration **Job 1-4** (in PART A) for example, relates to the text in **Job 1, Step 4.**

SAFETY FIRST!

- Before carrying out any of the work in this chapter, be sure to read and understand **Chapter 1, Safety First!**
- Be sure to read any safety notes supplied with any of the materials for equipment you purchase in connection with the work described in this chapter.
- If you are not sure about your competence or skills in carrying out any of the work described in this chapter, have the work carried out by your FIAT dealership.

PART A: ENGINE

PART A: Contents

Job 1. OHV cylinder head - removal.
Job 2. OHV cylinder head - refitting.
Job 3. OHV cylinder head - dismantling and overhaul.
Job 4. OHC cylinder head - removal.
Job 5. OHC cylinder head - refitting.
Job 6. OHC cylinder head - dismantling and servicing.
Job 7. OHC cylinder head - valve clearance adjustment.
Job 8. OHV engine, timing chain and sprockets - removal.
Job 9. OHV engine, timing chain and sprockets - refitting.
Job 10. OHC engine, timing belt - removal and replacement.

Job 11. OHV and OHC engine and transmission - removal downwards.
Job 12. OHV engine - removal upwards.
Job 13. Engine, all types - refitting.
Job 14. Engine mountings - replacement.
Job 15. Engine/transmission - separation.
Job 16. Engine/transmission - reconnection.
Job 17. OHV Engine - dismantling.
Job 18. OHV Engine - reassembly.
Job 19. OHC Engine - dismantling.
Job 20. OHC Engine - reassembly

Job 1. OHV cylinder head - removal.

☐ **Step 1:** Familiarise yourself with drawing **Job 1-1**, showing the cylinder head components referred to in the following text.

> **SAFETY FIRST!**
>
> • *Disconnect both battery leads, negative terminal first.*

☐ **Step 2:** Drain the cooling system. See **PART C: COOLING SYSTEM**.

☐ **Step 3:** Remove the air cleaner, carburettor, spacer block and gasket. See **PART F: FUEL AND EXHAUST SYSTEM**.

☐ **Step 4:** Remove all five nuts and washers holding the exhaust manifold and ducting to the cylinder head. The rocker cover has already been removed from this engine.

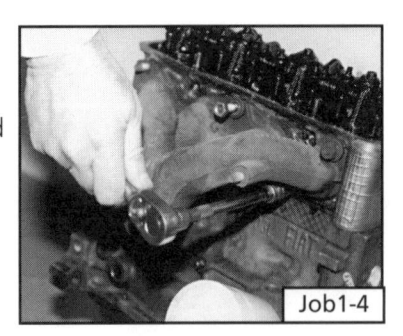

Job1-4

☐ **Step 5:** Remove the distributor and leads, paying particular attention to **PART D: IGNITION**.

☐ **Step 6:** Remove the water temperature sender unit cable from the sender unit in the cylinder head. (See **Job 1-15 (b)** for position on head.)

☐ **Step 7:** Remove the thermostat housing from the cylinder head. (See **Job 1-15, (a)** for position.)

☐ **Step 8:** Disconnect all water hoses from the cylinder head.

☐ **Step 9:** Note alternator cable positions and disconnect. Remove the alternator after undoing the three nuts and bolts.

☐ **Step 10:** Undo and remove the rocker cover securing nuts, spring washers and packers. Then lift off the rocker cover and gasket.

☐ **Step 11:** Unscrew the four rocker post nuts evenly a few turns at a time until loose. Remove the nuts and spring washers and pull the rocker shaft assembly clear of the studs.

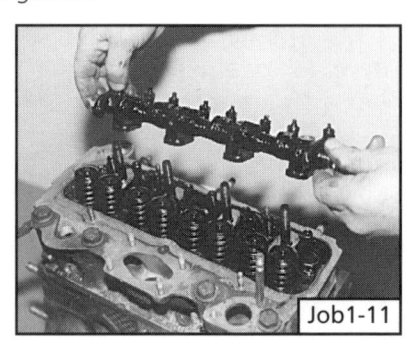

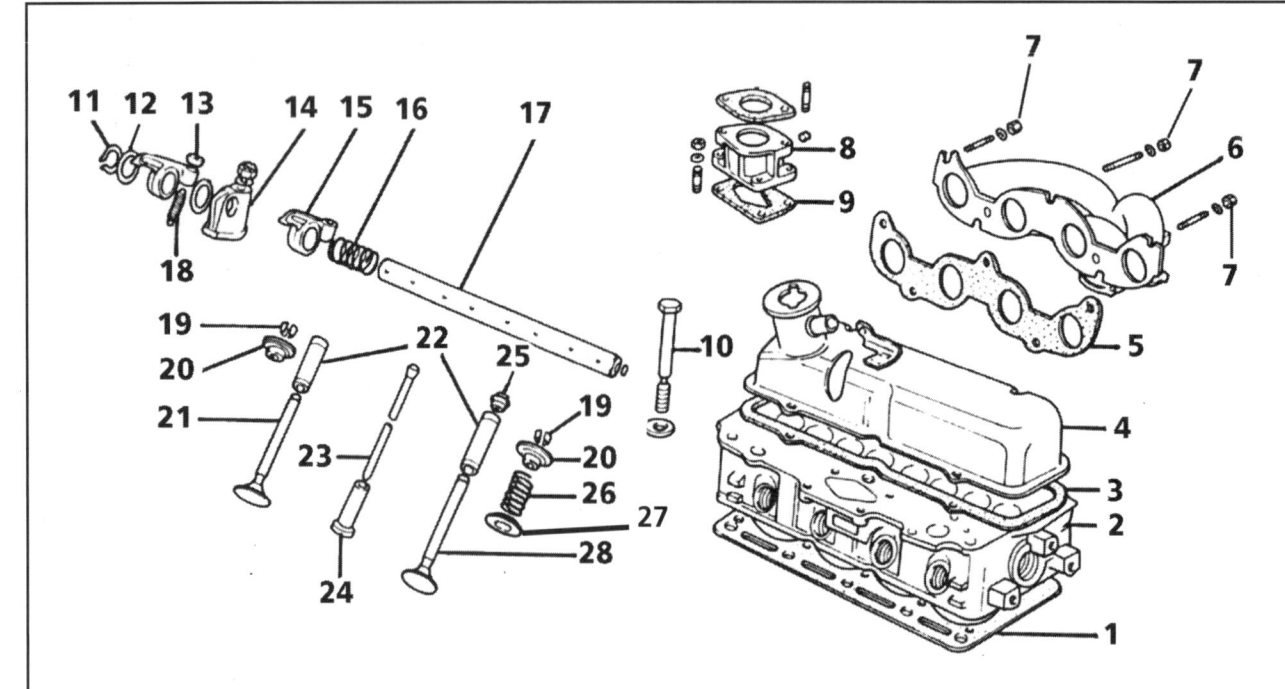

Job1-11

1 - Cylinder head gasket.
2 - Cylinder head.
3 - Rocker cover gasket.
4 - Rocker cover.
5 - Exhaust manifold gasket.
6 - Exhaust manifold.
7 - Exhaust manifold studs with nuts and washers.
8 - Spacer block.
9 - Gasket.
10 - Cylinder head bolt.
11 - Circlip.
12 - Washer.
13 - Locknut.
14 - Pedestal.
15 - Rocker.
16 - Spring.
17 - Rocker shaft.
18 - Adjusting screw.
19 - Collets.
20 - Cap.
21 - Exhaust valve.
22 - Valve guide.
23 - Push rod.
24 - Cam follower.
25 - Oil seal.
26 - Valve spring.
27 - Valve spring seat.
28 - Inlet valve.

Job 1-1

CHAPTER 6 PART A: ENGINE

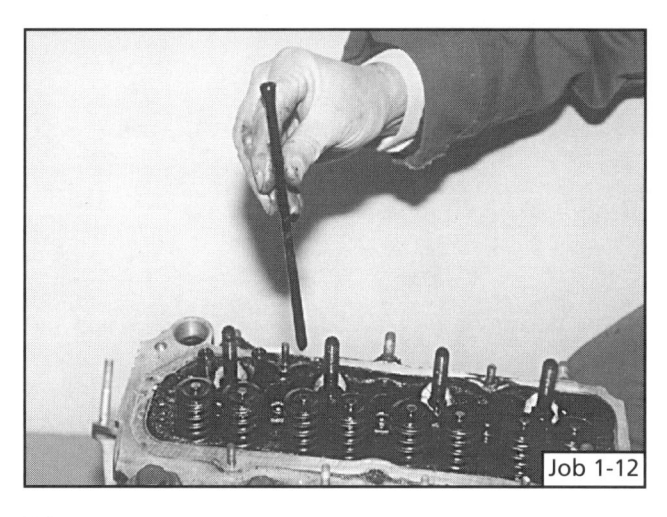

❑ **Step 12:** Remove the pushrods one at a time, keeping them in the correct order.

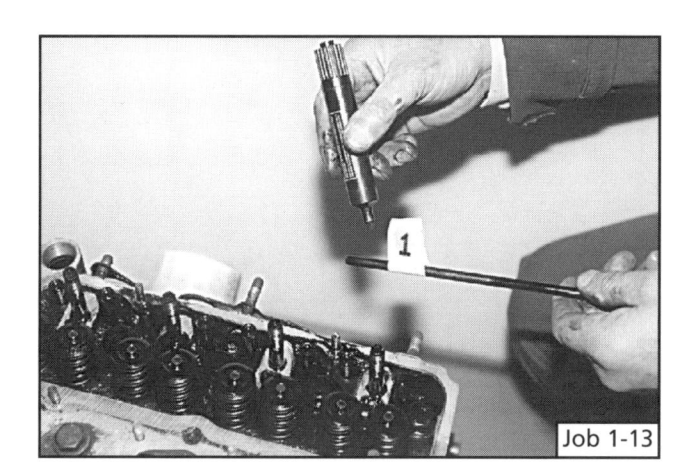

making it easy! ❑ **Step 13:** So that you don't confuse the order in which the pushrods were fitted, put masking tape around the end of each one as it is removed and number it. No. 1 is at the timing chain end.

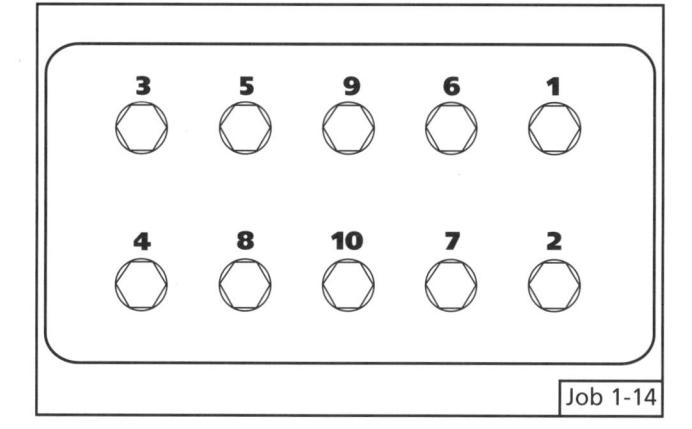

❑ **Step 14:** Unscrew the cylinder head bolts half a turn at a time and in the order shown.

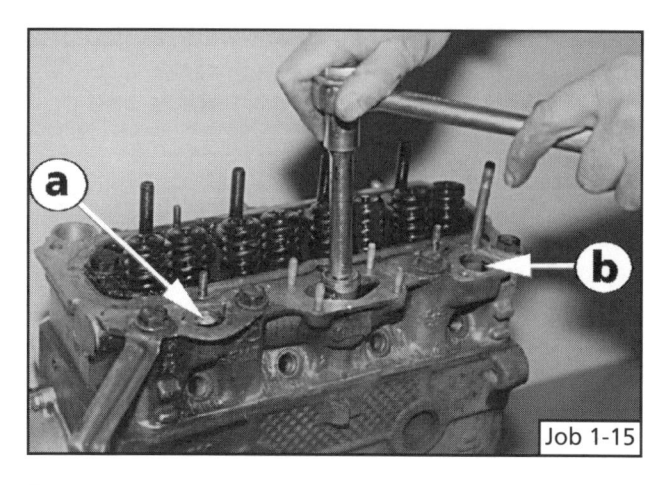

ⓘ **Step 15:** INSIDE INFORMATION: Don't forget the bolt hidden inside the inlet manifold. When free, remove all bolts and washers. ⓘ

❑ **Step 16:** You will also have to remove the water pipe bracket previously held by two of the bolts.

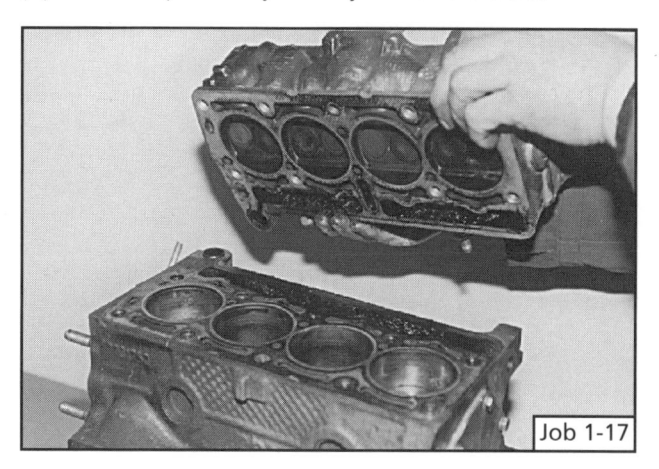

❑ **Step 17:** The cylinder head is now ready to be removed.

making it easy! • If the head is stuck, use a wooden hammer shaft or something similar, as a lever in one of the exhaust ports to break the seal.

CHAPTER 6 PART A: ENGINE

71

Protect the bores and main waterways by plugging with clean rag. (For cylinder head overhaul, see *Job 3. OHV cylinder head dismantling and overhaul*.)

Job 2. OHV cylinder head - refitting.

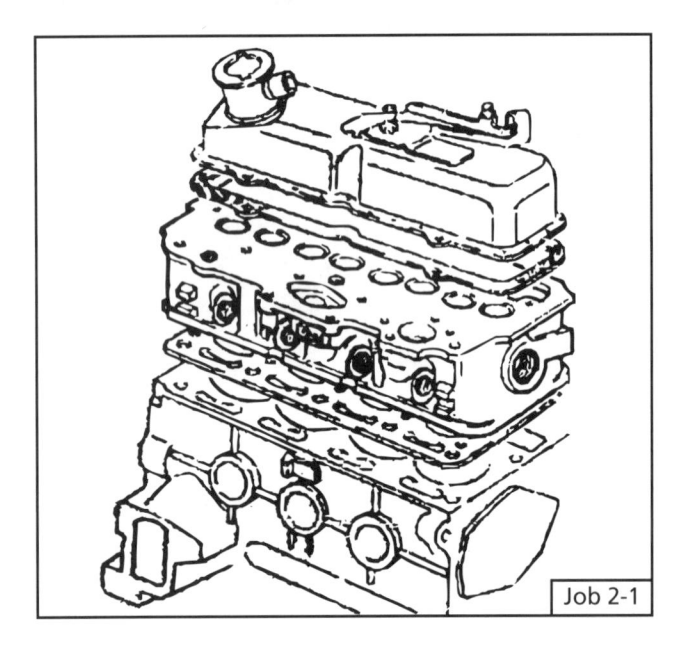

Job 2-1

Job 2-4

☐ **Step 1:** Make sure you have all the gaskets you will need, from your FIAT dealership. All the gaskets should be renewed.

☐ **Step 2:** Ensure that cylinder head and block surfaces are thoroughly cleaned. Remove the rag from the cylinder bores and ensure that the bores and piston crowns are perfectly clean. Apply a coating of new engine oil to the cylinder walls.

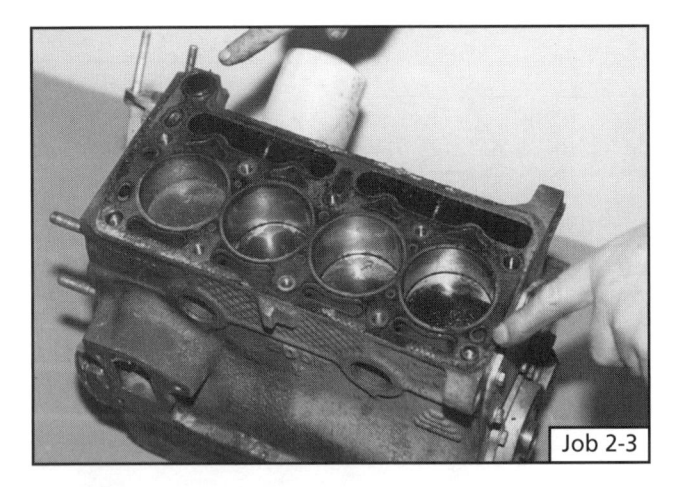

Job 2-3

☐ **Step 3:** Make sure that the two cylinder head locating dowels are properly fitted in the recessed bolt holes at the front and rear of the cylinder block.

☐ **Step 4:** Correctly locate a new gasket over the dowels with the word "ALTO" facing upwards. Important note: The cylinder head gasket should be fitted dry, with no oil or grease being applied to any of the mating surfaces.

☐ **Step 5:** Carefully lower the cylinder head into position.

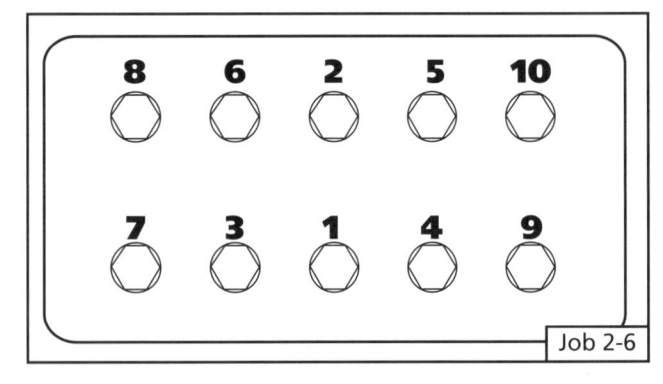

Job 2-6

☐ **Step 6:** The securing bolts may now be loosely fitted to the cylinder head.

i INSIDE INFORMATION: Don't forget the cylinder head bolt inside the inlet manifold. (See *Job 1, Step 15*.) Also note that two of the bolts, next to the temperature sender unit position, also secure the water pipe bracket. (See *Job 1, Step 16*.) *i*

You can now refit the sender unit.

☐ **Step 7:** Using a torque wrench tighten the cylinder head bolts a little at a time in the order shown above until all reach their specified torque requirement. See *Chapter 3, Facts and Figures*.

☐ **Step 8:** Fit the pushrods in the same order as removed, lubricating the ends beforehand.

☐ **Step 9:** Fully unscrew the rocker arm adjusters and lower the rocker gear carefully onto the four studs in the cylinder head, ensuring that all the rocker ball ends are located in the pushrod cups.

i INSIDE INFORMATION: Spinning the pushrods between your fingers helps to ensure proper location in the tappets. *i*

☐ **Step 10:** Refit the nuts and washers to the studs and tighten progressively to the specified torque. See *Chapter 3, Facts and Figures*.

❑ **Step 11:** Adjust the valve clearances. See *Job 7*.

Job 2-12

❑ **Step 12:** Refit the exhaust manifold and ducting, the alternator and the thermostat housing.

❑ **Step 13:** Refit the distributor. See **PART D: IGNITION**.

Job 2-14

❑ **Step 14:** Refit the rocker cover, using a new gasket.

ℹ **INSIDE INFORMATION:** Avoid distortion of the rocker cover by not over-tightening the bolts. Over-tightening distorts the pressed-steel cover and causes leaks! ℹ

❑ **Step 15:** Refit the carburettor and the air cleaner. See **PART F: FUEL AND EXHAUST**.

❑ **Step 16:** Reconnect all the water hoses, remake the electrical connections and connect the battery.

❑ **Step 17:** Refill the cooling system, using the correct **FL Paraflu** anti-freeze solution. See *Chapter 3, Facts and Figures*.

Job 3. OHV cylinder head - dismantling and overhaul.

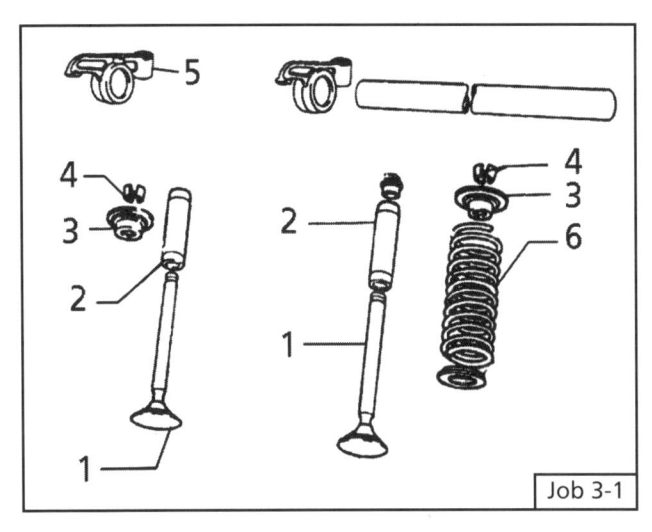

Job 3-1

❑ **Step 1:** The most important items to note here are the valves themselves (**1**), valve guides (**2**), caps (or valve retainers) (**3**) and collets (**4**), the rocker arms (**5**) and valve springs (**6**) - sometimes two fitted, one inside the other.

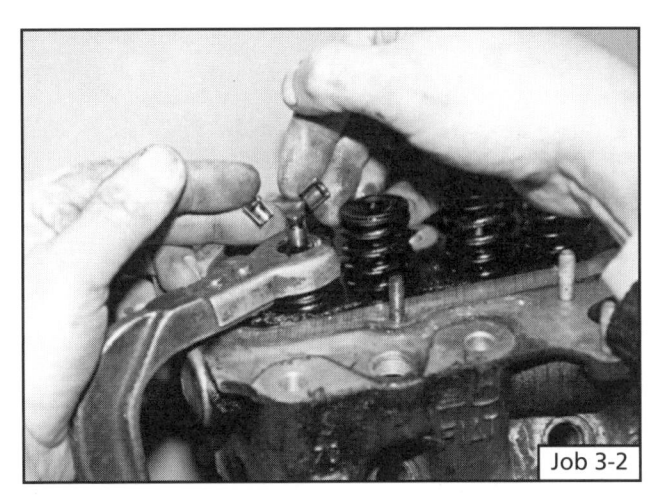

Job 3-2

❑ **Step 2:** Use a suitable valve spring compressor to compress each spring in turn to allow the removal of the split collets from the valve stems. Take care not to lose the collets when releasing the spring compressor.

making it easy!
• Keep the valves in their correct order by pushing their stems through some cardboard and numbering them, number one being at the timing chain end.
• Another means of identification is to label each valve with masking tape which you can write on with a biro or felt pen.

CHAPTER 6 PART A: ENGINE

73

CHAPTER 6 PART A: ENGINE

Job 3-3

❑ **Step 3:** The valve spring caps, springs and spring seats can all be lifted clear and the valves withdrawn from their guides.

Job 3-4

❑ **Step 4:** INSIDE INFORMATION: The valves should slide freely out of their guides. Any resistance may be caused by a build up of carbon, or a slight burr on the stem where the collets engage. This can usually be removed by careful use of fine wet-or-dry paper, allowing you to withdraw the valves without scoring their guides. *i*

Keep the valves in their correct order.

❑ **Step 5:** Re-insert each valve into its guide, keeping hold of the valve end. Try to move the valve from side to side. Try again from the other end of the valve guide. If *any* movement can be felt, the guide is worn and must be replaced by your FIAT dealer or specialist workshop.

❑ **Step 6:** The cylinder head is made of light alloy and is easily damaged when being cleaned. Use a rotary wire brush for the combustion chambers and ports, but no sharp objects such as screwdrivers should be used. The machined surfaces must have all traces of old gasket removed by use of a not too sharp straight edge - take *great* care not to dig it in!. Then wash down with paraffin to remove old oil and dirt, and dry off with a clean rag.

At all costs, avoid gouging the cylinder head. This can be very expensive to put right!

making it easy! ∏ Try using a safe solvent, such as carburettor cleaner, or proprietary gasket remover, to loosen old gasket material.

❑ **Step 7:** Clean the carbon from the valves with a rotary wire brush and wash them in paraffin. This is a cleaned-up valve next to a typically carboned-up one. Wash the valve springs, caps, seats and collets and dry.

Job 3-7

making it easy! • Clean the flat ends of the valve heads back to the shiny metal. Now the sucker on the end of your valve grinding stick won't keep falling off when you grind-in the valves!

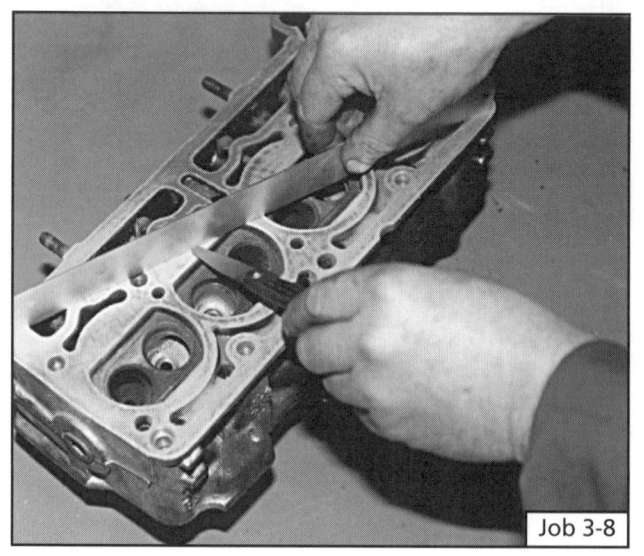

Job 3-8

❑ **Step 8:** The cylinder head should be checked for distortion by use of a straight edge and feeler gauge. At the same time check for excessive corrosion. If you are in doubt, or if the old gasket had blown, have the cylinder head refaced by your FIAT agent or engine specialist.

❑ **Step 9:** Examine the valve seats for pitting or burning. Also, check the valve seats in the cylinder head. Small pits can be removed by grinding the valves onto their seats. The seats in the cylinder head will have to be recut (again, by your local FIAT agent if the pitting is too deep), and new valves fitted.

FACT FILE: VALVE GRINDING

☐ **Step 10:** Apply a small quantity of coarse grinding paste evenly round the valve seat. A valve grinding stick with a suction pad slightly smaller than the valve head should be selected. Put a dab of moisture onto the suction pad and press the grinding stick to the first valve.

☐ **Step 11:** Lower the valve stem into its guide and, holding the grinding stick between the palms of your hands, rub your hands together (like a bushman making a fire), rotating the valve and grinding the two seats together. Lift the valve regularly, say every ten or so turns, to allow the grinding paste to be redistributed. When you can feel the paste wearing smooth, remove the valve and wipe all the surfaces clean.

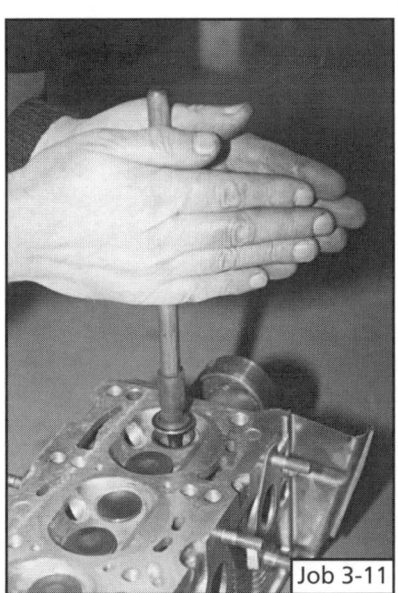

IMPORTANT NOTE: Make sure that no paste is allowed to enter the guide. This would cause a lot of wear to the valve stem and guide.

• A complete ring of grey contact area should be visible on the valve head and its seat in the cylinder head. If necessary, start off with coarse paste to remove the deeper pits, and finally use fine paste to obtain a smooth finish. If pitting is too bad, you could have the valve face and the valve seats resurfaced or, in worse cases, the valve and/or valve seat (in the cylinder head) will have to be replaced. Consult your FIAT dealer or engine specialist if in doubt.

i INSIDE INFORMATION: A narrow contact band means more seat pressure and longer life. A wide band allows rapid valve burning. *i*

Now repeat this operation on the remaining seven valves.

☐ **Step 12:** Wash the whole cylinder head again using paraffin and an old brush, making sure that all traces of grinding paste are removed, then dry off. Use compressed air if available.

SAFETY FIRST!

• *Treat compressed air with respect. Always wear goggles to protect your eyes.*

• *Never allow the airline nozzle near any of the body apertures.*

☐ **Step 13:** The valve stems must be amply lubricated with clean engine oil and then located in their respective guides, after pushing new oil seals onto the tops of the guides. Temporarily wrap sellotape around the tops of the valve stems so that the seal slides over the collets groove.

i **Step 14:** INSIDE INFORMATION: Check the valve springs' height against new ones if possible, but if not, check them against each other. If any are shorter than the others, play safe and replace the complete set. After a long time in use, they are bound to have suffered fatigue which could cause valve failure. *i*

☐ **Step 15:** Place the valve spring seat over the guide, and then position the spring, with the tighter coils towards the seat, followed by the cap. Compress the spring enough to allow you to engage the split cotters with the valve stem.

i INSIDE INFORMATION: Use a little grease to keep the collets in place, see *Job 6, Step 16*. Slowly release the compressor, checking that the collets are correctly located. Tap the end of each valve stem with a soft hammer to bed the collets in. With all the valves in place, the cylinder head is ready for refitting as described in *Job 2*. *i*

Job 4. OHC cylinder head - removal.

i INSIDE INFORMATION: Allow the engine to cool right down before starting work, or you will run the risk of causing cylinder head distortion. *i*

CHAPTER 6 PART A: ENGINE

75

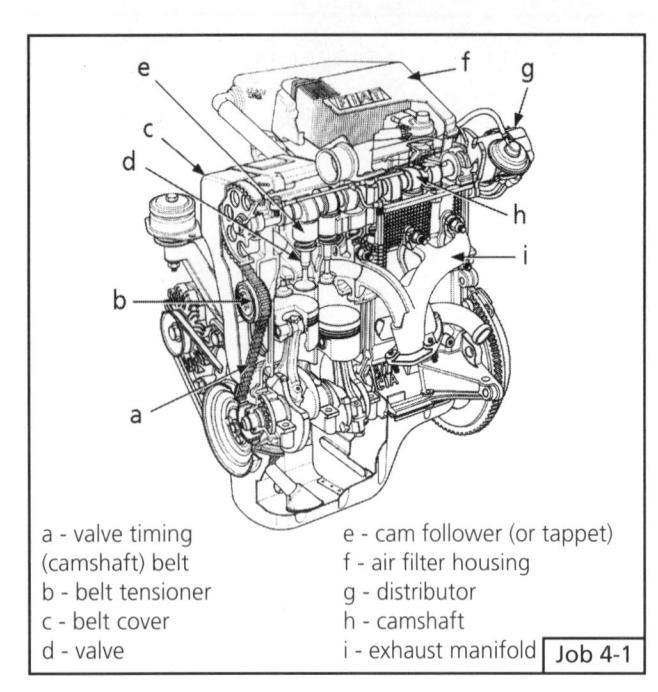

CHAPTER 6 PART A: ENGINE

a - valve timing (camshaft) belt
b - belt tensioner
c - belt cover
d - valve
e - cam follower (or tappet)
f - air filter housing
g - distributor
h - camshaft
i - exhaust manifold

Job 4-1

❏ **Step 1:** This is the layout of the major components of the FIRE Overhead Camshaft (OHC) engine as it is covered in **Jobs 4, 5, 6, 7** and **10**.

❏ **Step 2:** Disconnect the battery earth lead. Remove the air cleaner and disconnect the accelerator and choke controls.

❏ **Step 3:** Drain the cooling system (engine COLD) and disconnect the coolant hoses from the head.

❏ **Step 4:** Disconnect the hoses from the fuel pump and carburettor and blank off with a bolt of suitable size.

❏ **Step 5:** Disconnect the vacuum and coolant hoses from the inlet manifold and cylinder head.

❏ **Step 6:** Disconnect the leads from the fuel cut off solenoid (when fitted), the coolant temperature switch and the (smaller) low tension leads from the coil.

❏ **Step 7:** Remove the distributor cap and leads and place to one side.

❏ **Step 8:** Unbolt the timing belt cover and remove. See **Job 7**. Remove the distributor. See **PART D: IGNITION**.

❏ **Step 9:** Put number one piston at TDC as described in **Job 10, Steps 5** and **6**.

❏ **Step 10:** Slacken the timing belt tensioner and remove the belt from the sprockets. See **Job 10**.

❏ **Step 11:** Unbolt the inlet manifold and, if you prefer, remove it complete with the carburettor.

Job 4-11

❏ **Step 12:** On the opposite side of the engine, take off the hot air ducting from the exhaust manifold studs - two locknuts.

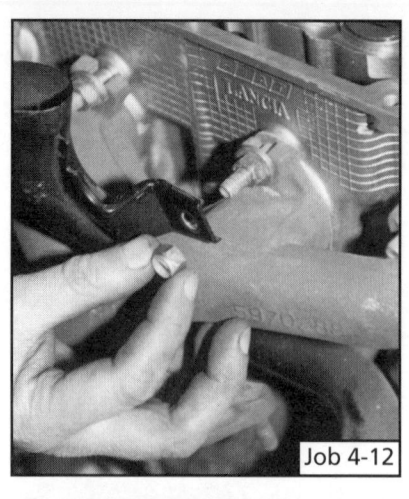

Job 4-12

❏ **Step 13:** Disconnect the exhaust downpipe bracket. Unbolt the manifold from the cylinder head and tie to one side (in the engine bay), or remove if you prefer.

Job 4-13

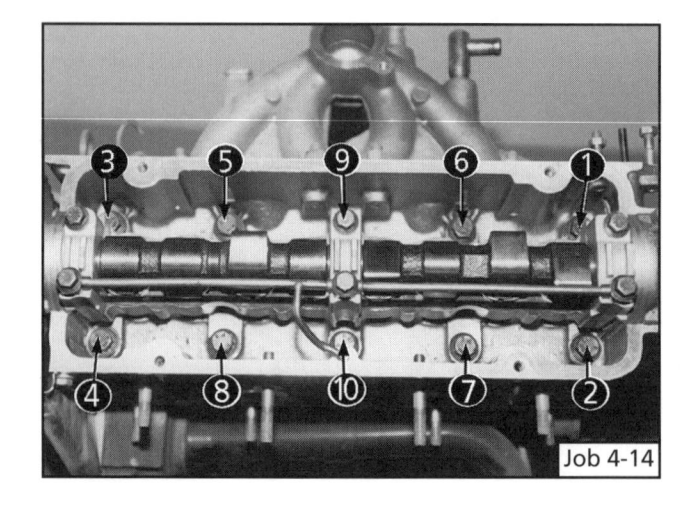

Job 4-14

❏ **Step 14:** Unscrew the cylinder head bolts half a turn at a time in the order shown, until all are loose.

❏ **Step 15:** Now remove the bolts and their washers from the cylinder head.

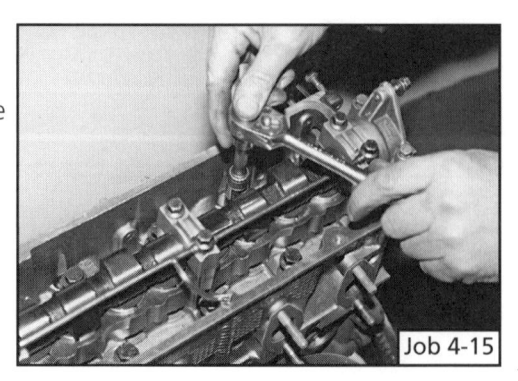

Job 4-15

76

❑ **Step 16:** The cylinder head is now ready for removal. Never attempt to use a wedge between the cylinder head and block. This causes a lot of damage.

making it easy!
- If the head is stuck, use a wooden hammer shaft or something similar, as a lever in the exhaust ports to break the seal.

Job 4-16

Job 5. OHC cylinder head - refitting.

❑ **Step 1:** The illustration below shows the layout of the cylinder head components. The valve cover gasket is re-usable unless damaged, in which case it must be replaced.

❑ **Step 2:** Before refitting, make sure that the cylinder head and block surfaces have been thoroughly cleaned and that the bolt holes in the cylinder block are clear to their bottoms.

❑ **Step 3:** Align the camshaft sprocket timing mark (arrowed) with the one on the cylinder head.

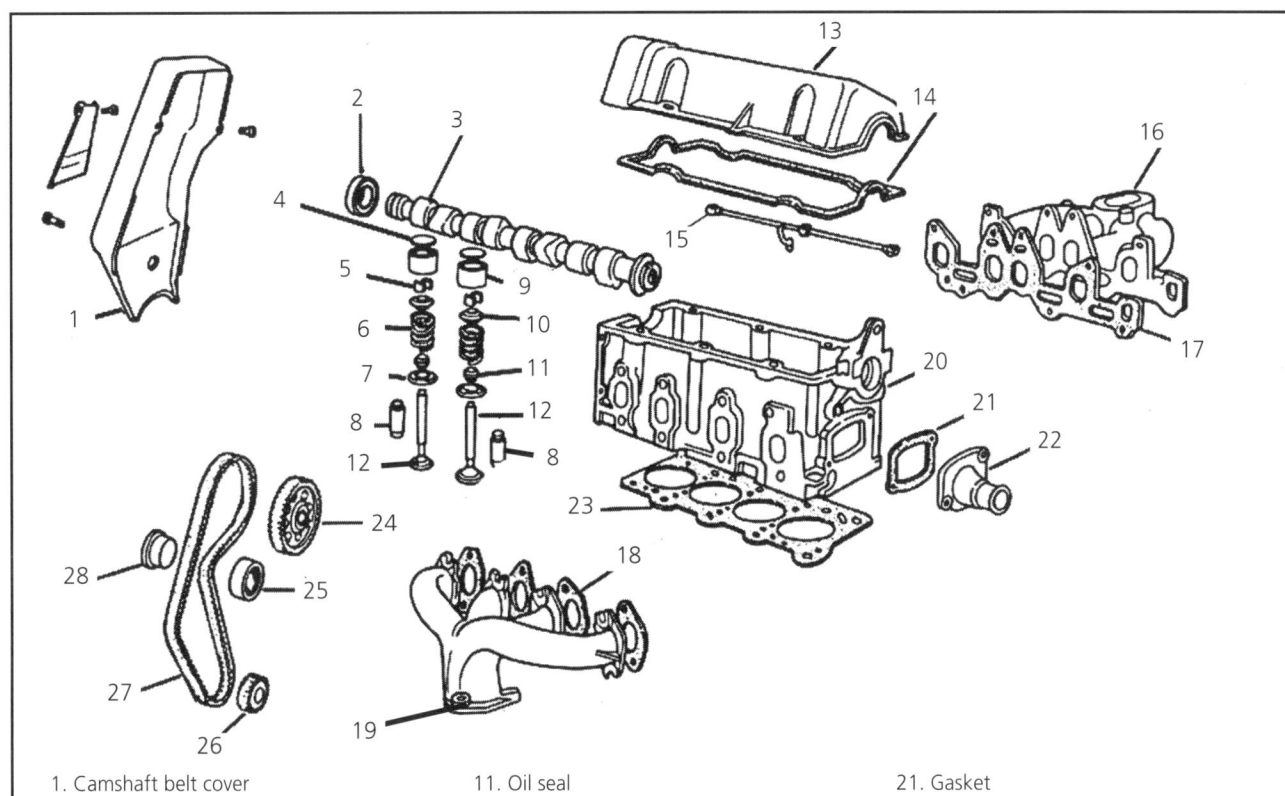

Job 5-3

1. Camshaft belt cover
2. Oil seal
3. Camshaft
4. Shim
5. Collets
6. Valve spring
7. Bottom valve spring cap
8. Valve guide
9. Tappet
10. Top valve spring cap
11. Oil seal
12. Valve
13. Camshaft cover
14. Cover gasket
15. Oil pipe
16. Inlet manifold
17. Inlet manifold gasket
18. Exhaust manifold gasket
19. Exhaust manifold
20. Cylinder head
21. Gasket
22. Thermostat housing
23. Cylinder head gasket
24. Camshaft pulley
25. Bearing
26. Crankshaft pulley
27. Camshaft drivebelt
28. Hub

Job 5-1

CHAPTER 6 PART A: ENGINE

77

CHAPTER 6 PART A: ENGINE

Job 5-4

❑ **Step 4:** Make sure that the two aligning dowels are in place, at opposite ends of the block.

Job 5-5

❑ **Step 5:** The new cylinder head gasket is fitted dry. Any oil or grease could cause it to blow. Place it over the dowels on the cylinder block with the word 'ALTO' facing upwards.

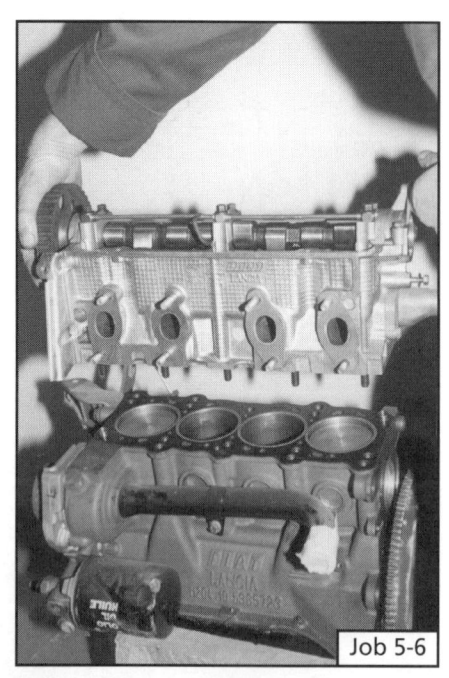

❑ **Step 6:** Place the cylinder head carefully on the block, locating it with its positioning dowels.

Job 5-6

SAFETY FIRST!

● Make sure you don't trap your fingers between the cylinder head and block!

i **Step 7:** INSIDE INFORMATION: The cylinder head bolts must be cleaned, dipped in engine oil and drained for thirty minutes before fitting. This stops them 'hydraulicing' when being screwed home and allows them to be 'torqued' down evenly. *i*

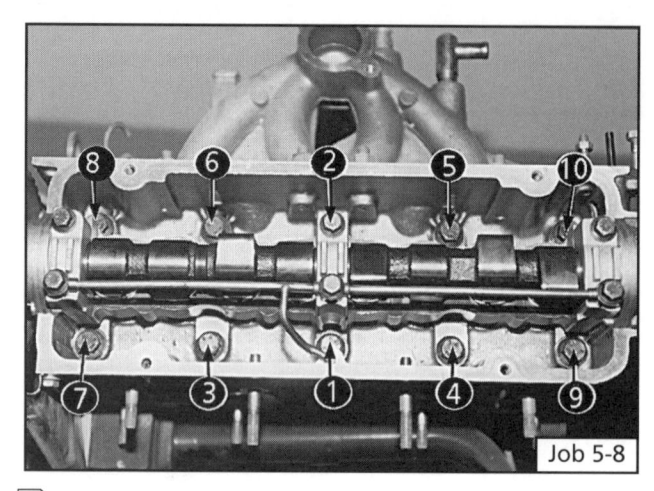

Job 5-8

❑ **Step 8:** Fit the cylinder head bolts and their washers finger tight, then tighten them in the sequence shown here, in the procedure described below.

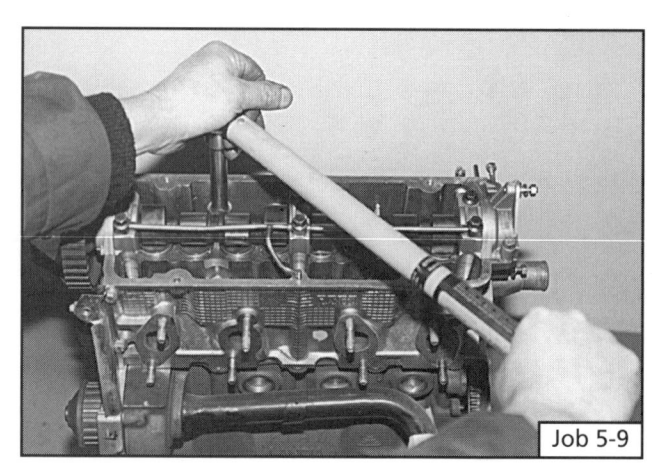

Job 5-9

❑ **Step 9:** First, tighten the bolts to the torque figure shown in **Chapter 3**.

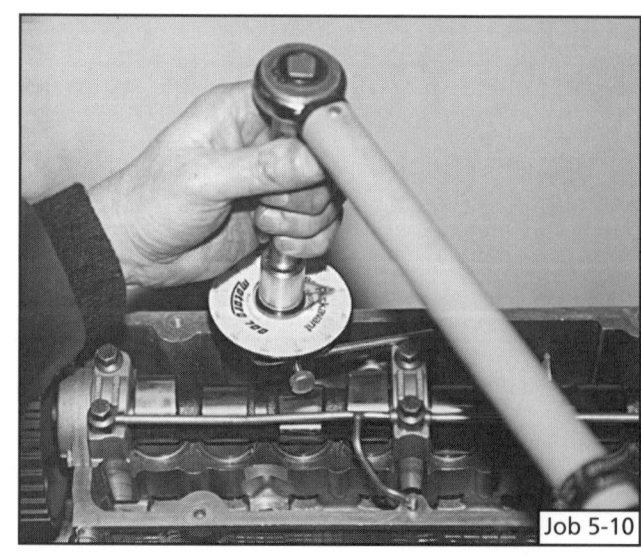

Job 5-10

❑ **Step 10:** Then use an angle gauge to turn each bolt the number of degrees given in **Chapter 3, Facts and Figures**.

78

❏ **Step 11:** Refit the inlet manifold using a new gasket and be careful to position the accelerator cable bracket 14 to 16 mm from the alternator terminal clamp. Before the manifold nuts are tightened, insert the large serrated washer (if one is fitted) between the bracket and the manifold. Tighten the manifold nuts evenly to the correct torque. See *Chapter 3, Facts and Figures.*

❏ **Step 12:** Refit the exhaust manifold with a new gasket and tighten to the correct torque. The downpipe bracket can now be reconnected.

Job 5-13

❏ **Step 13:** Making sure the timing marks are aligned, follow the instructions in *Job 10* for fitting a new timing belt DON'T re-use the old one! Remember: Timing belts should be replaced periodically - refer to *Chapter 5.*

❏ **Step 14:** Refit the camshaft cover, timing belt cover and distributor cap and leads.

❏ **Step 15:** Reconnect all controls, all hoses and remaining leads.

❏ **Step 16:** Fill the cooling system (see *Chapter 5, Job 17*) with the correct dilution of new **FL Paraflu** anti-freeze solution. See *Chapter 3, Facts and Figures.*

❏ **Step 17:** Refit the air cleaner.

Job 6. OHC cylinder head - dismantling and servicing.

Job 6-1

❏ **Step 1:** The cylinder head is partly stripped as it is being removed from the engine. Only the camshaft and valves remain to be dismantled at this stage.

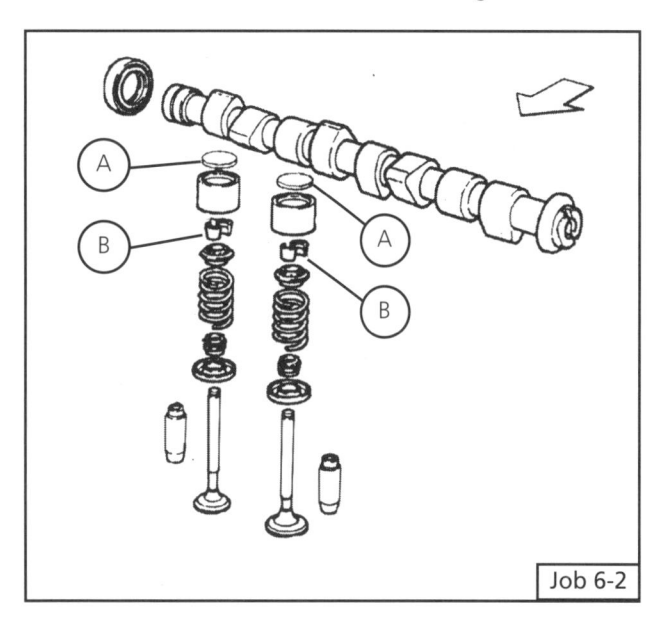

Job 6-2

❏ **Step 2:** This is the general layout of the valve gear. Take careful note of the tappet shims (**A**) and valve collets (**B**).

Job 6-3

❏ **Step 3:** Undo the camshaft sprocket fixing bolt and remove the sprocket.

CHAPTER 6 PART A: ENGINE

79

> *making it easy!* • Pass a steel bar through one of the sprocket holes to prevent rotation when undoing the camshaft sprocket bolt.
> • Avoid damage to the cylinder head by putting a piece of wood under the end of the bar.

❑ **Step 4:** Mark the camshaft bearing caps, so that you can refit them in the same positions.

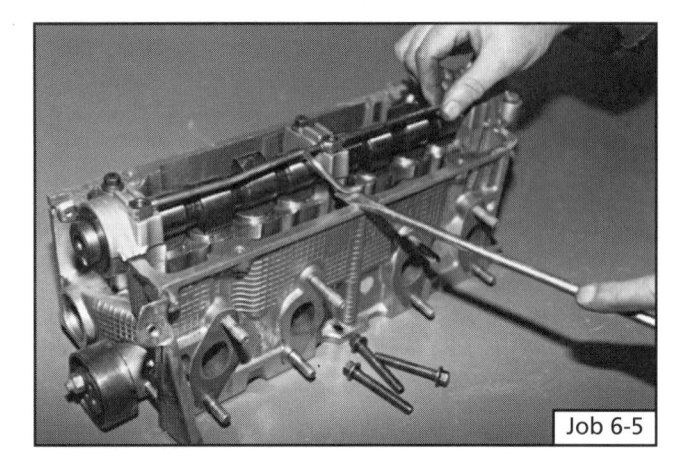

Job 6-5

❑ **Step 5:** Unbolt and remove the oil feed pipe - carefully prise out the stub using a screwdriver, as shown after removing the relevant bolts.

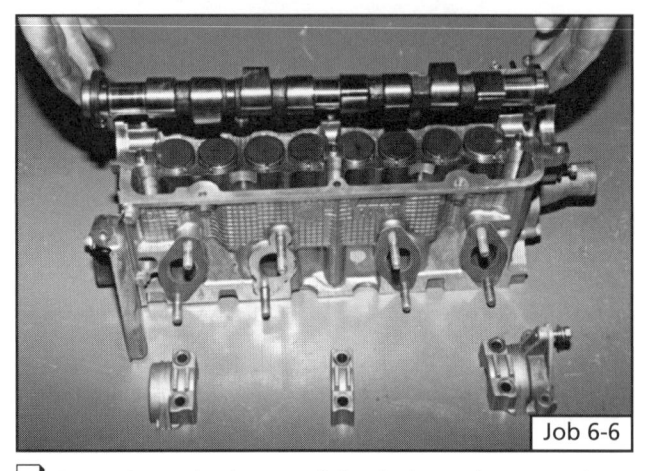

Job 6-6

❑ **Step 6:** Undo the remaining bolts and remove the bearing caps. Carefully remove the camshaft from the cylinder head, without disturbing the shims and cam followers beneath.

i INSIDE INFORMATION: 1) Note that the oil in the engine will tend to make the cam followers tricky to lift. Try prising carefully with a pair of screwdrivers, one each side to lift evenly.

2) If the valve grinding or seat cutting has taken place, or the valves, camshaft or cam followers have been changed, the original shims will no longer give the correct clearances. See *Job 7* for adjustment. *i*

Job 6-7

❑ **Step 7:** Now remove cam followers (or tappets), keeping them in the correct order for refitting. They will be complete with their shims at this stage.

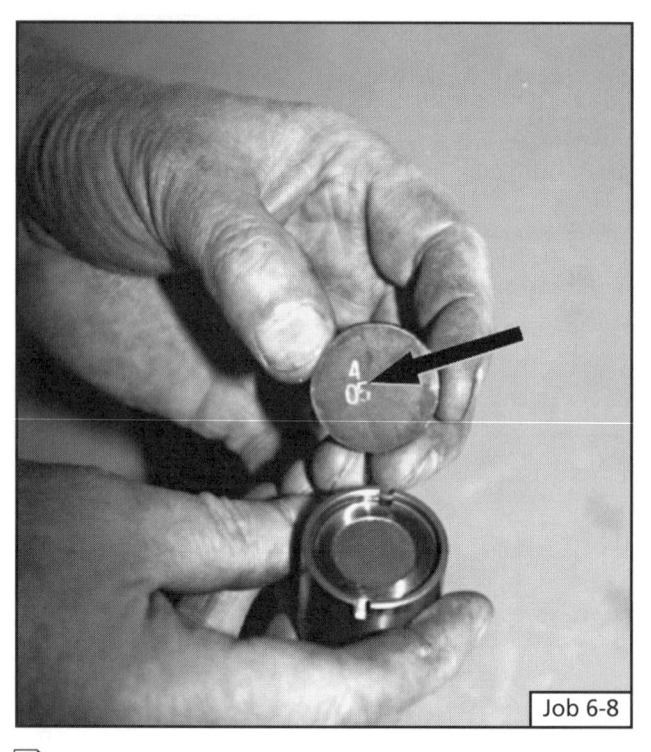

Job 6-8

❑ **Step 8:** The shims can each be removed, if necessary, but be sure to keep them with their correct 'partners'. Each shim is marked with its thickness (arrowed).

❑ **Step 9:** Use a suitable valve spring compressor to compress each spring in turn to allow the removal of the split collets from the valve stems. Take care not to lose the collets when releasing the spring compressor.

Job 6-9

Job 6-10

❑ **Step 10:** The valve spring caps, springs and spring seats can all be lifted clear and the valves withdrawn from their guides. Keep the valves in their correct order.

making it easy!
- Keep the valves in their correct order by pushing their stems through some cardboard and numbering them, number one being at the timing belt end.
- An alternative means of identification is to label each valve with masking tape.

❑ **Step 11:** INSIDE INFORMATION: The valves should slide freely out of their guides. Any resistance may be caused by a build up of carbon, or a slight burr on the stem where the collets engage. This can usually be removed by careful use of fine wet-or-dry paper, allowing you to withdraw the valves without scoring their guides.

❑ **Step 12:** The cylinder head is made of light alloy and is easily damaged when being cleaned. Use a rotary wire brush for the combustion chambers and ports, but no sharp objects such as a screwdriver should be used. The machined surfaces must have all traces of old gasket removed by use of a not too sharp straight edge. Then wash down with paraffin to remove old oil and dirt and dry with clean rag. *At all costs*, avoid gouging the cylinder head. This can be very expensive to put right.

making it easy!
- Try using carburettor cleaner or proprietary gasket remover, to loosen old gasket material.

❑ **Step 13:** The cylinder head should be checked for distortion by use of a straight edge and feeler gauge. At the same time check for excessive corrosion. If you are in doubt, or if the old gasket had blown, have the cylinder head refaced by your FIAT agent or engine specialist.

The valves should be checked for side movement in their guides. Anything but the very slightest tells you that the valve guides are in need of replacement. Your local FIAT agent or engine specialist should do this job. Examine the valve seats for pitting or burning, and also check their mating seats in the cylinder head. Small pits can be removed by grinding the valves onto their seats. The seats in the cylinder head will have to be recut, again, by your local agent if the pitting is too deep, and new valves fitted.

IMPORTANT NOTE: 'Unleaded' engine valve seats are too hard for valve grinding to make much impression on them. You can only grind out the smallest of blemishes by hand.

❑ **Step 14:** Clean the carbon from the valves with a rotary wire brush and wash them in paraffin. Wash the valve springs, caps, seats and collets and dry them.

making it easy!
- Clean the valve heads back to shiny metal.
- Now the sucker on the end of your valve grinding stick won't keep falling off!

❑ **Step 15:** Grind in the valves. The process is the same as on OHV cylinder heads. See *Job 3, Step 10-on*.

Job 6-16

❑ **Step 16:** INSIDE INFORMATION: It can be tricky to re-fit the collets. Put a dab of grease on the collet, put a dab on the end of your screwdriver, pick up the collet and 'stick' it in place on the stem of the valve.

❑ **Step 17:** Reassemble the rest of the cylinder head in the reverse order. Remember to oil the camshaft bearings and use a new camshaft oil seal. However, the valve seats are hardened (for use with unleaded fuel) and the process will be much slower. See your FIAT agent if there is any visible pitting or burning on the valve faces or seat.

Job 7. OHC cylinder head - valve clearance adjustment.

i INSIDE INFORMATION: Adjustment must always be made with the engine cold. *i*

☐ **Step 1:** Remove the camshaft cover and the spark plugs. Jack up a front wheel and engage top gear. Turning the wheel will rotate the engine and therefore the camshaft. (If the cylinder head is detached and on the bench, turn the camshaft by gripping the camshaft sprocket.)

☐ **Step 2:** The inlet and exhaust valves use different clearances which are checked when each cam lobe is pointing directly away from its follower. See *Chapter 3, Facts and Figures.*

☐ **Step 3:** The order of the valves in the cylinder head is:
- *Inlet* - 2-3-6-7
- *Exhaust* - 1-4-5-8

from the timing cover end.

Job 7-4

☐ **Step 4:** Select a feeler blade which is about the thickness of the correct valve clearance and insert it between the heel of the cam and the cam follower shim when the cam lobe is uppermost. If necessary, select different thicknesses of feeler blade until a small amount of drag can be felt as the blade is pushed in and out. Record the total blade thickness. This is the valve clearance for this valve.

☐ **Step 5:** Rotate the camshaft and repeat this operation on each of the remaining seven valves, noting their respective clearances. Those which have clearances within limits obviously don't need any further attention.

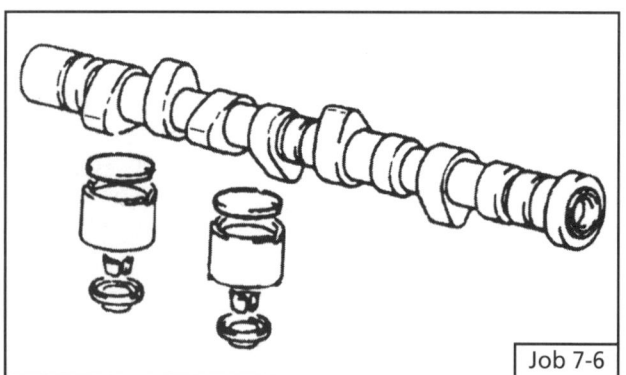

Job 7-6

☐ **Step 6:** The remaining valves will now need to have their shims changed for thicker or thinner ones, bringing their clearances to within the specifications shown in *Chapter 3, Facts and Figures.*

☐ **Step 7:** In theory, a special tool is needed to depress the cam follower and allow extraction of the shim. This is available to your FIAT dealer, or you will have to make a lever with a fork that locates nicely on the rim of a cam follower allowing removal of the shim by prising it from the follower.

i INSIDE INFORMATION: In practice, you would probably spend longer making the tool than removing and refitting the camshaft a couple of times, after first measuring and noting all of the valve clearances, so that you can calculate the amount of increase or decrease in shim thickness needed. You should also note that some shims can be *extremely* awkward to shift, even with the camshaft removed. And far more awkward with it in place! We recommend camshaft removal! *i*

☐ **Step 8:** The thickness of a shim is engraved on it in 'mm'. If this is worn away, you will have to measure the thickness with a metric micrometer - or have your FIAT dealer do it for you.

☐ **Step 9:** Where a clearance is too small with the thinnest shim in position, the valve should be removed and the stem ground just sufficiently to make the correction. Your FIAT dealer can do this, keeping the end square and retaining a smooth finish.

Job 8. OHV engine. Timing chain and sprockets - removal.

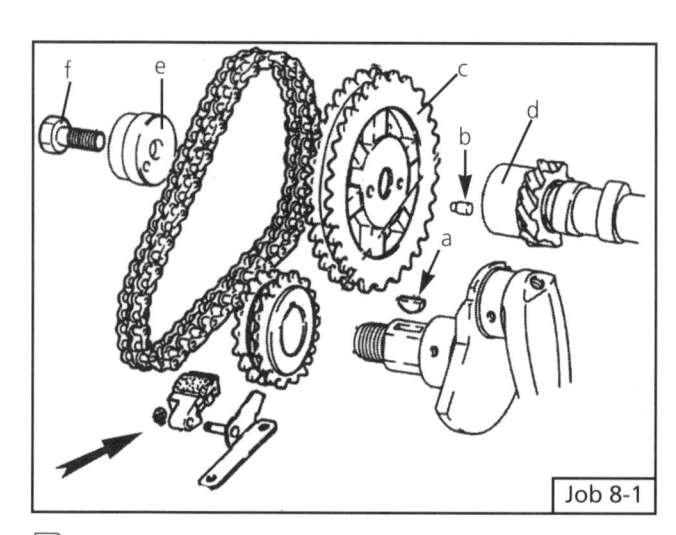

Job 8-1

☐ **Step 1:** Take note that on early OHV Pandas, there was no timing chain tensioner fitted (arrowed). On these engines, the tensioners are incorporated in the chain links.

☐ **Step 2:** If yours is a later OHV-engined Panda, a timing chain tensioner will have been added. See *Job 8-1,* arrowed.

i INSIDE INFORMATION: When an early - type of chain needs replacement, you may wish to convert to the later type. See **Job 8-16** for the tensioner mounting points. **i**

❏ **Step 3:** Slacken the alternator mounting bolts and remove the drive belt.

❏ **Step 4:** Unscrew the crankshaft pulley bolt.

i INSIDE INFORMATION: Prevent the engine turning by engaging a low gear and asking a helper to apply the foot brake firmly. If this fails, remove the starter motor and prevent the flywheel ring gear from turning with a large screwdriver. **i**

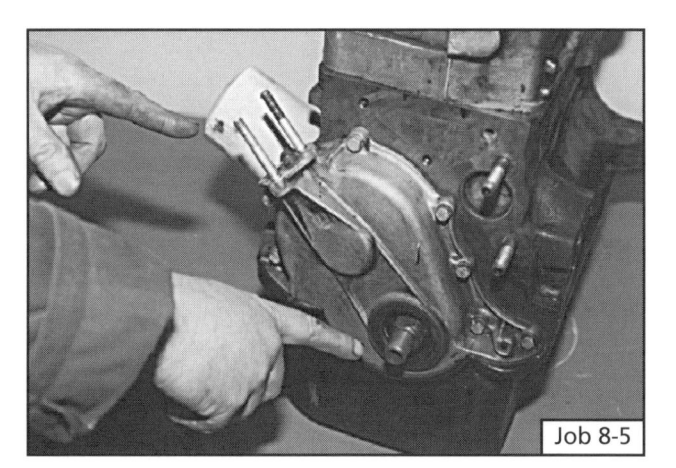

Job 8-5

❏ **Step 5:** Disconnect the fuel pump hoses, unbolt the pump and remove it together with the spacer and pushrod. The left hand is pointing out the fuel pump mounting bolts; the right hand is pointing to the crankshaft pulley position.

Job 8-6

❏ **Step 6:** With the aid of suitable lifting apparatus, raise the engine just enough to take the weight off the right hand mounting. Undo and remove the mounting. Loosen the timing cover bolts.

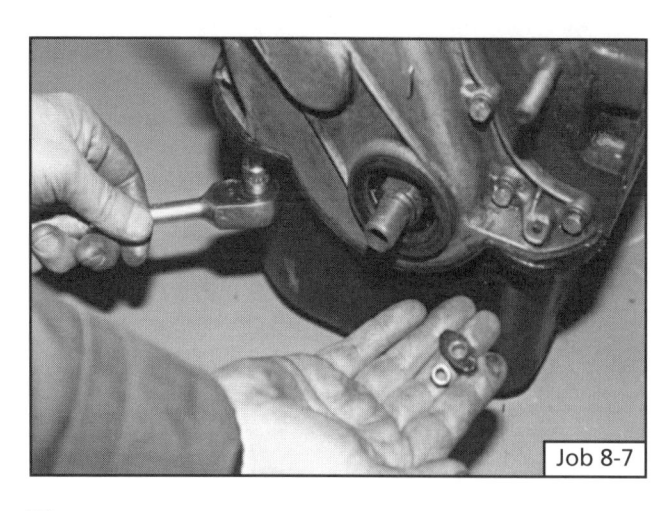

Job 8-7

❏ **Step 7:** After draining the oil, slacken the sump bolts removing all but the back four or five bolts.

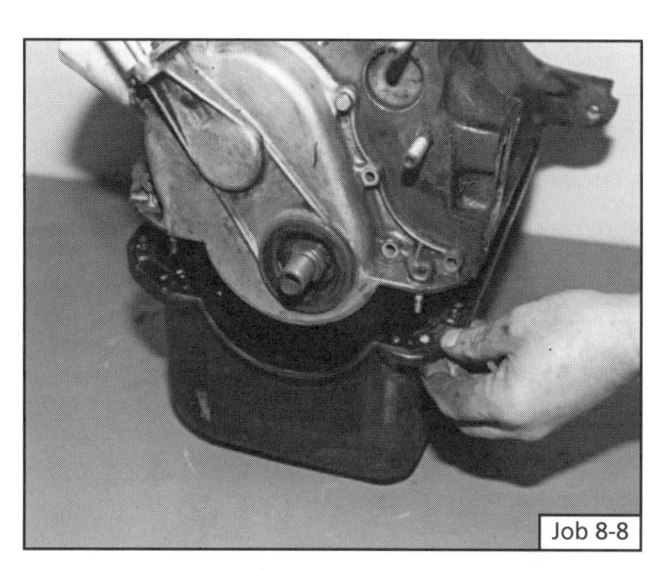

Job 8-8

❏ **Step 8:** Carefully lower the sump enough to clear the timing cover. Avoid damaging the sump gasket.

Job 8-9

❏ **Step 9:** The timing cover bolts can now be removed and the cover lifted away.

CHAPTER 6 PART A: ENGINE

83

CHAPTER 6 PART A: ENGINE

Job 8-10

❑ **Step 10:** Note the timing marks on both chain sprockets - a 'dot' on the camshaft pulley and a line on the crankshaft pulley.

Job 8-11

❑ **Step 11:** Later engines are fitted with a separate chain tensioner which is mounted on the No. 1 main bearing cap and secured by the cap bolts. Before proceeding to Step 13, release the tension by pushing on the plunger to compress the spring and turn the lever on the end in an anti-clockwise direction, looking from the left in this illustration.

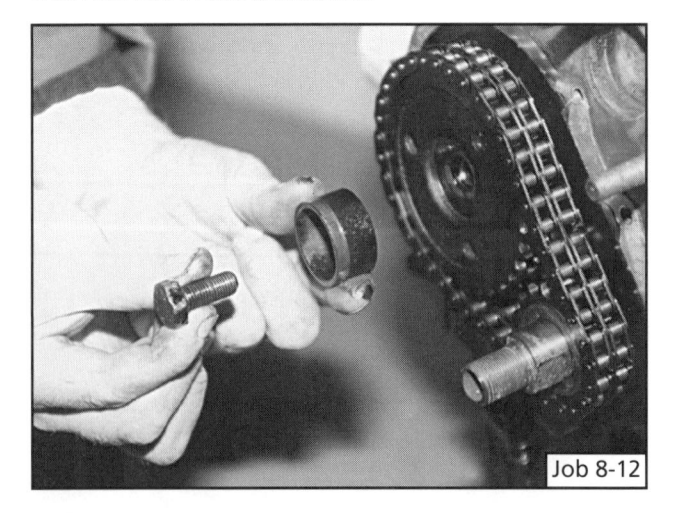

Job 8-12

❑ **Step 12:** Undo the camshaft sprocket securing bolt. This also releases the fuel pump drive cam.

Job 8-13

❑ **Step 13:** Use two large screwdrivers as levers to release the sprockets, then carefully pull the sprockets off their shafts. Lift the chain and sprockets clear.

❑ **Step 14:** Remove the woodruff key from the crankshaft (see illustration **Job 8-1, a**) and put in a safe place. The camshaft uses a dowel peg (see **Job 8-1, b**) for sprocket location.

Job 8-15

❑ **Step 15:** You can now examine the tensioner for wear on its slipper surface.

84

Job 8-16

❑ **Step 16:** If badly grooved, the tensioner is removed by undoing the two front main bearing cap bolts. The sump will have to be completely removed first.

❑ **Step 17:** Unlock the tensioner by turning the lever on the end in a clockwise direction.

Job 9. OHV engine. Timing chain and sprocket - refitting.

FACT FILE: TIMING CHAIN TENSIONER

• Where the separate type of tensioner is fitted, check the chain contact pad for signs of wear.

• It is usually best to replace the tensioner when the chain is renewed.

❑ **Step 1:** Turn the crankshaft until the woodruff key slot is uppermost. Insert the key and lightly tap fully home if it is a tight fit, leaving the forward edge slightly lower than the back.

❑ **Step 2:** Tap the crankshaft sprocket into position, making sure that the groove locates properly with the woodruff key.

❑ **Step 3:** Turn the camshaft so that the timing dimple on its sprocket will align correctly, when fitted, with the straight line on the crankshaft sprocket. See *Job 8, Step 10*.

❑ **Step 4:** To replace the tensioner (where fitted, and when necessary) see *Job 8, Steps 15, 16, and 17*. Release the new or replacement tensioner before fitting. See *Job 8-11*.

❑ **Step 5:** Fit the chain to the crankshaft sprocket. If it's the early type, without a separate tensioner, make sure that the chain is held with the self-tensioning links facing the cylinder block.

❑ **Step 6:** Locate the camshaft sprocket teeth with the upper chain loop, still retaining correct alignment of the two timing marks.

❑ **Step 7:** Locate the camshaft sprocket (see *Job 8-1, c*) with the camshaft (see *Job 8-1, d*) and secure it by fitting the fuel pump (*Job 8-1,e*) cam on its locating dowel (*Job 8-1, b*). Fit the fuel pump drive cam (*Job 8- 1, e*) and the retaining bolt (*Job 8-1, f*) and tighten to the specified torque. See **Chapter 3, Facts and Figures.**

❑ **Step 8:** Where a separate tensioner is fitted, unlock the tensioner by turning the lever on the end in a clockwise direction.

❑ **Step 9:** Rotate the engine two full turns clockwise and check that the timing marks on the sprockets are exactly aligned. See *Job 8, Step 10*. Number 4 piston should now be at top-dead centre on the compression stroke.

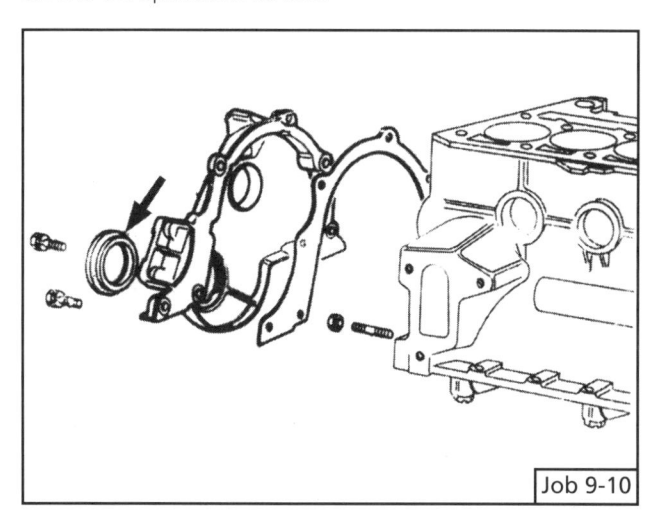

Job 9-10

❑ **Step 10:** Remove the old seal (arrowed) from the timing cover by levering it out from the inside. Clean off all traces of old gasket and sealant from the cover.

❑ **Step 11:** Fit the new seal squarely into its hole and tap home.

❑ **Step 12:** Clean the mating surface on the cylinder block.

❑ **Step 13:** Smear a little grease on the timing cover to locate the gasket and fit the timing cover to the block, ensuring that the fuel pump pushrod bush is in place. Screw the bolts in finger-tight.

CHAPTER 6 PART A: ENGINE

Job 9-14

❑ **Step 14:** Clean the pulley hub and coat with clean engine oil. Push the pulley onto the crankshaft end and carefully locate its groove over the woodruff key (location slot, arrowed).

❑ **Step 15:** Centralise the cover seal on the pulley and tighten the cover securing bolts.

❑ **Step 16:** Tighten the crankshaft pulley nut to the correct torque. See **Chapter 3, Facts and Figures.**

❑ **Step 17:** Refit the sump and refill with oil.

❑ **Step 18:** Refit the alternator drive belt and fuel pump.

Job 10. OHC engine. Timing belt - removal and replacement.

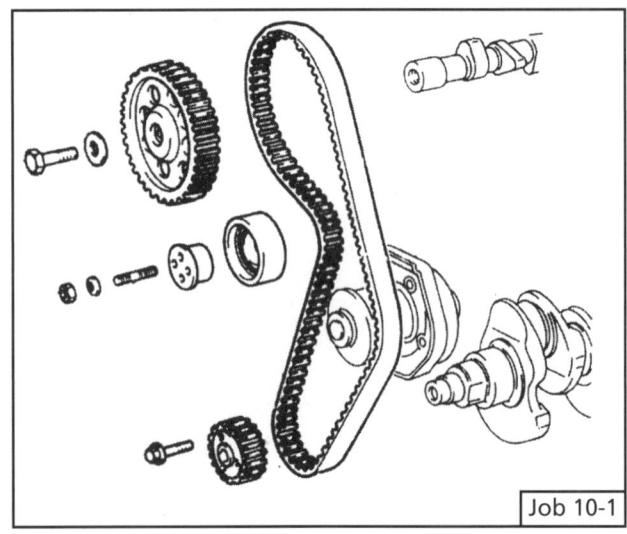

Job 10-1

❑ **Step 1:** These are the principal components concerned with timing belt removal and replacement.

IMPORTANT NOTE: FIAT strongly recommend that you should NEVER re-use a timing belt. Removal and re-application of the belt's tension can lead to premature failure. ALWAYS fit a new one!

❑ **Step 2:** Disconnect the battery earth. Remove the air cleaner, remove the spark plugs and take off the alternator drive belt.

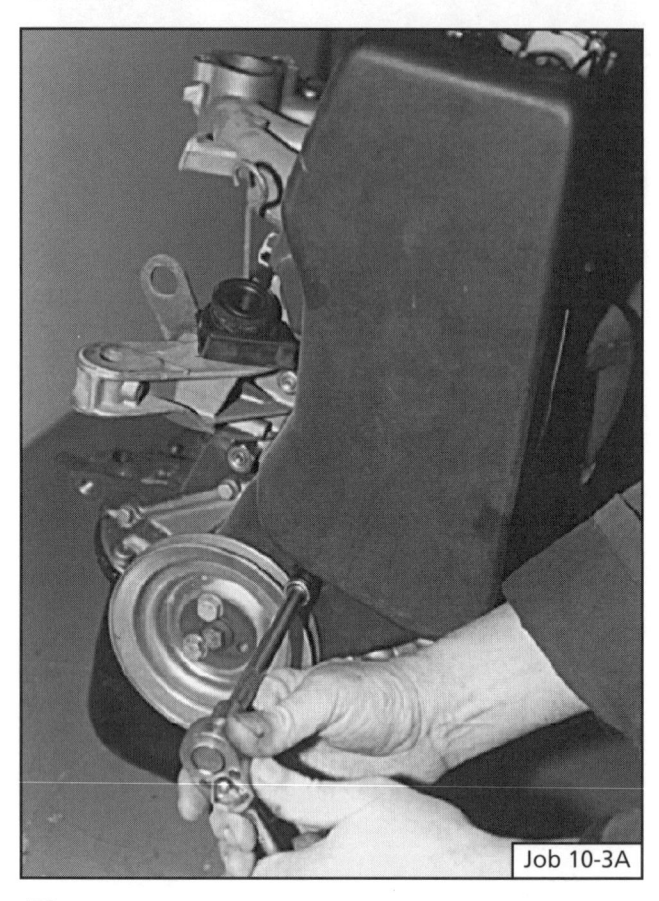

Job 10-3A

❑ **Step 3A:** Remove the timing belt cover, not forgetting the bolt at the bottom.

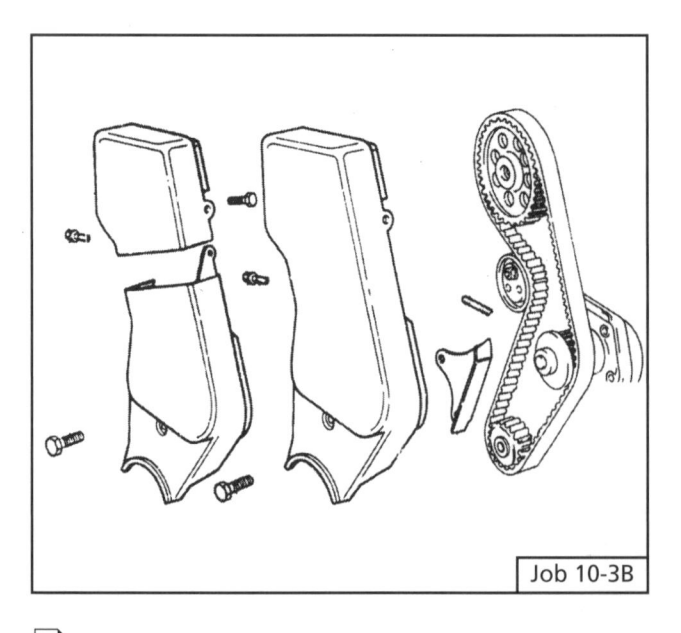

Job 10-3B

❑ **Step 3B:** Take note of the different cover types used on different models.

86

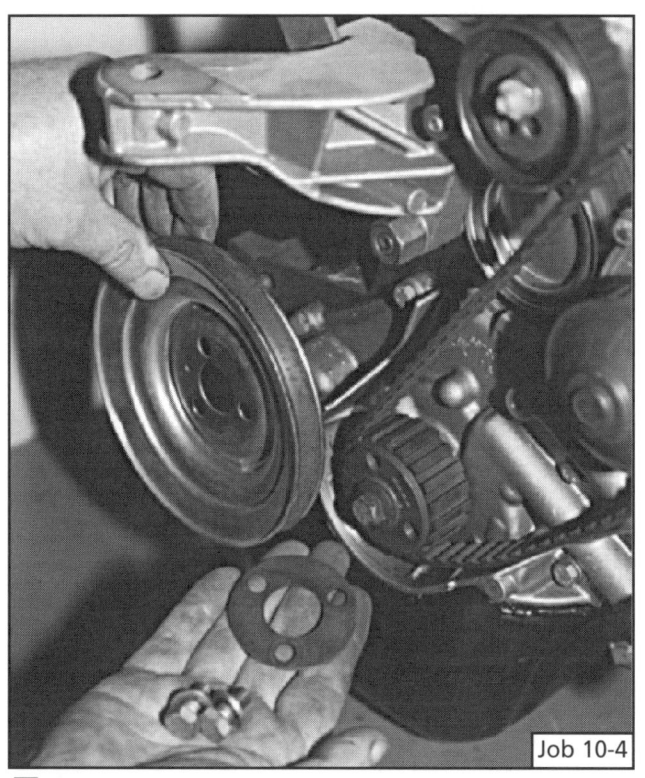

❑ **Step 4:** Unbolt and remove the crankshaft pulley.

❑ **Step 5:** Using a spanner on the crankshaft bolt, turn clockwise until the camshaft sprocket timing mark (arrowed) is aligned with the mark on the cylinder head.

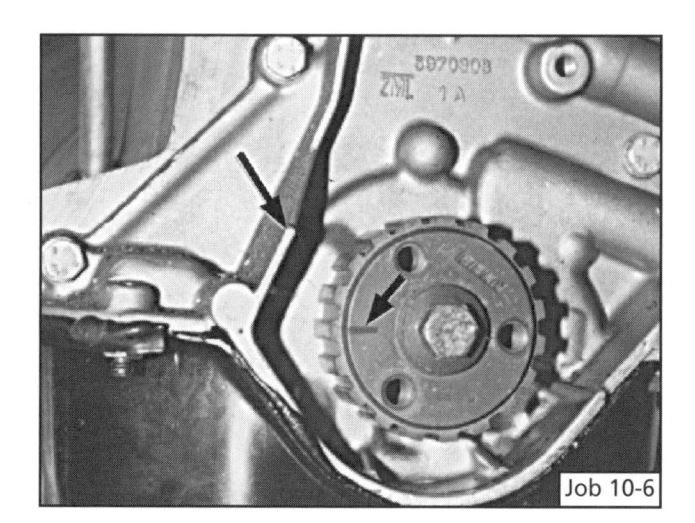

❑ **Step 6:** Also, make sure that the timing mark on the crankshaft pulley is aligned with the mark on the oil pump cover (see arrows).

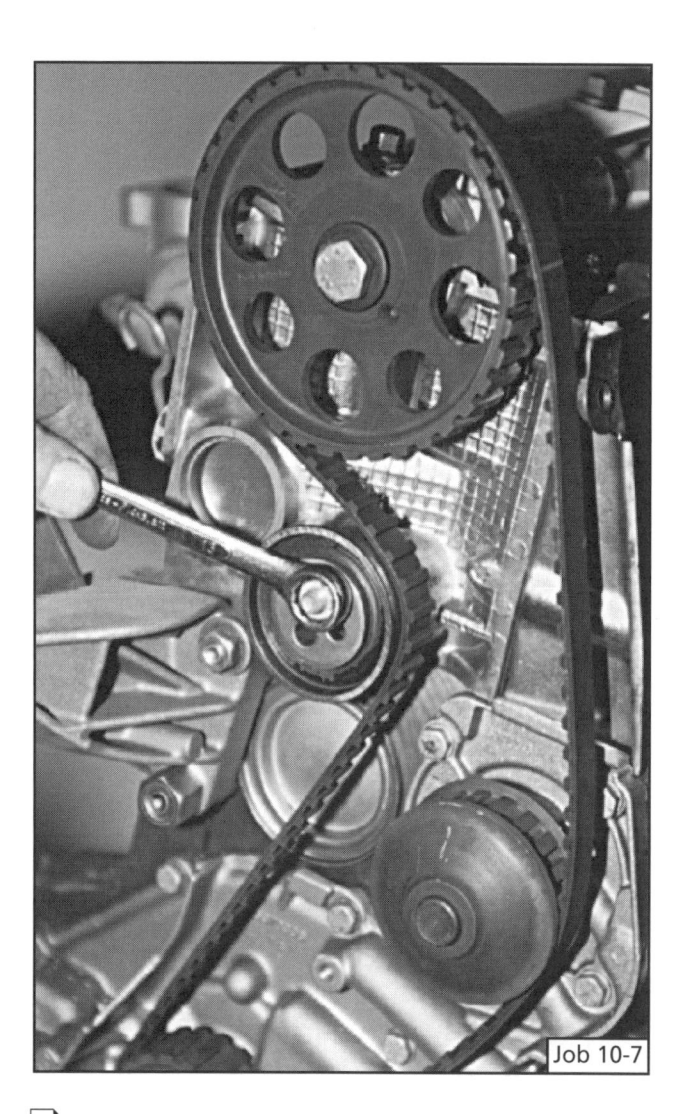

❑ **Step 7:** Slacken the timing belt tensioner nut...

❑ **Step 8:** ...move the pulley away from the belt by turning it.

i **INSIDE INFORMATION:** Retighten the nut to temporarily retain this position, to make it easier to refit the belt, later. *i*

Job 10-9

❑ **Step 9:** Remove the old belt.

❑ **Step 10:** The new belt must be fitted with the arrows printed on the outside of the belt pointing in the direction of engine rotation. Ensure that the timing marks are still aligned.

Job 10-11

❑ **Step 11:** Engage the belt with the crankshaft sprocket first, then in turn, the coolant and camshaft sprockets. Finally, feed it round the tensioner pulley. Also, as a double-check that the belt is not 'out', ensure that the yellow lines on the belt align exactly with the timing marks on the camshaft sprocket and crankshaft sprocket.

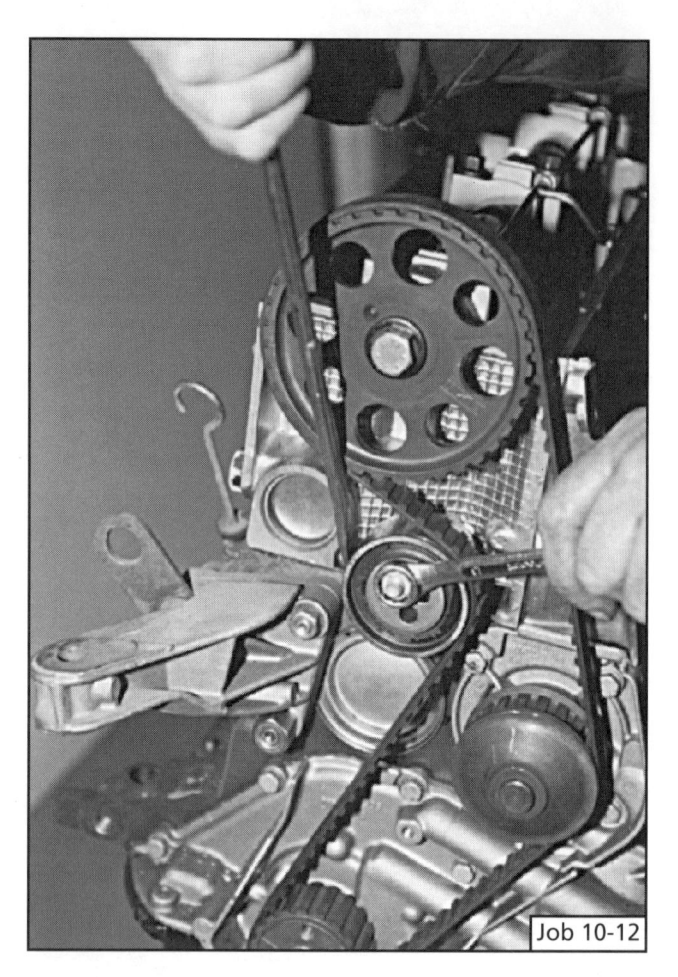

Job 10-12

❑ **Step 12:** Slacken the tensioner nut and push the pulley onto the belt until taut. Check that the timing marks are still correctly aligned. Still pressing the pulley against the belt, tighten its locking nut.

i **INSIDE INFORMATION:** If you can't put enough pressure on the tensioner with your fingers, carefully use a long screwdriver as a lever. Alternatively, insert two bolts into the two holes in the tensioner and turn with a lever. *i*

Job 10-13

❑ **Step 13:** Turn the engine through two complete turns clockwise. If correctly tensioned, you should just be able to twist the belt through a quarter of a complete turn (i.e. through 90 degrees) with your thumb and finger at the centre of its longest run. Re-adjust if necessary.

❏ **Step 14:** Refit the timing belt cover, crankshaft pulley, alternator drive belt, spark plugs and air cleaner.

Job 11. OHV and OHC. Engine and transmission - removal downwards.

FACT FILE: REMOVAL- UP OR DOWN

• With OHV engines only, removal may be upwards, the driveshafts being disconnected from the final drive and the whole unit being lifted up and out of the engine compartment. See *Job 12*.

• The alternative for OHV engines - and the ONLY option for OHC 'FIRE' engines - is downwards, the driveshafts staying with the unit which is lowered to the ground. The front of the car is raised and the unit pulled out from underneath.

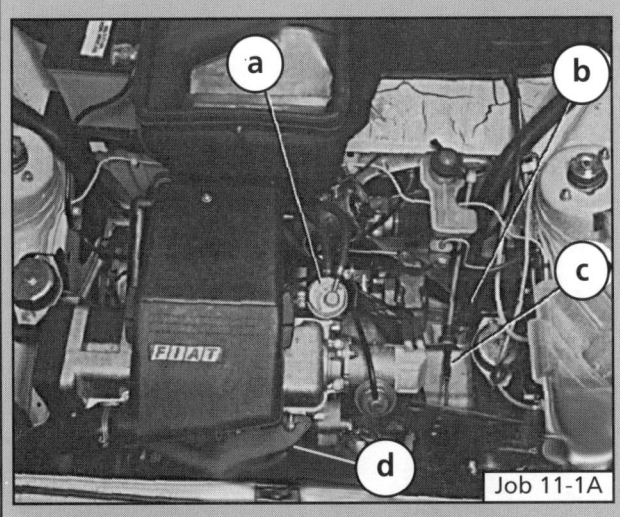

Fuel pipe from pump. **a**

Reversing light switch cable. **b**

Job 11-1A

Clutch cable. **c**

Coolant pipes. **d**

❏ **Step 1A:** It pays to familiarise yourself with the positions of the main components to be disconnected. Illustrations *a* to *d* show the layout in the OHC 'FIRE' engine bay.

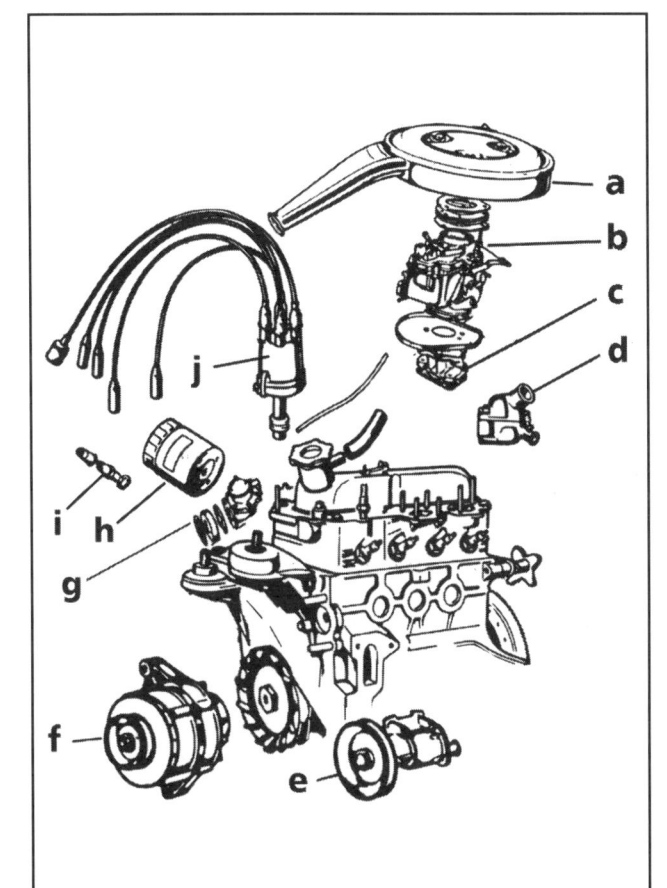

a - air filter
b - carburettor
c - spacer block
d - thermostat housing
e - water pump
f - alternator
g - fuel pump
h - oil filter
i - oil pressure sender unit
j - distributor

Job 11-1B

❏ **Step 1B:** These are the main ancillaries to be removed from the OHV 903cc engine. The air filter has a rectangular shape on later vehicles.

❏ **Step 2:** Remove the bonnet.

❏ **Step 3:** Disconnect the battery earth lead.

❏ **Step 4:** Remove the spare wheel and the coolant expansion tank.

❏ **Step 5:** Drain the cooling system. See *PART C: COOLING SYSTEM.*

❏ **Step 6:** Drain the engine oil.

❏ **Step 7:** Remove the air cleaner.

CHAPTER 6 PART A: ENGINE

89

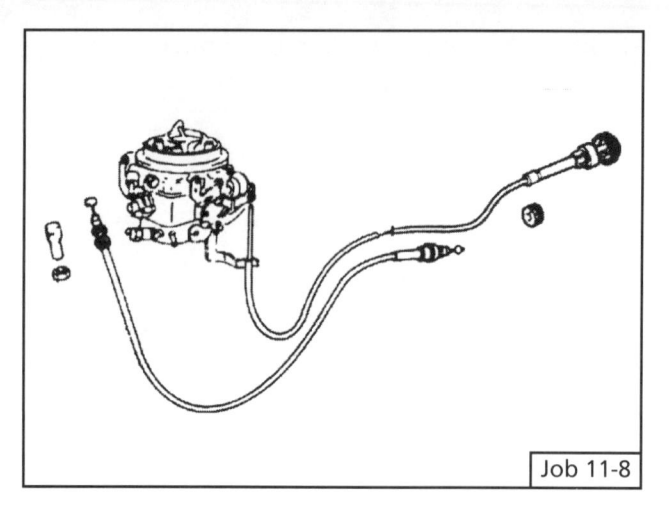

CHAPTER 6 PART A: ENGINE

Job 11-8

❏ **Step 8:** Fully slacken the throttle cable adjustment at the carburettor and disconnect from the throttle quadrant. Release the inner and outer choke cables from the carburettor and tie back.

❏ **Step 9:** Disconnect the idle cut out device cable (arrowed), when fitted.

❏ **Step 10:** Don't forget the heated air hose, from the exhaust manifold to the underside of the air cleaner, at the front. NOTE - if this hose is damaged or split, replace it. If this hose is damaged it can cause poor running - or even no running! - in cold weather.

Job 11-9

❏ **Step 11:** Disconnect the hoses from the fuel pump (see **Step 11-1A**), plugging the ends. Disconnect the carburettor fuel return hose.

❏ **Step 12:** Disconnect the radiator hoses, and heater hoses from the engine.

❏ **Step 13:** Disconnect the leads from the radiator fan, starter motor and alternator.

❏ **Step 14:** Take the lead off the water temperature sender unit, just above No. 1 spark plug and take the lead off the oil sender unit, as shown here on a 'FIRE' engine.

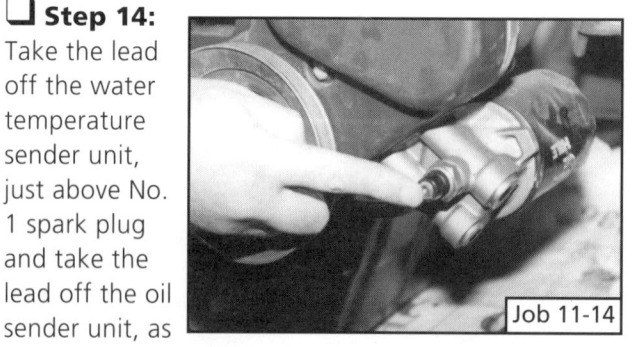

Job 11-14

❏ **Step 15:** Disconnect the LT and HT leads, from coil to distributor. The low tension (LT) lead is arrowed. Remove the distributor cap complete with plug leads.

Job 11-15

Job 11-16

❏ **Step 16:** Unbolt the exhaust system from its manifold (arrowed), disconnect the flexible mountings and remove the whole system.

❏ **Step 17:** Disconnect the clutch cable from the release lever (see **Step 11-1A**) and the reversing light switch, mounted on the transmission casing.

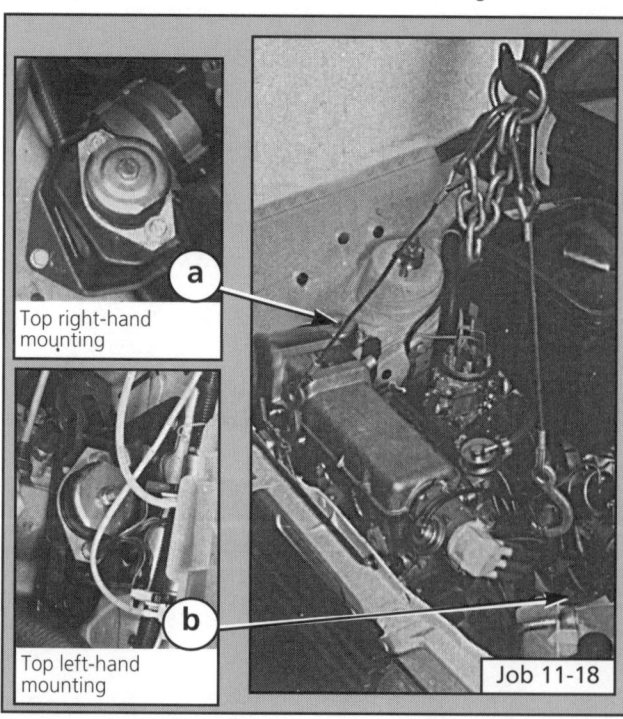

Top right-hand mounting
Top left-hand mounting
Job 11-18

❏ **Step 18:** Using an engine hoist on the engine lifting lugs (or a trolley jack from beneath), take the weight off the engine. Disconnect the top mountings **a** and **b**.

❑ **Step 19:** Note the location of parts (**a**) and (**b**), beneath the car.

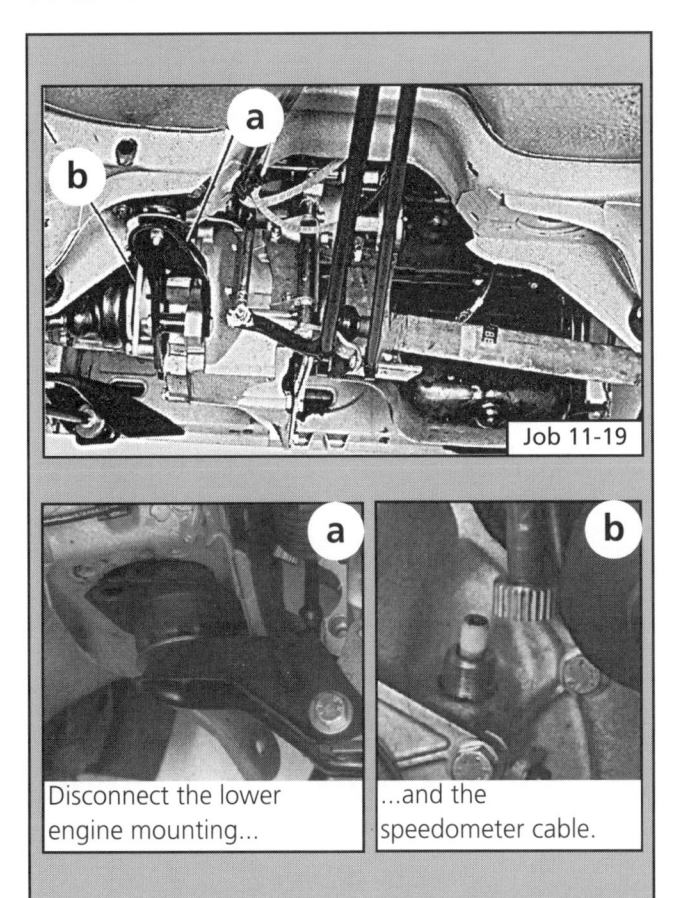

Job 11-19

Disconnect the lower engine mounting...

...and the speedometer cable.

❑ **Step 20:** Disconnect the gearchange control rod from the flexible joint at the gearbox selector shaft (arrowed) and tie out of the way.

Job 11-20

❑ **Step 21:** Support the body under the frame with axle stands and jacks ...

❑ **Step 22:** ...and remove the front wheels.

❑ **Step 23:** Loosen the driveshaft to hub nuts. See *PART G: STEERING AND SUSPENSION.*

i INSIDE INFORMATION: These are very tight and will require a good deal of leverage. It is essential to undo the hub nuts while the vehicle is still on the ground. They are (should be!) extremely tight! *i*

❑ **Step 24:** Raise the front of the car simultaneously with the engine, until you have sufficient room for the engine to be pulled out from underneath and make sure that the rear wheels are chocked, front and back.

❑ **Step 25:** Make doubly sure that the body is properly supported on axle stands.

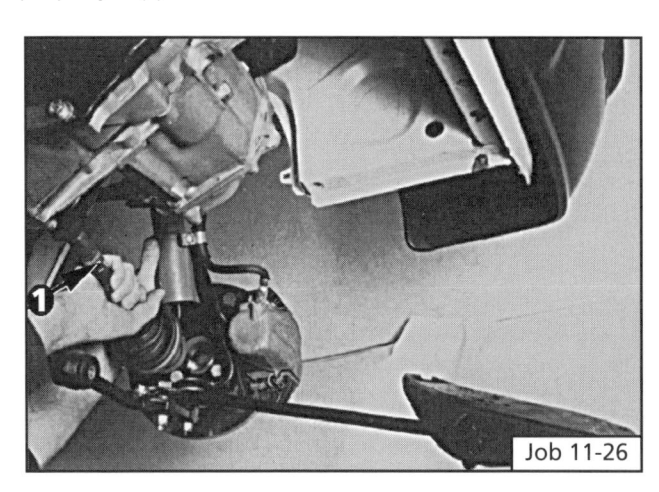

Job 11-26

i **Step 26:** INSIDE INFORMATION: Before removing the hub nuts, fix the drive shafts (*Job 11-26, 1*) to prevent them coming out of the differential internal casing. *i*

❑ **Step 27:** Disconnect both front suspension track control arms at their inboard ends and pull down. See *PART G: STEERING AND SUSPENSION.*

❑ **Step 28:** disconnect the steering tie rod balljoints from the steering arms. See *PART G: STEERING AND SUSPENSION.*

❑ **Step 29:** Disconnect the radius rods from the track control arms. See *PART G: STEERING AND SUSPENSION.*

❑ **Step 30:** Unbolt the brake calipers and release the hose ties. Tie the calipers clear. See *PART H: BRAKES.*

❑ **Step 31:** Remove the remaining engine/transmission mountings. See *Step 18.*

❑ **Step 32:** Remove the two clamp bolts from the lower ends of the suspension struts and tap the hub carriers downwards. Tap or press the driveshafts out of the hubs.

CHAPTER 6 PART A: ENGINE

☐ **Step 33:** Make a final check that nothing remains connected. Lower the power unit to the ground, preferably onto a suitable trolley.

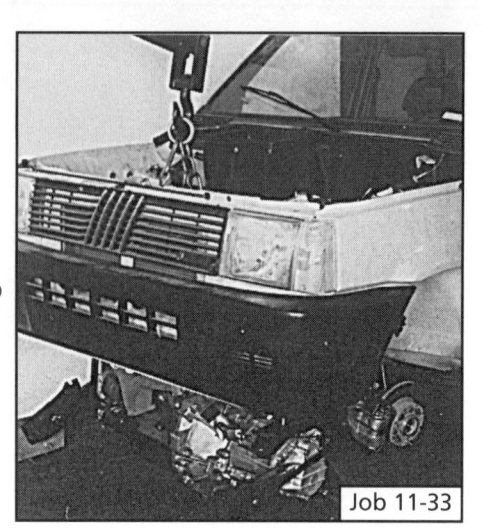

Job 11-33

☐ **Step 34:** Taking great care not to disturb the propped body, pull the power/transmission assembly clear.

Job 11-34

4x4 MODELS ONLY

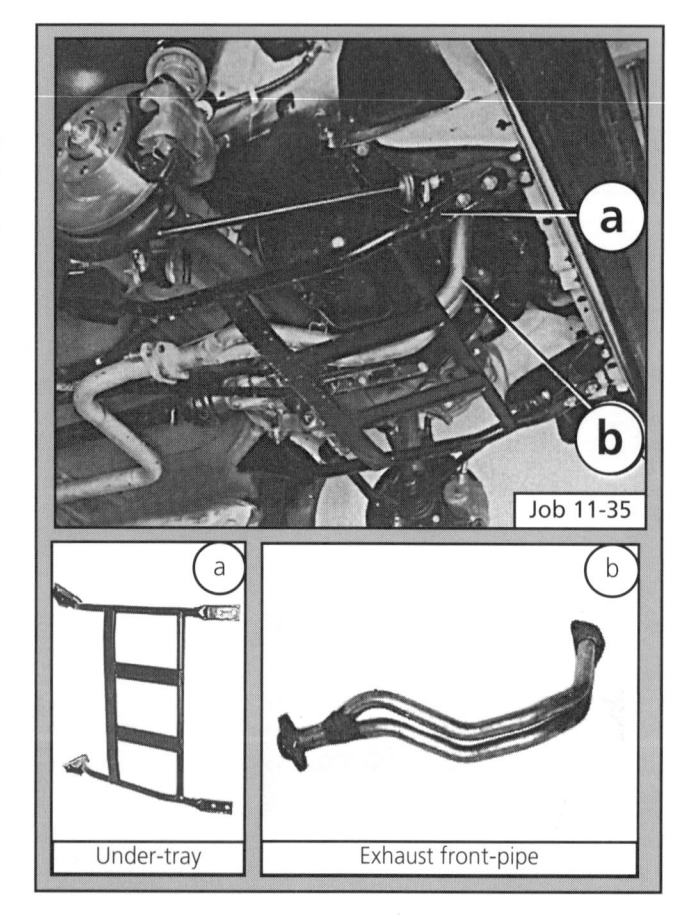

Job 11-35

Under-tray | Exhaust front-pipe

☐ **Step 35:** The removal and refitting of the power unit for the Panda 4x4 version is the same as that of the other versions illustrated in **Steps 1 to 32** with the exception of the components shown here in **Jobs 11-35** and **11-36**.

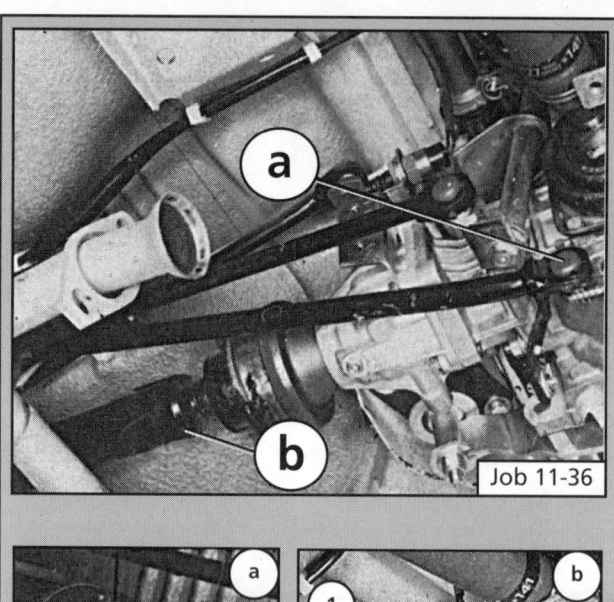

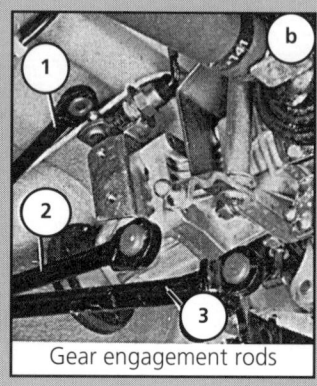

Job 11-36

Rear propshaft joint | Gear engagement rods

Key for picture b

1 - Rear transmission engagement rod

2 - Gear engagement control rod

3 - Gear selector control rod

☐ **Step 36:** Take note of the rear propshaft (**a**) and gear engagement controls (**b**) to be disconnected on 4x4 models.

Job 12. OHV engine - removal upwards.

OHV ENGINES ONLY: OHC 'FIRE' engines can ONLY be removed downwards. See **Job 11**.

☐ **Step 1:** Carry out **Steps 1 to 21** in **Job 11, Removal downwards**.

☐ **Step 2:** Remove the front roadwheels.

☐ **Step 3:** From under the car, unbolt the bottom mounting arm from the transmission and exhaust pipe. Unbolt the flexible mounting.

☐ **Step 4:** Unbolt the brake calipers and release the hose ties. Tie calipers clear.

❑ **Step 5:** Using a balljoint splitter, disconnect the tie rod ends from the steering arms and the track control arm lower balljoints from the hub carriers.

❑ **Step 6:** Unscrew the gaiter-to-transmission retaining bolts. Some oil loss will occur.

❑ **Step 7:** Disconnect the radius rods from the track control arms.

❑ **Step 8:** Pull the hub carriers outwards while a helper supports the driveshafts, then tie them up.

❑ **Step 9:** Remove the radiator. See **PART C: COOLING SYSTEM, Job 3**.

❑ **Step 10:** Attach the lifting gear to the engine and take the weight. Disconnect the mountings.

❑ **Step 11:** Lift the complete unit up and out of the engine bay.

Job 13. Engine, all types - refitting.

Refitting is the reversal of whichever method was chosen for removal, but these tips might help.

making it easy! • **Step 1:** When lowering from above, the power unit should be at a steep angle so that the transmission will pass under the left hand side member and allow the sump to clear the right hand engine mounting.

❑ **Step 2:** Wait until the car's weight is on its wheels and the lifting gear removed, then tighten the engine mounting and also tighten the front suspension bolts to their specified torque. See **Chapter 3, Facts and Figures**.

❑ **Step 3:** Fill the cooling system with the correct **FL Paraflu** anti-freeze solution. See **Chapter 3, Facts and Figures**.

❑ **Step 4:** Fill the engine with the correct grade and quantity of **FL** engine oil. See **Chapter 3, Facts and Figures**.

❑ **Step 5:** Replace any lost transmission oil.

❑ **Step 6:** Reconnect the battery.

❑ **Step 7:** Adjust the clutch pedal. See **Chapter 5, Servicing Your Car, Job 23**.

Job 14. Engine mountings - replacement.

IMPORTANT NOTE: There are several different types of engine mounting in use. All are self-explanatory and the commonest are shown here.

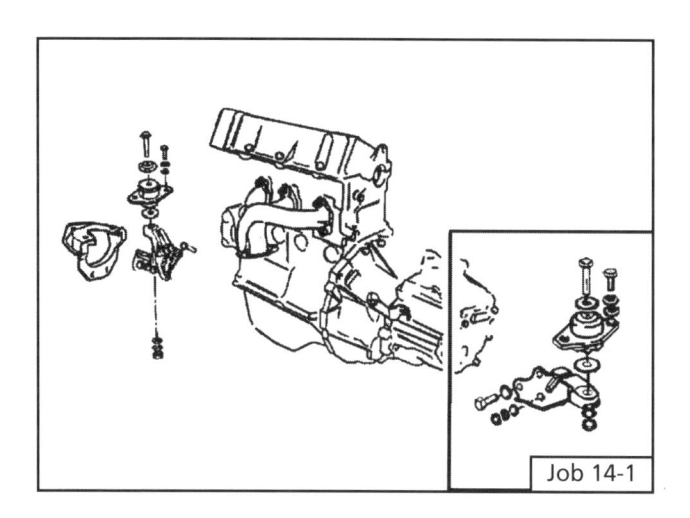

Job 14-1

❑ **Step 1:** Familiarise yourself with the engine and gearbox mounting layout.

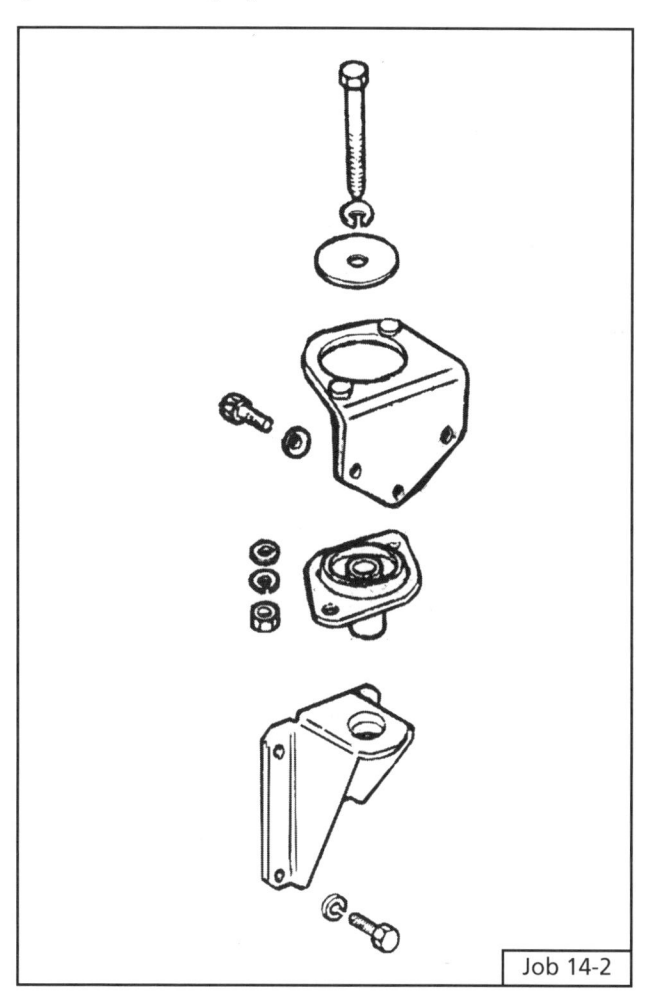

Job 14-2

❑ **Step 2:** This is a common layout of the engine's front mountings.

CHAPTER 6 PART A: ENGINE

93

CHAPTER 6 PART A: ENGINE

❑ **Step 3:** Support the engine/transmission underneath with a jack, or above with a hoist until the weight is just off the transmission-end mountings.

❑ **Step 4:** Remove the old and fit new mountings one at a time.

ℹ **INSIDE INFORMATION:** If you unbolt the whole of the rear mounting bracket, be sure to replace any bolts that pass into the gearbox casing, to prevent oil leakage. ℹ

❑ **Step 5:** Remove the engine support.

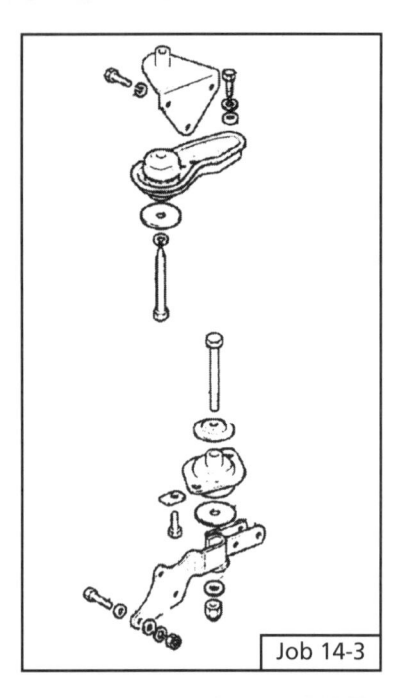

Job 14-3

Job 15: Engine/transmission - separation.

This Job assumes that the engine and transmission have been removed from the car, as described in earlier Jobs.

making it easy!
❑ **Step 1:** Before starting work, clean the unit with paraffin or proprietary engine cleaner.
• It's easier - and safer - to work in clean conditions!

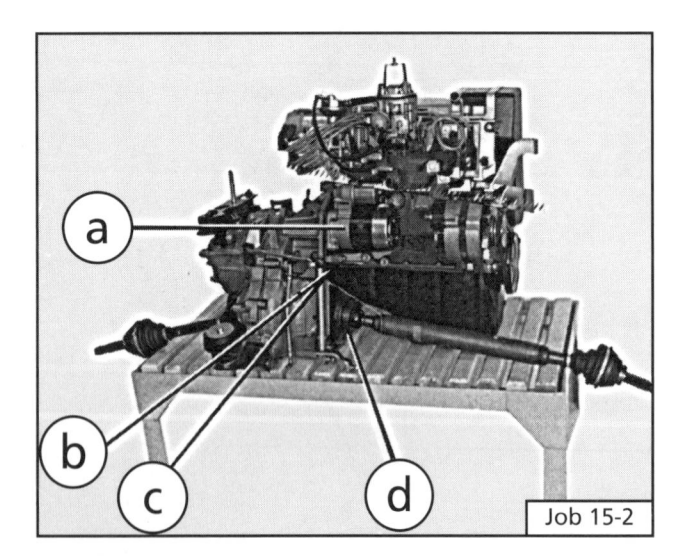

Job 15-2

❑ **Step 2:** These are the major components referred to in this and subsequent Steps. Remove the starter motor (a). See **PART E: ELECTRICAL AND INSTRUMENTS, Job 3.**

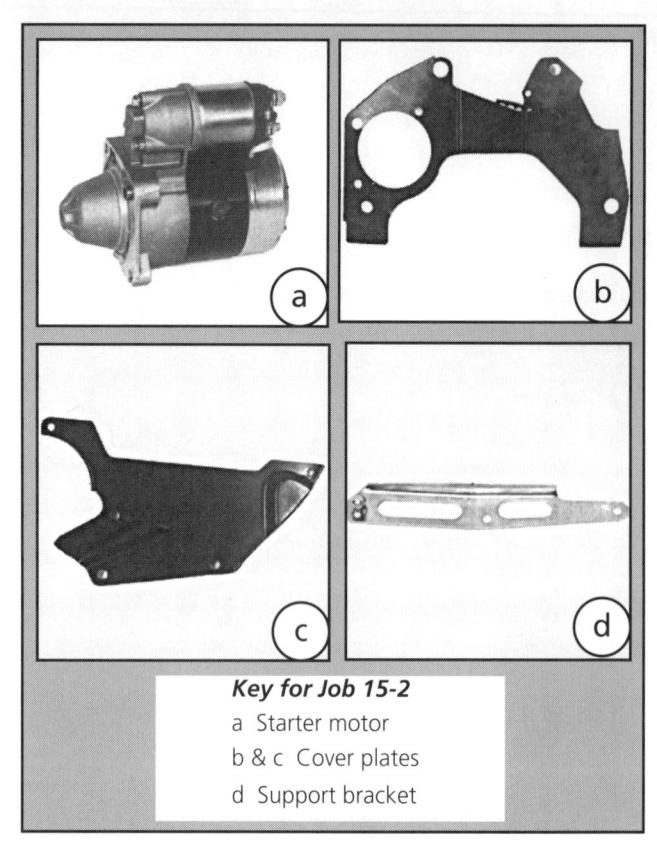

Key for Job 15-2
a Starter motor
b & c Cover plates
d Support bracket

❑ **Step 3:** Remove the cover plates from the flywheel housing (see **Job 15 -2, b** and **Job 15 -2, c**).

❑ **Step 4:** Remove the engine and transmission mounting brackets and the support bracket (**Job 15-2, d**).

❑ **Step 5:** Unscrew the flywheel housing to engine bolts, and, supporting its weight, withdraw the transmission in a straight line.

❑ **Step 6:** Make sure the positioning dowels are still secure in their holes.

Job 15-7

❑ **Step 7:** Disconnect the driveshafts if still attached to the transmission. See **PART B: TRANSMISSION AND CLUTCH, Job 5.**

Job 16: Engine/transmission - reconnection.

❑ **Step 1:** Offer the transmission to the engine, holding it in correct alignment. Engage the splined input shaft with the clutch driven plate. It should pass through easily provided that the splines are aligned and the driven plate is properly centred. See **PART B: TRANSMISSION AND CLUTCH, Job 3.**

❑ **Step 2:** Once the alignment dowels are properly locating the engine to the transmission, draw them together using two connecting bolts.

❑ **Step 3:** Fit the remaining bolts, at the same time locating the lifting eyes.

❑ **Step 4:** Refit the flywheel housing cover plate and mounting brackets.

❑ **Step 5:** Refit the starter motor.

Job 17: OHV Engine - dismantling.

❑ **Step 1:** Familiarise yourself with the major bottom-end engine components shown below in illustration **Job 17-1**.

❑ **Step 2:** Remove the water pump. See **PART C: COOLING SYSTEM, Job 1**.

❑ **Step 3:** Unbolt and remove the clutch from the flywheel.

❑ **Step 4:** Remove the cylinder head as described in **Job 1**.

❑ **Step 5:** Remove the dipstick and guide tube.

❑ **Step 6:** With the engine over on one side, unbolt and remove the sump.

❑ **Step 7:** Check the connecting rods (see **Step 1, part 6**) and their big end bearing caps to make sure that each is marked with matching numbers or punch marks, starting with No.1 at the timing cover end. Mark if necessary. Undo the big-end bolts and remove the caps, loosen them if stubborn with a soft faced mallet. Keep the caps in their original order.

❕ INSIDE INFORMATION: **Step 8:** Remove shell bearings by pressing on the side opposite the location slot in the connecting rod and cap. Keep them in their correct order if they are to be reused. ❕

❑ **Step 9:** Withdraw the piston/conrod assemblies from the tops of their bores, keeping them in order.

❑ **Step 10:** Position a block of wood inside the crankcase to stop crankshaft movement. Undo the crankshaft pulley nut and remove the pulley.

❑ **Step 11:** Remove the timing chain and sprockets. See **Job 8**.

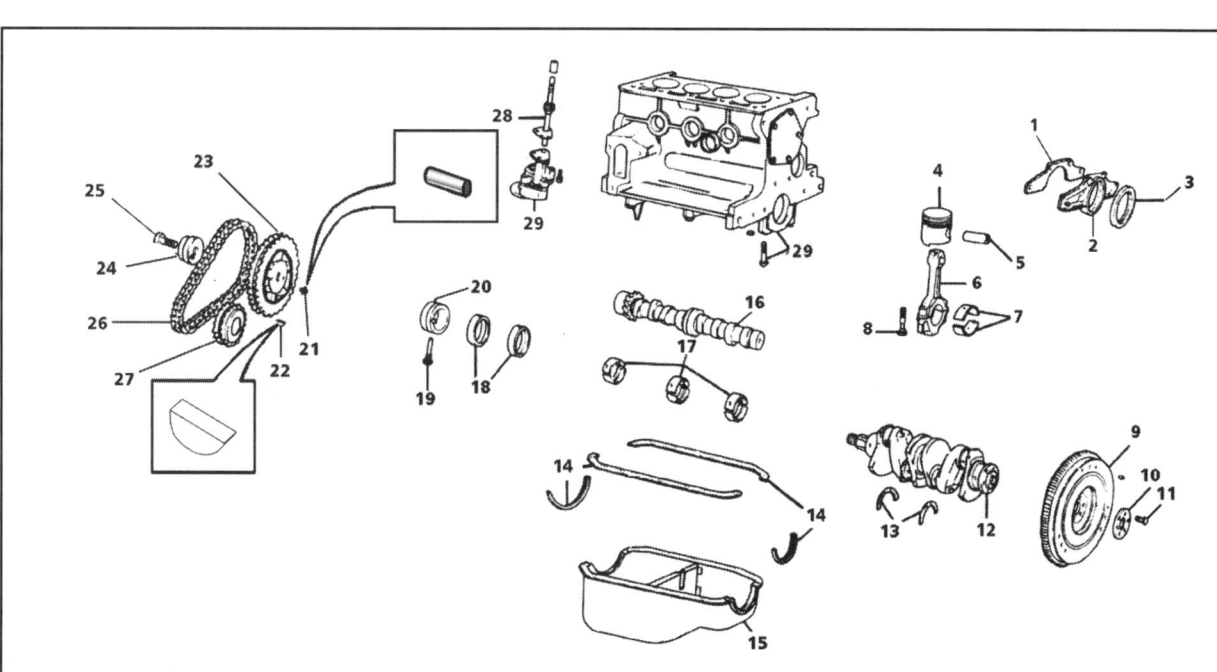

1 - core plug
2 - rear oil seal carrier
3 - rear oil seal
4 - piston
5 - gudgeon pin
6 - conrod
7 - big-end bearings
8 - big-end bolts
9 - flywheel
10 - washer
11 - fly wheel bolt
12 - crankshaft
13 - crankshaft thrust washers
14 - sump gaskets
15 - sump
16 - camshaft
17 - main (crankshaft) bearings
18 - camshaft bearings
19 - retaining bolt
20 - front camshaft bearing
21 - dowel
22 - woodruff key
23 - camshaft sprocket
24 - fuel pump cam
25 - cam sprocket bolt
26 - timing chain
27 - crankshaft sprocket
28 - oil pump driveshaft
29 - oil pump

Job 17-1

☐ **Step 12:** Unbolt the oil pump and remove.

☐ **Step 13:** Remove the locking screw from the camshaft front bearing and withdraw the camshaft. Take care that the cam lobes do not damage the bearings as the camshaft is pulled through.

☐ **Step 14:** Remove the cam followers, keeping them in their correct order.

☐ **Step 15:** Undo the securing bolts, remove the flywheel and the rear engine plate.

☐ **Step 16:** Stand the block in the upside down position, unbolt and remove the crankshaft rear oil seal carrier.

☐ **Step 17:** Make sure the main bearing caps are numbered and note which way round they are fitted, then undo their bolts and remove them. Keep the bearing shells with their caps and the centre thrust washers in their correct positions.

☐ **Step 18:** Lift the crankshaft away from the cylinder block and recover the other halves of the main bearing shells.

Job 18. OHV Engine - reassembly.

Checking for Wear

GENERAL
All parts must be thoroughly cleaned for inspection - still keeping them in the right order for reassembly in case they are to be re used. Check each component as follows:

CYLINDER BLOCK
Look for any cracks in the casting, particularly at bolt holes and between cylinders. Check the bores for score marks, caused by burned pistons or broken rings. Check for a wear ridge just below the top of the bore where the top piston ring ends its travel. If any of these defects are present in any of the cylinders, all should be rebored. Ask your FIAT agent or engine specialist to inspect and measure the bores for wear if you are unsure. It is sometimes possible to 'glaze bust' the bores and fit new piston rings, assuming the pistons to be in good condition. All of this work must be carried out by your FIAT agent, who will supply the pistons when reboring and who must also fit the pistons to your connecting rods as the gudgeon pins are a press fit into the connecting rod small ends - which have to be heated - not a DIY job.

CRANKSHAFT
Check all the mains journals and crankpins for any signs of wear ridges round the circumference or scoring of the surface. Check for ovality with a suitable micrometer, 0.025 mm being the maximum permissible. Check the shell bearings, they should have an even dull grey finish. If this has worn through to the copper coloured backing, or if the crankshaft has any of the previously mentioned faults, the crankshaft should be reground by your specialist who will also supply the new shell bearings and thrust washers.

CAMSHAFT
Check the bearings in the cylinder block and replace if there are excessive wear signs. Once installed, the centre and rear ones should be reamed out to size, your FIAT agent has a suitable tool. The front bearing is already reamed. Check each cam lobe for wear, this can be quite rapid once started. The cam followers should also be checked, particularly where they contact the cam lobe. If you are replacing the camshaft, fit new followers as well.

TIMING CHAIN AND SPROCKETS
The timing chain should be changed as a matter of course during a complete overhaul but check the sprockets for tooth wear at the same time and renew as necessary.

i **INSIDE INFORMATION:** If your timing chain is one of the self tensioning type (early engines), fit the later type with a separate tensioner. See **Job 13**. *i*

CYLINDER HEAD. See **Job 3**.

ROCKER SHAFT AND ROCKERS.
i **INSIDE INFORMATION:** Check the shaft for wear at the rocker pivot points. Check the rocker bushes for wear by positioning the rockers on a 'new' part of the shaft and rocking sideways. *i*

Check the rocker ends where they contact the valve stem for damage to the case hardening. Check the adjusting screw ball and thread. Check the pushrods for straightness and the ball and socket for wear.

OIL PUMP
Unscrew the four bolts holding the two parts of the pump body together. Wash all the parts in paraffin and dry them. Check the gear teeth for wear, visually and by rocking the gears together. By using a feeler gauge, check that the clearance between the gear teeth and the pump body does not exceed 0.14 mm. And with a straight edge across the top of the body, check that the gear end float does not exceed 0.105 mm. If either is the case, fit a new pump.

Engine Reassembly

PART A - CRANKSHAFT

☐ **Step A1:** Make sure the bearing seats in the block are perfectly clean and locate the main bearing shells so that their tabs engage with the slots.

☐ **Step A2:** Apply some grease to the smooth side of the thrust washers (see *Job 17-1, part 13*) and stick them in position either side of the centre main bearing.

☐ **Step A3:** Oil the shells liberally with fresh engine oil and lower the crankshaft into position.

☐ **Step A4:** Fit the remaining halves of the shells into the bearing caps and position the remaining halves of the thrust washers on either side of the centre main cap with grease.

☐ **Step A5:** Oil the crank journals and position the caps the right way round and in the correct order.

☐ **Step A6:** Screw the bolts in finger tight and check that the crankshaft rotates freely and smoothly.

☐ **Step A7:** Tighten the bolts evenly and progressively until the specified torque setting is reached. See *Chapter 3, Facts and Figures.* Check again that the crankshaft rotates smoothly.

☐ **Step A8:** Check the crankshaft end float by using a feeler gauge between the thrust washer and the crankshaft. Thicker washers are available if required. See *Chapter 3, Facts and Figures.*

☐ **Step A9:** Fit the rear oil seal carrier (with its new seal), using a new gasket. Lubricate the seal with fresh engine oil.

☐ **Step A10:** Fit the rear engine plate.

i **Step A11:** INSIDE INFORMATION: Check the flywheel for score marks or micro cracking on the clutch contact surface. Deep score marks or cracking would be too much to machine out, making a new flywheel necessary. *i*

Position numbers 1 and 4 big-end crankpins at TDC, then fit the flywheel with the TDC mark facing upwards. Tighten the bolts to their specified torque. See *Chapter 3, Facts and Figures.*

PART B - CAMSHAFT

☐ **Step B1:** Oil the cam followers and refit in their original positions.

☐ **Step B2:** Oil the camshaft bearings (see *Job 17-1, parts 18* and *20*) and install with care, avoiding damage to the bearings by the cam lobes.

☐ **Step B3:** Fit the front bearing (see *Job 17-1, part 18*), chamfer first, and secure with the locking bolt. Lubricate the cam lobes.

PART C - OIL PUMP

☐ **Step C1:** Position the gasket on the crankcase mounting.

☐ **Step C2:** Locate the driveshaft in the pump and offer the assembly to the crankcase allowing the driveshaft and camshaft gears to mesh. Fit the mounting bolts.

☐ **Step C3:** Fit the oil return pipe.

i INSIDE INFORMATION: The sump cannot be fitted until the timing cover is in place and the pistons and connecting rods fitted. *i*

PART D - TIMING CHAIN AND SPROCKETS

See *Job 13.*

PART E - PISTON/CONNECTING ROD ASSEMBLIES.

IMPORTANT NOTE: The pistons and connecting rods are to be fitted as assemblies. Their dismantling and reassembly is a job for your FIAT agent - not a DIY job.

☐ **Step E1:** Make sure the bores and pistons are clean. Position the piston ring gaps at equal intervals round the pistons circumference and lubricate well. Make sure the rings are fitted with the word TOP upwards.

☐ **Step E2:** Locate the upper half of the big-end shell bearing in the conrod, making sure that the mating surfaces are clean.

☐ **Step E3:** Locate a ring clamp over the piston rings and tighten enough to close the ring gaps, but not too tight! Lubricate the rings so that they can slide in the ring clamp more easily.

❏ **Step E4:** Position the assembly in its correct bore with the piston arrow pointing towards the timing cover and the connecting rod number facing away from the camshaft.

Job 18-E5

❏ **Step E5:** With the ring clamp touching the cylinder block, use a hammer shaft to gently tap the piston through and into the bore.

❏ **Step E6:** Lubricate the crankpin and the big-end shell and draw the conrod down the bore so that the big-end locates with the crankpin.

❏ **Step E7:** Fit the other half of the big-end shell to the bearing cap and lubricate. Offer the cap to the connecting rod and make sure that the numbers match. Screw in the fixing bolts and tighten progressively to the correct torque. See **Chapter 3, Facts and Figures.**

❏ **Step E8:** Fit the remaining piston/conrod assemblies.

❏ **Step E9:** Prepare the sump for refitting by positioning the cork strips (see **Job 17-14**) in each end and trimming them just proud of the flange.

❏ **Step E10:** Position the side gaskets and apply gasket cement where they contact the cork strips.

❏ **Step E11:** Position the sump and screw in the bolts and nuts. Tighten progressively. Check that the drain plug is tight.

PART F - CYLINDER HEAD
❏ **Step F1:** Stand the engine on its sump and fit the cylinder head. See **PART A: ENGINE, Job 2, Steps 2 to 8.**

PART G - ANCILLARY COMPONENTS
❏ **Step G1:** Refit the exhaust manifold and ducting, the alternator and the thermostat housing.

❏ **Step G2:** Refit the distributor. See **PART D: IGNITION.**

❏ **Step G3:** Refit the carburettor and the air cleaner. See **PART F: FUEL AND EXHAUST SYSTEMS.**

❏ **Step G4:** Fit a new oil filter.

❏ **Step G5:** Refit the coolant pump - check for play in the bearings and for any sign of leaking.

❏ **Step G6:** Refit the dipstick tube.

❏ **Step G7:** Fit the clutch. See **PART B: TRANSMISSION AND CLUTCH, Job 4.**

PART H - INSTALLATION AND INITIAL START-UP
❏ **Step H1:** Reconnect the engine to the transmission. See **Job 20.**

❏ **Step H2:** Refit the complete unit to the car. See **Job 16.**

i **Step H3:** INSIDE INFORMATION: Before fitting the spark plugs and with a fully charged battery, turn the engine on the starter until the oil warning light goes out.

This primes the lubrication system and gives more immediate oil pressure on initial start up after overhaul - a critical time in the life of an engine. *i*

❏ **Step H4:** Fit the spark plugs and speed up the slow running adjustment screw by a complete turn before starting the engine.

❏ **Step H5:** Allow the engine to warm up on fast idle until it reaches working temperature and then slow it down to its normal speed.

❏ **Step H6:** Stop the engine and allow it to cool, check the oil and coolant levels and look for any leaks.

❏ **Step H7:** Avoid over-revving or over-loading the engine during its settling down period of 600 miles, then retighten the head as follows: Using the correct sequence, slacken each head bolt by one quarter of a turn and immediately retighten it to the specified torque. Adjust the tappets. See **Chapter 3, Facts and Figures.**

IMPORTANT NOTE: Some FIAT cylinder head gaskets do not need re-torquing after a bedding-down interval. Check with your supplier.

Job 19. OHC Engine - dismantling.

❑ **Step 1:** Familiarise yourself with the layout of the FIRE engine components, shown below.

❑ **Step 2:** Remove the cylinder head. See **Job 4**. Remove the distributor. See **PART D: IGNITION, Job 1**. Remove the thermostat housing.

❑ **Step 3:** Remove the distribution pipe from the coolant pump and remove the pump. Discard the oil filter.

❑ **Step 4:** Remove the fuel pump (when a mechanical pump is fitted), its spacer block and pushrod. See **PART F: FUEL AND EXHAUST SYSTEMS, Job 5**.

❑ **Step 5:** Remove the alternator and drive belt.

❑ **Step 6:** Lock the flywheel and undo the crankshaft nut, and remove the crank pulley.

❑ **Step 7:** Remove the clutch and then the flywheel.

❑ **Step 8:** Unbolt and remove the sump.

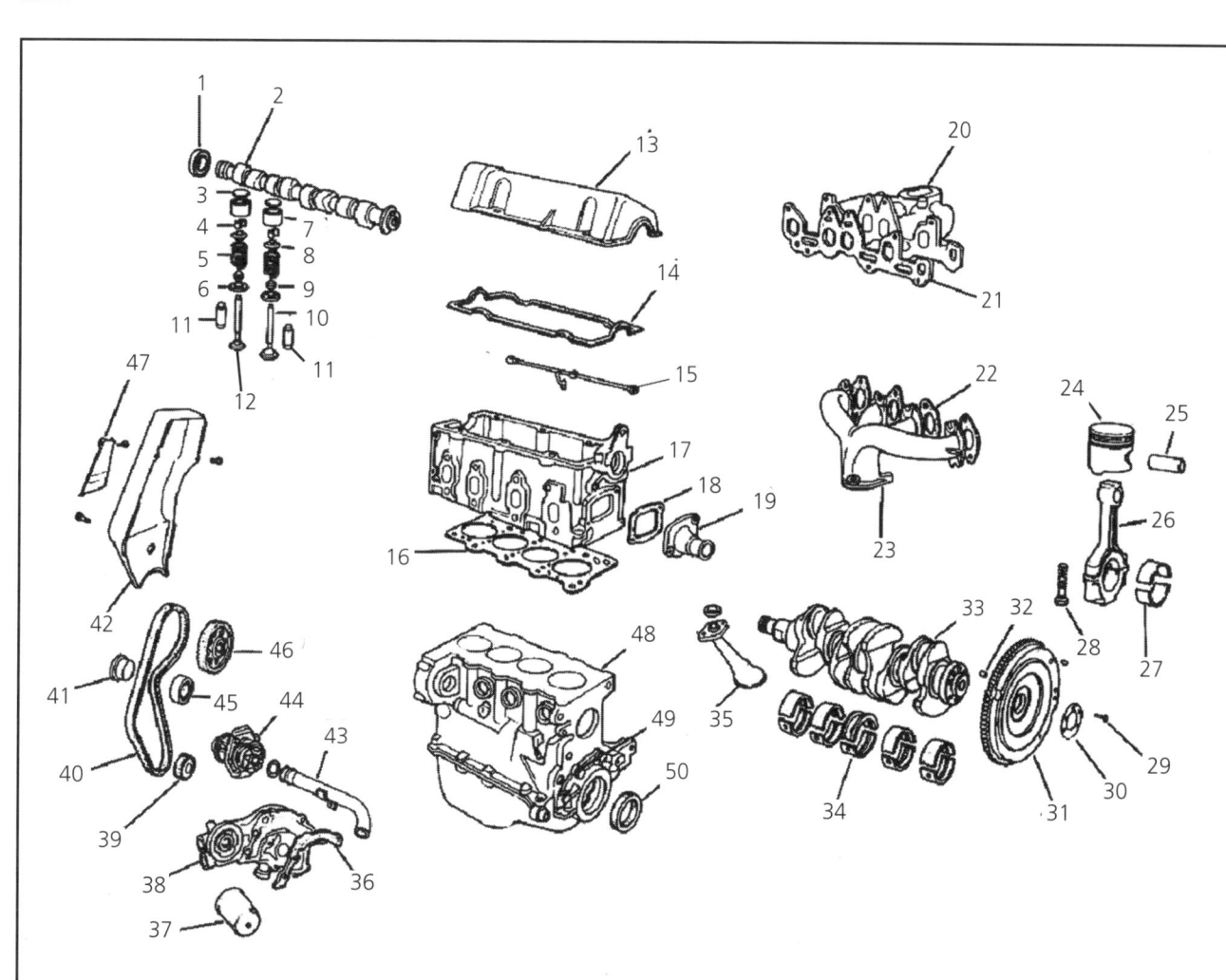

1 - oil seal
2 - camshaft
3 - shim
4 - collets
5 - valve spring
6 - bottom spring cap
7 - tappet
8 - top spring cap
9 - oil seal
10 - inlet valve
11 - valve guides
12 - exhaust valve
13 - camshaft cover
14 - camshaft cover gasket
15 - oil pipe
16 - cylinder head gasket
17 - cylinder head

18 - thermostat gasket
19 - thermostat/housing
20 - inlet manifold
21 - gasket
22 - gasket
23 - exhaust manifold
24 - piston
25 - gudgeon pin
26 - conrod assembly
27 - big-end bearing shells
28 - conrod bolt
29 - bolt
30 - washer
31 - flywheel
32 - dowel
33 - crankshaft
34 - crankshaft bearings

35 - oil pump pick-up
36 - gasket
37 - oil filter
38 - oil pump
39 - crankshaft pulley
40 - camshaft belt
41 - hub
42 - camshaft belt cover
43 - coolant pipe
44 - coolant pump
45 - cambelt tensioner
46 - camshaft pulley
47 - rear cover
48 - cylinder block
49 - oil seal housing
50 - oil seal

Job 19-1

CHAPTER 6 PART A: ENGINE

99

CHAPTER 6 — PART A: ENGINE

☐ **Step 9:** Remove the oil pump and pickup assembly.

☐ **Step 10:** Remove the engine back plate and timing index plate.

☐ **Step 11:** Lay the engine on its side and undo the big-end bolts.

☐ **Step 12:** Remove the bearing caps and half shells and keep them in order.

ℹ **INSIDE INFORMATION:** Make sure the caps have numbers matching those on their mating conrods. It is essential they are kept together. ℹ

☐ **Step 13:** Withdraw the piston/conrod assemblies upwards from their bores and keep them in the order they were fitted in.

☐ **Step 14:** Turn the cylinder block upside down and remove the rear crankshaft seal and carrier.

☐ **Step 15:** Undo the main bearing cap bolts and remove the caps. They are numbered from the front (timing belt end) - centre one identified by the letter 'C'.

☐ **Step 16:** Lift out the crankshaft and retrieve the bearing shells and thrusts, keeping them in order in case they are re-used.

Job 20. OHC Engine - reassembly.

Checking for Wear

GENERAL
As the checks carried out on the cylinder block and crankshaft are common to most engines, read **Job 18, Checking For Wear.** If the oil pressure is suspect, it is best to change the pump as servicing is restricted to washing out the pump, checking the relief valve and changing the seal.

Engine Reassembly

PART A - CRANKSHAFT

☐ **Step A1:** Make sure the bearing seats in the block are perfectly clean and locate the main bearing shells so that their tabs engage with the slots.

☐ **Step A2:** Position the thrust washers either side of the centre web - held in place by the bearing shell. Then carry out **Steps A3** to **A8** of **Job 18, PART A.**

☐ **Step A3:** Fit the rear oil seal carrier (with its new seal - see **Job 19-1, parts 1, 12** and **13**), using RTV instant silicone gasket. Lubricate the 'bearing' surfaces of the oil seal with fresh engine oil.

PART B - PISTON/CONNECTING ROD ASSEMBLIES
Refer to **Job 18, PART E** and carry out **Steps E1** to **E3**, noting that the arrow on the piston crown must point to the camshaft drivebelt end. Continue with **Steps E5** to **E8**.

PART C - COMPLETE THE REASSEMBLY

☐ **Step C1:** Fit a new seal to the oil pump and fit the pump, using a new gasket.

☐ **Step C2:** Fit the pump pickup/ filter assembly using a new sealing washer.

☐ **Step C3:** Fit the engine backplate and fit the flywheel. Use a locking fluid on the flywheel bolts and tighten them to their correct torque. See **Chapter 3, Facts and Figures.**

☐ **Step C4:** Refit the sump using a smear of RTV silicone on the gasket and refit the flywheel housing cover plate.

☐ **Step C5:** Fit the crankshaft sprocket, locating it on its integral key. Tighten the securing bolt to its specified torque. See **Chapter 3, Facts and Figures.**

☐ **Step C6:** Fit the new clutch, see **PART B: TRANSMISSION AND CLUTCH, Job 3. Clutch Replacement.**

☐ **Step C7:** Refit the cylinder head. See **PART A: ENGINE, Job 5.**

☐ **Step C8:** Refit the coolant pump using RTV silicone gasket.

☐ **Step C9:** Refit the timing belt rear cover. Refit the tensioner and lock it away from the tensioned position.

☐ **Step C10:** Fit the new timing belt. See **Job 10.**

☐ **Step C11:** Refit the crankshaft pulley.

☐ **Step C12:** Refit the alternator and new drive belt.

☐ **Step C13:** Refit the oil dipstick.

☐ **Step C14:** Refit the fuel pump and pushrod, using a new gasket on each side of the spacer block.

☐ **Step C15:** Refit the thermostat housing, using a new gasket.

☐ **Step C16:** Using a new seal, fit the coolant pipe to the back of the coolant pump.

☐ **Step C17:** Lubricate the sealing ring and screw on a new oil filter cartridge.

☐ **Step C18:** Follow **Job 18, PART H - INSTALLATION AND INITIAL START-UP** to complete the installation and initial start up.

PART B: TRANSMISSION AND CLUTCH

PART B: Contents

Job 1. Transmission - removal (with engine in car).
Job 2. Transmission - refitting (with engine in car).
Job 3. Clutch - replacement.
Job 4. Clutch cable - replacement.
Job 5. Driveshaft - removal.
Job 6. Driveshaft - refitting.
Job 7. Inner 'c.v.' (spider) joint - replacement.
Job 8. Outer driveshaft constant velocity joint - replacement.
Job 9. Front hub/bearings - replacement.
Job 10. 4x4 Propshaft universal joint replacement.
Job 11. 4x4 Propshaft c.v. joint - replacement.

Job 1. Transmission - removal (with engine in car).

Refer to the illustrations in **PART A: ENGINE, Jobs 11, 12 and 13** in connection with this Job.

IMPORTANT NOTE: If you intend fully removing the driveshaft (see **Step 15**), slacken the hub nut before raising the car. See **Job 9**.

❏ **Step 1:** Drain the transmission oil.

❏ **Step 2:** Remove the spare wheel and disconnect the battery.

❏ **Step 3:** Disconnect the reverse light leads and the speedometer drive from the transmission.

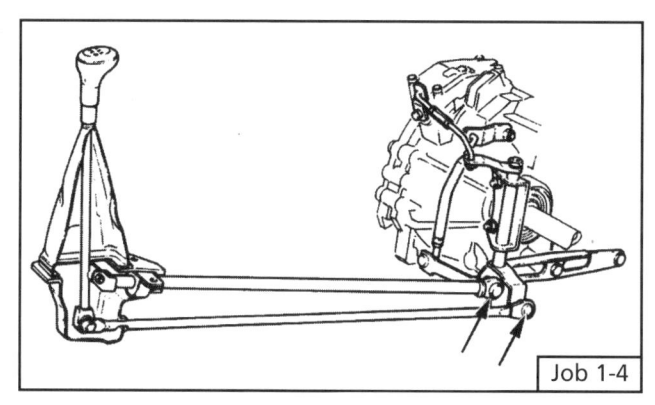

❏ **Step 4:** Disconnect the gearchange linkage by levering off the linkrod ball ends and spring clips (arrowed).

❏ **Step 5:** While underneath, unbolt the bottom mounting arm from the exhaust pipe and transmission. Unbolt the flexible mounting.

❏ **Step 6:** Disconnect the exhaust from its manifold.

❏ **Step 7:** Disconnect the starter and remove it.

❏ **Step 8:** Support the car in the raised position and remove the road wheels.

❏ **Step 10:** Unbolt the brake calipers and tie clear.

❏ **Step 11:** Undo the nuts on the track control arm balljoints and tie rod ends and part them with a suitable splitter. Disconnect the radius rods from the control arms. See **PART G: STEERING AND SUSPENSION**.

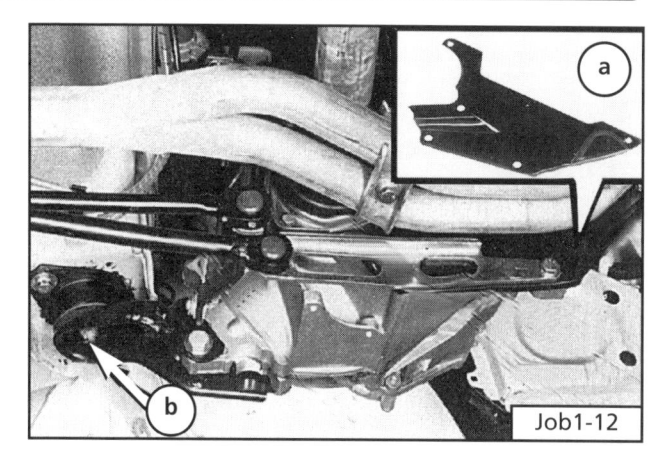

❏ **Step 12:** Remove the five bolts securing the flywheel housing cover plate (**a**).

i INSIDE INFORMATION: Don't forget the bolt high up by the driveshaft. *i*

❏ **Step 13:** Disconnect the clutch cable from the lever on the transmission.

❏ **Step 14:** Unscrew the gaiter retaining bolts on the inboard ends of the driveshafts.

❏ **Step 15:** Free the brake flexible hoses from their retainers on the suspension struts. Pull the hub carriers outwards to free the driveshafts from the transmission. Catch the oil spill! (Alternatively, remove the driveshaft from the hub.) See **Job 5**.

❏ **Step 16:** Take the weight of the engine on a version of FIAT's engine support, positioned above the car, or carefully take the weight on a jack or hoist.

CHAPTER 6 PART B: TRANSMISSION

101

❏ **Step 17:** Unscrew the flywheel housing to engine bolts.

❏ **Step 18:** Support the transmission with a trolley jack and undo the transmission mounting (illustration *Job 1-12*, position *b*).

❏ **Step 19:** Once you are sure that nothing remains connected, the transmission can be removed.

❏ **Step 20:** With a helper operating the trolley jack, carefully pull the transmission from the engine and lower to the ground.

Job 2. Transmission - refitting (with engine in car).

IMPORTANT NOTE: Refer to the illustration in **PART A: ENGINE, Jobs 11, 12 and 13** in connection with this Job.

❏ **Step 1:** Refitting is the reverse of removal. Before starting, make sure that the clutch driven plate is still centralised. See *Job 3*.

❏ **Step 2:** Fill the transmission with the correct grade of new FL oil. See **Chapter 3, Facts and Figures.**

❏ **Step 3:** Check the clutch adjustment. See **Chapter 5, Servicing Your Car, Job 23.**

❏ **Step 4:** When the brake calipers have been refitted, pump the brake pedal until its normal solid feel is restored.

❏ **Step 5:** Use a self-grip wrench to reconnect the gear rod balls and sockets. Use new driveshaft nuts, tightened to the correct torque and staked into the shaft grooves with a punch. See *Jobs 5* and *6*.

Job 3. Clutch - replacement.

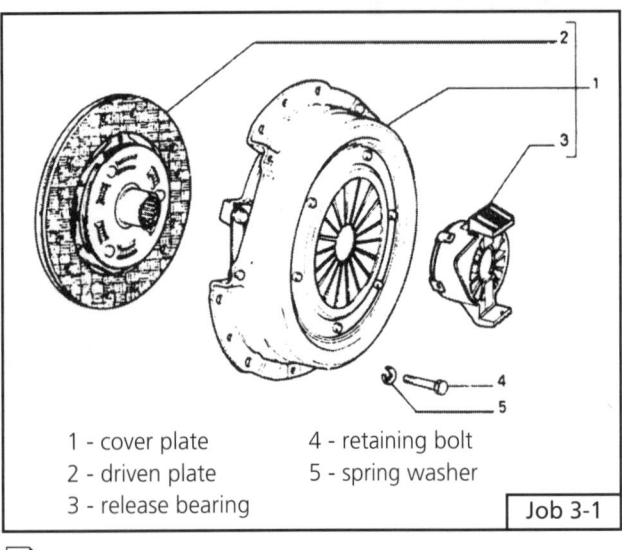

1 - cover plate
2 - driven plate
3 - release bearing
4 - retaining bolt
5 - spring washer
Job 3-1

❏ **Step 1:** The first three numbers are the parts you will need to obtain, from your FIAT dealership.

FACT FILE:
● We strongly recommended that all three main components: clutch cover, driven plate and release bearing are replaced after a high mileage, ensuring longer life and smoother operation.
● If one is worn, they are all likely to be, so save yourself another big stripdown in the near future!

❏ **Step 2:** Remove the transmission. See **PART B: TRANSMISSION AND CLUTCH, Job 1.**

❏ **Step 3:** Unscrew the clutch cover bolts (see *Job 3-1, part 4*) progressively until the spring pressure is released, then remove the bolts.

❏ **Step 4:** Ease the cover off its dowels and catch the driven plate as it falls.

❏ **Step 5:**
INSIDE INFORMATION: Check the inside of the clutch bell housing for contamination by oil. This indicates a leak from either the crankshaft rear seal or the gearbox input shaft seal (illustrated). A faulty seal should be replaced without delay. Oil can cause judder and slip. Here, the seal (inset) is being replaced. See **PART A: ENGINE, Job 19** for the position of the rear crankshaft seal.

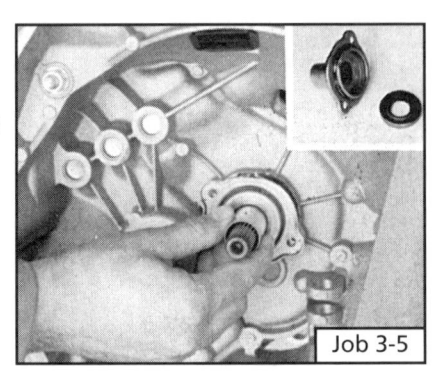

❏ **Step 6:** Check the surface of the flywheel that mates with the clutch, for scoring, or significant micro cracking caused by excessive heat generated by clutch slip. Replace the flywheel if in doubt.

❏ **Step 7:**
Check the release fork pivot, inside the bellhousing, for wear. Replace the bushes (inset) if necessary, lubricating with a small quantity of molybdenum disulphide grease.

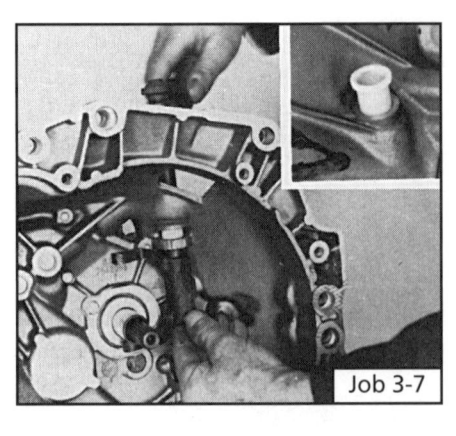

❏ **Step 8:** Clean oil or the protective film from the clutch cover and flywheel faces.

❏ **Step 9:** Offer the driven plate to the flywheel with the side having the greatest hub projection facing outwards.

☐ **Step 10:** Locate the clutch cover on the flywheel dowels and screw in the fixing bolts finger tight.

☐ **Step 11:** Use an aligning tool to make sure that the clutch is centralised, otherwise the gearbox will not relocate on the engine and damage can be caused to the centre plate.

i INSIDE INFORMATION: There is no spigot bush or bearing in the crankshaft end, but there is an indentation which you can 'feel' with a normal clutch alignment tool allowing you to centralise the driven plate between the clutch cover release fingers. *i*

☐ **Step 12:** Tighten the cover bolts evenly to the correct torque. See **Chapter 3, Facts and Figures.**

☐ **Step 13:** Smear a little 'copper' grease on the release bearing guide and the gearbox input shaft.

☐ **Step 14:** Refit the transmission. See **Job 2.**

Job 4. Clutch cable - replacement.

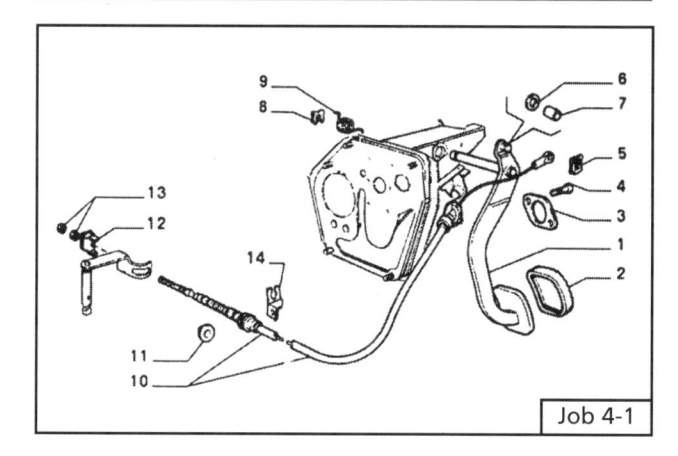

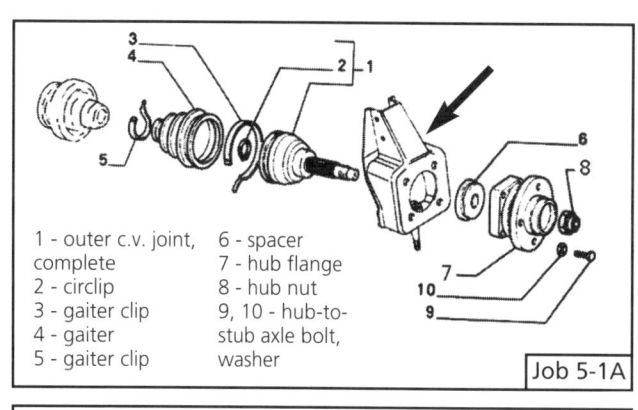

1 - outer c.v. joint, complete
2 - circlip
3 - gaiter clip
4 - gaiter
5 - gaiter clip
6 - spacer
7 - hub flange
8 - hub nut
9, 10 - hub-to-stub axle bolt, washer

Job 5-1A

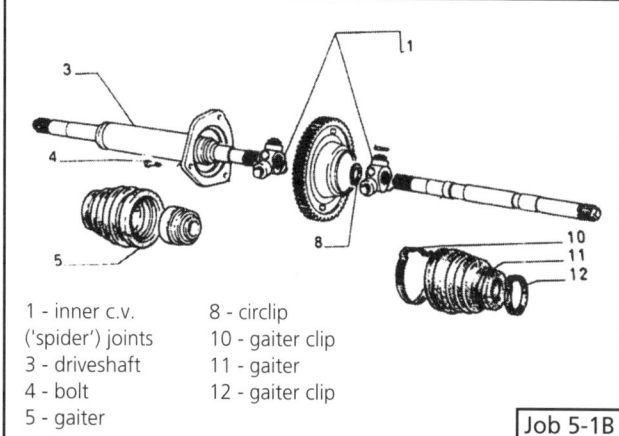

1 - inner c.v. ('spider') joints
3 - driveshaft
4 - bolt
5 - gaiter
8 - circlip
10 - gaiter clip
11 - gaiter
12 - gaiter clip

Job 5-1B

☐ **Step 1B:** ...and this, between the inner c.v. joint and the driveshafts and differential.

☐ **Step 2:** Slacken the driveshaft nut (see **Job 5, Step 1A, part 8**) using a long bar - it is very tight. A helper may need to apply the foot brake very firmly.

☐ **Step 3:** Raise the car on the side to be worked on and support it securely. Remove the road wheel.

☐ **Step 4:** Unbolt the brake caliper and tie clear, not putting any strain on the flexible hose. See **PART H: BRAKES.**

☐ **Step 5:** Disconnect the tie rod end from the steering arm using a balljoint splitter. See **PART G: STEERING AND SUSPENSION.**

☐ **Step 6:** Remove the driveshaft nut and washer.

☐ **Step 7:** Place a suitable container under the inboard end of the driveshaft and unscrew the bolts (see illustration, **Job 7-1B, part 4**) holding the gaiter retainer in place. Pull the gaiter (see **Job 5-1B, part 5**) back and allow the oil to drain.

☐ **Step 1:** From under the bonnet, slacken the cable adjusting nut. Disconnect the cable from the release lever and outer cable bracket.

☐ **Step 2:** From inside the car. Disconnect the cable from the foot pedal by removing the securing clip (see **Job 4-1, part 5**) and pulling the cable end off its pivot.

☐ **Step 3:** Unbolt the forked cable retaining plate from the bulkhead. Pull the cable out from inside the car.

☐ **Step 4:** Fit the new cable in the reverse order and adjust. See **Chapter 5, Servicing Your Car, Job 23.**

Job 5. Driveshaft - removal.

☐ **Step 1A:** This drawing shows the relationship between the outer constant velocity (c.v.) joint and the hub and stub axle assembly...

☐ **Step 8:** Unscrew the bolts securing the hub carrier (**Job 5-1A,** arrowed) to the clamp at the base of the suspension strut.

☐ **Step 9:** Use a splitter tool to disconnect the suspension balljoint below the hub carrier. Disconnect the radius rod from the track control arm.

☐ **Step 10:** Pull the stub axle carrier outwards, allowing the inboard end of the driveshaft to part from the transmission. Remove the entire assembly, complete with hub.

CHAPTER 6 PART B: TRANSMISSION

103

❑ **Step 11:** Push the splined outboard end of the driveshaft (see **Job 5-1A, part 2**) through the hub. If stiff, use a three legged puller.

Job 6. Driveshaft - refitting.

❑ **Step 1:** Refit in the reverse order, tightening all nuts and bolts to their correct torque. See **Chapter 3, Facts and Figures.** If you don't have a suitably large torque wrench for the driveshaft end nut, use a socket with a long bar (at least 450 mm - 18 in.) to tighten fully. Stake the nut into the groove with a punch. Drive straight to your nearest FIAT dealer or specialist and have the torque/tightness of this nut checked before using the car.

❑ **Step 2:** Fit the road wheel and replace the lost transmission oil.

Job 7. Inner 'c.v.' (spider) joint - replacement.

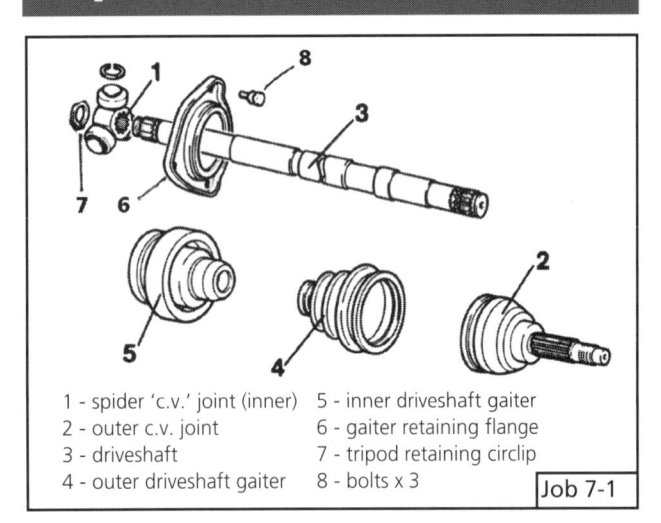

1 - spider 'c.v.' joint (inner)
2 - outer c.v. joint
3 - driveshaft
4 - outer driveshaft gaiter
5 - inner driveshaft gaiter
6 - gaiter retaining flange
7 - tripod retaining circlip
8 - bolts x 3

Job 7-1

❑ **Step 1:** Note the arrangement of the inner driveshaft components.

❑ **Step 2:** With the driveshaft removed from the car (see **Job 5**), remove the circlip and pull the spider from the driveshaft or press the shaft out.

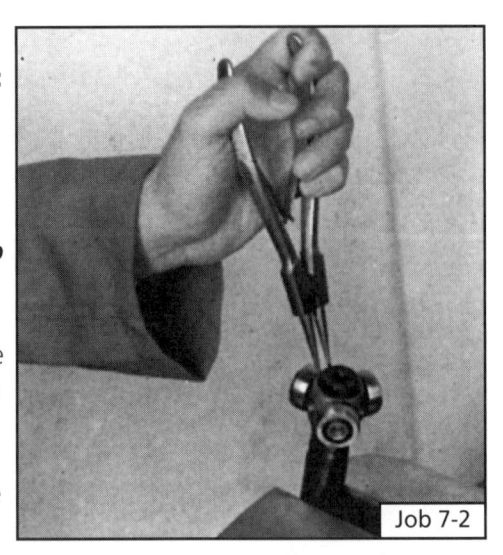

Job 7-2

❑ **Step 3:** Remove the inner gaiter and retainer flange from the driveshaft.

❑ **Step 4:** After obtaining a new spider, if necessary, (available as a complete replacement item from your FIAT dealership), fit the new gaiter and its retainer to the shaft, followed by the spider and circlip. No lubrication is required prior to refitting the driveshaft.

Job 8. Outer driveshaft constant velocity joint - replacement.

❑ **Step 1:** Refer to illustration **Job 5-1A**.

Job 8-2

Job 8-3

❑ **Step 2:** Remove the gaiter retaining clip ...

❑ **Step 3:** ...and pull the gaiter clear.

❑ **Step 4:** Remove the circlip and pull the shaft from the CV joint.

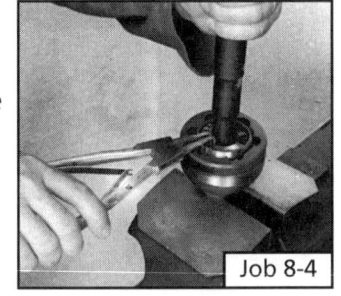

Job 8-4

❑ **Step 5:** Fit the new gaiter onto the shaft, followed by the new CV joint and circlip. Pack the joint with the grease supplied or with **FL Tutela MRM2** grease.

❑ **Step 6:** Pull the gaiter over the joint and secure with the retaining band. The driveshaft assembly is now ready for refitting.

Job 9. Front hub/bearings - replacement.

IMPORTANT NOTE: FIAT Panda hub bearings have a much longer service life because they are factory built into the hub. The bearing races cannot be replaced separately. Refer to drawing **Job 5-1A**.

❑ **Step 1:** While a helper applies the footbrake very firmly, (vehicle still on its wheels) slacken the driveshaft nut using a socket and long bar for extra leverage. Slacken the wheel nuts.

❑ **Step 2:** Jack up the appropriate side of the car and support with an axle stand. Remove the road wheel.

❑ **Step 3:** Release the brake hose from the suspension strut. Unbolt the brake caliper and tie clear, supporting its weight.

❏ **Step 4:** Disconnect the tie rod end from the steering arm using a balljoint splitter.

❏ **Step 5:** Remove the driveshaft nut and washer (see *Job 5-1A, part 8*).

❏ **Step 6:** Undo the bolts securing the hub carrier at the base of the suspension strut.

❏ **Step 7:** Using the splitter tool, disconnect the suspension balljoint below the hub carrier. Disconnect the radius rod.

❏ **Step 8:** Pull the hub carrier downwards and outwards, simultaneously pushing the driveshaft inwards, through the carrier. A three legged puller might be needed to move the shaft.

❏ **Step 9:** Unscrew the wheel alignment stud and brake disc fixing bolt. Remove the disc. Unbolt the hub/flange assembly.

❏ **Step 10:** The new bearings come with a new hub/flange as a complete assembly.

Job 9-10

❏ **Step 11:** Fit the hub assembly to the stub axle carrier - this one illustrated while off the car.

❏ **Step 12:** Refit the brake disc.

❏ **Step 13:** Push the hub carrier onto the driveshaft end and loosely fit the nut and washer.

Job 9-11

❏ **Step 14:** Refit the hub carrier to the base of the suspension strut and the suspension control arm balljoint.

❏ **Step 15:** Reconnect the tie rod end balljoint to the steering arm. Tighten the nut to the correct torque. See *Chapter 3, Facts and Figures.*

❏ **Step 16:** Refit the brake caliper. tightening the bolts to the correct torque. Reconnect the radius rod.

❏ **Step 17:** A helper's heavy right foot is again required on the brake pedal to allow you to fully tighten the driveshaft nut. See *Job 6, Step 1*. Stake the nut into the shaft groove with a punch.

❏ **Step 18:** Fit the roadwheel, lower the car to the ground - check the hub nut torque prior to replacing hub cap.

IMPORTANT NOTE: (For rear hubs see **PART G: STEERING AND SUSPENSION, Job 12**).

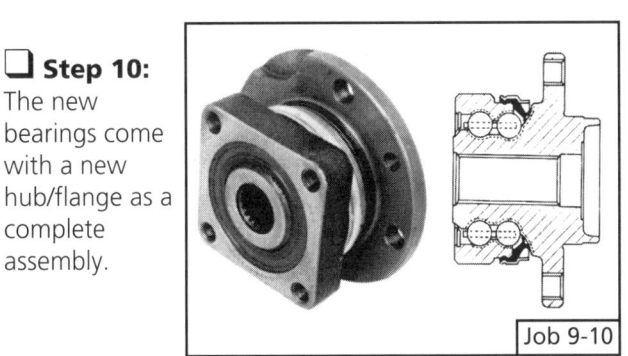

Job 10. 4x4 Propshaft universal joint - replacement.

❏ **Step 1:** The component parts of the propshaft assembly are shown below.

❏ **Step 2:** Undo the six allen screws securing the coupling to the power unit.

Job 10-2

Job 10-3

Job 10-4

❏ **Step 3:** Unbolt the universal joint from the rear axle.

❏ **Step 4:** Undo the shield/centre mounting screws (arrowed) and remove the shield and the propshaft from the car.

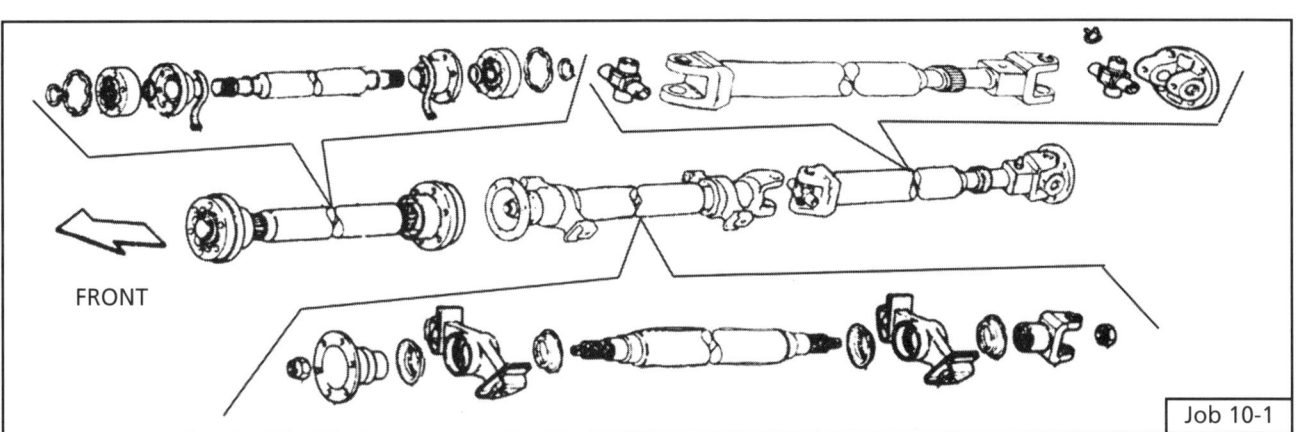

FRONT

Job 10-1

CHAPTER 6 PART B: TRANSMISSION

105

Step 5: INSIDE INFORMATION: Before dismantling, mark each component so that it is reassembled in the same order, thus retaining the propshaft balance.

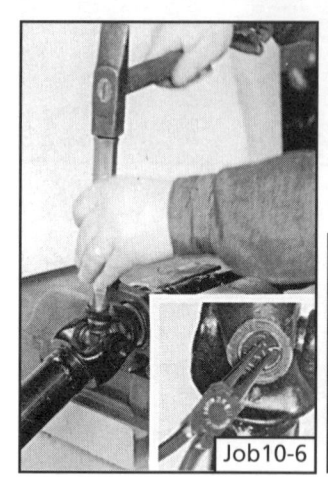

Step 6: Remove the circlips securing the needle roller cups in the yokes (see *inset*) and knock out the universal joint spider using a suitable drift.

Step 7: Position the spider within the yoke. Engage the needle roller cups squarely in their holes and press in slowly and carefully, at the same time engaging the spider pins in the cups.

Step 8: Press the cups in until they are flush with the yoke.

Step 9: Using a spacer of slightly smaller diameter, press one cup in just far enough to allow engagement of the retaining circlip in its groove. Repeat this operation on the other side.

Step 10: Repeat **Steps 7** to **9** to assemble the other half of the universal joint.

Step 11: Check the clearance between the spider pins and the needle bearings. This should be between 0.01 and 0.04 mm. Rubber shims are available from your FIAT dealer but unless you have a dial gauge, this is a check that will have to be carried out, if necessary, by your FIAT dealer.

Job 11. 4x4 Propshaft c.v. joint - replacement.

You would need a special press the length of the front section of the propeller shaft to refit the new c.v. joint to the shaft. We recommend that the propshaft c.v. joints are replaced by your FIAT dealer, who will have the correct equipment.

PART C: COOLING SYSTEM

PART C: Contents

Job 1. Water pump - replacement.
Job 2. Thermostat - replacement.
Job 3. Radiator - removal and replacement.
Job 4. Cooling fan and switch - removal, refitting and testing the switch.

Job 1. Water pump - replacement.

Step 1: Drain the cooling system.

Step 2: Remove the water hoses from the pump.

Step 3: Slacken the alternator securing and adjusting nuts and push the alternator towards the engine. Remove the drive belt.

Step 4A: Unbolt the pump (arrowed) and remove. It's fitted to the side of the block on OHV engines.

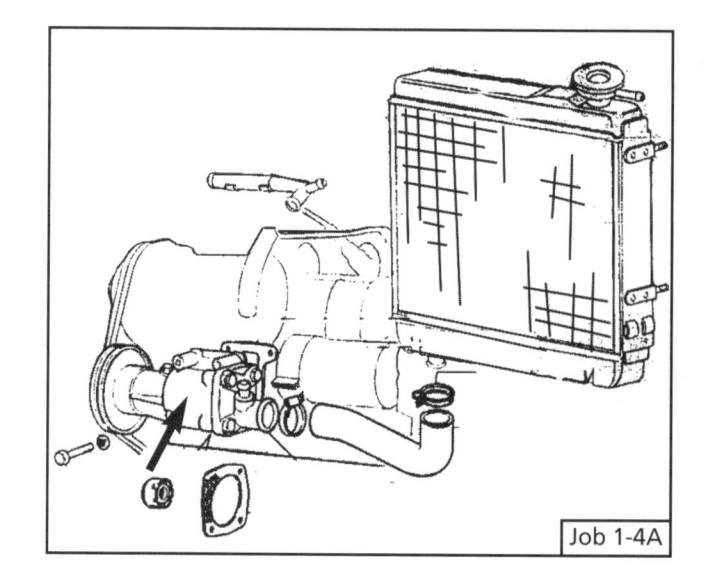

1 - water pump
3, 4, 5 - fixings
7 - bolt
8 - seal
9 - pipe
10 - gasket
11 - thermostat
12 - bolt

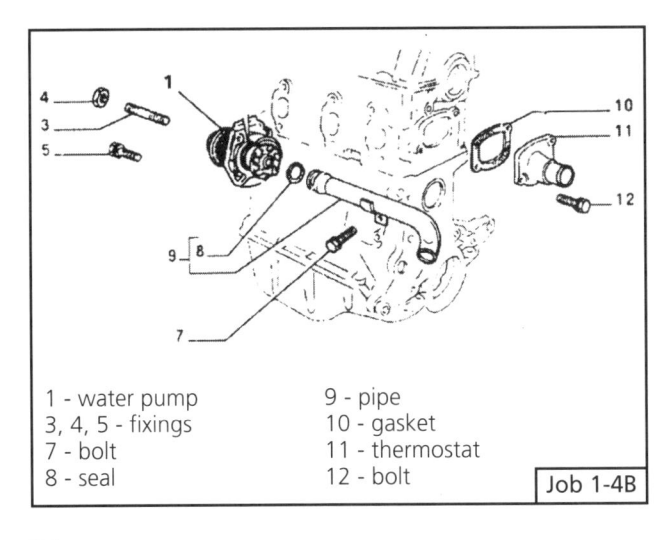

Job 1-4B

❏ **Step 4B:** This is the location on OHC 'FIRE' engines.

❏ **Step 5:** Refitting is the reverse of removal. Adjust the drive belt. Fill the cooling system. See *Chapter 5, Servicing Your Car* and see *Chapter 3, Facts and Figures*.

Job 2. Thermostat - replacement.

❏ **Step 1:** Drain the cooling system.

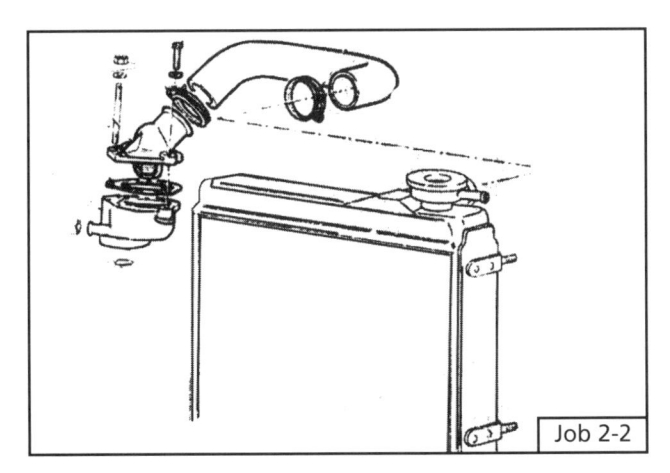

Job 2-2

❏ **Step 2:** Disconnect the hoses from the thermostat housing. This is the arrangement on OHV engines.

❏ **Step 3:** Unbolt and remove the housing and thermostat assembly. See *Job 1, Step 4B* for the location of the 'FIRE' engine thermostat.

❏ **Step 4:** Clean the mating surface on the cylinder head. Fit the new thermostat and gasket.

❏ **Step 5:** Refill the cooling system. See *Chapter 5, Servicing Your Car* and see *Chapter 3, Facts and Figures*.

Job 3. Radiator - removal and refitting.

❏ **Step 1:** Drain the cooling system.

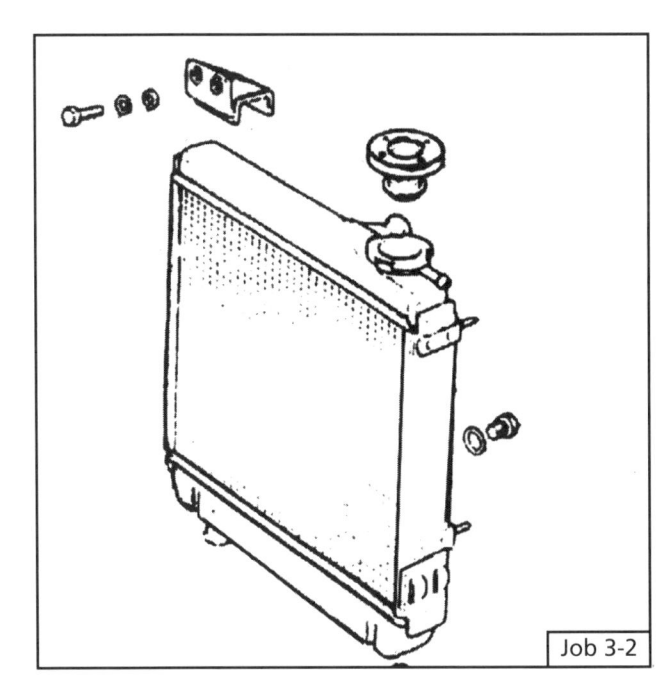

Job 3-2

❏ **Step 2:** Disconnect the radiator hoses and thermostatic switch leads. This is the earlier radiator - thermostat switch arrowed. See *Job 4-1, part 9* for the later type.

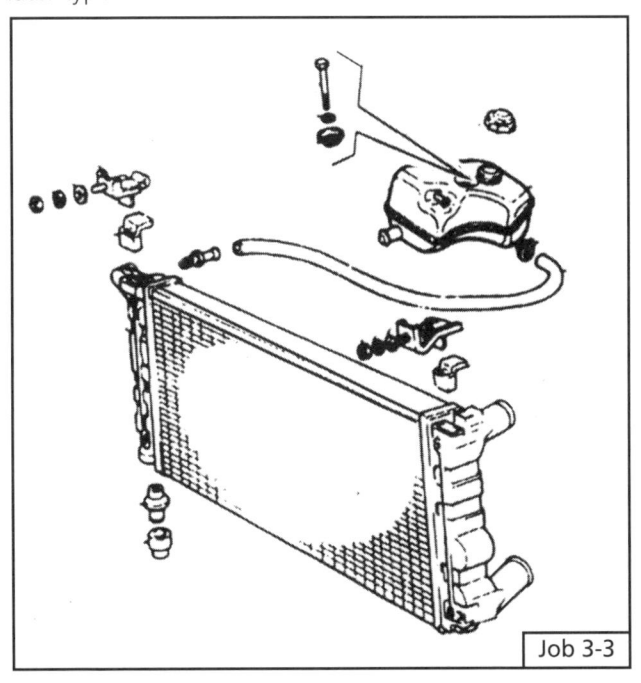

Job 3-3

❏ **Step 3:** Undo the bolts securing the radiator top clamps and remove the clamps. This is the 4x4 radiator with separate header tank. Non-4x4, later radiators fit in a similar way. See illustration *Job 4-1*.

❏ **Step 4:** Lift the radiator and fan assembly out of the bottom insulators.

❏ **Step 5:** Unbolt the fan assembly and remove from the radiator.

❏ **Step 6:** Refit in reverse order

❏ **Step 7:** Refill the cooling system. See *Chapter 5, Servicing Your Car* and see *Chapter 3, Facts and Figures*.

CHAPTER 6 PART D: IGNITION

Job 4. Cooling fan and switch - removal, refitting and testing the switch.

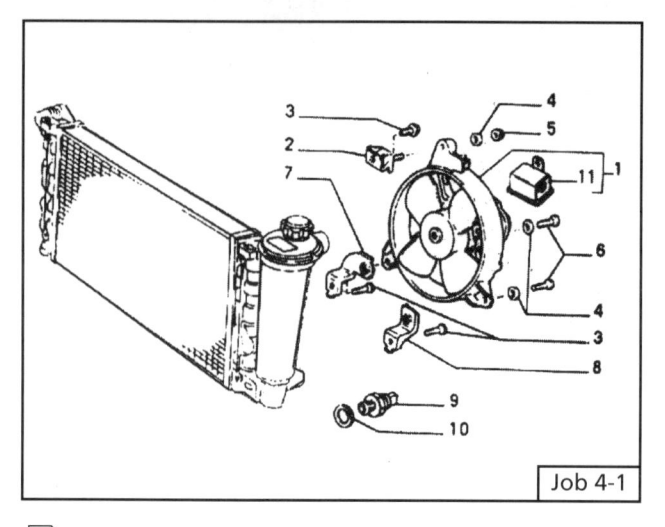

□ **Step 1:** Undo the electrical connections.

□ **Step 2:** Undo the mounting nuts and bolts (see *Job 4-1, parts 5 and 6*) and remove the complete assembly from the radiator.

□ **Step 3:** The thermostatic switch (see *Job 4-1, part 9*) which controls the fan is located in the radiator bottom tank - but see *Job 3-2*, (arrowed) for the earlier type.

□ **Step 4:** To remove, drain the cooling system, disconnect the switch and unscrew it from the radiator.

□ **Step 5:** INSIDE INFORMATION: Test the switch using a test bulb with two leads. Connect one to a battery terminal and the other to one of the switch terminals. Now connect a wire between the remaining switch and battery terminals.

□ **Step 6:** Lower the switch into water until the thread is just covered and the terminals remain dry.

□ **Step 7:** Heat the water slowly. The bulb should light just below boiling point (90 to 94 degrees Celsius) and go out when the temperature falls below 85 to 89 degrees Celsius.

Step 8: Refit with a new washer (see *Job 4-1, part 10*) but do not over tighten.

Job 4-1

PART D: IGNITION

PART D: Contents

Job 1. Distributor - removal and refitting.

Job 2. Ignition coil - replacement.

Job 1. Distributor - removal and refitting.

IMPORTANT NOTE: For further information on distributor replacement on OHC 'FIRE' engines, also see **Chapter 5, Servicing Your Car, Job 30.**

□ **Step 1:** Turn the engine in a clockwise direction with a spanner on the crankshaft pulley nut until the timing marks are in alignment. See **Chapter 5,** again.

□ **Step 2:** Remove the distributor cap and check that the rotor contact is pointing at the number one segment inside the cap. If the rotor is pointing at number four, turn the engine another full turn and check that the rotor is now pointing at number one segment in the distributor cap, with the timing marks again in alignment.

□ **Step 3:** Mark the alignment of the rotor with the distributor body, and the alignment of the distributor base with the engine. Use typist's correction fluid.

□ **Step 4:** Disconnect the LT lead (the thin, low-tension lead) from the distributor, and detach the vacuum pipe (*Job 1-5A, part 9*).

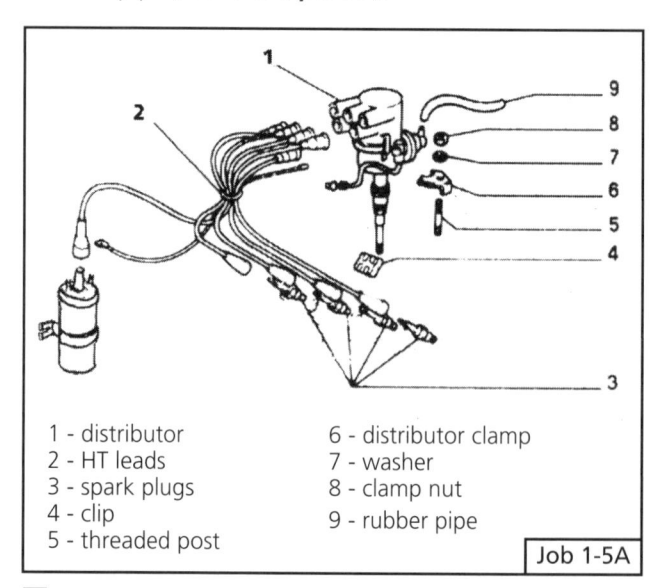

1 - distributor
2 - HT leads
3 - spark plugs
4 - clip
5 - threaded post
6 - distributor clamp
7 - washer
8 - clamp nut
9 - rubber pipe

Job 1-5A

□ **Step 5A:** OHV ENGINES: Undo the distributor clamp nut and remove the clamp.

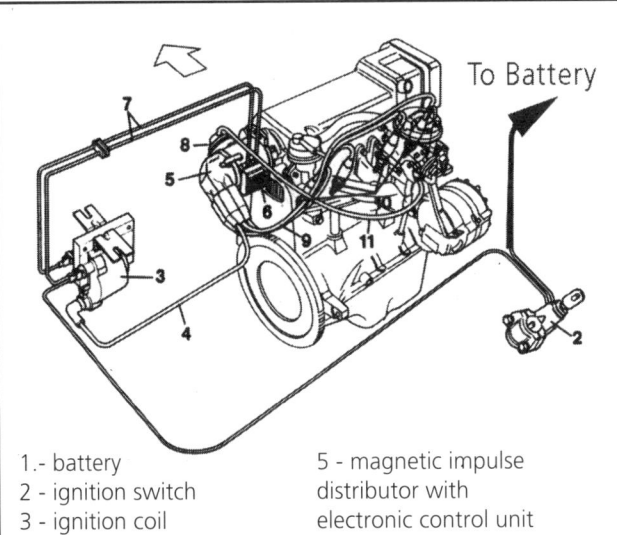

Step 10: Refit the LT lead and distributor cap and leads. Reconnect the vacuum pipe.

Step 11: Start the engine and check the ignition timing. See **Chapter 5, Servicing Your Car.**

Job 2. Ignition coil - replacement.

Step 1: Disconnect all leads (**Step 2, part 2** is the HT lead), taking note of their terminal positions. See **Job 1-5A** for the position of the coil on OHV engines and **Job 1-5B** for 4x4 breakerless ignition engines.

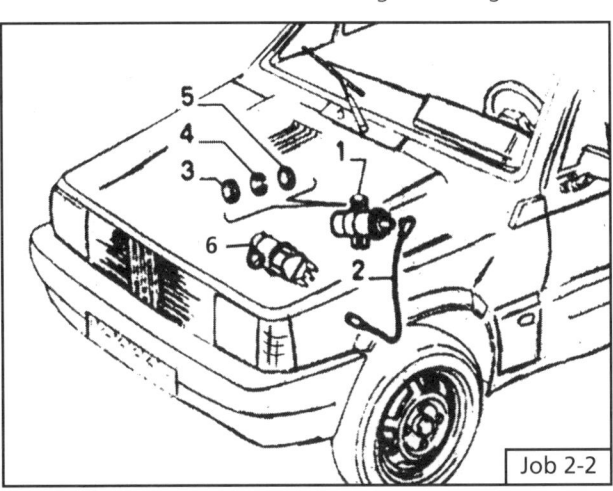

1.- battery
2 - ignition switch
3 - ignition coil
4 - HT lead connecting (3) and distributor (5)
5 - magnetic impulse distributor with electronic control unit
6 - distributor electronic control unit.
Job 1-5B

Step 5B: For reference, this is the layout of the 4x4's breakerless ignition layout and the position of the distributor on all **OHC 'FIRE'** engines.

Step 6: After marking its position, remove the distributor from the cylinder head. If the driveshaft is displaced, just push it back. No timing is lost.

Step 7: Refit by holding the distributor over its mounting hole with the mark on its base aligned with the one on the cylinder head and the rotor aligned with the mark on the body.

Step 8: Push the distributor home, turning the rotor very slightly if necessary to engage the driveshaft splines (OHV engine). The OHC drive has an off-centre location and only fits one way.

Step 9: Align the distributor with the mark on the cylinder head and refit the clamp plate and nut.

Job 2-2

Step 2: Undo the two sets of fixing nuts and washers (3, 4, 5) remove the coil, and its bracket. This is the position on **OHC 'FIRE'** engines. **Part 6** shows the distributor position.

Step 3: Transfer the mounting bracket (**Step 2, part 1**) to the new coil and fit in reverse order.

PART E: ELECTRICAL AND INSTRUMENTS

PART E: Contents

Job 1. System checks.
Job 2. Alternator - removal and refitting.
Job 3. Starter motor - removal and refitting.
Job 4. Fuel gauge sender unit - replacement - early types.
Job 5. Electric fuel pump/fuel gauge sender unit - replacement.
Job 6. Instruments - removal and refitting.
Job 7. Speedometer cable - replacement.
Job 8. Instrument panel lights - replacement.
Job 9. Rear light - unit replacement.
Job 10. Headlight unit - replacement.
Job 11. Windscreen wiper motor (front) - replacement.
Job 12. Tailgate wiper motor - replacement.
Job 13. Windscreen washer pumps - replacement.
Job 14. Radio aerial - replacement.

Job 1. System checks.

Step 1: Decide whether you have enough knowledge or information to do this work yourself, or whether to consult your FIAT dealer or auto-electrician. You can waste money and cause further damage if you don't know what you're doing!

PORTER MANUALS *Auto-Electrics Manual* explains everything in a simple-to-follow style.

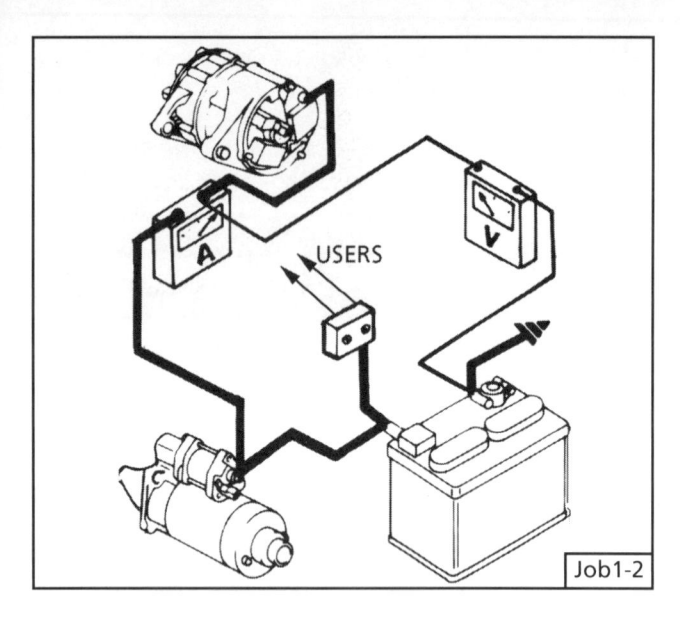

❑ **Step 2:** Before assuming that a flat battery is 'dead', have the charging system checked. This is the set-up for checking the maximum charge rate on Pandas with built-in electronic regulator.

❑ **Step 3:** You should check the battery voltage only after the car has been unused for at least two hours.

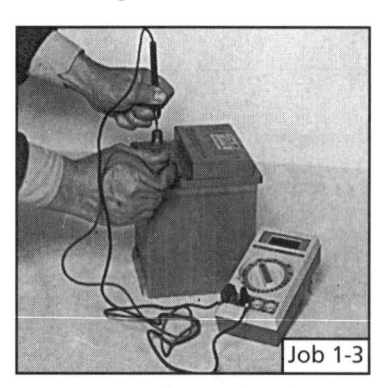

Job 2. Alternator - removal and refitting.

❑ **Step 1:** Disconnect the plugs and leads from the back of the alternator.

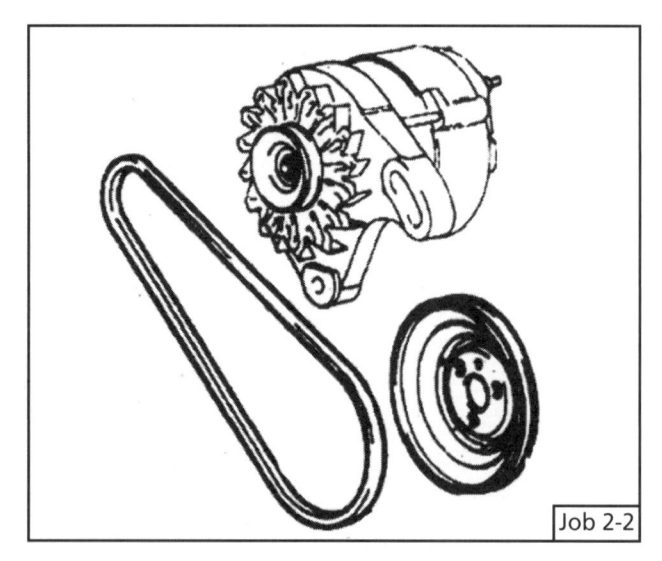

❑ **Step 2:** Slacken all mounting nuts. Push the alternator towards the engine and remove the drive belt.

❑ **Step 3:** Undo the mounting nuts and remove the alternator from its mountings.

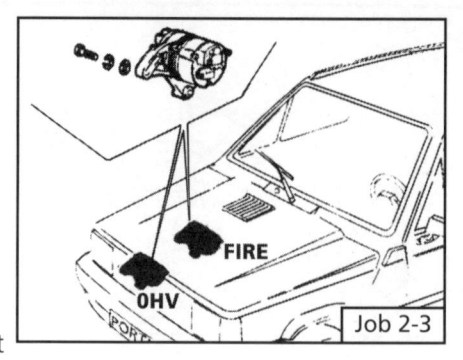

❑ **Step 4:** Refit in reverse order and adjust the drive belt. See **Chapter 5, Servicing Your Car, Job 27.**

Job 3. Starter motor - removal and refitting.

❑ **Step 1:** Disconnect the battery earth lead from the negative terminal.

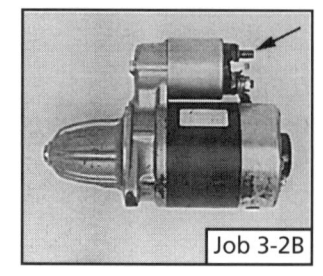

❑ **Step 2A:** Disconnect the cables from the starter solenoid (arrowed).

❑ **Step 2B:** This is the solenoid cable connection screw (arrowed) on the Hitachi starter motor fitted to Selecta (automatic gearbox) models.

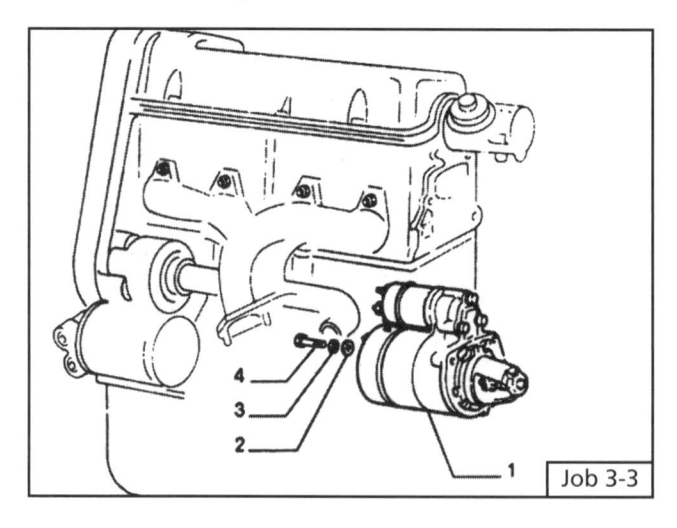

❑ **Step 3:** Undo the mounting bolts (**2**, **3** and **4**) and remove the starter (**1**).

❑ **Step 4:** Refit in reverse order, ensuring that all the electrical connections are clean.

❑ **Step 5:** You should also check that all terminal ends are tight and clean - very common problem areas!

IMPORTANT NOTE: Read **Chapter 1, Safety First!** before carrying out any work on the fuel system.

Job 4. Fuel gauge sender unit - replacement - early types.

EARLY MODELS ONLY

This job relates to cars with a mechanical fuel pump, mounted on the engine block.

❑ **Step 1:** Remove the fuel tank. (See **PART F: FUEL AND EXHAUST SYSTEMS, Job 6**).

❑ **Step 2:** Release the sender unit securing ring (arrowed) by removing the nuts and remove the sender unit from the tank.

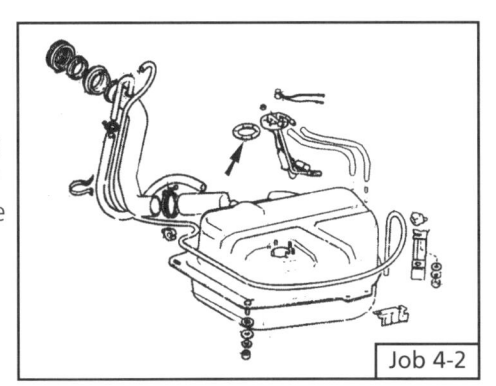

Job 4-2

❑ **Step 3:** Fit the new unit in reverse order using a new sealing ring.

❑ **Step 4:** Refit the fuel tank. (See **PART F: FUEL AND EXHAUST SYSTEMS, Job 6**).

Job 5. Electric fuel pump/fuel gauge sender unit - replacement.

LATER MODELS ONLY

This job relates to cars with an electric fuel pump. For the earlier, mechanical pump, see **PART F, Job 5**.

❑ **Step 1:** Disconnect the battery terminals.

❑ **Step 2:** Fold the rear seat fully forwards, pull back the luggage compartment mat and raise the cover from the floor panel to reveal the pump unit.

❑ **Step 3:** As the system may still be pressurised, the following must be done with care. Undo the nut and remove the hose union retaining plate. While covering with a rag to mop up any spillage, carefully and SLOWLY remove the two hose unions (arrowed) from the front of the pump. Note the fuel union "O" rings.

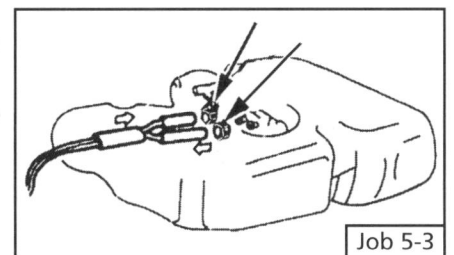

Job 5-3

❑ **Step 4:** Disconnect all wiring connectors.

❑ **Step 5:** Unscrew the large ring nut and carefully remove the assembly and its sealing ring from the fuel tank.

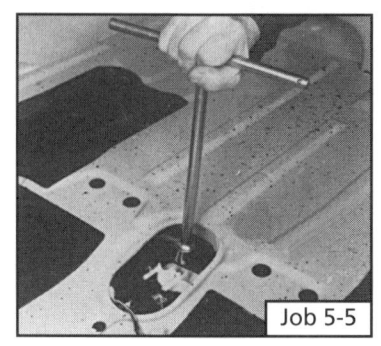

Job 5-5

making it easy! • Use an oil filter removing tool, similar to the special FIAT tool being used here.

i **Step 6:** INSIDE INFORMATION: If separating the pump and sender unit for renewal, take written note of the correct positions of the components as they are removed. This will help in reassembly. *i*

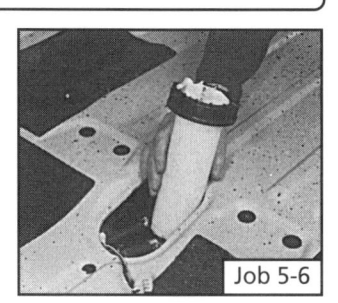

Job 5-6

❑ **Step 7:** Refitting is the reverse of removal but you must use a new sealing ring. Check that the pump wiring connectors are properly reconnected. Fit new 'O' rings to the fuel hoses and remember to tighten the clamp nut.

❑ **Step 8:** Reconnect the battery and start the engine. Check for fuel leaks.

❑ **Step 9:** Once satisfied that you've done a good job, reposition the hatch cover, floor mat and rear seat.

Job 6. Instruments - removal and refitting.

❑ **Step 1:** Disconnect the battery terminals.

❑ **Step 2:** Lever out the horn button from the steering wheel centre - unscrew from behind the wheel, as shown, when appropriate - and remove the two contact springs.

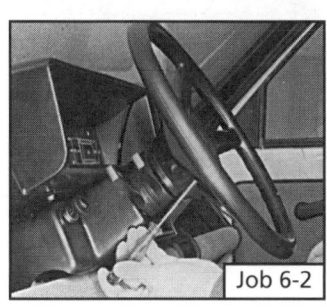

Job 6-2

❑ **Step 3:** Undo the steering wheel securing nut and set the steering in the straight ahead position.

SAFETY FIRST!

• As you bang the steering wheel towards you with your hands, to get it off the splines, take care to leave the centre nut on loosely so the wheel can not hit you in the face!

CHAPTER 6 PART E: ELECTRICAL

111

❏ **Step 4:** Remove the wheel from the inner column splines.

❏ **Step 5:** Remove the heater control knobs. These can be very stiff to pull off.

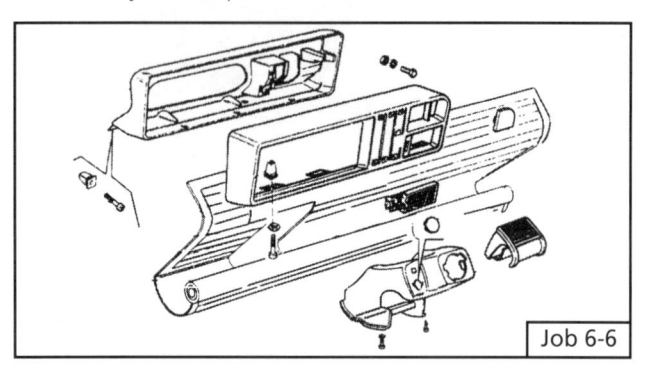

Job 6-6

❏ **Step 6:** Undo the three screws from under the instrument panel. Pull the panel out by squeezing the plastic cable retainer far enough to disconnect the speedometer drive.

❏ **Step 7:** Note the wiring plug positions and disconnect. Remove the instrument panel.

❏ **Step 8:** Refit the instrument panel in the reverse order. Refit the steering wheel, correctly positioned on its splines with the road wheels in the dead-ahead position and tighten the nut to the specified torque. See *Chapter 3, Facts and Figures*.

❏ **Step 9:** Refit the contact springs and the horn push. Reconnect the battery.

Job 7. Speedometer cable - replacement.

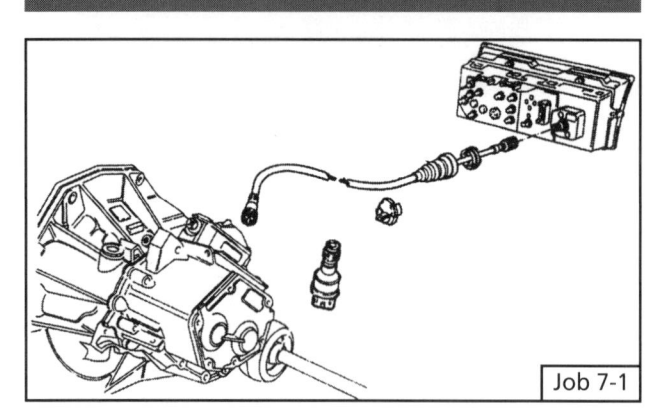

Job 7-1

❏ **Step 1:** Undo the speedometer cable knurled nut on the transmission unit.

❏ **Step 2:** Withdraw the instrument panel and disconnect the cable. See *Job 6*.

❏ **Step 3:** Withdraw the cable through the bulkhead grommet.

❏ **Step 4:** Refit in reverse order, avoiding sharp bends in the cable. Be sure to re-site the bulkhead grommet.

Job 8. Instrument panel lights - replacement.

❏ **Step 1:** Remove the instrument panel. See *Job 6*.

❏ **Step 2:** Capless-type bulbs are mounted in small holders which locate in the back of the instrument panel by a push and turn motion.

Job 9. Rear light unit - replacement.

❏ **Step. 1:** Undo the two mounting screws and remove the light unit. If water is getting in, replace the gasket (arrowed).

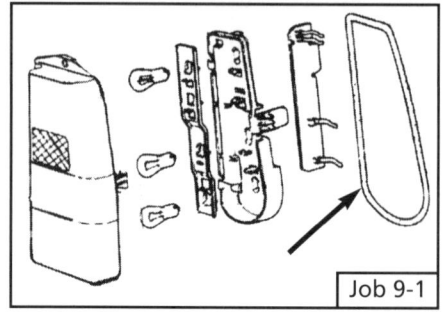

Job 9-1

❏ **Step 2:** Access to the bulbs is gained by depressing the retaining clip and releasing the bulb holder. See *Chapter 5, Servicing Your Car, Job 7*.

Job 10. Headlight unit - replacement.

❏ **Step 1:** Remove the wiring plugs and the rubber cover from the back of the light unit.

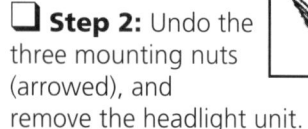

❏ **Step 2:** Undo the three mounting nuts (arrowed), and remove the headlight unit.

Job 10-2

❏ **Step 3:** Refit in reverse order.

❏ **Step 4:** Headlight alignment should be carried by your FIAT dealer who has the correct beam setting equipment. For headlight bulb replacement, see *Chapter 5, Servicing Your Car, Job 7*.

Job 11. Windscreen wiper motor (front) - replacement.

❏ **Step 1:** Carefully pull the wiper arm (**3**) from its splined spindle (**4**).

❏ **Step 2:** From under the bonnet, pull out the insulating strip from the bulkhead.

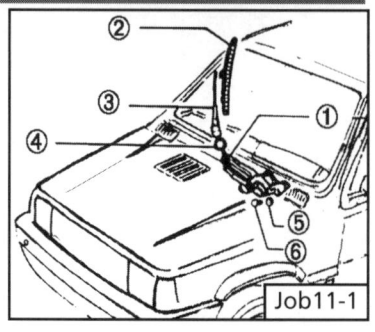

Job 11-1

112

❑ **Step 3:** Disconnect the wiring plug. Undo the motor and wheelbox (see *Job11-1, part 1*) mountings (see *Job11-1 parts 5* and *6*) and remove the complete unit from the car.

❑ **Step 4:** Refit in reverse order.

Job 12. Tailgate wiper motor - replacement.

❑ **Step 1:** Remove the wiper arm (**9**).

❑ **Step 2:** From inside the tailgate, remove the wiper motor cover.

❑ **Step 3:** Undo the wheelbox spindle nut (*Job 12, parts 1, 6, 7* and *8*) and unbolt the assembly (see *Job 12-1, part 1*). Withdraw enough to disconnect the wiring plug and remove the unit. Refit in the reverse order.

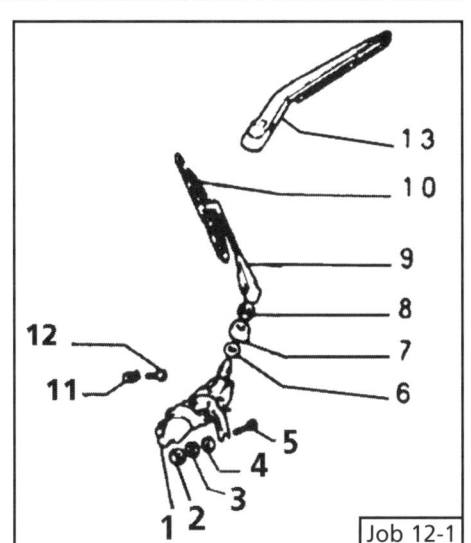

Job 13. Windscreen washer pumps - replacement.

EARLY MODELS WITH 'PLASTIC BAG' RESERVOIRS
The pump is moulded into the bag and the whole lot has to be replaced if the pump fails.

LATER MODELS WITH RIGID RESERVOIR

❑ **Step 1:** Disconnect the wires and washer tubing from both pumps and remove the fluid reservoir.

❑ **Step 2:** Pull out the defective pump. The replacement pushes into the hole in the reservoir and clips into the reservoir body. Refit the reservoir and remake the connections.

❑ **Step 3:** Check that all pipe connections are good and that the one-way valve (see *Job 13-1, arrowed*) for the rear washer works okay. If it takes a long time for water to pump through, replace the valve.

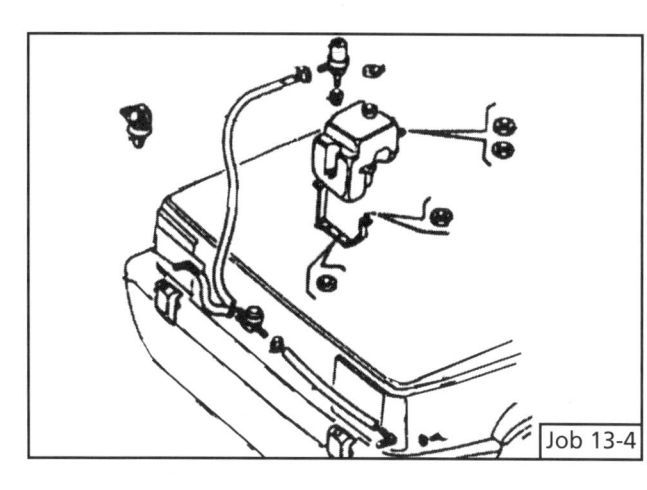

❑ **Step 4:** This is the headlight washer layout, when fitted. The pump unclips from the reservoir.

Job 14. Radio aerial - replacement.

❑ **Step 1:** From under the bonnet, release the fuse box and move aside. Partially remove the weather strip for access.

❑ **Step 2:** Remove the left-hand top door hinge cover.

ℹ **Step 3:** INSIDE INFORMATION: Unplug the old aerial cable from the radio and leave in place. Cut the old cable where it joins the aerial. Use insulation tape to attach the new aerial cable's radio-end and use the old cable to pull it through the correct route. Plug the new cable into the radio. ℹ

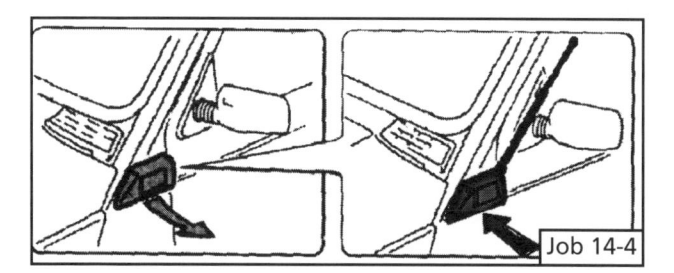

❑ **Step 4:** Fit the new aerial to the A-pillar, when originally fitted there, in the position shown.

❑ **Step 5:** This is the order in which the aerial parts are fitted to the body.

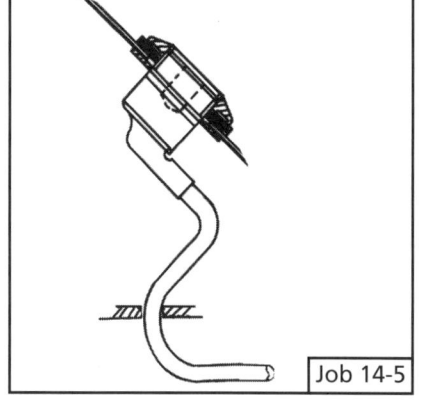

❑ **Step 6:** Refit all parts removed in exactly the same order.

CHAPTER 6 PART E: ELECTRICAL

PART F: FUEL AND EXHAUST SYSTEMS

PART F: Contents

Job 1. Carburettor - removal and refitting.
Job 2. Accelerator cable, carburettor engine - replacement.
Job 3. Accelerator cable, IAW injection engine - replacement.
Job 4. Choke cable - replacement.
Job 5. Fuel pump, (mechanical) - replacement. (For electric pump, see *PART E: ELECTRICAL AND INSTRUMENTS, Job 5.*).
Job 6. Fuel tank - removal and refitting.
Job 7. Fuel breather valves - replacement.
Job 8. Lambda sensor - replacement.
Job 9. Purge valves - replacement.
Job 10. Purge valve hose float valves - replacement.
Job 11 Exhaust system - replacement.

Job 1. Carburettor - removal and refitting.

☐ **Step 1:** Remove the air cleaner (**B**).

☐ **Step 2:** Disconnect the water hoses from the throttle valve plate block and tie them up high to prevent draining.

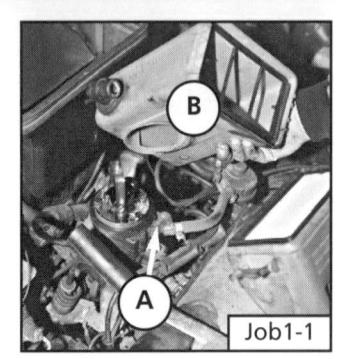

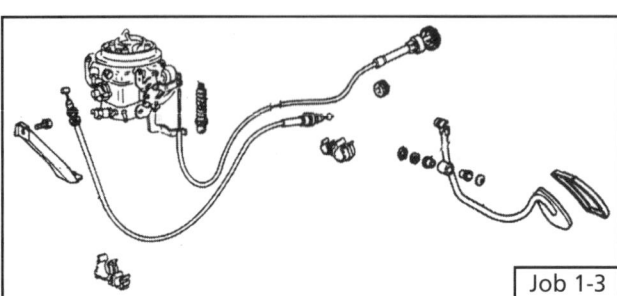

making it easy! • Ensure that delivery and return fuel lines are identified for refitting in the correct positions.

☐ **Step 5:** Unscrew the mounting nuts (holding the carburettor to the spacer) and remove the carburettor.

☐ **Step 6:** Refit in the reverse order, cleaning both flanges and fitting a new gasket.

Job 2. Accelerator cable, carburettor engine - replacement.

☐ **Step 3:** Disconnect the throttle and choke controls.

☐ **Step 4:** Disconnect the fuel lines from the carburettor stubs (see *Job 1-1*) and plug the ends.

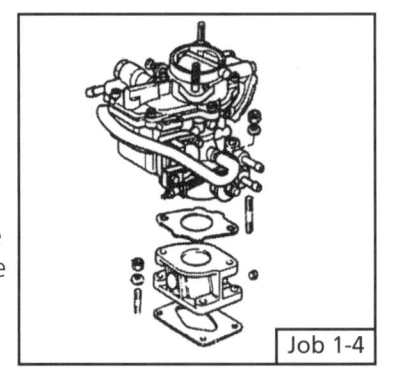

☐ **Step 1:** Fully slacken the cable adjustment and disconnect from the carburettor. See *Job 1, Step 3* for the earlier type of cable.

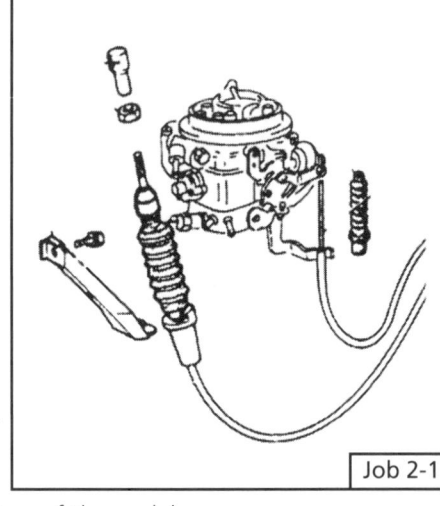

☐ **Step 2:** From inside the car, unhook the cable from the fork at the top of the pedal arm.

☐ **Step 3:** Free the bulkhead grommet and remove the cable.

SAFETY FIRST!

• The high pressure pipework on a fuel injection system can retain its pressure for days even after the engine has been switched off.
• When you disconnect the pipework, a jet of fuel can be emitted under very high pressure - strong enough to penetrate the skin or damage the eyes.
• NEVER work on the fuel pipework when the engine is running.
• ALWAYS place a rag over a union while it is being undone until all the pressure has been let out of the system.
• You are recommended to wear strong rubber gloves and goggles when disconnecting the fuel injection system's high pressure pipework. Always disconnect VERY slowly, letting pressure out progressively.

❏ **Step 4:** Refit in reverse order, using the nuts at the outer cable end to adjust so that there is the smallest amount of free movement.

❏ **Step 5:** Check that when the pedal is fully depressed, the lever at the carburettor is back against its stop.

Job 3. Accelerator cable, IAW injection engine - replacement.

❏ **Step 1:** Loosen the two locknuts (illustration *Job 3-1, part 2*).

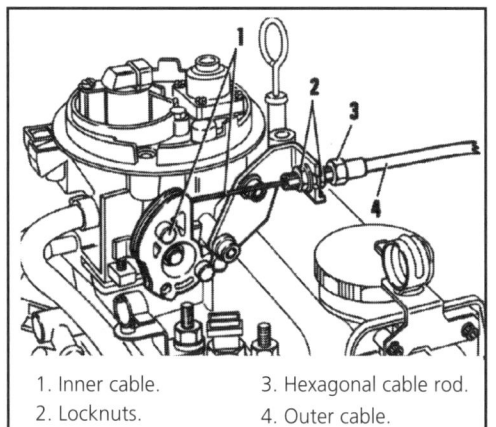

❏ **Step 2:** Detach the hexagonal cable rod (*Job 3-1, part 3*), from its support bracket and the inner cable, from the quadrant.

1. Inner cable.
2. Locknuts.
3. Hexagonal cable rod.
4. Outer cable.

Job 3-1

❏ **Step 3:** From inside the car, unhook the cable from the fork at the top of the pedal arm. (See *Job 2.*)

❏ **Step 4:** Free the bulkhead grommet and remove the cable.

❏ **Step 5:** Refit in reverse order, using the lock nuts and the hexagonal rod, to adjust the smallest amount of free movement.

❏ **Step 6:** Check that the butterfly valve opens fully when the accelerator pedal is fully depressed.

Job 4. Choke cable - replacement.

❏ **Step 1:** Release both inner and outer cables at the carburettor end. See *Job 1* and *Job 2.*

❏ **Step 2:** Remove the claw-type fixing from behind the dash board.

❏ **Step 3:** Release the bulkhead grommet and withdraw the cable.

❏ **Step 4:** Fit the replacement in the reverse order and adjust by pulling the choke knob out about 4 mm, setting the choke at the carburettor end to its fully-open position and tightening the pinch bolt on the inner cable. Check that the choke is fully open ('off') when the knob is pushed fully in - most important!

Job 5. Fuel pump (mechanical) - replacement.

EARLY MODELS ONLY

For the later, electric fuel pump, see *PART E: ELECTRICAL AND INSTRUMENTS, Job 5.*

❏ **Step 1:** Disconnect the fuel hoses from the pump.

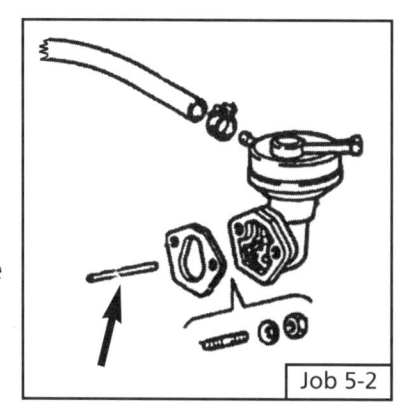

❏ **Step 2:** Undo the two mounting nuts and washers and carefully remove the fuel pump. Retrieve the two gaskets and spacer and the pump operating pushrod (arrowed) and bush.

Job 5-2

❏ **Step 3:** Refit in the reverse order, taking care that with the pushrod fully retracted, it projects between 1.0 mm and 1.5 mm beyond the spacer block outer gasket. Adjustment can be made by varying the gasket thickness, available from your FIAT dealer.

Job 6. Fuel tank - removal and refitting.

IMPORTANT NOTE: Read *Chapter 1, Safety First!* before carrying out this work.

❏ **Step 1:** Plan ahead! Run the fuel in the tank as low as possible before you start this job.

❏ **Step 2:** Jack up the rear of the car and support on axle stands. Remove the right hand rear wheel.

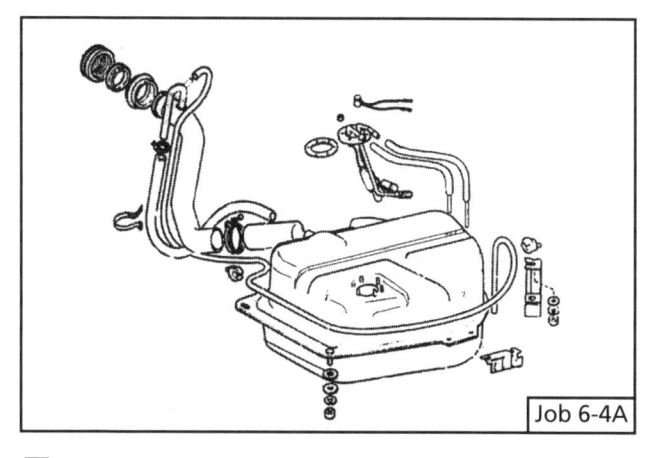

Job 6-4A

❏ **Step 3:** Disconnect the breather hoses and filler pipe from the tank.

❏ **Step 4A: EARLY MODELS WITH STEEL TANKS:** From under the car, undo the mounting nuts from the tank flange and lower sufficiently to allow disconnection of the electrical leads and fuel lines. Lower the tank to the ground.

CHAPTER 6 PART F: FUEL AND EXHAUST

115

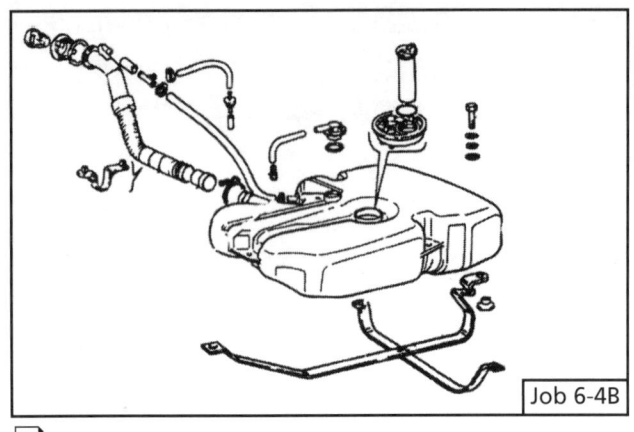

CHAPTER 6 PART F: FUEL AND EXHAUST

Job 6-4B illustration

❑ **Step 4B:** LATER MODELS WITH PLASTIC TANKS: Disconnect the pump and sender unit. See **PART E: ELECTRICAL AND INSTRUMENTS, Job 5.** Disconnect all pipes and hoses. Unbolt the straps and lower the tank to the ground.

❑ **Step 5:** Refitting is in reverse order. Ensure that the fuel lines and electrical connections are sound.

Job 7. Fuel breather valves - replacement.

1992-ON ONLY

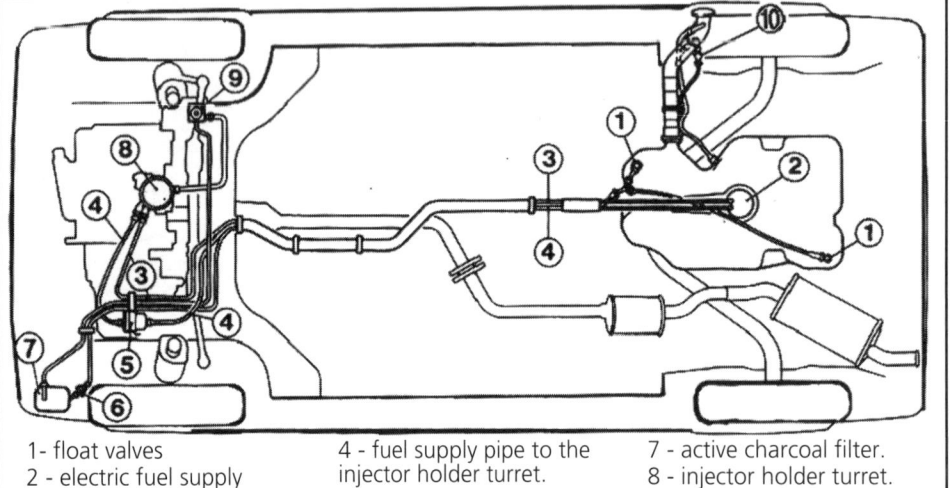

Job 7-1 illustration

1- float valves
2 - electric fuel supply pump.
3 - fuel return pipe.
4 - fuel supply pipe to the injector holder turret.
5 - fuel filter cut out valve.
6 - 2 way petrol vapour breather valve.
7 - active charcoal filter.
8 - injector holder turret.
9 - petrol vapour solenoid
10 - breather/safety valve.

❑ **Step 1:** Locate the breather/safety valve (**10**) under the top of the filler neck.

❑ **Step 2:** Slacken the retaining clips and disconnect the valve.

i **Step 3:** INSIDE INFORMATION: Test the valve by blowing through it. This should *i* possible in one direction only. Replace if faulty *i*

❑ **Step 4:** Refit in reverse order, making sure that the valve is the right way round, so that you could blow into the tank but not the other way.

❑ **Step 5:** Now locate the two-way petrol vapour breather solenoid valve (**Job 7-1, part 6**) which is fitted in line from the charcoal filter to the injection turret. (See **Chapter 5** for filter replacement.)

i INSIDE INFORMATION: When replacing valves, the two-way breather valve (see **Job 7-1, part 6**) is connected the right way round when the LIGHT BLUE side is connected to the pipe leading to the charcoal filter and the BLACK side to the fuel tank float valves. The safety valve (see **Job 7-1, part 10**) is connected the right way when the WHITE side faces the tank. *i*

Job 8. Lambda sensor - replacement.

i INSIDE INFORMATION: On models with the earlier type of catalytic converters, the sensor is located in the exhaust manifold. On later models it is screwed into the exhaust's front downpipe. In this case you will have to jack up and securely support your car in order to work from underneath. *i*

❑ **Step 1:** Trace the wiring back from the sensor and release it from any securing clips until you reach the main loom and then disconnect it.

❑ **Step 2:** Ensure that the sealing ring is in good condition and lightly lubricate the thread with an anti-seize agent before refitting in reverse order. See **Job 11, Step 30.**

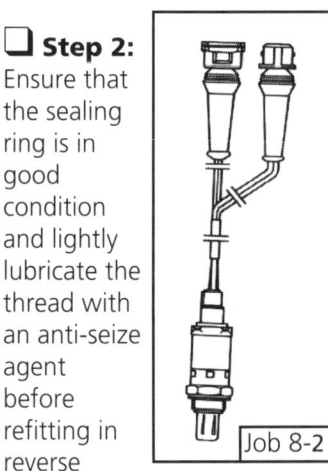

Job 8-2 illustration

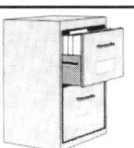

FACT FILE: LAMBDA SENSOR

• The Lambda sensor is very easily damaged and should not be knocked or dropped.

• We recommend that you have your FIAT dealer test your Lambda sensor and replace it if necessary.

• No cleaners should be used on it.

Job 9. Purge valves - replacement.

❑ **Step 1:** Disconnect the battery earth lead.

116

☐ **Step 2:** Refer to illustration **Job 7-1.** Locate both purge valves on the right hand suspension turret. Disconnect the outlet hose from the upper valve and the inlet hose from the lower valve.

☐ **Step 3:** Unplug the wiring connector from each valve, undo the mounting nuts and remove the two hoses as an assembly.

☐ **Step 4:** Refit in the reverse order making sure that your connections are sound.

Job 10. Purge valve hose float valves - replacement.

Refer to illustration **Job 7-1.**

☐ **Step 1:** Remove the fuel tank. See **Job 6.**

☐ **Step 2:** Disconnect the hose from the valve and carefully remove the valve from its sealing grommet.

☐ **Step 3:** When refitting, check the condition of the grommet and take care not to displace it while easing the valve back into position.

☐ **Step 4:** Refit the fuel tank. See **Job 6.**

Job 11. Exhaust system - replacement.

☐ **Step 1:** The manifold is mounted on the side of the cylinder head and has ducting attached to it which supplies hot air to the carburettor at low temperatures. It is secured by five studs and nuts. When refitting, always use a new gasket. See **PART A: ENGINE.**

☐ **Step 2:** Disconnect the downpipe from the manifold and release the flexible mountings. Remove the compete system from the car.

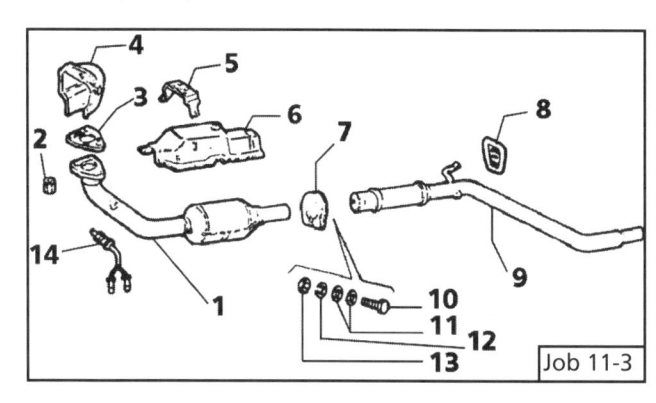

☐ **Step 3:** If not replacing the whole system, undo the clamp (**parts 3, 7** and **10** to **13**). Use penetrating oil and tap with a hammer to help part the sections. This is the later system with a catalytic converter in the front pipe and a Lambda sensor (**14**).

☐ **Step 4:** Refit by loosely assembling the complete system and attaching to the car. Align the system ensuring sufficient clearance along its length, then tighten all the clamps.

PART G: STEERING AND SUSPENSION

PART G: Contents

Job 1. The systems explained.
Job 2. Tie rod - replacement.
Job 3. Track control arm - replacement.
Job 4. Front suspension strut - replacement.
Job 5. Track rod end balljoint - replacement.
Job 6. Steering rack gaiter - replacement.
Job 7. Steering rack - replacement.
Job 8. Rear axle - removal and refitting.
Job 9. Rear leaf spring - replacement.
Job 10. Rear shock absorber - replacement.
Job 11. Rear suspension overhaul - 'Omega' type.
Job 12. Rear hub bearings - replacement.
Job 13. Steering wheel - removal/replacement.

Job 1. The systems explained.

☐ **Point 1A:** All Panda front suspension layouts are virtually identical. This is the front shock absorber strut and its attachments to the hub carrier (two bolts) and the bodywork, at the top.

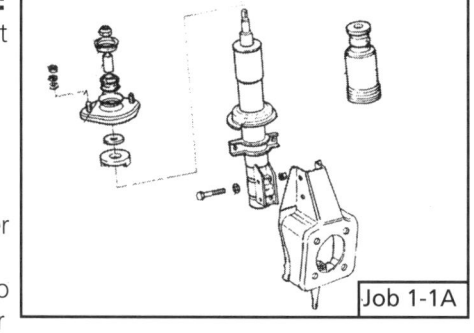

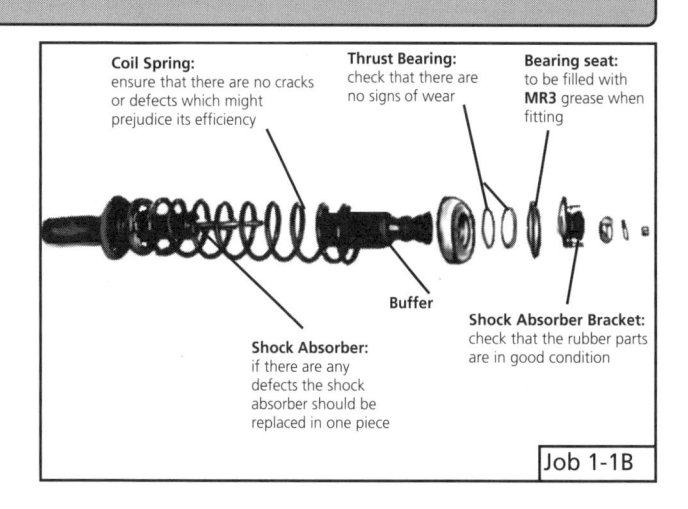

Coil Spring: ensure that there are no cracks or defects which might prejudice its efficiency

Thrust Bearing: check that there are no signs of wear

Bearing seat: to be filled with MR3 grease when fitting

Buffer

Shock Absorber: if there are any defects the shock absorber should be replaced in one piece

Shock Absorber Bracket: check that the rubber parts are in good condition

☐ **Point 1-B:** The shock absorber is surrounded with a coil spring.

117

CHAPTER 6 PART G: SUSPENSION

❑ **Point 1C:** You must NEVER remove the central nut holding the coil spring onto the strut (**a**) without using a purpose-made coil spring compressor, located on the coils as shown.

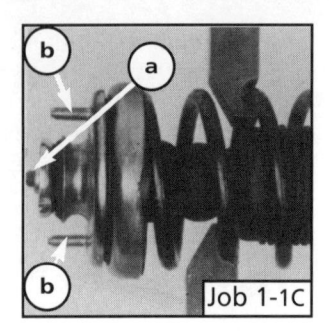

Job 1-1C

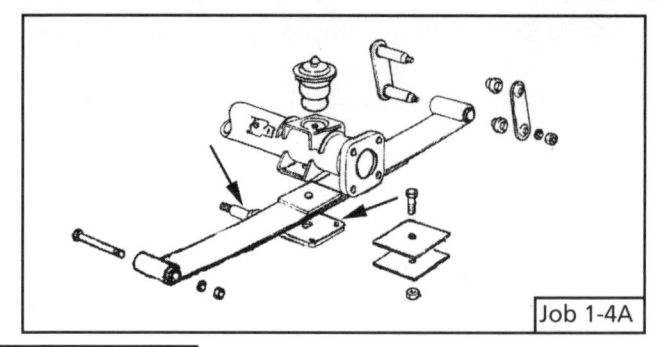

Job 1-4A

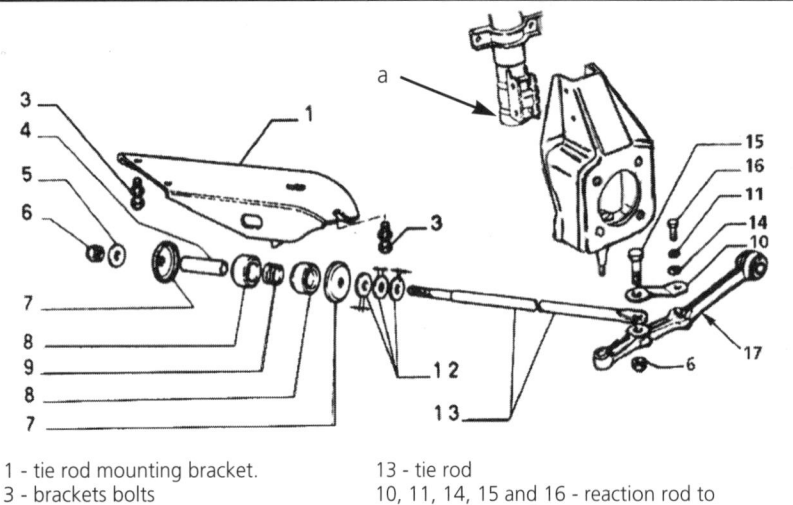

❑ **Point 4A:** Up to 1986, all Pandas had rear leaf spring suspension and 4x4 Pandas were always fitted with this type of suspension. The bracket (arrowed) is the shock absorber mounting plate, used on non-4x4 models only. The 4x4 shock absorber bolts to a bracket on the axle.

1 - tie rod mounting bracket.
3 - brackets bolts
4 to 12 - tie rod fixings, buffers, shims and spacer.
13 - tie rod
10, 11, 14, 15 and 16 - reaction rod to track control arm fixings.
17 - track control arm (arrowed).

Job 1-2

❑ **Point 2:** These are the components that can be purchased separately from your FIAT dealership when overhauling the lower front suspension components.

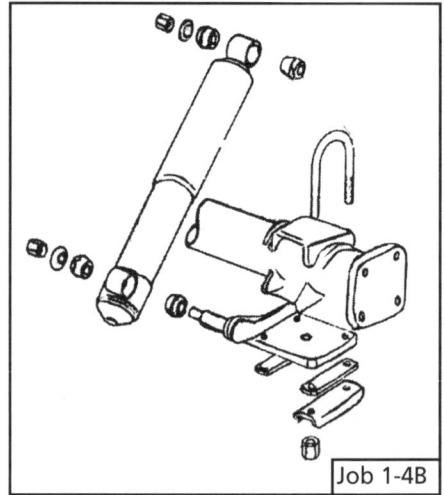

❑ **Point 4B:** These are the rear shock absorber mountings and spring shackle plates on all non-4x4 rear leaf spring suspension Pandas.

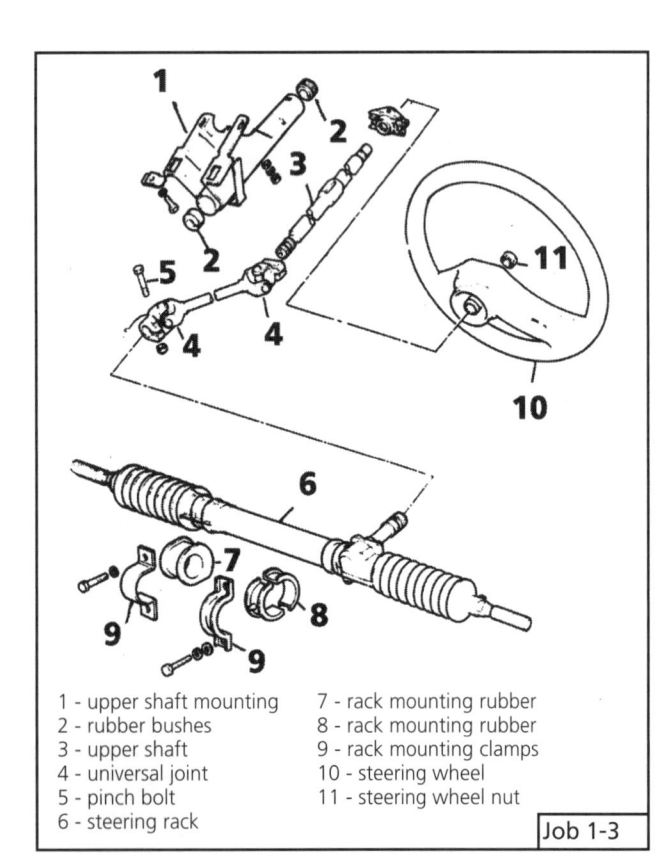

Job 1-4B

1 - upper shaft mounting
2 - rubber bushes
3 - upper shaft
4 - universal joint
5 - pinch bolt
6 - steering rack
7 - rack mounting rubber
8 - rack mounting rubber
9 - rack mounting clamps
10 - steering wheel
11 - steering wheel nut

Job 1-3

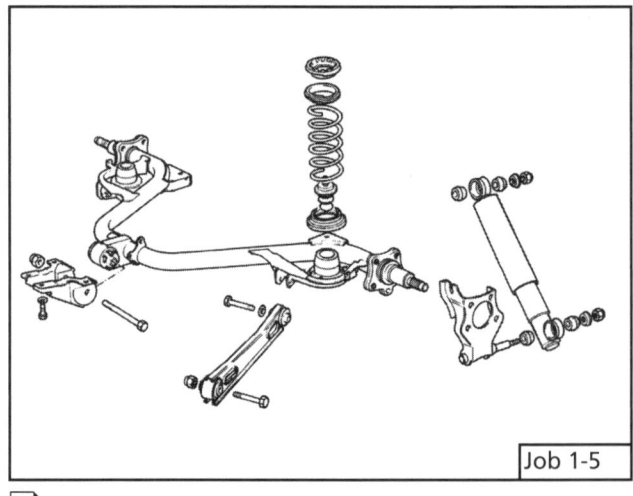

Job 1-5

❑ **Point 5:** From 1986, a completely new rear suspension system was introduced called 'Omega'. These are the component parts.

IMPORTANT NOTE: New shock absorbers should ONLY be fitted in front - or rear-pairs to ensure safe handling and braking.

❑ **Point 3:** These are the components which are available separately from your FIAT dealership for the steering system. The Track Rod Ends (see later) are fitted to the outer ends of the steering rack.

Job 2. Tie rod - replacement.

See illustration **Job 1-2** for details of the components referred to here.

❏ **Step 1:** Disconnect the outer end of the tie rod from the track control arm by undoing the nut and bolt (see **Job 1-2, parts 4** to **12**).

Job 2-2

❏ **Step 2:** Disconnect the inner end of the rod from its mounting bracket on the body.

ℹ INSIDE INFORMATION: When refitting the original tie rod, make sure that the shims (see **Job 2-2, part 12**) are all replaced so that the castor angle is not altered when refitting. However, if any replacement parts are fitted, have the castor angle checked and re-set at your FIAT dealership. ℹ

Job 3. Track control arm - replacement.

Refer to illustration **Job 1-2** for the components described in this Job.

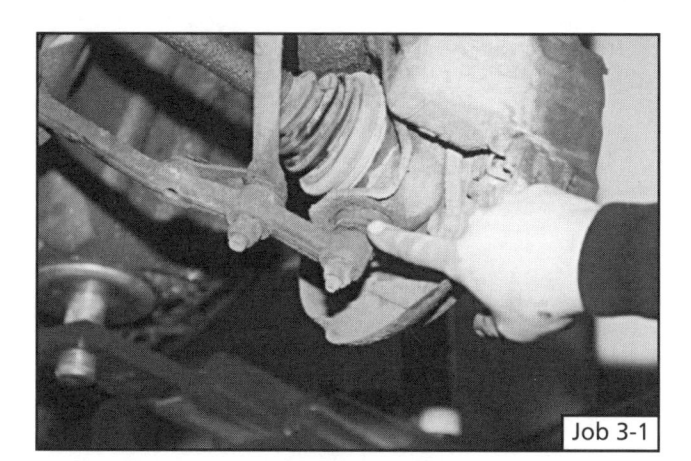

Job 3-1

❏ **Step 1:** You will have to use a ball joint splitter to remove the outer end of the track control arm from the ball joint on the bottom of the hub. If the rubber shroud is damaged, you must replace the ball joint.

❏ **Step 2:** Detach the tie rod from the track control arm. (See **Job 1-2 parts 6** and **15**.)

❏ **Step 3:** Undo and remove the pivot bolt at the inner end of the track control arm and remove the arm.

IMPORTANT NOTE: If the track control arm is damaged or distorted or if the rubber bush has deteriorated, a new track control arm must be obtained from your FIAT dealer and fitted.

Job 4. Front suspension strut - replacement.

Refer to illustrations **Job 1-1A**, **Job 1-1B** and **Job 1-1C**.

❏ **Step 1:** Place the front of the car on axle stands and remove the road wheel.

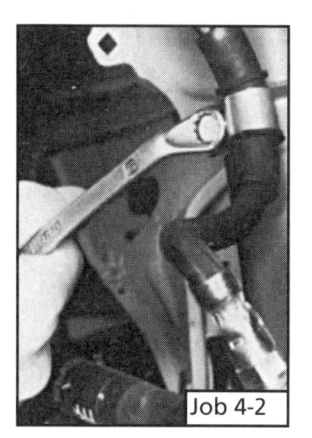

Job 4-2 *Job 4-3*

❏ **Step 2:** Disconnect the flexible hydraulic brake hose clip from the suspension strut so as not to stretch the hose.

❏ **Step 3:** Detach the steering arm. Undo the bolts (arrowed)

❏ **Step 4:** Undo the hub carrier clamp bolts (also see illustration **Job 1-2, point a**) and slide the carrier down and off the strut.

❏ **Step 5:** From under the bonnet, undo the two nuts securing the strut upper mounting to the turret, (**Job 1-1C,** arrows **b**).

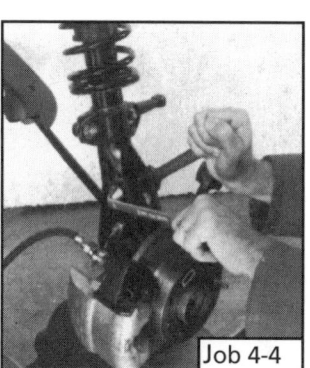

Job 4-4

❏ **Step 6:** Lower the strut from under the wing.

❏ **Step 7:** Using two coil spring compressors spread over as many coils as possible, compress the spring until the ends are free of their seats.

❏ **Step 8:** Undo the large nut at the top of the strut spindle. Remove the mounting, the clamped spring and gaiter.

CHAPTER 6 PART G: SUSPENSION

119

CHAPTER 6 PART G: SUSPENSION

FACT FILE: CHECKING FOR WEAR
- Before refitting the top mounting, you should check the condition of the thrust bearing.
- Clean and check the bearing for signs of wear and replace it if necessary.
- Pack the bearing seat with **Tutela MR3** grease when assembling.

SAFETY FIRST!
- NEVER undo the centre nut (see illustration **Job1-1, part C**) without using a suitable spring compressor.
- The power contained within the spring is enormous and extremely dangerous.
- If you are not trained or experienced in this part of the Job, leave it to your FIAT dealer.

☐ **Step 8:** Reassemble in reverse order. Release the spring clamps evenly to ensure proper engagement with the top and bottom seats.

☐ **Step 9:** Refit the complete assembly in reverse order.

SAFETY FIRST!
- New struts should always be fitted in pairs to ensure good handling and safe braking.

☐ **Step 10:** Repeat the whole operation on the other side.

Job 5. Track rod end balljoint - replacement.

☐ **Step 1:** Support the front of the car on axle stands and remove the roadwheel on the side to be worked on.

Job 5-2

☐ **Step 2:** Slacken the locknut on the (TRE) Track Rod End (arrowed) with an open-ended spanner.

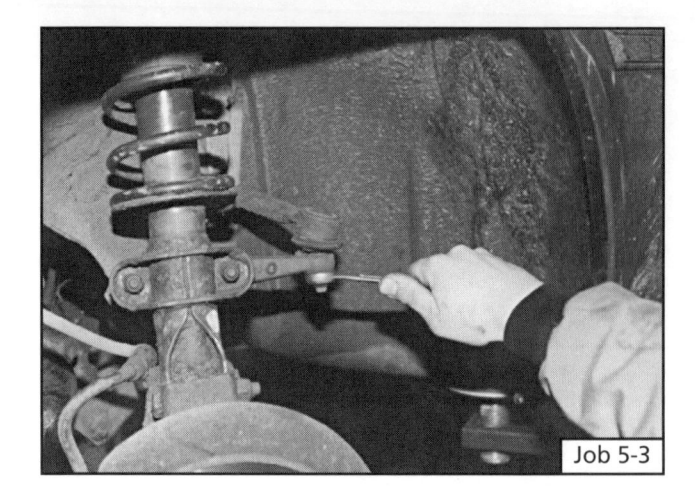

Job 5-3

☐ **Step 3:** Slacken the balljoint stud nut...

Job 5-4

☐ **Step 4:** ...and release the stud using a splitter tool.

ℹ️ **Step 5:** INSIDE INFORMATION: A sharp blow to the side of the eye often momentarily distorts the eye and releases the pin. Remove the nut. ℹ️

Job 5-5

☐ **Step 6:** Disconnect the balljoint from the steering arm and unscrew from the tie bar - count the turns!

☐ **Step 7:** Clean and grease the tie bar threads before fitting the new balljoint to prevent

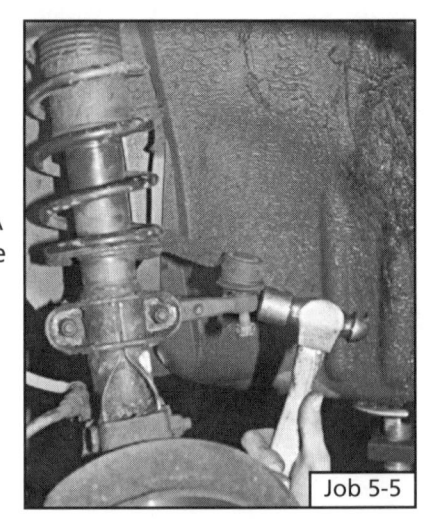

Job 5-6

120

future seizure. Fit the new balljoint in reverse order, screwing on the same number of turns and, before using the car further, take it to your FIAT dealership or tyre specialist to have the front wheel alignment set. This is NOT a job you can do at home but it DOES need doing as soon as possible! Misaligned track can lead to rapid tyre wear and uneven breaking.

Job 6. Steering rack gaiter - replacement.

❏ **Step 1:** Remove the Track Rod End (TRE) balljoint. See *Job 5*.

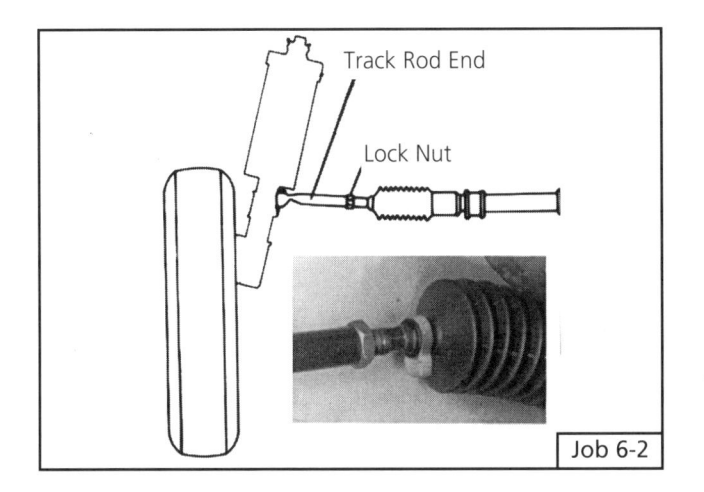

Job 6-2

❏ **Step 2:** Undo the securing clips and remove the gaiter (inset).

❏ **Step 3:** Wipe away contaminated grease and replace with new. Secure the new gaiter in position at both ends with new bands or screw-type clips.

❏ **Step 4:** Complete the reassembly in reverse order.

❏ **Step 5:** Clean and grease the tie bar threads before fitting the new balljoint to prevent future seizure. Fit the new balljoint in reverse order and, before using the car further, take it to your FIAT dealership or tyre specialist to have the front wheel alignment set. This is NOT a job you can do at home but it DOES need doing as soon as possible!

i INSIDE INFORMATION: While the TRE is detached, check it by swivelling it. If it is seized or is loose and worn, replace it now. Also, replace it if you accidentally damaged the TRE gaiter while removing it. *i*

Job 7. Steering rack - replacement.

Refer to illustration *Job 1-3*.

❏ **Step 1:** Raise the front of the car and support on axle stands. Remove the road wheels.

❏ **Step 2:** Undo the Track Rod Ends (TRE) balljoint nuts (see *Job 5*), then part the balljoints from the steering arms with a splitter tool.

❏ **Step 3:** Locate the column lower coupling to the splined pinion next to the front pedals, inside the car. Undo and remove the pinch bolt (arrowed).

Job 7-3

❏ **Step 4:** From under the bonnet, undo the bolts and remove the rack mounting clamps.

❏ **Step 5:** Supporting the steering rack, lower it away from the bulkhead to disengage from the column coupling and withdraw it from beneath a wheel arch.

Job 7-4

making it easy ❏ **Step 6:** The replacement rack should be 'centred' before installation.
• Measure the total travel of a track rod end when moved from lock to lock. Go back half this distance and your rack is centred. Check again after fitting.

❏ **Step 7:** Place the steering wheel in the dead ahead position and engage the rack pinion splines with the column coupling.

❏ **Step 8:** Continue refitting in reverse order of removal.

❏ **Step 9:** Clean and grease the tie bar threads before fitting the new balljoint to prevent future seizure. Fit the new balljoint in reverse order and, before using the car further, take it to your FIAT dealership or tyre specialist to have the front wheel alignment set. This is NOT a job you can do at home but it DOES need doing as soon as possible!

Job 8. Rear axle - removal and refitting.

LEAF-SPRING MODELS ONLY

Refer to illustrations *Job 1-4A* and *Job 1-4B*.

CHAPTER 6 PART G: SUSPENSION

❑ **Step 1:** Raise the rear of the car and support safely under a structural area of the bodywork.

❑ **Step 2:** Remove the road wheels.

❑ **Step 3:** Release the handbrake cables from their axle tube retainers and disconnect from the levers on the brake backplates.

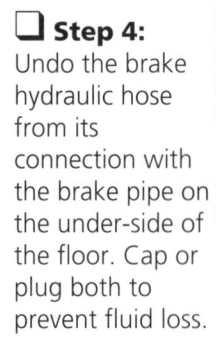

❑ **Step 4:** Undo the brake hydraulic hose from its connection with the brake pipe on the under-side of the floor. Cap or plug both to prevent fluid loss.

❑ **Step 5A: 4x4 MODELS ONLY:** Unbolt the shock absorbers from the axle casing.

❑ **Step 5B:** Undo the axle-to-spring 'U' bolts and release all the shackle plates, including the shock absorber mounting on non-4x4 models.

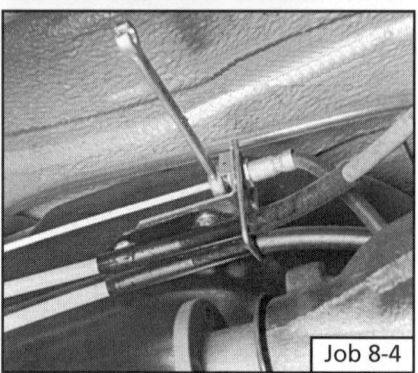

❑ **Step 6:** Remove one buffer from a side box member. Lift the axle and bring out sideways between the side member and road spring. Refit in reverse order. Bleed the rear brake hydraulics. See **PART H: BRAKES**.

IMPORTANT NOTE: After refitting, do not tighten the bolts right up until the weight of the vehicle is back on its rear wheels, such as on wheel ramps.

Job 9. Rear leaf spring - replacement.

Refer to illustration **Job 1-4A** and **Job 1-4B**.

❑ **Step 1:** Raise the rear of the car, leaving the road wheels just touching the ground.

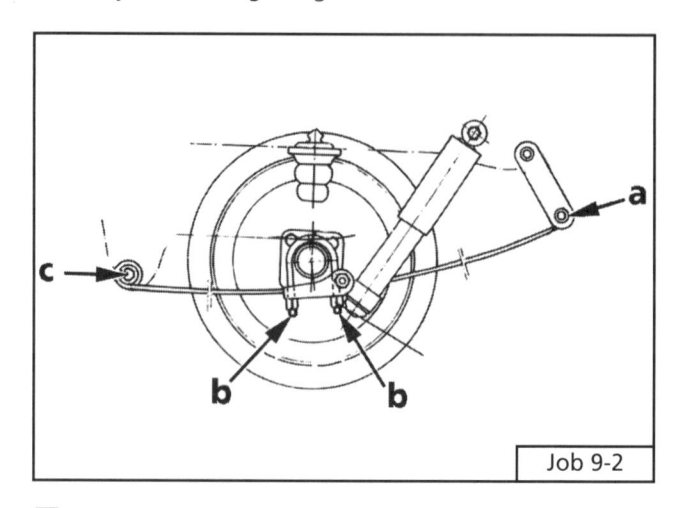

❑ **Step 2:** Undo the rear swinging shackle bolt (**a**) and remove it.

❑ **Step 3:** Undo the 'U' bolts (**Job 9-2, b**) and lower the spring.

❑ **Step 4:** Undo the front fixed shackle bolt (**Job 9-2, c**) and remove the spring.

❑ **Step 5:** Refit in reverse order and note that you may have to replace the spring on the other side if the ride height is not the same on both sides.

IMPORTANT NOTE: After refitting, do not tighten the bolts right up until the weight of the vehicle is back on its rear wheels, such as on wheel ramps. Recheck the 'U'-bolts for tightness after a test run.

Job 10. Rear shock absorber - replacement.

❑ **Step 1:** Undo the top and bottom mountings (arrowed) on all models and remove the old unit from the car.

❑ **Step 2:** Refit in reverse order.

❑ **Step 3:** Check the bushes - renew if necessary.

SAFETY FIRST!

● Always replace shock absorbers in pairs to ensure safe handling.

making it easy! ● To reduce the risk of shearing off the mounting pins, soak the threads with Releasing Fluid several times over a couple of days before removal.

Job 11. Rear suspension overhaul - 'Omega' type.

COIL-SPRUNG REAR SUSPENSION MODELS ONLY

Refer to *Job 1-5*.

❑ **Step 1:** If either of the reaction rods (*Job 1-5,* arrowed) is damaged, or the bushes are worn, the whole reaction rod will have to be replaced.

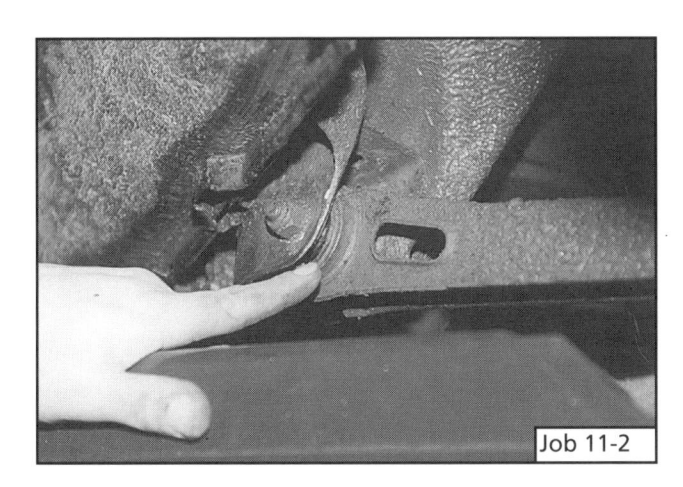

Job 11-2

❑ **Step 2:** Reaction rods are held with a bolt and locknut at each end.

making it easy! ● These nuts and bolts can corrode heavily. Soak several times with Releasing Fluid over a couple of days before attempting the remove.
● If necessary, cut between bracket and bush with a padsaw - a tedious business!

❑ **Step 3:** If a coil spring breaks, replace them both.

i **INSIDE INFORMATION:** FIAT coil springs have either a YELLOW or GREEN stripe, to assist matching. Both must be of the same colour. *i*

❑ **Step 4:** Support the rear of the body, with the wheels off the ground. Remove the wheels and support the axle beam with a trolley jack and support bar.

Job 11-4

❑ **Step 5:** Disconnect one end of the reaction rods and the shock absorbers. Lower the axle sufficiently to remove and replace the springs.

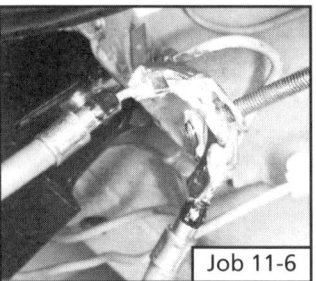

Job 11-6    Job 11-7

❑ **Step 6:** If the axle beam has to be removed completely, disconnect the handbrake cable, just in front of the central axle mounting...

❑ **Step 7:** ...and disconnect the adjacent rigid pipe from the flexible hose and remove the flexible hose from the bracket.

❑ **Step 8:** The bolt passing through the central bush and bracket is removed and the axle will come free. If the flexible bush is worn or has deteriorated, the complete axle tube will have to be replaced.

Job 11-8

Job 12. Rear hub bearings - replacement.

IMPORTANT NOTE: FIAT Panda hub bearings have a much longer service life because they are factory built into the hub. The bearing races cannot be replaced separately.

❑ **Step 1:** Raise the rear of the car and support on stands. Remove the rear wheel.

❑ **Step 2:** Unscrew the road wheel alignment spigot and brake drum fixing bolt and pull off the brake drum. See **PART H: BRAKES.** Remove the brake shoes.

CHAPTER 6 PART H: BRAKES

Step 3: 4x4 MODELS ONLY. Remove the bolt fixing the drive shaft to the wheel hub.

Job 12-3

Step 4: Undo the bolts holding the hub and brake backplate to the axle.

Job 12-4

Step 5: Take out the wheel hub retaining nut. Remove the hub/bearing assembly (arrowed). On 4x4 models, you may need a puller to get the hub off the driveshaft splines. On non-4x4 models, you may need a puller to remove the hub nut cap, or tap all around it with a hammer and drift.

Job 12-5

Step 6: Check the end of the stub axle, where the bearing fits. If there are any signs of distortion, cracks or wear, the axle tube will have to be replaced.

Step 7: Fitting the new hub/bearing assembly is carried out in the reverse order.

For front hubs and bearings. See *PART B: TRANSMISSION AND CLUTCH, Job 9.*

Job 13. Steering wheel - removal/replacement

See *PART E: ELECTRICAL AND INSTRUMENTS Job 6, Instruments - removal and refitting on page 105.*

PART H: BRAKES

PART H: Contents

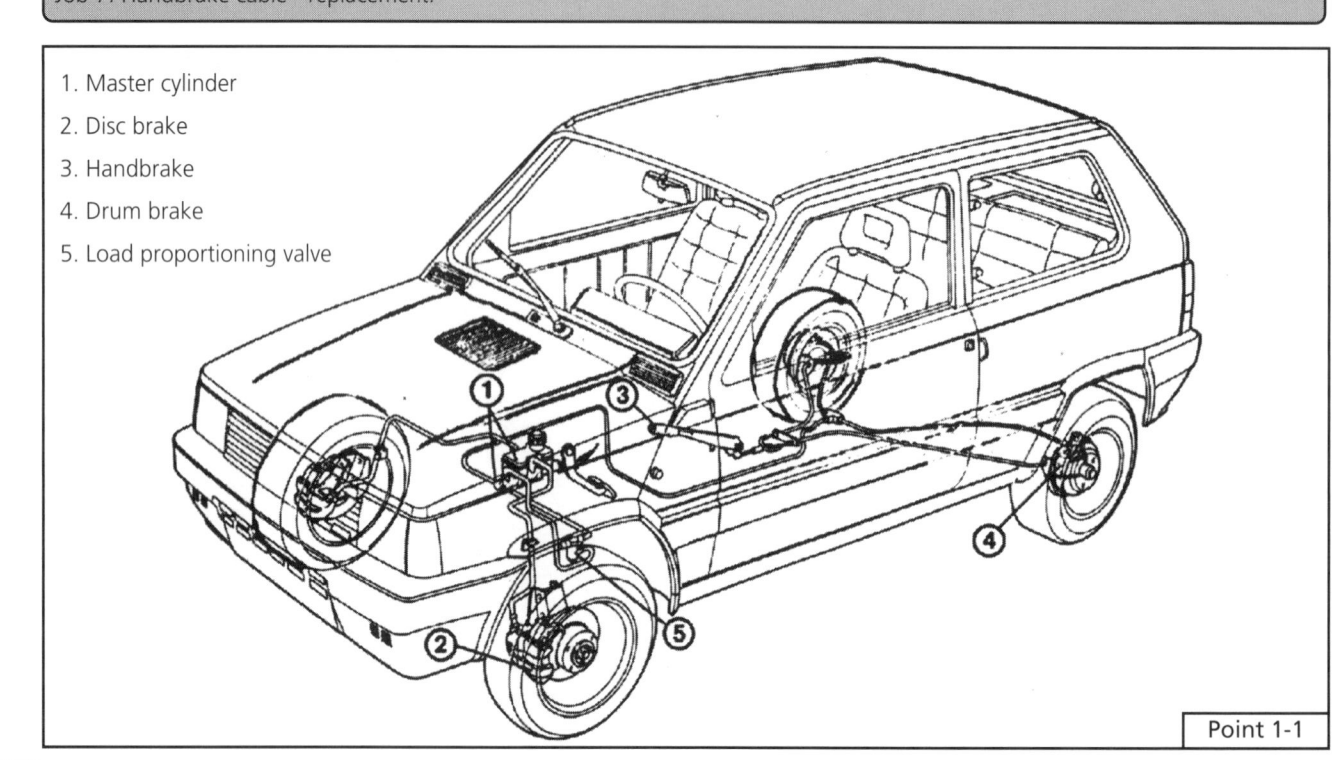

Job 1. Understanding Panda brakes.
Job 2. Disc brake pads - replacement.
Job 3. Disc brake calipers - replacement.
Job 4. Brake disc - replacement.
Job 5. Brake shoes - replacement.
Job 6.. Wheel cylinder - replacement.
Job 7. Handbrake cable - replacement.
Job 8. Master cylinder - replacement.
Job 9. Load proportioning valve - replacement.
Job 10. Servo-check, remove and refit.
Job 11. Flexible hoses - replacement.
Job 12. Metal pipes - replacement.
Job 13. Brake bleeding.

1. Master cylinder
2. Disc brake
3. Handbrake
4. Drum brake
5. Load proportioning valve

Point 1-1

Job 1. Understanding Panda brakes.

❏ **Point 1:** Illustration **Job 1-1** shows the layout of the standard model braking system. (Obviously, the brake pedal and master cylinder are on the other side on right-hand drive cars.)

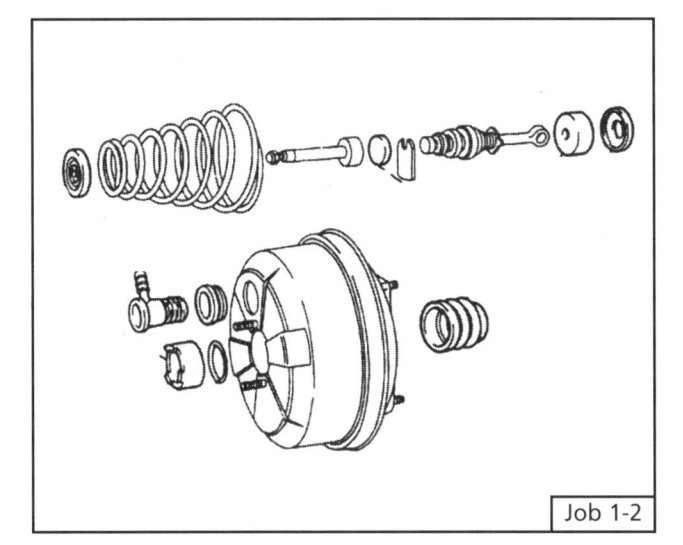

Job 1-2

❏ **Point 2:** 4x4, Selecta (automatic) and very late manual models also have a brake servo unit, situated behind the master cylinder.

❏ **Point 3:** Selecta front brakes are of a different type and rear wheel cylinders are larger than those fitted to other Pandas.

Job 2. Disc brake pads - replacement.

IMPORTANT NOTE: Copper-impregnated grease should be lightly smeared on the edge of the caliper piston where it touches the pad and on all sliding surfaces to prevent seizure.

PART A - CALIPER WITHOUT INSPECTION OPENING

The amount of dismantling needed in order to replace the brake pads of this caliper type is the same as for checking them. Therefore, see **Chapter 5, Servicing Your Car, Job 49.**

PART B - CALIPER WITH INSPECTION OPENING

i INSIDE INFORMATION: The brake pads should be replaced before the friction material thickness falls to no less than 1.5 mm. This can be seen through the opening in the caliper body - although you'll see better if you swing the caliper away, as shown. *i*

❏ **Step B1:** Slacken the front wheel bolts, raise the front of the car and support on axle stands. See **Chapter 1, Safety First!** Remove the front wheels.

❏ **Step B2:** Undo the lower guide bolts of the caliper cylinder housing. Slacken the top bolt but don't remove it.

❏ **Step B3:** Unplug the sensor wiring if fitted. Swing the cylinder housing upwards and tie it clear.

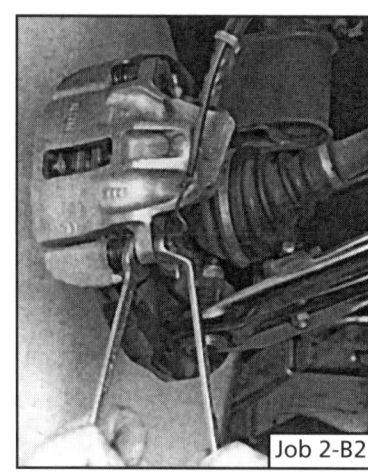

Job 2-B2

❏ **Step B4:** Remove the pads, complete with anti-rattle springs.

❏ **Step B5:** Using a spray on brake cleaner, clean away all dirt and dust, taking care not to inhale it. See **Chapter 1, Safety First!**

❏ **Step B6:** Loosen the cap on the master cylinder, push in the caliper pistons to allow for extra thickness of the new pads, syphoning off excess fluid from the reservoir to prevent spillage - often a flat blade has to be used to lever the pad back - retracting the piston.

❏ **Step B7:** Reassemble in the reverse order, tightening new cylinder housing bolts to the specified torque. See **Chapter 3, Facts and Figures.**

IMPORTANT NOTE: Always use new FIAT caliper mounting bolts - they are of a special self-locking type - when refitting the caliper.

❏ **Step B8:** Pump the brake pedal to bring the pads into contact with the discs and top-up the brake fluid.

❏ **Step B9:** Refit the road wheels and lower the car to the ground.

Job 3. Disc brake calipers - replacement.

See **Chapter 5, Servicing Your Car**, for illustrations relating to this job.

❏ **Step 1:** Slacken the front wheel bolts, raise the front of the car and support on axle stands. See **Chapter 1, Safety First!** Remove the front wheels.

❏ **Step 2:** Clean dirt from the union at the caliper end of the flexible hose and undo the union. Cap, plug or clamp the exposed pipe end to prevent fluid loss. If clamping, use only a purpose-built brake hose clamp.

❏ **Step 3:** Refit the wheels, lower the car to the ground, and tighten the wheel bolts.

CHAPTER 6 PART H: BRAKES

PART A - CALIPER WITHOUT INSPECTION OPENING

☐ **Step A1:** Remove the spring clips and locking blocks and remove the caliper brake pads.

☐ **Step A2:** Check the condition of the brake hose, replace it if showing signs of cracking or perishing or if it has rubbed or chaffed against any other component, then fit the new caliper in reverse order and bleed the front brake circuit. See *Part H, BRAKES, Job 13.*

PART B - SELECTA MODELS WITH INSPECTION OPENING

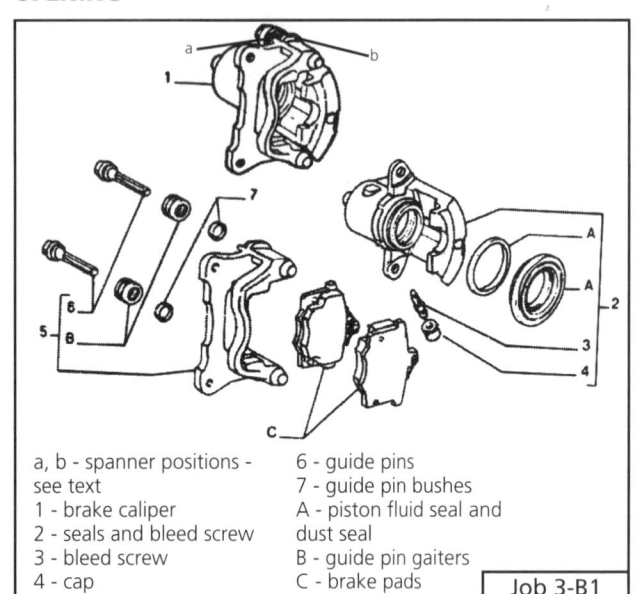

a, b - spanner positions - see text
1 - brake caliper
2 - seals and bleed screw
3 - bleed screw
4 - cap
6 - guide pins
7 - guide pin bushes
A - piston fluid seal and dust seal
B - guide pin gaiters
C - brake pads

Job 3-B1

☐ **Step B1:** Gently pull the caliper outwards to ease the piston a little way back into its bore, or use a flat blade to lever pad and piston back into the bore. Prevent each guide pin from turning, using a slim, open-ended spanner (*point a*) while unbolting the upper and lower guide bolts (*point b*). Lift off the caliper.

☐ **Step B2:** Check the condition of the brake hose (see *Step A2*), replace it if need be, then fit the new caliper in reverse order. Use NEW guide pin bolts tightened to the torque specified in **Chapter 3, Facts and Figures**, then bleed the front brake circuit. See *Job 13.*

☐ **Step B3:** Refit the wheels, lower the car to the ground, and tighten the wheel bolts.

Job 4. Brake disc - replacement.

☐ **Step 1:** Remove the caliper and pads. See **Job 3.**

☐ **Step 2:** Unbolt and remove the caliper support bracket, when fitted.

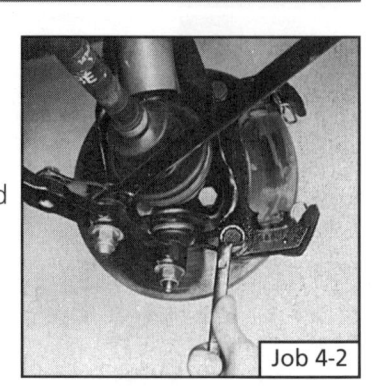

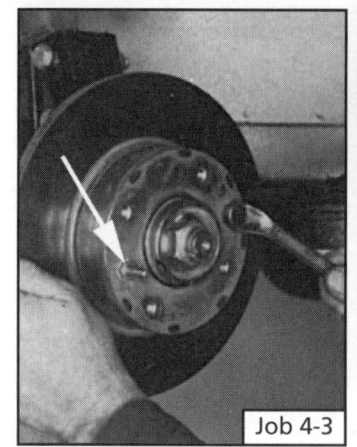

Job 4-2

Job 4-3

Job 4-4

☐ **Step 3:** Undo the fixing bolt and wheel locating spigot (arrowed)...

☐ **Step 4:** ...and remove the disc.

☐ **Step 5:** Refit in reverse order.

Job 5. Brake shoes - replacement.

i **INSIDE INFORMATION:** The brake shoe linings are bonded to the brake shoes. When the lining thickness is down to a minimum of 1.5 mm replace the shoes as a complete axle set. Work on one side at a time so that you have always got the other side as a visual guide. *i*

☐ **Step 1:** Jack up the rear of the car and support on stands.

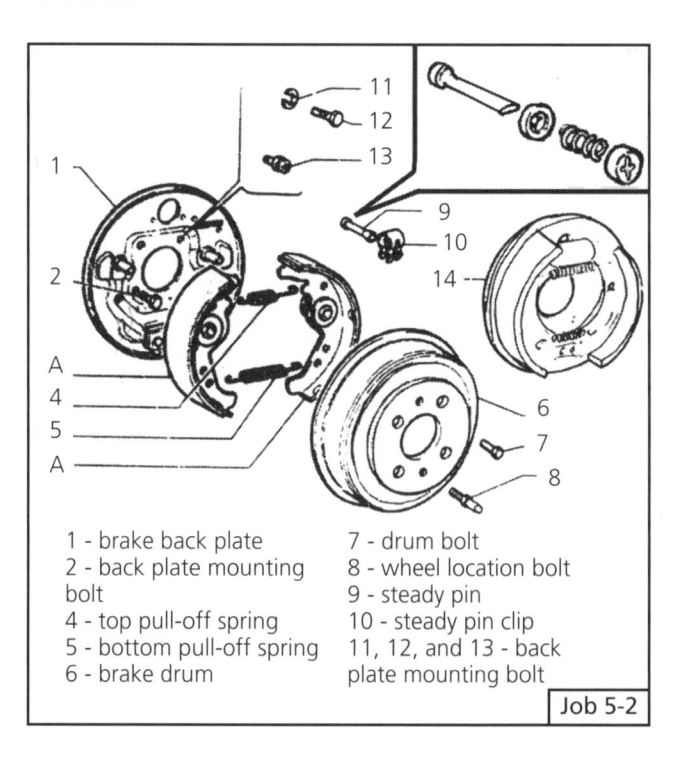

1 - brake back plate
2 - back plate mounting bolt
4 - top pull-off spring
5 - bottom pull-off spring
6 - brake drum
7 - drum bolt
8 - wheel location bolt
9 - steady pin
10 - steady pin clip
11, 12, and 13 - back plate mounting bolt

Job 5-2

☐ **Step 2:** Unscrew the drum securing bolts (**7** and **8**) and remove the drum (**6**). See **Chapter 5, Servicing Your Car.**

CHAPTER 6 PART H: BRAKES

Job 5-3

☐ **Step 3:** Wash the brake dust away with FIAT brake cleaner, taking care not to inhale any brake dust.

☐ **Step 4:** Undo the shoe steady pin by levering off the spring (*Job 5-2, part 10*) ...

Job 5-4

☐ **Step 5:** ... and removing the pin through the rear of the backplate. The earlier type is shown in illustration *Job 5-2, inset*

Job 5-5

☐ **Step 6:** Use self-locking grips to hold the top spring while you disengage it.

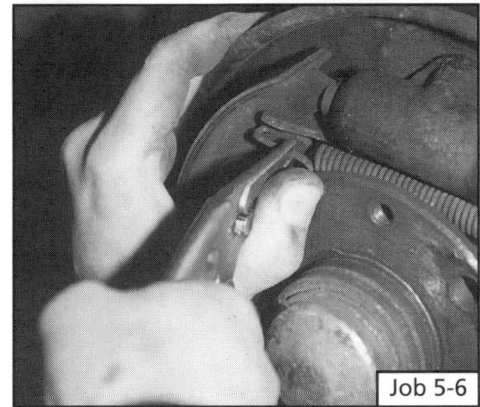

Job 5-6

☐ **Step 7:** Use larger grips to unhook the bottom of the shoe - to take the pressure off the spring - and remove the spring.

Job 5-7

☐ **Step 8:** You now have to turn the cut-outs on the hub flange (arrowed) so that the auto-adjusters clear the flange.

Job 5-8

i **Step 9:** INSIDE INFORMATION: While the shoes are off, check the wheel cylinder for leaks - peel back each rubber shroud - and push the pistons to-and-fro to make sure that they move freely. Replace if any problems are found. *i*

Job 5-9

Job 5-10

☐ **Step 10:** When reassembling, put a smear of lithium - based brake grease (not ordinary grease!) on all the working contact surfaces including those shown on the backplate, except the wheel cylinder piston ends.

127

CHAPTER 6 PART H: BRAKES

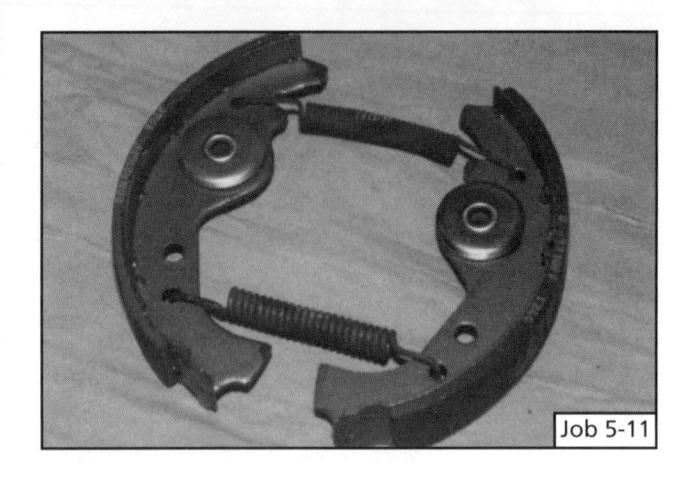

Job 5-11

☐ **Step 11:** Ensure that the springs are in the correct positions.

☐ **Step 12:** Do not forget to fit the shoe retaining pins and securing clips.

making it easy!
- **Step 13:** Compare with the other side for correct assembly.
- Repeat the whole operation on the second side using your first one as a guide if necessary.

☐ **Step 14:** Centralise and align the shoes by tapping them towards the centre of the hub with a soft mallet. This moves them against the pressure of the self adjuster springs.

☐ **Step 15:** Clean the dust from the drums and check their condition. Use a piece of fine emery cloth to deglaze them. Refit the brake drums and securing bolts.

☐ **Step 16:** Pump the brake pedal a few times to bring the linings into contact with the drums. Refit the road wheels and lower the car to the ground. Check the wheel nuts for tightness.

Job 6. Wheel cylinder - replacement.

☐ **Step 1:** Remove the brake shoes. See *Job 5*.

☐ **Step 2:** Disconnect the brake pipe from the back of the wheel cylinder (see *point a*) and seal the pipe end.

Job 6-2

☐ **Step 3:** Undo the fixing bolts (*Job 6-2*, arrowed) and remove the wheel cylinder from the backplate.

☐ **Step 4:** Fit the new cylinder to the backplate and connect the brake pipe. We strongly recommend that you do not attempt to overhaul a seized, leaking or damaged wheel cylinder. Replace it with a new unit from your FIAT dealership.

☐ **Step 5:** Refit the brake shoes, drum and road wheel.

☐ **Step 6:** Bleed the rear brake hydraulics. See *Job 13*.

Job 7. Handbrake cable - replacement.

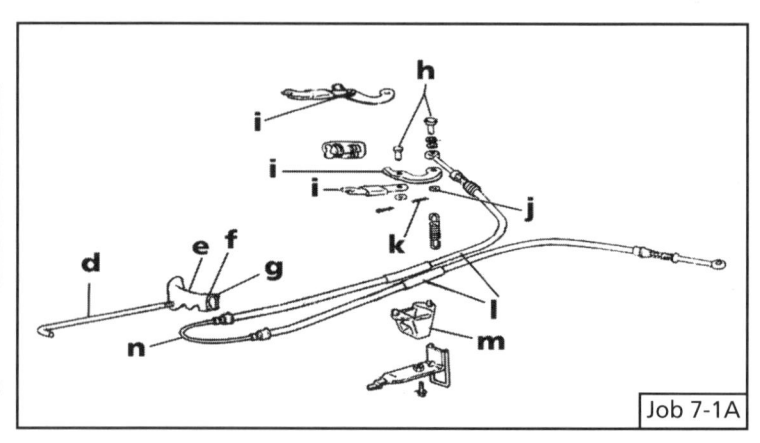

Job 7-1A

a - release button
b - handbrake lever
c - toothed sector
d - adjuster rod
e - cable anchorage
f - adjuster nut
g - locknut
h - clevis pin
i - brake shoes operating lever
j - washer
k - split pin
l - inner and outer cable
m - axle bracket
n - inner cable
o - cover
p - backplate grommet

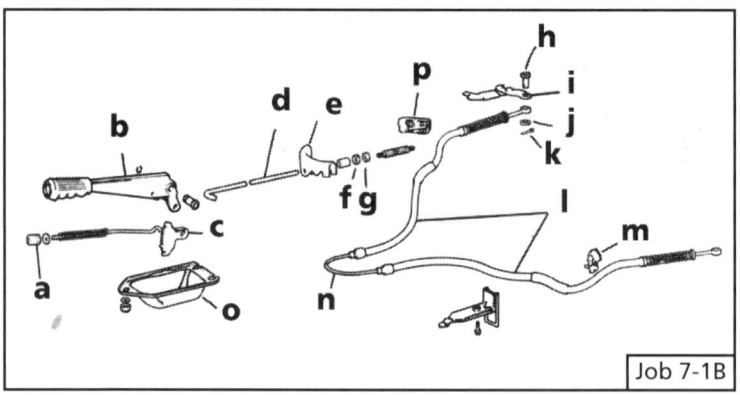

Job 7-1B

☐ **Step 1A:** The handbrake cables on earlier models, with leaf-spring suspension are different from those on later models with coil-spring. This is the earlier type. Two different types of brake shoes operating lever were used, as shown.

☐ **Step 1B:** This is the handbrake mechanism as fitted to Pandas from 1986-on.

128

❑ **Step 2:** Chock front and back of the front wheels and release the handbrake. Loosen the rear wheel nuts, raise the rear of the car and support securely. Remove the rear wheels.

❑ **Step 3:** Unscrew the adjuster nut and locknut and release the cable anchorage and cable from the adjuster rod.

❑ **Step 4:** Disconnect the cable from the axle tube brackets.

❑ **Step 5:** Disconnect the ends of the handbrake cable from the brake shoe operating levers. Straighten out the split pins and remove. Pull out the clevis pin.

❑ **Step 6:** Check the clevis pins (4 on earliest cars) and renew if excessively worn. Renew the brake shoes operating levers, if necessary. Grease on reassembly and use new split pins.

❑ **Step 7:** Fit the new cable in the reverse order.

❑ **Step 8:** Adjust the handbrake correctly. See **Chapter 5, Servicing Your Car, Job 51**.

Job 8. Master cylinder - replacement.

❑ **Step 1:** Raise the bonnet and cover the wings to protect them against a possible spillage of brake fluid. Brake fluid damages paintwork and some plastics.

❑ **Step 2:** Locate the master cylinder on the engine compartment bulkhead. Disconnect the leads from the reservoir cap, unscrew and remove the cap and float. Syphon out as much brake fluid as possible.

❑ **Step 3:** Unscrew the pipe unions and ease them clear of the master cylinder. Use a container to catch lost fluid.

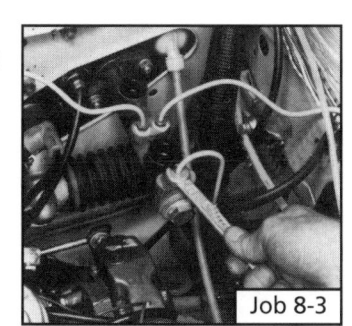

Job 8-3

❑ **Step 4:** Undo the mounting nuts and remove the master cylinder.

❑ **Step 5:** Fit the new cylinder in reverse order ensuring sound connections of the fluid pipe unions.

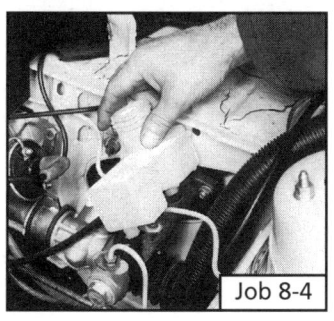

Job 8-4

❑ **Step 6:** Bleed the complete brake system. See **Job 13**. Wash away any spilt brake fluid with plenty of water, and wipe off.

Job 9. Load proportioning valve - replacement.

If the load proportioning valve becomes faulty, it cannot be overhauled but must be replaced. Its position varies slightly on different vehicles but can be found on the left-hand inner wing, inside the engine bay. Illustration **Job 9-1** shows the valve next to the master cylinder on the left-hand drive vehicle.

❑ **Step 1:** Unscrew each of the brake pipes (arrowed) from the valve and tape over the ends of the pipes to prevent any dirt from getting in. Unbolt the valve from the vehicle.

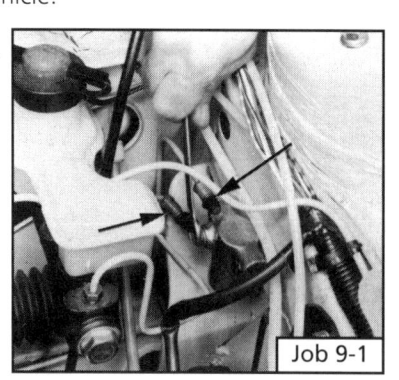

❑ **Step 2:** Fit the new valve as a direct replacement for the old one.

Job 9-1

❑ **Step 3:** Bleed the brakes as described in **Job 13**.

Job 10. Servo - check, remove and refit.

WHERE APPLICABLE

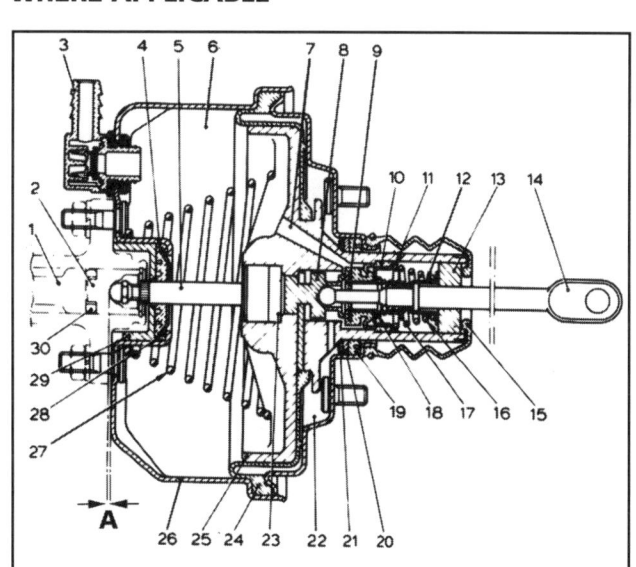

1 - master cylinder casing
2 - piston
3 - low pressure valve
4 - front seal
5 - hydraulic piston rod
6 - front chamber
7 - vacuum duct
8 - valve piston
9 - gasket centring ring
10 - valve
11 - valve cap
12 - spring retainer cap
13 - filter element
14 - control rod - brake pedal connection
15 - protective boot
16 - piston valve return spring
17 - valve return spring
18 - valve cap
19 - rear seal
20 - seal
21 - cap
22 - rear chamber
23 - reaction disc
24 - diaphragm
25 - control piston
26 - front cover
27 - return spring
28 - cap
29 - bush
30 - seal

Job 10-1

❏ **Step 1:** Take note of the component parts shown on page 129, as they relate to the following text.

ℹ **INSIDE INFORMATION:** Before condemning the servo for lack of efficiency, check the condition of the one way valve and the vacuum pipe connecting it to the inlet manifold.
• Ease the valve out of the front of the servo and disconnect the pipe from the inlet manifold.
• Check that you can only blow one way through the valve - from the servo end towards the inlet manifold.
• The vacuum pipe can suffer failure in many ways. Age can harden it until it cracks, causing an air leak which sometimes results in a whistling noise and rough slow running.
• Loose connections could also produce the same result.
• The other type of vacuum hose failure is an implosion, (where the hose is sucked flat by the vacuum). This is often the result of softening of the hose by oil contamination for example. This is not so easily detected as it rarely upsets the engine performance and resumes its normal shape shortly after stopping the engine.
• The inner lining can also deteriorate, causing a blockage. ℹ

❏ **Step 2:** Disconnect the wires from the reservoir cap, remove the cap and float. Syphon out as much fluid from the reservoir as possible.

❏ **Step 3:** Undo the pipe unions at the master cylinder, ease clear and plug the ends.

❏ **Step 4:** From inside the car, disconnect the servo pushrod from the pedal and undo the servo mounting nuts. Remove the servo and be careful not to spill fluid onto the paintwork.

❏ **Step 5:** Measure the projection of the servo piston pushrod. With the master cylinder fitted there should be a clearance of between 0.825 mm and 1.025 mm between the primary piston face and the end of the pushrod. Use the mating surfaces of the master cylinder and servo as the reference point. See **'A'**, in illustration **Job 10-1**.

❏ **Step 6:** Move the adjusting screw on the servo as necessary and apply locking fluid to the thread when finished.

❏ **Step 7:** Complete the reassembly in the reverse order and bleed the brakes. See **PART H: BRAKES, Job 13**.

Job 11. Flexible hoses - replacement.

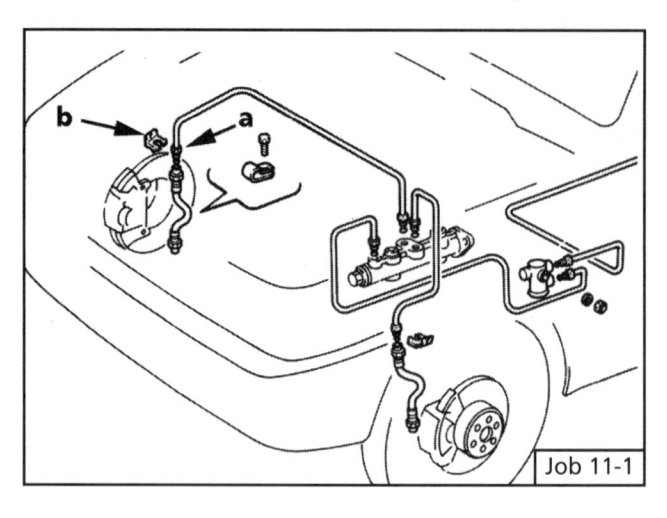

❏ **Step 1:** Unscrew the union on the end of the rigid pipe (**a**) where it screws into the flexible hose at the support bracket. Take care not to damage the bracket or tear it off the body.

❏ **Step 2:** Remove the clip (**Job 11-1, part b**) securing the hose to the bracket and take the hose from the bracket. You can now unscrew the other end of the flexible hose with a spanner.

❏ **Step 3:** Fit the new hose in the reverse order, making sure that it is not twisted when refitting the rigid hose.

making it easy!
• If the pipe starts to twist with the union, grip the pipe with a self - grip wrench as lightly as you can get away with and see if you can stop if from turning.

• If not, cut through the pipe with a junior hacksaw and replace the length of rigid pipe.

❏ **Step 4:** Check that the hose cannot chafe anywhere or be under tension, over the whole range of steering and suspension movement.

❏ **Step 5:** Bleed the hydraulics. See **Job 13**.

Job 12. Metal pipes - replacement.

☐ **Step 1:** Undo the unions at each end of the pipe. Patience and releasing fluid are often required because of the union seizing on its threads and on the pipe. A pipe spanner makes the job **much** easier!

☐ **Step 2:** Detach from the securing clips on bodywork or axle and remove.

i **Step 3:** INSIDE INFORMATION: Where possible, use the old pipe as a pattern to shape the new one prior to fitting. *i*

☐ **Step 4:** Follow the original route and secure the pipe in all of the body clips, renewing any damaged or missing ones.

☐ **Step 5:** Connect the unions and bleed the system. See *Job 13*.

i INSIDE INFORMATION: Unless the master cylinder has been disturbed, it will only be necessary to bleed the end of the car having work carried out on it. Start with the bleed screw furthest from the master cylinder. *i*

Job 13. Brake bleeding.

IMPORTANT NOTE: Take great care not to let the master cylinder run out of brake fluid. Otherwise you will introduce fresh air into the system and have to start again. Use ONLY fresh brake fluid from a previously unopened container.

A - WITH A HELPER

☐ **Step A1:** Push a tight-fitting length of plastic or rubber tubing onto the first bleed screw and immerse the other end in a small quantity of brake fluid contained in a glass jar.

Job 13-A1

☐ **Step A2:** Undo the bleed screw half-a-turn. Have your helper push the brake pedal smoothly and steadily to the floor and hold it there while you lock up the bleed valve. Then release the pedal slowly. Repeat several times, with the following suggested dialogue:

YOU. (*Open bleed screw*) "Open!"
HELPER. (*Pushes pedal down*) "Down!"
YOU. (*Close bleed screw*) "Closed!"
HELPER. (*Lets pedal up*) "Up!" - repeated, as necessary.

☐ **Step A3:** Top up the fluid reservoir frequently while repeating the bleeding operation until all the air is expelled and no bubbles appear in the jar.

☐ **Step A4:** Bleed the remaining screws - one at each brake - in the same way.

☐ **Step A5:** Go round again, if necessary, to obtain a firm brake pedal.

B - WITH A ONE-WAY BLEEDING KIT

☐ **Step B1:** Connect the one-way tube fitted with a non-return valve, securely to the bleeding screw. Open the screw one half turn.

☐ **Step B2:** Press the pedal all the way down and release slowly. Keep an eye on the fluid level in the reservoir and repeat several times.

☐ **Step B3:** Lock up the bleed screw and remove the tube. Bleed the remainder as required.

☐ **Step B4:** Go round again, if necessary, to obtain a firm brake pedal.

C - WITH A PRESSURE KIT

☐ **Step C1:** Attach the pressure kit to the brake reservoir.

☐ **Step C2:** Undo each bleed screw in turn and allow the fluid to flow until clear and free of bubbles, then lock up.

Job 13-C1

☐ **Step C3:** Go round again, if necessary, to obtain a firm brake pedal.

☐ **Step C4:** Remove the pressure kit.

SAFETY FIRST!

• After completing the bleeding operation and with your helper's foot firmly on the brake pedal, check all connections for leaks.
• Remember to top up the fluid, replace the master cylinder cap and reconnect the wires to it.

CHAPTER 6 PART H: BRAKES

131

PART I: BODY AND INTERIOR

PART I: Contents

Job 1. Bumpers - removal and refitting.
Job 2. Door trim panel - removal and refitting.
Job 3. Door locks and handles - removal and refitting.
Job 4. Window regulator - removal and refitting.
Job 5. Door - removal and refitting.
Job 6. Bonnet - removal and refitting.
Job 7. Bonnet lock and release cable.
Job 8. Tailgate and strut - removal and refitting
Job 9. Rear view mirrors.

Job 1. Bumpers - removal and refitting.

Job 1-1A

❑ **Step 1A:** This is the earlier bumper. Locate all of the fixing bolts and (after soaking the threads with releasing fluid) undo and remove including the domed bolt head covers.

i INSIDE INFORMATION: The square bolt shanks are supposed to be prevented from turning by square holes in the bumper. If they turn, you'll have to cut the nuts off. *i*

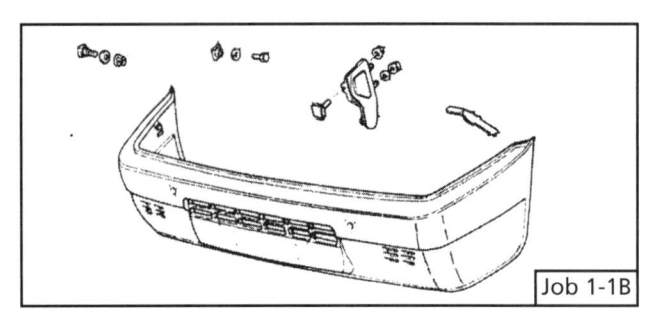

Job 1-1B

❑ **Step 1B:** These are the restyled-Panda bumper fixing bolts. There are two on each outer end, and two more brackets, each side of the grille (front) and number plate mounting (rear).

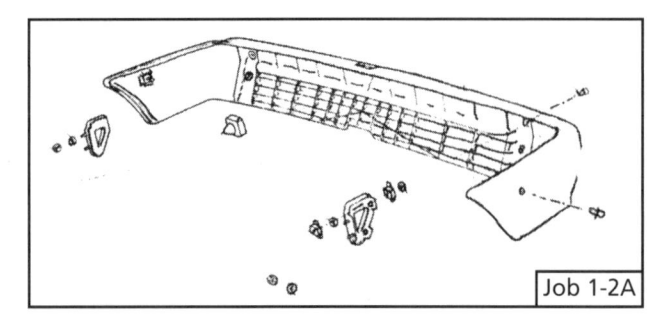

Job 1-2A

❑ **Step 2A:** Disconnect the number plate light leads before removing the rear bumper. This is the early type...

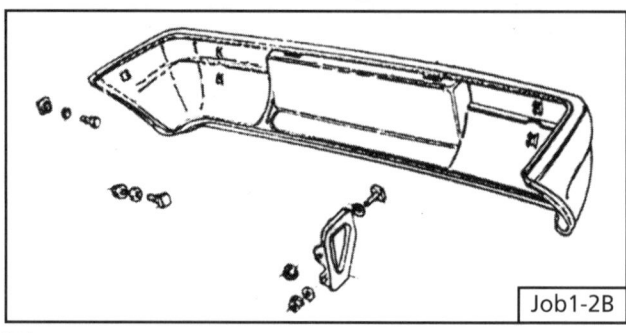

Job1-2B

❑ **Step 2B:** ...and this is the later, 'restyled' type.

❑ **Step 3:** Refit in reverse order and remember to transfer the number plate and light from the old rear bumper.

Job 2. Door trim panel - removal and refitting.

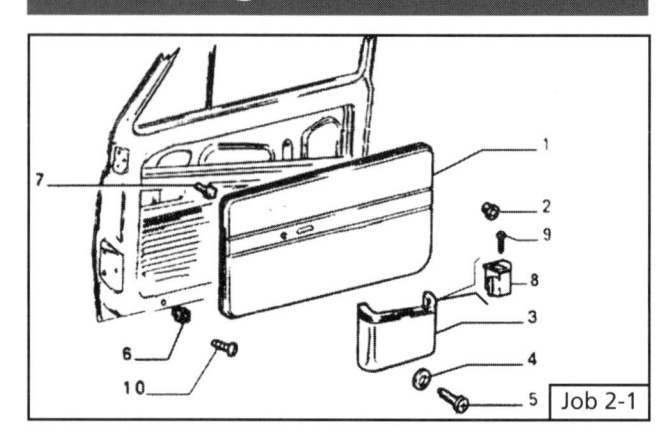

Job 2-1

❑ **Step 1:** Undo the screws (**5**) securing the door pocket (**3**) and remove.

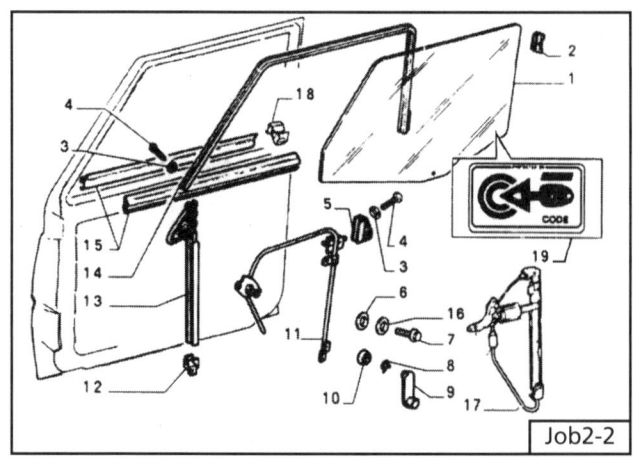

Job2-2

❑ **Step 2:** Remove the window regulator handle (**9**) by undoing the screw, or if no screw is fitted, by removing the spring clip (**8**). Push back the trim, look behind the handle and you'll see it.

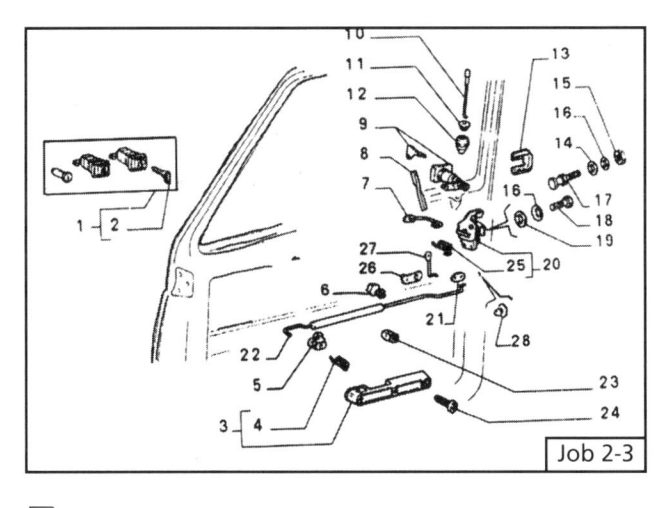

Job 2-3

☐ **Step 3:** Remove the door pull/remote lock handle far enough to be unhooked from the link rod by revolving it through a quarter turn.

☐ **Step 4:** Grip the edge of the door panel and carefully pull it back with a jerk to release it from its retaining clips. Alternatively, lever carefully next to each clip with a screwdriver.

☐ **Step 5:** Refit in the reverse order.

Job 3. Door locks and handles - removal and refitting.

☐ **Step 1:** Remove the door trim. See *Job 2*.

☐ **Step 2:** Undo the lock fixing screws from the edge of the door (see *Job 2-3, part 18*) and remove the lock (*part 20*).

☐ **Step 3:** To remove the exterior handle (see *Job 2-3, part 9*), release the forked spring clip (*part 13*) inside the door cavity.

☐ **Step 4:** Refit in reverse order.

Job 4. Window regulator - removal and refitting.

☐ **Step 1:** Remove the door trim as described in *Job 2*.

☐ **Step 2:** Refer to the illustration *Job 2-2* in connection with this Job.

☐ **Step 3:** Disconnect the door glass carrier clamps from the cable...

☐ **Step 4:** ...and remove the window winder cable from the pulleys.

☐ **Step 5:** Push on the winder handle temporarily and fully lower the glass.

☐ **Step 6:** Pull the winder handle back off the regulator and remove the two bolts holding the regulator to the door. Remove the regulator.

☐ **Step 7:** Take out the bolts and disconnect the door glass lower fixing and remove the glass carrier.

☐ **Step 8:** Carefully remove the weather strip from the upper edge of the door panel.

☐ **Step 9:** The glass can now be lifted out of the door frame, upwards and towards the outside of the door. Lift and turn the front corner of the glass first, so that the door glass comes out more easily.

IMPORTANT NOTE: The quarter light can be removed with the door glass still in place provided that the glass is first wound down.

☐ **Step 10:** Two screws hold the top of the quarter light to the front, sloping edge of the door frame. Remove the screws and take out the quarter light assembly.

Job 5. Door - removal and refitting.

☐ **Step 1:** Tap the top hinge cover towards the front of the car and remove it.

☐ **Step 2:** Use a felt pen to draw around the hinge so that it can be refitted in precisely the same position.

☐ **Step 3:** Prise out the cover plate over the two lower hinge bolts. Mark the position of the hinge with a felt pen through the aperture.

☐ **Step 4:** While an assistant supports the outer edge of the door, remove the bolts and lift the door away.

Job 6. Bonnet - removal and refitting.

☐ **Step 1:** Open the bonnet and support it with the bonnet stay (see illustration *Job 7-1, C*) firmly located in the bonnet, in position (**D**).

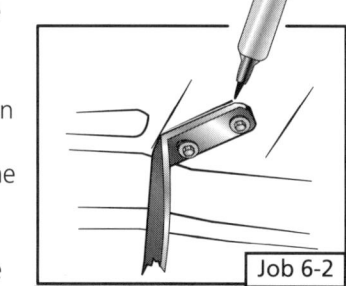

☐ **Step 2:** Use a felt pen to draw around each hinge where it bolts to the bonnet.

☐ **Step 3:** Take out the hinge bolts from one side of the bonnet and have an assistant carefully support the bonnet on that side while you take out the bolts from the other side. Lift the bonnet away.

Job 6-2

making it easy ☐ **Step 4:** When you and your assistant replace the bonnet, place a piece of cloth under each back corner so that it doesn't damage your car's bodywork.

CHAPTER 6 PART E: BODY AND INTERIOR

133

❑ **Step 5:** Align the hinge plates exactly with the felt pen marks you made when removing the bonnet, so that it fits correctly.

i INSIDE INFORMATION: The bonnet closing buffers (illustration **Job 7-1, B**) can be screwed up or down by hand, enabling the level of the bonnet to be adjusted in comparison with the height of each wing. *i*

Job 7. Bonnet lock and release cable.

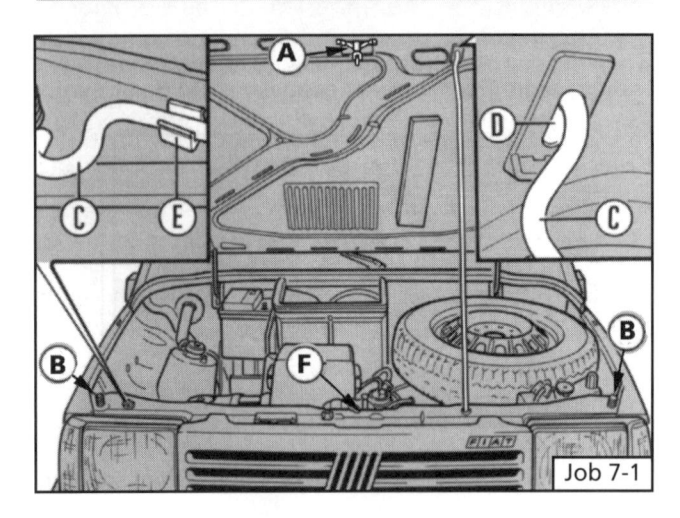

Job 7-1

❑ **Step 1:** Two small bolts locate the bonnet lock to the inside of the front rail (**F**). Before removing the lock, mark its position very accurately with a felt pen so that it can be replaced precisely.

❑ **Step 2:** When refitting the bonnet lock, its position has to be accurately set so that the bonnet striker (see **Job 7-1, A**) aligns with the lock.

❑ **Step 3:** The lock adjustment should be carried out in conjunction with the positioning of the rubber buffers described in **Job 6**.

SAFETY FIRST!

• **Step 4:** Make sure that the bonnet closes positively when it is pressed down and that the safety catch operates correctly.

❑ **Step 5:** When replacing the bonnet release cable, note that it has to be cut away from the bonnet lock with a pair of side cutters or pliers. It can then be detached from the bonnet release handle inside the passenger compartment and withdrawn through the bulkhead and into the car interior.

❑ **Step 6:** When fitting a new cable, start by locating it onto the bonnet release handle inside the car, pass it through the bulkhead and into the engine bay, then when the slack has been taken out of the cable it will have to be secured at the bonnet lock.

i INSIDE INFORMATION: Buy a new crimping tag from your FIAT dealer or purchase a solderless nipple from a bicycle accessories supplier in order to attach the cable. *i*

Job 8. Tailgate and strut - removal and refitting.

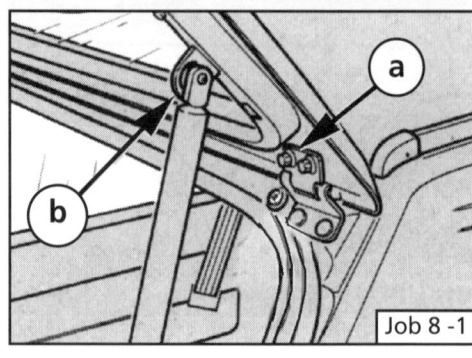

❑ **Step 1:** Use a felt pen to draw around the hinge plates where they fit against the inside of the tailgate (**a**) so that they can be refitted later in exactly the same position.

Job 8-1

❑ **Step 2:** Disconnect the following:
• the leads from the rear screen heater.
• the leads from the wiper motor.
• the plastic tube from the windscreen washer jet.

❑ **Step 3:** Have an assistant hold the tailgate open while you pull out the spring clips from the top of the strut (see **Job 8-1, b**) and the identical fixing at the bottom of the strut.

❑ **Step 4:** The hinge bolts can now be removed and the tailgate carefully lifted away.

making it easy! ❑ **Step 5:** When you and your assistant replace the tailgate, place a piece of cloth under each top corner so that it doesn't damage your car's bodywork.

Job 9. Rear view mirrors.

Interior Mirror

The interior mirror is held in place by a single screw.

Door Mirrors - non-adjustable

This type of door mirror is held in place with two clearly visible exterior cross-head screws.

Door Mirrors - remote

❑ **Step 1:** Pull off the rubber shroud from the control knob.

❑ **Step 2:** Undo the ring nut found beneath the shroud. Support the mirror from outside while the ring nut is disconnected and remove the mirror.

IMPORTANT NOTE: *Not all of the components listed here are fitted to all models.*

CHAPTER 7
WIRING DIAGRAMS

KEY: COMPONENT NUMBERS 1981-1986

00200	Alternator
00500	Battery
01001	Starter motor
01206	Windscreen wiper motor
01207	Rearscreen wiper motor
01400	Electric windscreen washer pump
01401	Electric rearscreen washer pump
01500	Radiator cooling fan
01504	Heater fan
02400	Ignition coil
03000	Engine oil pressure switch
03006	Handbrake warning light switch
03007	Brake lights switch
03008	Reversing light switch
03028	Radiator thermal switch
03029	Coolant overheating light switch
03054	External lights switch
03060	Rear foglight switch
03110	Heated rear window switch
03112	Rear window washer switch
03114	Heater fan switch
03110	Left door courtesy light switch
03319	Horn push button
03500	Ignition switch
03550	Hazard warning lights switch
04010	Direction indicators switch
04020	Headlights dipped and main beam switch
04032	Windscreen wash/wipe switch
04292	Heated rear window relay
04500	Windscreen wiper intermittent device
04581	Direction indicator flashers unit
04600	Distributor
04700	Water temperature sender unit
05004	Right front headlight, main and dipped beam, sidelight and direction indicator cluster
05005	Left front headlight, main and dipped beam, sidelight and direction indicator cluster
05412	Right front side indicator
05413	Left front side indicator
05640	Number plate light
05671	Rear sidelight, direction indicator brake light and reversing light cluster
05684	Left sidelight, direction indicator brake light and rear foglight cluster
06005	Courtesy light on rear view mirror with switch
06300	Sidelights warning light
06305	Main bean headlights warning light
06310	Rear foglight warning light
06315	Hazard warning lights warning light
06320	Direction indicators warning light
06337	Brake and handbrake warning light
06343	Engine oil pressure warning light
06345	Fuel reserve warning light
06355	Batter recharging warning light
06385	Heated rear windscreen warning light
06800	Horn
07003	Brake fluid level sensor
07050	Fuel gauge sender unit
07400	Fuel gauge
07415	Coolant temperature gauge
07461	Clock (if fitted)
09100	Heated rear windscreen element
59000	Cigar lighter
59010	Radio power lead (if fitted)
60220	Fusebox

KEY: COMPONENT NUMBERS 1986-ON

00200	Alternator
00203	Alternator
00208	Alternator with built-in regulator
00500	Battery
01001	Starter motor
01002	Starter motor
01206	Windscreen wiper motor
01207	Rearscreen wiper motor
01400	Electric windscreen washer pump
01401	Electric rearscreen washer pump
01402	Headlight washer pump
01405	Ignition coil
01500	Radiator cooling fan
01504	Heater fan
02405	Ignition coil
03000	Insufficient engine oil pressure warning light switch
03007	Brake lights switch
03008	Reversing lights switch
03015	Handbrake applied warning light switch
03028	Radiator thermal switch
03029	Coolant overheating thermal switch
03054	Main external lights switch
03060	Rear fog lights switch
03085	Micro-switch on pedal for accelerator pedal travel of 16-24mm
03086	Micro-switch on pedal for accelerator pedal travel of 3-7mm
03110	Heated rear windscreen switch
03114	Heater fan switch
03150	Rear drive engaged warning light switch
03305	Push button switch on right door pillar for courtesy light
03306	Push button switch on left door pillar for courtesy light
03315	Push button for electric windscreen washer pump
03319	Push button for horn
03336	Push button for headlight flashers
03500	Ignition switch
03511	Multiple switch on selector lever
03546	Rearscreen wash/wipe switch
03550	Hazard warning lights switch
04010	Steering column switch unit, direction indicators switch
04020	Steering column switch unit, headlights, main beam and dipped
04032	Steering column switch unit, windscreen wash/wipe control
04248	Headlight washer remote control switch with timer
04279	Starter inhibitor relay
04292	Heater rear windscreen relay
04305	Automatic transmission electronic control unit relay feed
04450	Remote control shunt to cut out lights in daytime
04500	Windscreen wiper intermittent device
04580	Flashers unit for direction indicators and hazard warning lights
04601	Distributor
04700	Coolant temperature sender unit
04730	Speedometer impulse generator
05004	Right main beam and dipped headlight with side light and direction indicator
05005	Left main beam and dipped headlight with side light and direction indicator
05671	Right rear light cluster: side light, direction indicator, brake light, reversing light
05684	Left rear light cluster: side light, direction indicator, brake light, rear fog light
06000	Light on rear view mirror with switch
06070	Ideogram light bulb
06080	Heater controls light bulb
06084	Instrument panel light bulb
06088	Cigar lighter light bulb
06104	Left side direction indicator
06105	Right side direction indicator
06108	Left no. plate light bulb
06109	Right no. plate light bulb
06300	Side lights warning light
06305	Main beam headlights warning light
06310	Rear fog lamps warning light
06315	Hazard warning lights warning light
06320	Direction indicators warning light
06343	Insufficient engine oil pressure warning light
06345	Fuel reserve warning light
06350	Coolant overheating warning light
06355	Battery recharging warning light
06366	Rear drive engaged warning light
06385	Heated rear windscreen warning light
06634	Timed buzzer signalling Park not engaged
06880	Horn
06887	Brake fluid and handbrake warning light
07003	Insufficient brake fluid level sensor
07012	Electronic clutch
07050	Fuel level gauge
07060	Idle cut out device
07400	Fuel level gauge
07415	Coolant temperature gauge
07460	Clock
08406	Relay and fuse box
08410	7.5 A fuse box
09100	Heated rear windscreen
09010	Radio (wiring)
10561	Automatic transmission electronic control unit
11062	Diagnostic socket
11065	Bridge as per legislation
40086	Join between dashboard cables and rear cables
40089	Join between dashboard cables and ceiling cables
59000	Cigar lighter
60000	Checking instrument
60120	Gear selector and engagement panel
70117	Right front earth
90003	Junction
A, B	Connector block

KEY: WIRING COLOUR CODES

A	Light Blue	AR	Light blue/Red	HV	Grey/Green
B	White	AV	Light blue/Green	LB	Blue/White
C	Orange	BG	White/Yellow	LG	Blue/Yellow
G	Yellow	BL	White/Blue	LN	Blue/Black
H	Grey	BN	White/Black	LR	Blue/Red
L	Blue	BR	White/Red	LV	Blue/Green
M	Brown	BV	White/Green	MB	Brown/White
N	Black	BZ	White/Violet	MN	Brown/Black
R	Red	CA	Orange/Light blue	NZ	Black/Violet
S	Pink	CB	Orange/White	RB	Red/White
V	Green	CN	Orange/Black	RG	Red/Yellow
Z	Violet	GN	Yellow/Black	RN	Red/Black
AB	Light blue/White	GL	Yellow/Blue	RV	Red/Green
AG	Light blue/Yellow	GR	Yellow/Red	SN	Pink/Black
AN	Light blue/Black	GV	Yellow/Green	VB	Green/White
		HG	Grey/Yellow	VN	Green/Black
		HN	Grey/Black	VR	Green/Red
		HR	Grey/Red	ZB	Violet/White

135

PART A: VEHICLES FROM 1981 - 1986

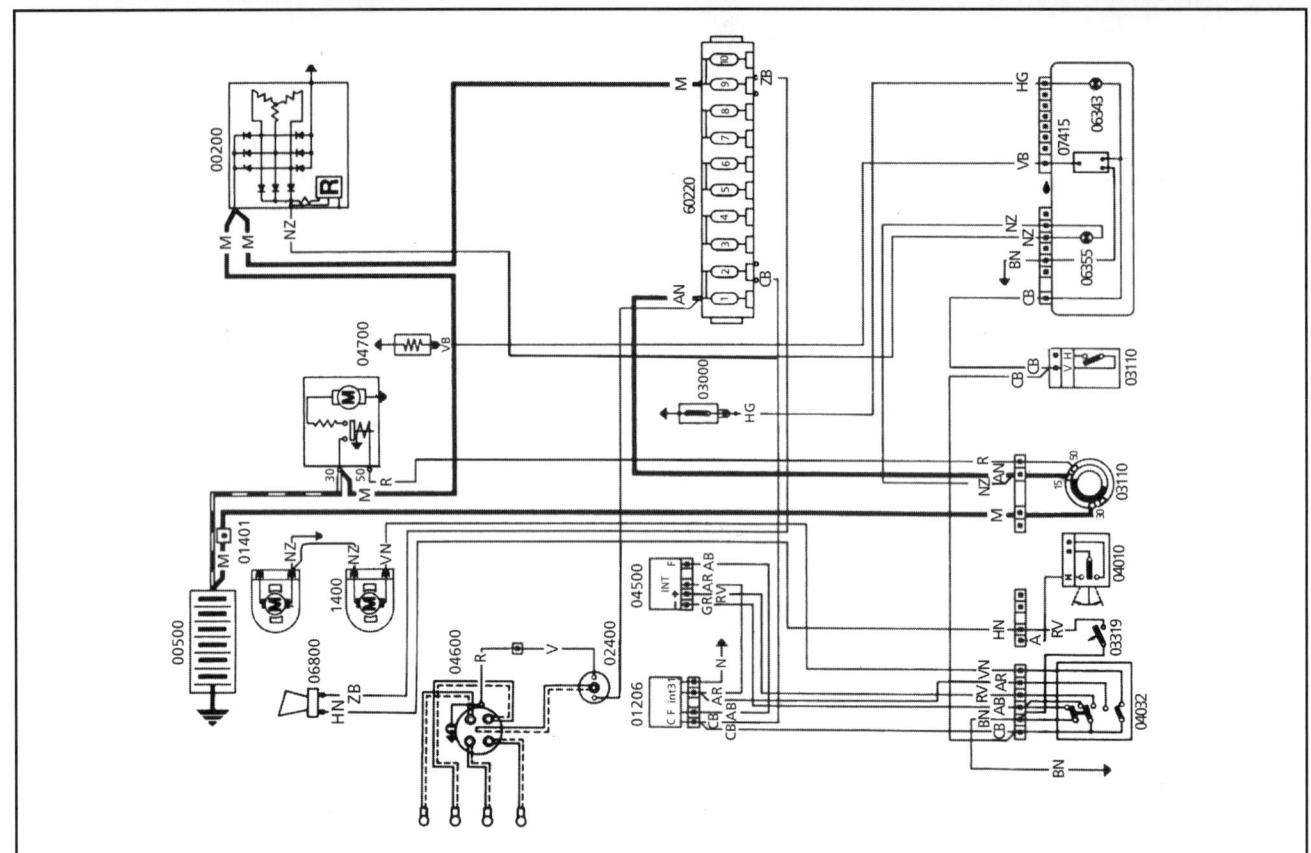

Diagram 1: 1981 - 1986 Starting - Ignition - Charging System - Coolant - Horn - Oil Pressure - Front Windscreen Wash/Wipe

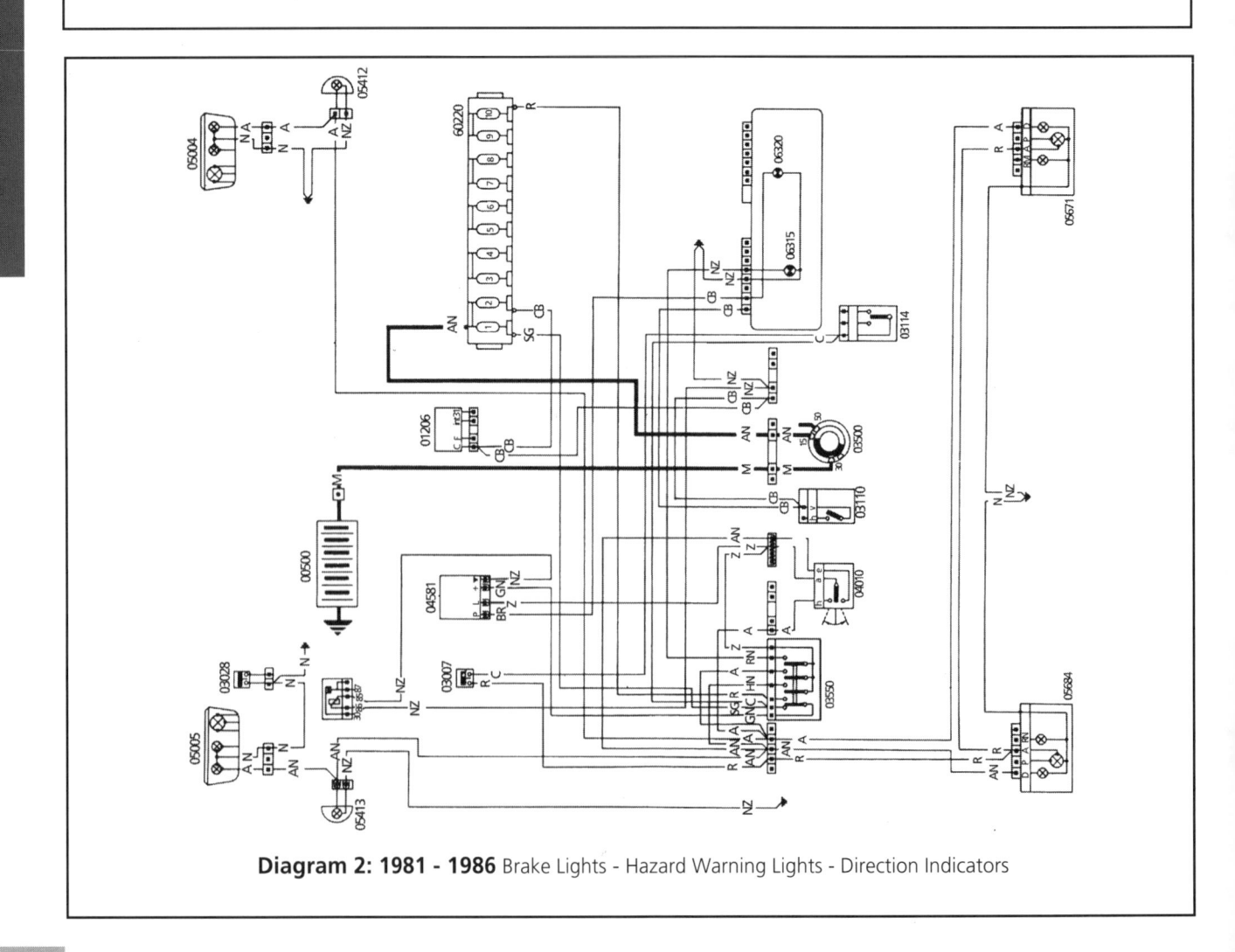

Diagram 2: 1981 - 1986 Brake Lights - Hazard Warning Lights - Direction Indicators

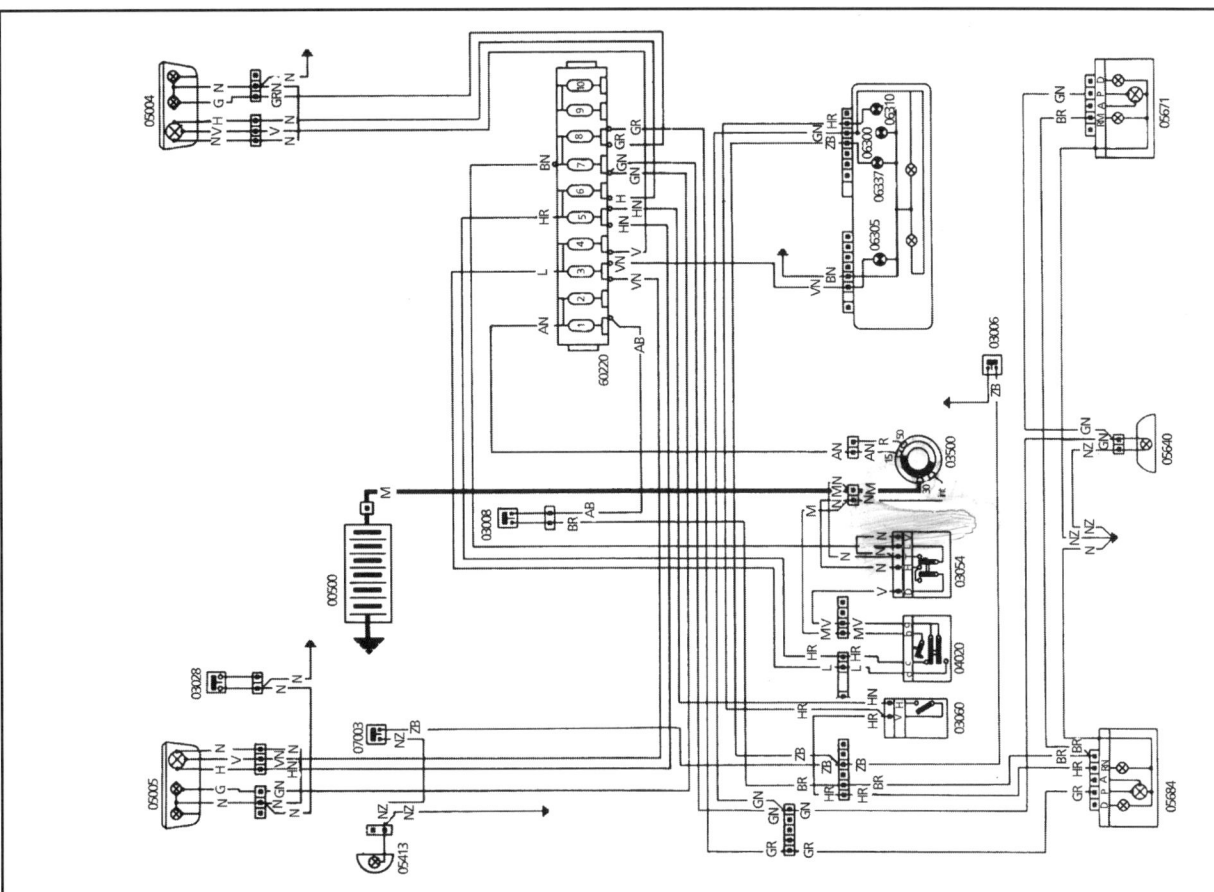

Diagram 3: 1981 - 1986 Sidelights - Headlights - Number Plate Light - Rear Foglight - Reversing Light - Brake Fluid and Handbrake Warning Lights

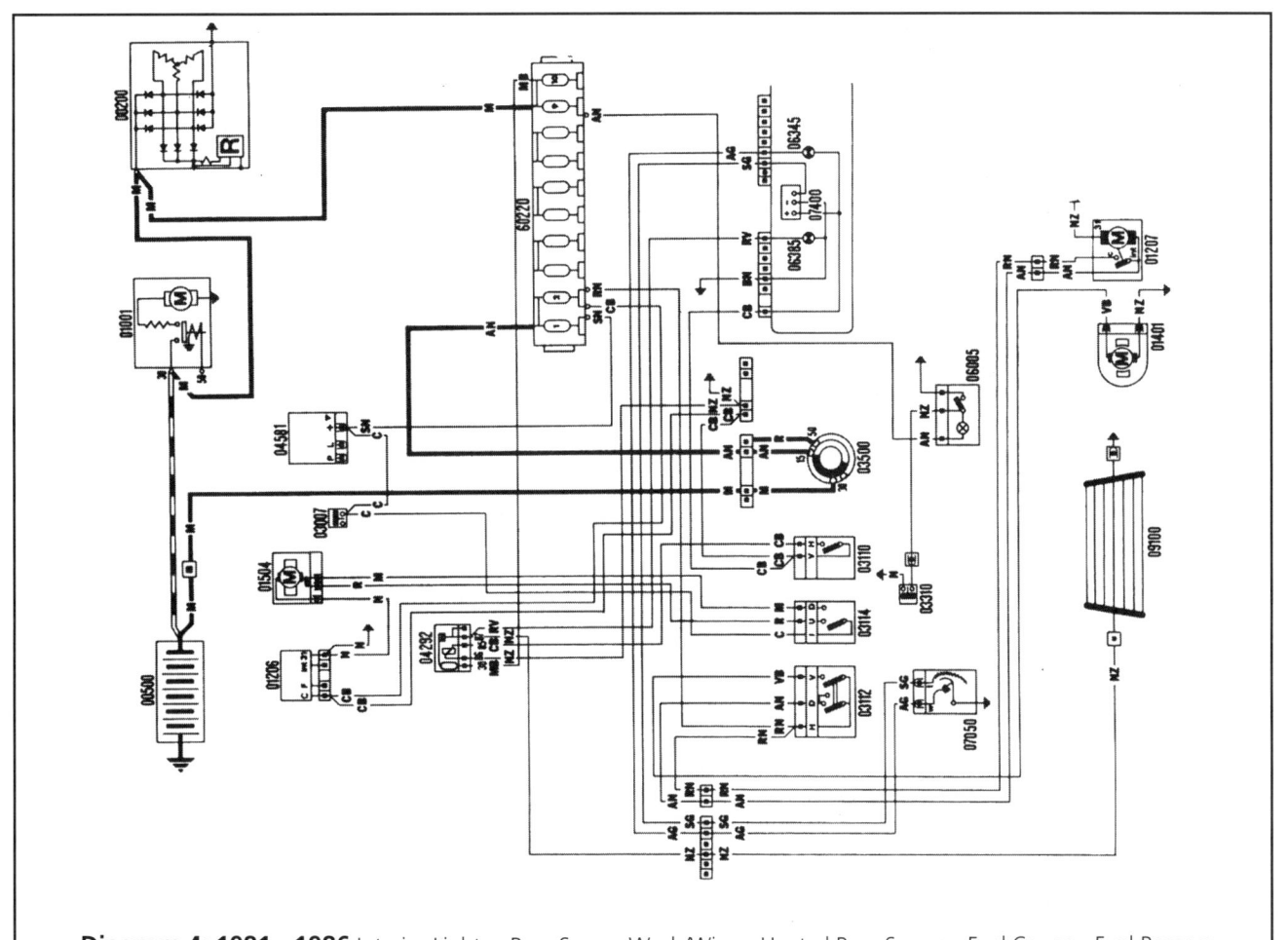

Diagram 4: 1981 - 1986 Interior Lights - Rear Screen Wash/Wipe - Heated Rear Screen - Fuel Gauge - Fuel Reserve

CHAPTER 7 WIRING DIAGRAMS

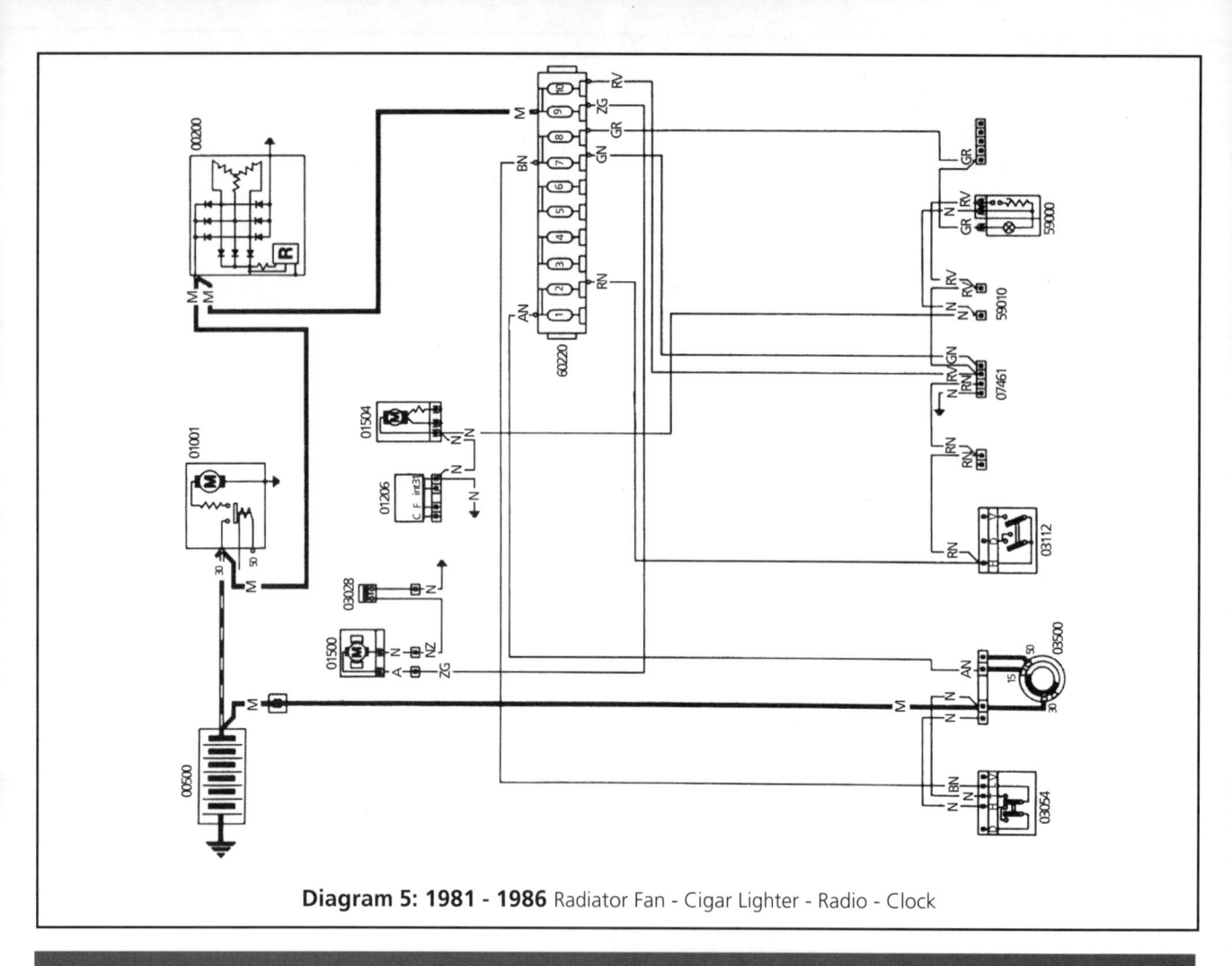

CHAPTER 7 WIRING DIAGRAMS

Diagram 5: 1981 - 1986 Radiator Fan - Cigar Lighter - Radio - Clock

PART B: VEHICLES FROM 1986 - ON

Latest vehicles (from about 1992-on) have a general 100A fuse, protecting the whole electrical system from major shorts. If this fuse blows, it is ESSENTIAL that the cause is put right before the fuse is replaced. To replace the fuse:

❏ **Step 1.** Disconnect the fuse container from the vehicle and cut the two bands (**6**) at the ends of the actual container (**2**).

❏ **Step 2.** Separate the two halves of the container (**2**), by pressing on the tabs (arrowed).

❏ **Step 3.** Undo the two nuts (**5**) and remove the fuse (**3**).

❏ **Step 4.** Fit the new fuse (**3**), after having checked that the amperage of the new fuse corresponds to the one of the fuse replaced, using the new bolts (**4**) and the nuts (**5**) which are part of the FIAT spares kit.

IMPORTANT NOTE: Take special care during the fitting to avoid mechanical stresses on the new fuse which could damage it irreparably.

❏ **Step 5.** Close the container (**2**) once again, lock it with the pull-in bands (**6**) and return the assembly to the correct position in the vehicle and secure it.

The shape of the container (**2**) may vary according to the version used. The method for replacing the general fuse is, however, the same, irrespective of the configuration of the container.

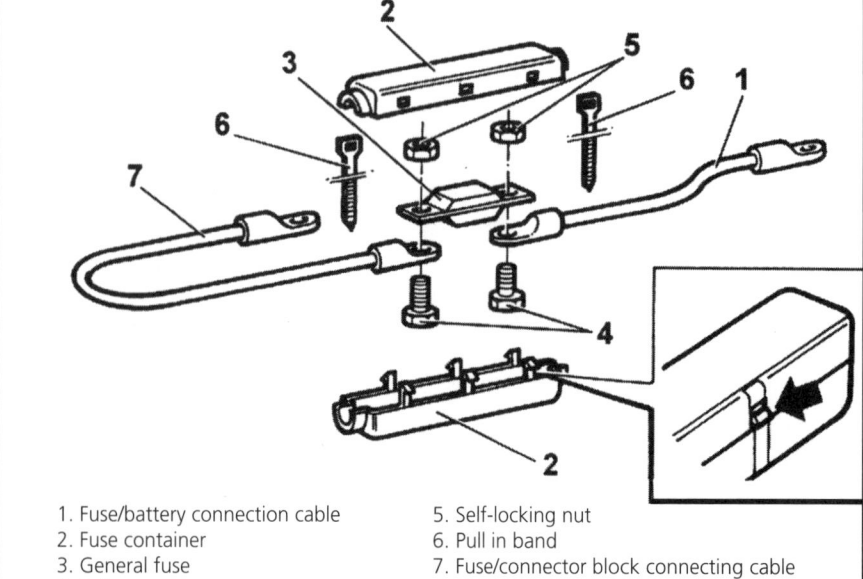

1. Fuse/battery connection cable
2. Fuse container
3. General fuse
4. Bolt
5. Self-locking nut
6. Pull in band
7. Fuse/connector block connecting cable

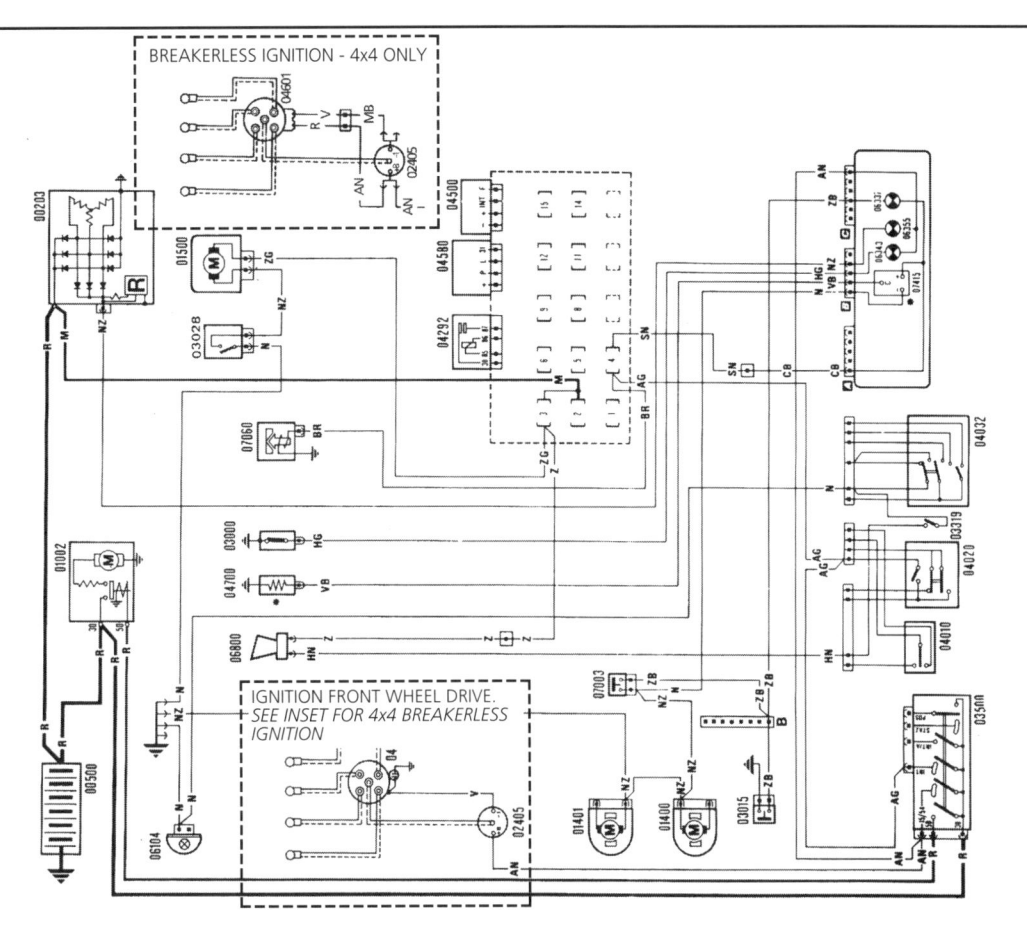

Diagram 1: 1986 - on Starting - Ignition - Charging System - Radiator Cooling Fan - Brake Fluid and Handbrake Warning Light - Horn - Idle Cut Out Device - Coolant Temperature Gauge - Oil Pressure Warning Light

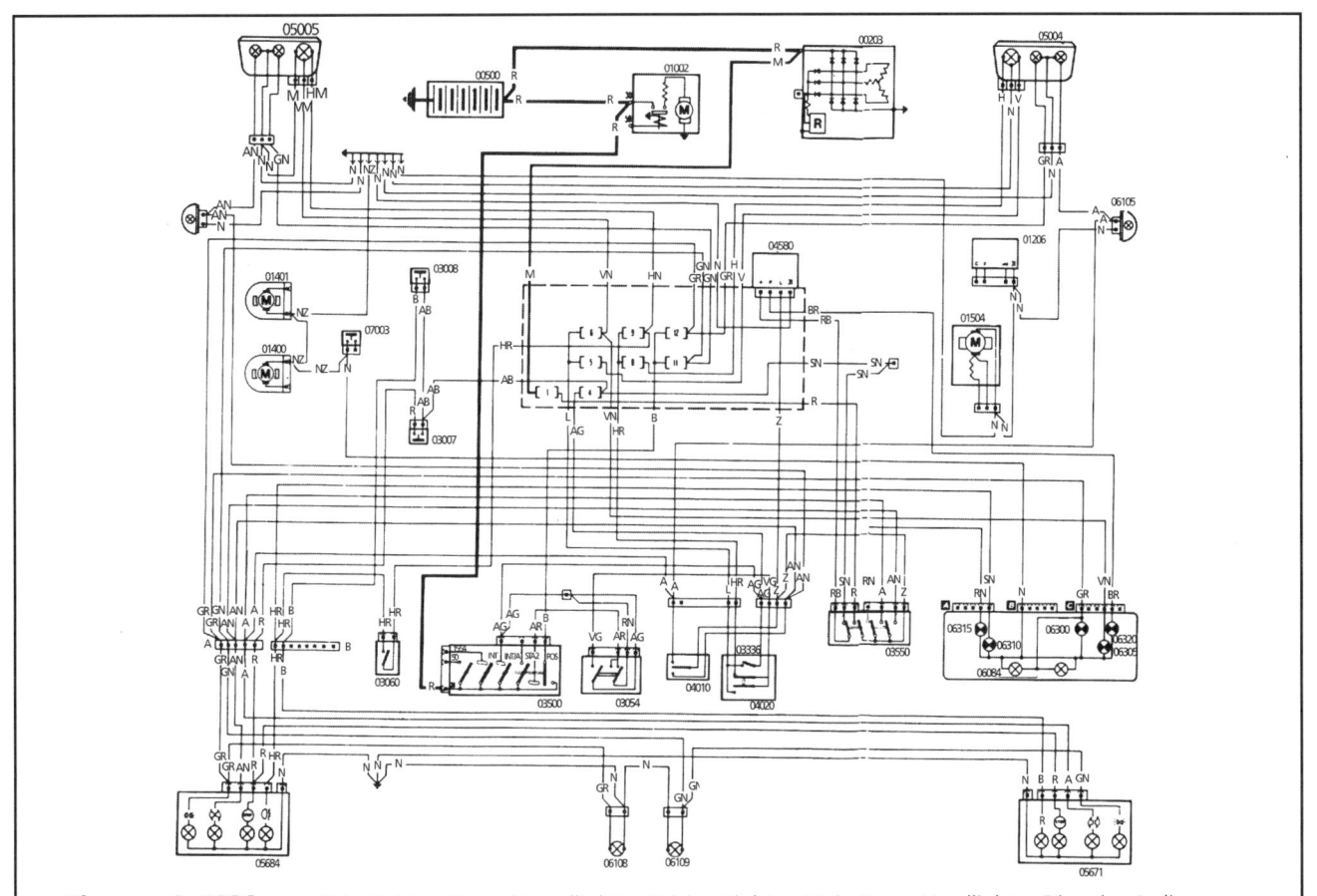

Diagram 2: 1986 - on Side Lights - Dipped Headlights - Driving Lights - Main Beam Headlights - Direction Indicators - Hazard Warning Lights - Brake Lights - Rear Foglights - Reversing Lights - Instrument Panel Light - No. Plate Light.

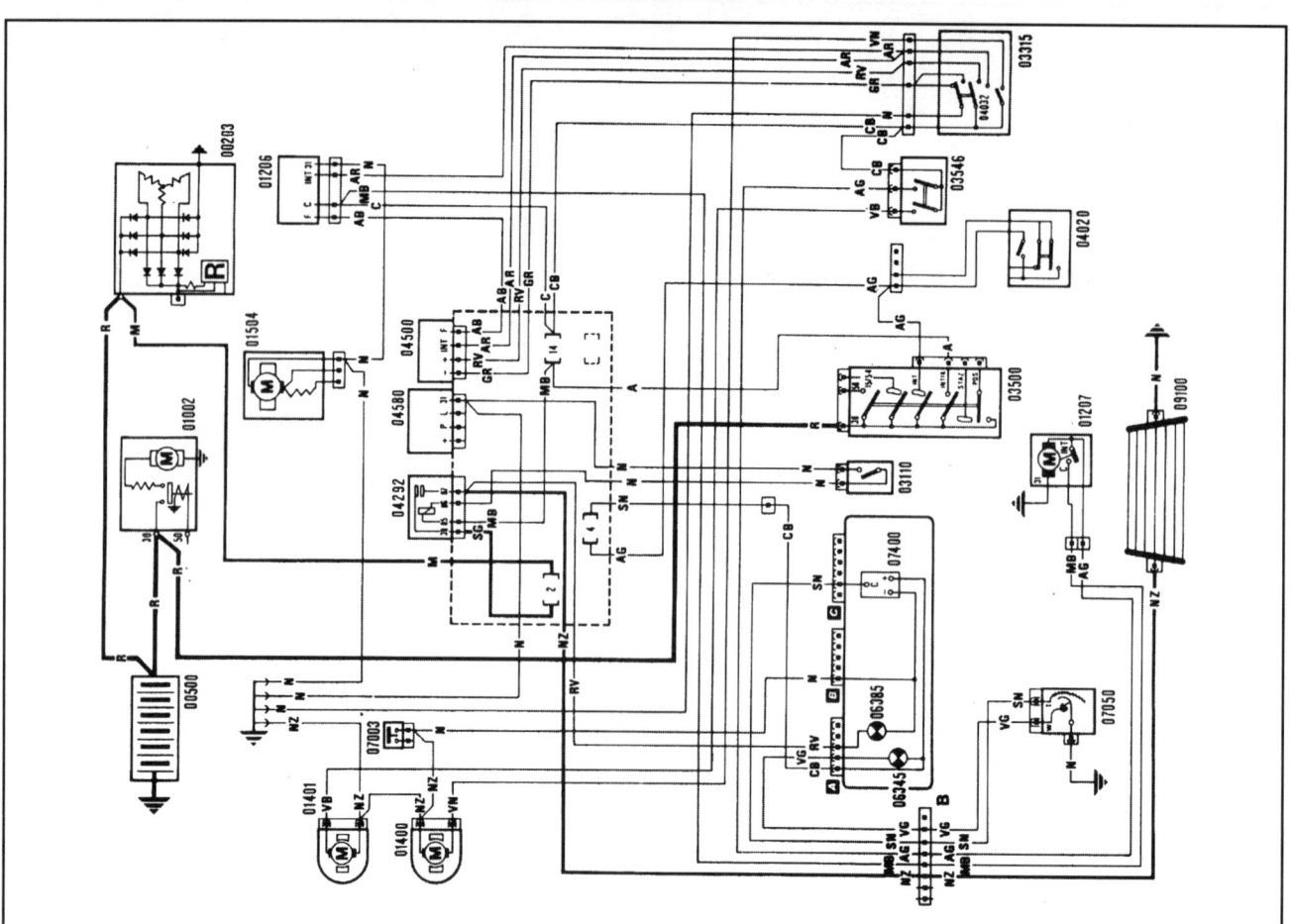

Diagram 3: 1986 - on Heated Rear Windscreen - Rear Screen Wiper with Electric Washer Pump - Windscreen Wiper with Electric Washer Pump - Fuel Gauge and Reserve Warning Light

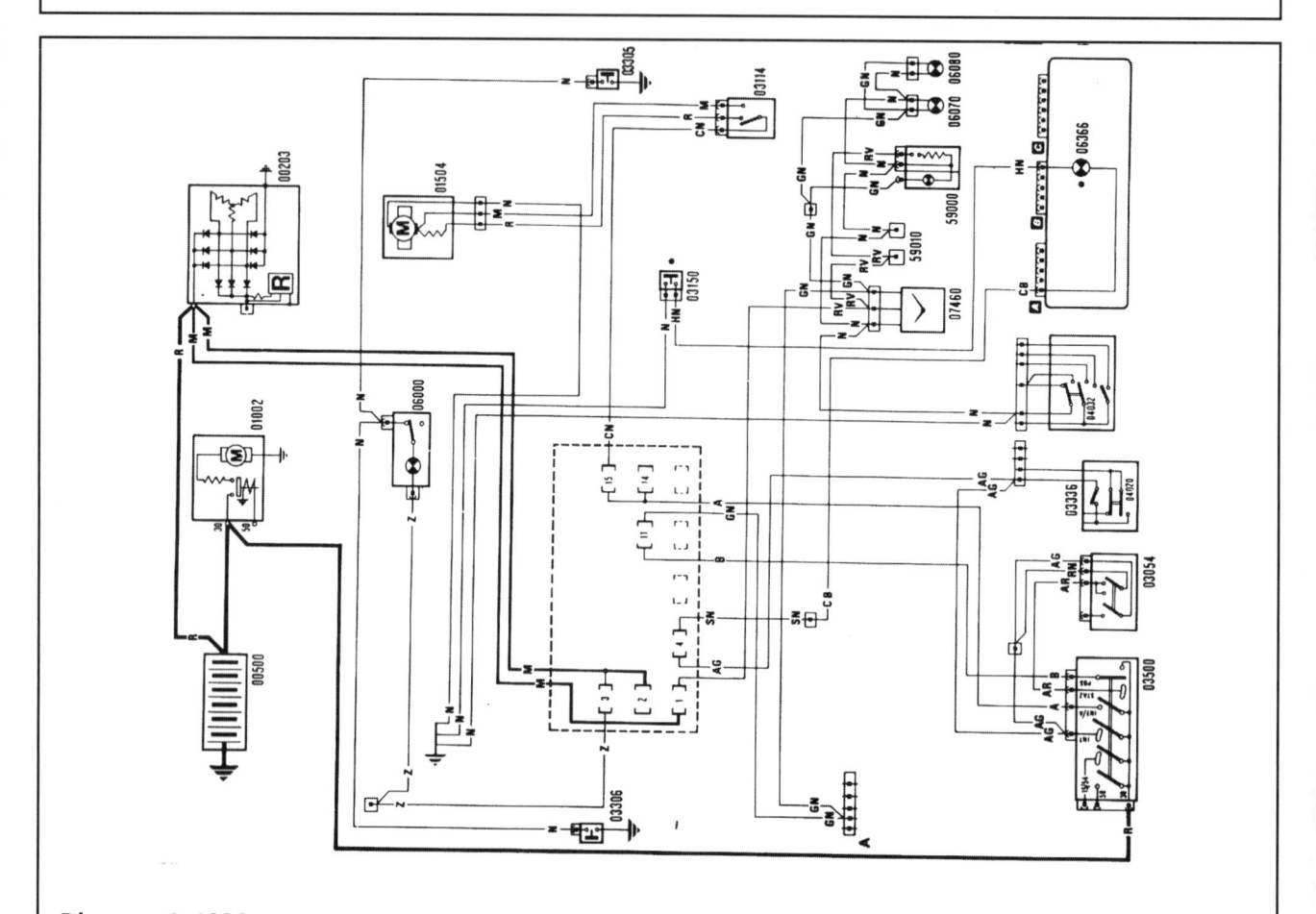

Diagram 4: 1986 - on Car Interior Fan - Courtesy Light - Cigar Lighter - Clock - Radio Wiring - Heater Controls Illumination - Rear Drive Engaged Warning Light

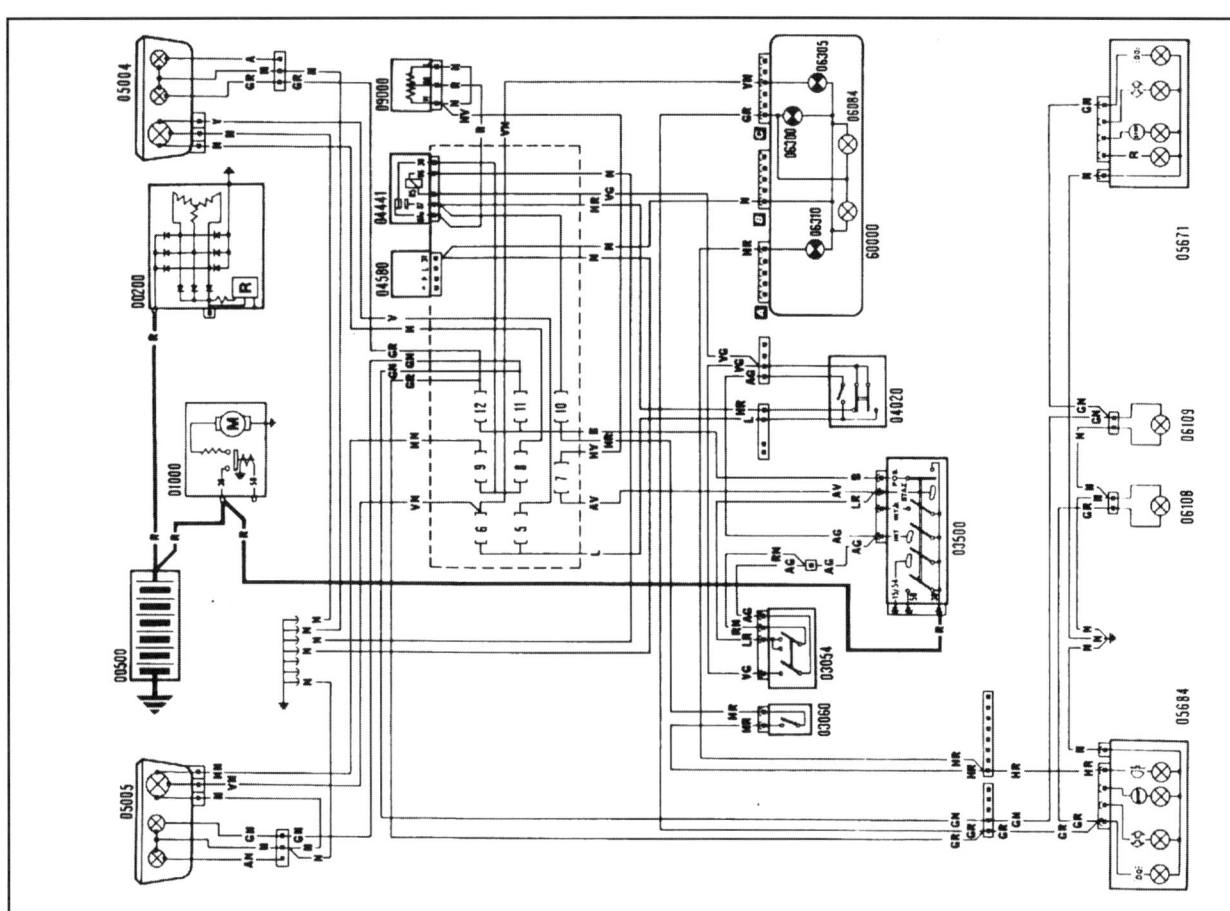

Diagram 5: 1986 - on RIGHT HAND DRIVE VERSION: Dipped Beams with DIM-DIP Device - Main Beam and Warning Lights - Flasher - Foglight and Warning Light

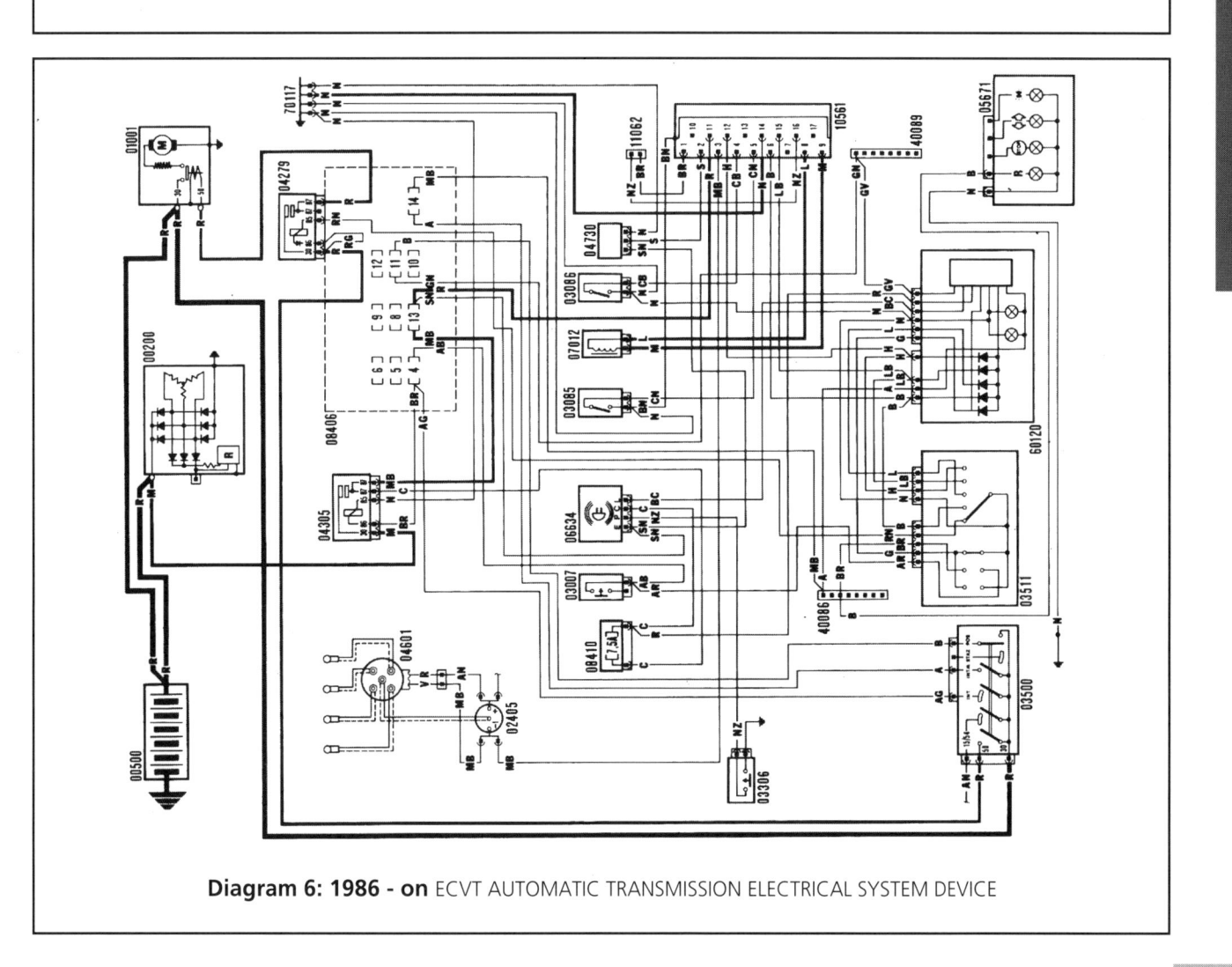

Diagram 6: 1986 - on ECVT AUTOMATIC TRANSMISSION ELECTRICAL SYSTEM DEVICE

CHAPTER 7 WIRING DIAGRAMS

141

CHAMPION 'READING' YOUR SPARK PLUGS

Champion explain how the condition of spark plug firing ends can act as a guide to the state of tune and general condition of the engine. The examples shown are assumed to be the correct grade for the engine.

NORMAL 
Core nose lightly coated with grey-brown deposits. Electrodes not burning unduly - gap increasing by about 0.01 mm every 1,000 miles approximately (with the use of unleaded fuel). Spark plugs correct for engine.

HEAVY DEPOSITS 
Possible causes: Fuel or oil additives. Excessive upper cylinder lubricant. Worn valve guides. Unvarying speed (stationary engine). Replace spark plugs.

CARBON FOULING 
Look for dull black sooty deposits. (Unleaded fuel carbon fouling can appear similar to oil fouling). Deposits can short circuit the firing end, weakening or eliminating the spark. Check for: Over-rich mixture, faulty choke or clogged air filter. Replace spark plugs.

OIL FOULING 
Deposits can short-circuit firing end, weakening or eliminating spark. Causes: worn valve guides, bores or piston rings, or while new engine is running-in. Replace spark plugs. Cure oiling problem.

OVERHEATING 
Likely causes are: Over-advanced ignition timing, or faulty distributor advance mechanism. Use of low octane fuel. Weak mixture. Discard spark plugs showing signs of overheating, and cure the cause.

INITIAL PRE-IGNITION 
Caused by serious overheating. Causes are those listed for overheating, but may be more severe. Corrective measures are urgently needed before engine damage occurs. Discard plugs in this condition.

SPLIT CORE NOSE 
(May first appear as hair-line crack). Probably caused by: Over-advanced ignition timing. Faulty.distributor advance mechanism. Use of low octane fuel. Weak mixture. Manifold air-leaks. Cooling system problems. Incorrect gap-setting technique.

FACT FILE: CORRECT INSTALLATION
- Make sure seating areas are perfectly clean.
- Insert plug finger tight to seat. Ensure plug 'spins' freely.
- PLUGS WITH SEATING GASKET: Tighten to relevant torque setting.
- PLUGS WITH TAPER SEATS: Tighten a further 1/16th turn ONLY - no further!
- Overtightening can damage cylinder head or make taper seat plugs impossible to remove.

RECOMMENDED FL LUBRICANTS
FOR YOUR FIAT PANDA

COMPONENT/ CAPACITY	PANDA 903cc	PANDA 750, 1000, 1.1 ie	PANDA 4x4 999cc	PANDA SELECTA 999cc and 1108cc
ENGINE CAPACITY	VS EUROPA 3.9 L	VS EUROPA 3.8 L	VS EUROPA 3.8 L	VS EUROPA 3.8 L
TRANSMISSION CAPACITY	TUTELA ZC90 2.4 L	TUTELA ZC90 2.4 L	TUTELA ZC90 2.4 L	TUTELA CVT 2.8 L (a)
DIFFERENTIAL(S) CAPACITY	FROM GEARBOX -	FROM GEARBOX -	FROM GEARBOX (b) 133 L 1.33 L	FROM GEARBOX -
STEERING BOX CAPACITY	TUTELA K854 100 g	TUTELA K854 100 g	TUTELA K854 100 g	TUTELA K854 100 g
CONSTANT VELOCITY JOINTS CAPACITY	TUTELA MRM2 95 g (each)	TUTELA MRM2 95 g (each)	TUTELA MRM2 95 g (each)	TUTELA MRM2 95 g (each)
TRANSMISSION SHAFT JOINTS CAPACITY	- -	- -	TUTELA MR2 50 g (each)	- -
BRAKE FLUID RESERVOIR CAPACITY	TUTELA PLUS 3 0.39 L	TUTELA PLUS 3 0.39 L	TUTELA PLUS 3 0.39 L	TUTELA PLUS 3 0.39 L
COOLANT CAPACITY	PARAFLU 11 5.2 L (c)	PARAFLU 11 5.2 L (c)	PARAFLU 11 5.2 L (c)	PARAFLU 11 5.2 L (c)
WINDSCREEN WASHER TANK CAPACITY	AREXONS DP1 3.5 L (d)	AREXONS DP1 3.5 L (d)	AREXONS DP1 3.5 L (d)	AREXONS DP1 3.5 L (d)

NOTES:
a) DRAIN/REFIL CAPACITY
b) FRONT DIFFERENTIAL: From gearbox REAR DIFFERENTIAL: 1.3 L TUTELA W140 MDA (API GL-5. SAE 85W-40, FIAT 9 55550
c) COOLING SYSTEM at a concentration of 50% coolant to 50% water
d) WINDSCREEN WASHER SYSTEM at a concentration of 50% DP1 to 50% water.

CHANGE PERIODS: See **Chapter 5, Service Intervals**

INDEX

A

Accelerator
  linkages and cables 114, 115
Aerial, maintenance 113
Air cleaner/filter 51, 52
  air temperature control 52
Alternator, drive belt . . . 44, 45, 110
Antifreeze 28
Auto-Biography 1
Automatic transmission, fluid . . . 41
Axle
  rear (4x4 only) 43
  rear 121, 122

B

Ball-joints
  steering and suspension 57
Battery
  disconnecting 30
  electrolyte 30
  safety 7
Bellows, steering gear (see *Gaiters*)
Bonnet
  cable 134
  lock 134
  removal and refitting 133
Brake . . . . 61 to 67, 124 to 131
  caliper . . . . 61 to 64
  cylinder (master) 129
  discs, front 61, 63, 126
  discs, rear 64, 126
  drums 64
  fluid, check level 29
  handbrake 66,128
  hoses/pipes 66, 130
  pads 34, 61, 62, 125
  proportioning valve 129
  safety 7
  servo 129
  shoes 126
Bulb renewal (see '*Lights*')
Bushes 58
Bumper
  removal and refitting 132

C

Cables
  accelerator 114, 115
  choke 115
  clutch 42, 103
  handbrake 66
Caliper, brakes (see '*Brakes*')
Camshaft belt 37,38
Capacities 16
Carburettor
  adjustment 53, 55
  removal 114
Catalytic converter 55
  safety 6
Choke 115
Clutch
  adjustment 42, 43, 101
  replacement 102
  cable 42, 103
Coil, ignition . . . 44, 45, 49, 50, 109
Coil spring 59
Contant Velocity (C.V.) joints
  (see '*Driveshaft*')
Contact breaker 46, 48
Contents 4
Cooling system. 28, 29, 38,
  106 to 108
  change coolant 39
  radiator pressure cap 28
Crankcase ventilation system . . 37
Cylinder head
  OHV . . . . 70 to 75
  OHC . . . . 75 to 82

D

Data . . . . 15 to 20
Disc, brakes (see '*Brakes*')
Distributor 108
  cap 45
  Ducellier (OHV) 47, 48
  Marelli (OHC) 48, 49
Doors
  Hinges 67
  Locks and handles 133
  removal and refitting 133
  Trim panels 132
Drivebelts
  alternator 44, 45, 110
  camshaft 37, 38
Driveshaft, gaiters 42
  replacing 103
  C.V. joints 104
Drum (see *Brakes*)

E

Electrical system . . . . . . 109 to 113
Electronic control module 55
  safety 7
Emergency starting 14
Emissions. . . . . 24, 53, to 55
  control 55
  legal limits 24
Engine bay layouts 27
Engine dismantling
  OHV 95
  OHC 99
Engine mountings 93
Engine oil (see "*Oil*")
  check level 28
Engine refitting 93
Exhaust manifold 56
Exhaust 56, 57
  system 56, 57, 116, 117
Expansion tank 39

F

Facts & Figures . . . . 15 to 20
Fast idle
  carburettor 52, 54
  fuel injection 55
Filter
  air 51, 52
  brake servo 129
  fuel 52
  fuel injection 55
  oil (see '*Oil filter*')
Fire Extinguisher 6
Fluoroelastomers, safety 8
Fuel guage 111
Fuel Injection 50,54, 55, 56
Fuel lines/pipes 51
Fuel pump
  electric 111
  mechanical 115
Fuel system . . . . 51 to 56
  breather valve 116
  evaporation control system . . . 55
Fumes, safety 6
Fuses 33, 138
Fuel tank 115

G

Gaiters 21, 59
Gearbox (transmission) . . . . 40 to 42
  oil (automatic) 40
  oil (manual) 40
Generator drive belt (see '*Alternator, drive belt*')

H

Handbrake 66, 128
Headlights (see '*Lights*')
  adjustment 67, 68
  bulb replacement 31, 32
Heater 11
Hoses/pipes (see *Pipes and hoses*)
HT leads 45
Hub
  front 104
  rear 123

I

Identification numbers 20
Idle speed adjustment (see '*Carburettor*')
Ignition system . . 44 to 51, 108,109
  coil 44, 45, 49, 50, 109
  safety 7
Ignition timing 50
Instruments . . . . 111 to 113
  panel lights 10

J

Jacking
  wheelchange 13, 14
  Safety 5
Jump leads (Jump starting) 16

L

Lambda sensor 55, 56, 115
Leaf springs 59, 122
Lights
  hazard warning 11
  headlights 10
  indicators 12, 32
  interior 12, 32
  MoT 21
  number plate 32
  reversing lights 32
  sidelights 12, 32
Locks and latches 9
Lubricants 142

M

Manifold fixings 56
Mirrors 11, 12, 134
Mixture adjustment (see '*Carburettor*')
Model years 15, 16
MoT, getting through . . . . . 21 to 24

N

Number plates (lighst) 32, 132

O

Oil change
  disposal 7, 8
  differential 40, 41, 43, 69
  gearbox 34, 40
  safety 7
Oil filler cap 21
Oil filter 35
Oil level
  engine 28
  gearbox 40, 41
  topping up 28

P

Pads, brake (see '*Brakes*')
Pipes and hoses
  brakes 66, 130
  radiator (cooling system) . . . 38, 39
Plastics, safety 7
Production changes 15
Proshaft, 4x4 models only . . 43, 105
Purge valves 115, 116

R

Radiator cap 107
Radius arm 58, 60
Raising the car 5
Rear axle (4x4 only) 43
Repair data 17
Road test, brakes and steering . . 68
Rotor arm 46

S

Safety First! . . . . 5 to 8
Seats 11, 12
  mountings 67
  runners 67
Seat belts (mountings) 67
Servicing Your Car . . . . . . 25 to 68
Shock absorbers 58, 60, 122
Shoes, brake (see '*Brakes*')
Sidelights (see '*Lights*')
Spark plugs 33, 51, 142
Speedometer cable 112
Starter motor 110
Steering . . . . . 57 to 59, 117 to 119
  rack gaiters 59, 121
Steering wheel 124
Suspension . . . 57 to 60, 117 to 120
  front 57,58
  rear 59
  rear leaf spring 122
  rear suspension 123
  strut 119

T

Tailgate wiper (see *Windscreen wipers*)
Tailgate and strut 134
Thermostat 107
Throttle cable and pedal (see "*Accelerator linkage and cables*")
Tie rod 119
Timing belt 37
  OHC . . . . 82 to 86
  OHV . . . . 86 to 89
Torque wrench settings 18, 19
Track control arm 58, 119
Track rod ends 58, 120
Transmission . . 89 to 93, 101 to 106
  removal 101
  seperation and reconnection 94
Transmission fluid 40
Tyre
  checking 7, 23, 30
  pressures 30, 31, 34

U

Universal joints 43, 59
Using your car . . . . 9 to 14

V

Vacuum unit, distributor . . . 47, 50
Valve clearances 36, 37
Vehicle Identification Numbers
  (VIN) 20

W

Washer fluid reservoir 30
Water pump 106
Wheel alignment 21
Wheel bearings 57, 59
Wheel bolts 60
Wheel changing 13, 14
Wheel cylinder 128
Windscreen, damage 22, 67
Window regulator 133
Windscreen washers 113
Windscreen wipers 112, 113
Wiring diagrams . . . . . . 135 to 140

143

MAINTAIN YOUR FIAT AS FIAT INTENDED

ADHESIVES • GASKETS • SEALANTS • VALETING • HAND CLEANERS

Plus a complete range of Plastic Padding bodyfillers and rust protection products

Loctite products are used by Fiat across a wide range of adhesive and sealing applications.

From the simplest repairs to a major rebuild, there's a Loctite product for the job.

Available from all good motor accessory retailers.

NEED EXPERT ADVICE ON USING YOUR LOCTITE PRODUCTS?
The Loctite HOTLINE is here to help!

Call (01707) 821173
Open Mon-Fri 9am-5pm

LOCTITE AUTO